Date Due

NOV 2 5 1986		FEB 2 5 2002	
FEB 1 3 1987		FEB 0 4 2004	
APR 1 9 1990			
FEB 26 1993			
JAN 2 4 1995			
JAN - 6 1998			
OCT 2 8 1998			
01-03-00			
DEC 0 1 1999			
DEC 1 0 1999			
NOV 3 0 2000			
FEB 1 1 2002			

The
Bre
of
Bo
and
Mi

The Breaking of Bodies and Minds

Torture, Psychiatric Abuse, and the Health Professions

3147263339

Edited by Eric Stover and Elena O. Nightingale, M.D.
American Association for the Advancement of Science

W. H. Freeman and Company
New York

Library of Congress Cataloging in Publication Data
Main entry under title:

The Breaking of bodies and minds.

   Bibliography: p.
   Includes index.
   1. Torture—Moral and ethical aspects.   2. Medical
ethics.   3. Psychiatric ethics.   4. Political prisoners—
Health and hygiene.   I. Stover, Eric.   II. Nightingale,
Elena O.   [DNLM: 1. Ethics, Medical.   2. Human Rights.
3. Psychiatry—USSR.   4. Torture.   WM 62 B828]
RA1122.8.B73   1985   174'.2   85-4512
ISBN 0-7167-1732-8
ISBN 0-7167-1733-6 (pbk.)

Printed in the United States of America
1 2 3 4 5 6 7 8 9 0 MP   3 2 1 0 8 9 8 7 6 5

Dedicated to the Memory of
Joelito Filártiga
and
Alexei Nikitin

Contents

Foreword

This is a rare, special, and sensitive book. It deals with a subject of vital worldwide importance that we would all prefer to avoid: the gross and pervasive violation of human rights. Such violations cause great suffering and, often, long-lasting mental and physical damage. There is nothing subtle nor doubtful about them. They are harmful to the victims and to the societies in which they occur. They are the ultimate abomination of the human spirit.

The tragic fact is that many millions of the world's people live in nations that condone or foster gross violations of human rights. The violation of these rights is so pervasive that we become habituated to it. What is today's shock is tomorrow's routine. Moreover, we have a virtuoso capacity for justifying harm to others, or at least for looking the other way. Violation of human rights has become so well organized, so systematic, so efficient, that it is now a kind of industry. We may indeed speak of the banality of evil. Even people in professions dedicated to humanitarian ends may be seductively drawn into this banality.

In view of the extraordinary diversity of human cultures, it is remarkable that we find evidence everywhere of respect for healers. What constitutes healing may vary considerably from one culture to another, but healers are generally perceived as good and kind, wise and helpful. In technologically advanced societies, there is unequivocal evidence that the capabilities of the health professions are growing, based on great advances in the sciences. Yet, here as elsewhere great power may be used both for good and for harm. From different parts of the world, we get disturbing reports of the collaboration of health professionals in physical and psychological torture. The other side of this coin is that many members of the healing professions are distinctly vulnerable themselves to such abuse in totalitarian countries. Their inherent compassion, their inclination to care for everyone regardless of position in society, their influence in the community as a force for human decency—all these admirable tendencies put them at risk of becoming victims in a cruel society.

This book brings together these instances of abuse in a careful, objective way, documenting their occurrence as well as humanly possible under the difficult circumstances of this subject. The most thoughtful and valuable perspectives of the health professions are brought to bear on these abuses. The authors make every effort to clarify the nature of the abuses, the contexts in which they are most likely to take place, the ways in which they are rationalized and pseudojustified, and above all the efforts that groups within the health professions are making to counteract such abuse and treat its victims.

The book raises very challenging and troublesome questions. How is it that members of the most humane and compassionate of all professions can participate in the most serious violations of human rights? What are the conditions under which such violations can occur? What can health professionals, scientific organizations, and other groups do to check this dangerous trend? In suggesting answers to these questions, the book offers insights on contemporary dilemmas of profound significance: the prevalence of repressive governments; human capacities to rationalize, deny, or obfuscate damaging behavior; the poignant conflict of loyalties experienced by decent people to other human beings and to larger organizations such as the state.

It is particularly appropriate that these highly respected authors—known for their humanity and integrity as well as for their professional stature—should put together this volume under the auspices of the American Association for the Advancement of Science (AAAS). Strong organizations covering wide sectors of science and technology such as the AAAS, the National Academy of Sciences, and certain medical organizations have taken an increasingly active role in preventing human rights violations and coming to the aid of people who suffer abuse. The sciences and science-based professions, through their most dynamic organizations, must use their formidable influence to strengthen human rights everywhere—and above all to minimize the abuse of human rights in the name of science and by the hands of science-based professionals. Such organizations must use their influence directly with their colleagues in each nation and indirectly with governments and with world opinion.

Given the well-earned respect for scientific achievement, these organizations are in a strong position to demand at least a decent minimum of respect for human individuality and decency everywhere. Beyond that, if the species is to survive in the face of the incredible technological power (especially of weapons) that it has created, the scientific community and the healing professions must use their talents, skills, and the respect given to them to improve the human condition. It is now more urgent than ever that we use the extraordinary human capacity for learning, communication, and attachment to one another to foster the bonds of mutual respect. We must cultivate tolerance for diversity, and a decent concern for our own status as a single, interdependent, worldwide vulnerable species.

On behalf of the scientific community and the healing professions, this book makes a useful step in that vital direction.

David A. Hamburg, M.D.

President
Carnegie Corporation of New York

President
American Association for
the Advancement of Science

Acknowledgements

This book grew out of our work with the Committee on Scientific Freedom and Responsibility of the American Association for the Advancement of Science. We have greatly benefited from research material generously provided by Amnesty International, Human Rights Internet, the World Medical Association, the World Psychiatric Association, and the United Nations Voluntary Fund for Victims of Torture. Several persons assisted in the preparation of this book; among them are Thomas Eisner, Rosemary Chalk, Arnost Kleinzeller, Arthur Herschman, Peggy Jarvis, David A. Hamburg, James Welsh, Kathie McCleskey, and Mary Ann Larkin. Our thanks to the contributing authors and especially to Richard Claude, whose incisive comments on international and domestic human rights law were invaluable. Finally, we are indebted to Jonathan Cobb and Heather Wiley, W. H. Freeman and Company, for their assistance, criticism, and encouragement throughout the final months of the book's preparation.

Eric Stover
Staff Officer

Elena O. Nightingale
Chair

Committee on Scientific
Freedom and Responsibility
American Association for
the Advancement of Science

Editors

Eric Stover is Staff Officer for the AAAS Committee on Scientific Freedom and Responsibility. He is a former member of the Research Department of Amnesty International in London and a former member of the Board of Directors of Amnesty International USA. He has written extensively on human rights and participated in fact-finding missions for the American Association for the Advancement of Science and Amnesty International.

Elena O. Nightingale, M.D., Ph.D., is Special Advisor to the President of the Carnegie Corporation of New York, Lecturer in Health Policy at Harvard University, Adjunct Professor of Pediatrics at Georgetown University, and Chair of the AAAS Committee on Scientific Freedom and Responsibility.

Contributors

Federico Allodi, M.D., is Head of the Transcultural Psychiatry Unit at the University of Toronto.

Sidney Bloch, M.D., is Consultant Psychiatrist and Honorary Clinical Lecturer in Psychiatry at the Warneford Hospital and the University of Oxford.

Paul Chodoff, M.D., is Clinical Professor of Psychiatry at George Washington University and a member of the Committee on International Abuse of Psychiatry of the American Psychiatric Association.

Richard P. Claude, Ph.D., is Professor of Government and Politics at the University of Maryland and founding editor of *Human Rights Quarterly*.

Ana Deutsch, M.A., is a practicing psychologist in Los Angeles, California and a member of the Los Angeles Medical Group of Amnesty International USA.

Roscius N. Doan, M.D., is Acting Medical Director of the Firecrest School in Seattle, Washington.

Albert R. Jonsen, Ph.D., is Professor of Ethics in Medicine at the University of California at San Francisco.

Kevin Klose is a correspondent and former Moscow Bureau Chief (1977–1981) for the *Washington Post*.

Cornelis Kolff, M.D., is Medical Director of the Seamar Health Center in Seattle, Washington.

Anatoly Koryagin, M.D., is a member of the unofficial Working Commission to Investigate the Use of Psychiatry for Political Purposes in the USSR. Sentenced to 12 years in 1981, he is now in Chistopol prison in Tatar Autonomous Republic, USSR. He is also an honorary member of the World Psychiatric Association, the American Psychiatric Association, and the Royal College of Psychiatrists (London).

Ellen Lutz, J.D., is at the Jurisprudence and Social Policy program, Boalt School of Law, University of California at Berkeley.

Ellen Mercer is Director of the Office of International Affairs of the American Psychiatric Association.

Michael Nelson, M.D., is a practicing psychiatrist in Boston, Massachusetts and a member of the Task Force on Human Rights of the American Psychiatric Association.

José Quiroga, M.D., is Adjunct Assistant Professor of Medicine and Public Health at the University of California at Los Angeles and Chairman of the Los Angeles Medical Group of Amnesty International USA.

Glenn R. Randall, M.D., is a physician in Oakland, California and former Chairman of the San Francisco Bay Area Medical Group of Amnesty International USA.

Peter Reddaway, Ph.D., is Senior Lecturer in Political Science at the London School of Economics and Political Science.

Walter Reich, M.D., is Director of Advanced Studies at the Staff College of the National Institute of Mental Health in Rockville, Maryland, Lecturer in Psychiatry at Yale University, Chairman of the Program in the Medical and Biological Sciences at the Washington School of Psychiatry, and Contributing Editor of *The Washington Quarterly*.

Leonard A. Sagan, M.D., is a senior scientist with the Electric Power Research Institute, Palo Alto, California. He is a former head of the Medical Committee of Amnesty International USA and was a rapporteur to the First International Conference for the Abolition of Torture (Paris, 1973).

Hazel Sirett is Assistant Editor for the Human Rights Internet, an international communications network and clearinghouse on human rights in Washington, D.C.

Maria Victoria Zunzunegui, M.A., is a biostatistician at the School of Public Health, University of California at Berkeley.

Introduction:
The Breaking of
Bodies and Minds

Eric Stover and Elena O. Nightingale

I'm thrown to the ground in the cell. It's hot. My eyes are blindfolded. The door opens and someone says that I'm to be moved. Two days have gone by without torture.

The doctor came to see me and removed the blindfold from my eyes. I asked him if he wasn't worried about my seeing his face. He acts surprised. "I'm your friend. The one who takes care of you when they apply the machine. Have you had something to eat?"

"I have trouble eating. I'm drinking water. They gave me an apple."

"You're doing the right thing. Eat lightly. After all, Gandhi survived on much less. If you need something call me."

"My gums hurt. They applied the machine to my mouth."

He examines my gums and advises me not to worry, I'm in perfect health. He tells me he's proud of the way I withstood it all. Some people die on their torturers, without a decision having been made to kill them; this is regarded as a professional failure.[1]

Jacobo Timerman

Jacobo Timerman was held without charge from 1977 to 1979 and tortured by the Argentine military. In exile, Timerman published a compelling account of the horrors he suffered and witnessed while under secret detention. His testimony and those of other political refugees are vivid reminders that today many of the world's governments condone acts of great cruelty as a means of maintaining power. For the victims—whether imprisoned in a secret detention center in Santiago or in a special psychiatric hospital in Moscow—brutality knows no ideology because its goal is the same: to silence dissent through the destruction of healthy bodies and minds.

It is alarming that state-sanctioned brutality exists at all, but it is doubly alarming that accounts such as Timerman's reveal that health personnel participate in this brutality. Health professionals are trained to heal, but some among them, for various reasons, directly or indirectly use their knowledge and skills to inflict needless pain and suffering. These collaborators in abuse are not simply mad doctors bent on satisfying their own sadistic desires; they include apparently normal health professionals. Some falsify medical certificates and autopsy reports of persons tortured or killed while in official custody, design new methods of abuse, or act as torturers themselves. Others diagnose political and social nonconformists, although mentally well, as suffering from serious psychiatric conditions and confine them involuntarily in psychiatric hospitals. Whether these health professionals participate knowingly or not, their misuse of medicine acts to legitimize brutality.

Grim as this picture of professional abuse may seem, today it is being counterbalanced by the vigorous efforts of a growing number of health professionals and other people to end the exploitation of medicine as a punitive weapon of the state. Several international health associations have recently adopted codes of ethics to prevent their members from participating in torture and other forms of abuse. European, North American, and Latin American medical teams are now studying the effects of torture and developing treatment and rehabilitation programs for victims and their families.[2] Courageous health practitioners living under repressive regimes are calling attention to or treating the victims of human rights abuses, often leaving themselves open to government reprisals by doing so. When such reprisals have occurred, their colleagues overseas have responded by protesting to government authorities.

In an attempt to generate greater awareness of these issues, the American Association for the Advancement of Science (AAAS) Committee on Scientific Freedom and Responsibility sponsored a symposium on medical ethics and torture in January 1981; this book is a result of that event. Through case history and analysis, its contributors focus on the role of health professionals in the use and prevention of both torture and psychiatric abuse as forms of political repression. Because the relationship between the health professions and the phenomena of torture and psychiatric abuse can only be fully understood when the actors—victims, survivors, perpetrators, and healers—are examined in the context of the political, social, and ethical forces that guide their actions, these contributors include not only psychiatrists and other physicians but also political scientists, journalists, and human rights workers.

No one country or region of the world has a monopoly on ill-treating its citizens. In certain US jails, for example, treatment of prisoners has characteristically included beatings and tear-gas sprayings.[3] Sometimes the treatment has been more vicious. A Federal court in 1983, for example, heard charges brought against a former Texas sheriff and three former deputies who, between 1976 and 1980, handcuffed prisoners to chairs, placed towels over their faces, and poured water on the cloth until the prisoners gave what the officers considered confessions.[4] The government attorney handling the case charged that the officers frequently applied this treatment to blacks, to people who appeared to be "hippies," and to those whose cars bore the bumper sticker of a particular Houston rock station.

The subject of this book, however, is not the *arbitrary* and *sporadic* misuse of authority, such as occurs in the United States and some other countries, but torture and psychiatric abuse as *systematic* means of political control. According to Amnesty International, such extreme violations of human rights are systematically or tacitly condoned in nearly one-third of the world's nations.[5] The aim of the authors is to explore both how repressive governments have enlisted the aid of medical practitioners in suppressing dissent and what steps need to be taken to prevent such professional complicity, and ultimately, to end the abuses themselves.

In this exploration, examples of professional complicity in physical and mental abuse are drawn from many countries. But the primary emphasis of the articles on torture (Part I) is on such ill-treatment as it exists in Latin America, and the focus of the articles on psychiatric abuse (Part II) is on this form of ill-treatment as it exists in the Soviet Union. These two regions receive the most attention because physical and mental abuse is particularly widespread, systematic, and well documented in them. For decades, military governments in Latin America have used physical torture to interrogate political prisoners and to create a national climate of fear with the object of deterring both armed and peaceful opposition. Since early in this century, Soviet authorities have used psychiatry to imprison and treat dissidents for nonexistent mental illnesses in an effort to discredit their political and social views.

In these two regions of the world, as well as elsewhere, torture and psychiatric abuse are not the only forms of ill-treatment that medical personnel may participate in. Health professionals may act in an incompetent or negligent manner toward those in their care, resulting in abuse of patients. Furthermore, poor sanitary conditions and inadequate health supplies may inhibit the health professional's ability to provide the best possible care and thereby result in relative abuse of patients. The concern here, however, is not with isolated or occasional abuses resulting from poor practice nor is it with poor medical care resulting from a lack of proper resources, but rather with the improper use of medicine, with flagrant and deliberate abuses of professional ethics in the service of torture and psychiatric abuse.

Although the discussions of torture and psychiatric abuse are grouped separately, it is important to recognize that they are not separate aberrations. Physical or mental torture may take place in any setting—whether it be a prison cell, a secret detention center, a psychiatric hospital, or a backyard. Indeed, involuntary confinement to a psychiatric hospital without adequate legal safeguards and professional care may result in torture. Likewise, acts of torture may require the use of psychiatric knowledge if the torturer is to obtain the desired results. What distinguishes torture from psychiatric abuse is that torture usually occurs in prisons and other places under the control of nonmedical personnel, whereas psychiatric abuse is a form of imprisonment in which psychiatrists usually are responsible for the facility's physical conditions, a patient's medical care and treatment, and the patient's length of stay.

To provide a background to the articles in this book, we now examine the definitions of torture and other forms of cruel, inhuman, or degrading treatment or punishment used by various international organizations. These definitions are important because they reflect the essential moral, legal, and ethical considerations that now guide actions taken by the international community to prevent such practices. These definitions also form the bases for the actions, detailed in the volume's conclusion, that medical groups and other organizations need to take to end torture and psychiatric abuse. We also review the historical context in which torture and psychiatric abuse have developed in order to understand why certain governments today continue to condone such acts as a means of political and social control.

What is Torture?

Torture is the deliberate infliction of pain by one person on another in an attempt to break down the will of the victim. Because cultures vary, not all practices considered torture in one society will be considered so in another.[6] However, certain aspects of torture appear to be universal. It is generally acknowledged, for example, that the physiology of the human nervous system is the same for all people regardless of race, climate, or culture. All human nervous systems respond to beatings, electric shocks, prolonged hanging by the arms or feet, and the injection of drugs in similar ways. It can also be argued that everyone, with rare exception, views torture as inherently wrong. Nothing negates one's sense of what it means to be human more than the deliberate infliction of unnecessary pain and humiliation on a helpless victim.

Amnesty International defines torture as "the systematic and deliberate infliction of acute pain in any form by one person on another or on a third person in order to accomplish the purpose of the former against the will of the latter."[7] Using similar language, the World Medical Association defines torture as "the deliberate, systematic, or wanton infliction of physical or mental suffering by one or more persons acting alone or on the orders of any authority to force another person to yield information, to make a confession, or for any other reason."[8] * In 1984, the United Nations adopted a convention against torture in which torture is defined as

> any act by which severe pain or suffering, whether physical or mental, is intentionally inflicted on a person for such purposes as obtaining from him or a third person information or a confession, punishing him for an act he or a third person has committed or is suspected of having committed, or intimidating or coercing him or a third person, or for any reason based on discrimination of any kind, when such pain or suffering is inflicted by or at the instigation of or with the consent or acquiescence of a public official or other person acting in an official capacity.[9]

All of these definitions make explicit the essential features of torture. First, the infliction of torture requires at least two persons—the perpetrator and the victim. Second, the torturer has effective physical control over his or her victim. Third, although infliction of severe or acute physical pain and mental suffering is integral to the process of torture, the purpose of torture is to break the will of the victim and ultimately to destroy his or her humanity. Finally, torture usually entails purposeful, systematic activity. The torturer's intent is, variously, to obtain information, a confession, or a recantation from the victim or a third party, to punish the victim, or to intimidate the victim or others.

Distinctions are often made, however, as to the degree to which certain forms of abuse constitute torture specifically, as distinct from other forms of "ill-treatment" or "cruel, degrading, or inhuman treatment or punishment." It can be argued, for example, that one blow to a detainee's body should be considered "ill-treatment," while continued beatings for, say, 48 hours constitute "torture."[10] Similarly, solitary confinement or other isolation in itself is not generally regarded as torture or ill-treatment under international law. However, Amnesty International argues that when courts and international organizations examine complaints of solitary confinement, they should take into account the age, sex, and state of health of the prisoner as well as the length of such confinement and its known or likely physical or

---

* For this and other statements on torture and psychiatric abuse that have been adopted by various organizations, see Appendix A.

mental effects on the prisoner, and determine their rulings accordingly. These distinctions remain purposely vague—at least in language adopted by the United Nations—in the hope that the scope of its application, particularly by governments, will be "interpreted so as to extend the widest possible protection against abuses, whether physical or mental."[11]

The word "torture" in this book is used in accordance with the definition accepted by the United Nations. "Ill-treatment" is used synonymously with the more legally correct phrase "cruel, inhuman, or degrading treatment or punishment" to describe practices that are also strictly prohibited by international law. For example, involuntary confinement in a psychiatric hospital is not necessarily in itself torture. However, if such confinement includes the systematic infliction of severe physical pain or mental suffering, then such treatment is torture.

The Forms and Consequences of Torture

To understand the consequences of torture, one must possess accurate information about the physical, psychological, or psychiatric-pharmacological techniques used. Physical torture includes such practices as prolonged beatings, the application of electric shocks, burning with lighted cigarettes, suspension of the body in mid-air, near suffocation by submersion in water, and forced standing for prolonged periods of time. Threats and sham executions are direct forms of psychological torture, but all types of torture could be said to be psychological because they inevitably produce psychological distress in the victim. Psychiatric-pharmacological torture includes forced overdoses of psychotropic drugs or toxic agents that cause severe pain, internal injury, disorientation, anxiety, or other disturbances of well-being.

Although each of these forms of torture appears to fit neatly into a prescribed category, the victim's experience of pain cannot be separated into a purely physical or mental realm. In terms of the character of stress experienced, the physical assault of burning the body with lighted cigarettes and the psychological assault implicit in sensory deprivation techniques fall at points on a single physical-psychological continuum.[12]

Central to the practice of torture, whether it is inflicted directly on the body or through psychological disorientation or deprivation, is the torturer's immediate intent to undermine the stability of both the physical and mental well-being of the victim. The victim, Timerman writes, "is shunted so quickly from one world to another that he is unable to tap a reserve of energy so as to confront the unbridled violence."[13] With the victim's normal thought processes disrupted, the torturer begins to probe for information or a

Confessions of Torture

Few torturers ever publicly admit to their deeds. One of the exceptions is Julio César Cooper, who witnessed many acts of torture while an officer in the Uruguayan Army and who carried out acts of torture in 1972, until he refused to participate further. The following excerpts are taken from a statement made by Lieutenant Cooper (LC) to Amnesty International (AI) in 1979.

LC: In my own case (and I would consider it typical of the general attitude of an officer at the time) torture was regarded as a means to an end. The objective was to obtain a confession from the detainee, purely and simply. The authorities constantly enjoined on us the need to obtain confessions in order to save the lives of military personnel who might be in danger of attack by revolutionary groups. . . . However, subsequently the idea began to lose its force and changed into the application of torture for its own sake, as part of a routine, and also as an act of vengeance against the detainee.

LC: . . . torture is applied in a way that leaves practically no margin for the detainee to demonstrate his innocence. From the moment of the detainee's arrival at the detention centre torture is applied—the prisoner can't avoid it and, given the human condition, in many cases the detainee would prefer to invent and attribute to himself responsibilities which are not real, provided he could be free of torture.

AI: . . . what possibility is there of rectification or denial of statements made under torture?
LC: I can perhaps answer the question by citing a case. In October 1972 four doctors who had been imprisoned in our barracks were brought before the military judge. Their statements had been extorted by torture. Before the judge they retracted the statements, and the judge ordered their release. The decree was not respected by the military authorities, and the four doctors were once more imprisoned at the Sixth Cavalry Regiment. I was able to observe that, immediately on their arrival at the barracks, they were subjected to a whole series of tortures, which resulted in the case of one doctor (Dr. Isern) in a fractured ankle. Following this it is unlikely that any detainee would actually deny his statements before a military judge. It would be absurd, since the denial would entail immediate torture to rectify the denial.

confession. It may be obtained during the first session or the fifteenth. For a person cast back in a cell after torture, there is always the fear that the tormentors will return. Physical discomfort, terror, anxiety, and desolation merge with thoughts of survival or possibly suicide. The victim is alone with the knowledge that family and friends are out of reach—that he or she is "at the mercy of those whose job it is to have no mercy."[14]

Torture: Past and Present

Second to murder, torture is the most egregious violation of human rights one human being can inflict on another. Unfortunately, torture's history is probably as long as that of murder. For centuries, torture was in many countries a part of the legal process, and it was not completely forbidden until 1808, when Napoleon's *Code d'instruction criminelle* ended secret juristic procedures.

In the Roman Empire, civil and criminal courts sanctioned torture as a means of extorting confession in trials of treason or sorcery and permitted masters to use torture to discipline slaves. Early European travelers to the kingdoms of the Asian monarchs reported that torture was a legally accepted and regularly used method of extracting information and punishing offenders. Japanese and Chinese criminal codes, for example, permitted torture of the accused when confession was required before punishment could be meted out. During the Middle Ages in Europe, judges of the Inquisition presided over the torture of suspected heretics in order to extort confessions and incriminate accomplices.[15] In the sixteenth century, Spanish conquerors of Mexico, Peru, and other parts of the Americas tortured captive Indians in their thirst for gold, while Englishmen led raiding parties on African villages to capture slaves, often torturing village leaders to discover the whereabouts of other villagers. Vagrants and debtors were punished by torture in the reigns of Henry VIII, Edward VI, and Elizabeth I.[16] During colonial times in British North America, so-called witches and pagans were tortured by dunkings and other punishments to make them recant their beliefs.

It is clear today that torture in the twentieth century is not a lingering practice from a more barbaric age. Although torture was virtually eliminated in Europe by the end of the nineteenth century, in the first half of this century, Hitler's concentration camps and Stalin's Gulag Archipelago institutionalized torture to a point where soldiers and prison guards inflicted it at will.[17] Partly as a reaction to the Nazi atrocities, public acceptance of torture declined in the postwar years. And in 1948, the United Nations

A torture rack in the Judges' Room of the Palace of the Inquisition, Cartegena, Colombia, circa 1550. (Courtesy of Robin Biellik.)

General Assembly adopted the Universal Declaration of Human Rights, which pledges signatory governments to uphold the rights and fundamental freedoms contained in the charter. Article 5 of the declaration states: "No one shall be subjected to torture or to cruel, inhuman or degrading treatment or punishment,"[18] and that governments may not, under any circumstances, allow their citizens to be tortured or ill-treated. Nevertheless, at least 66 governments today practice or tacitly condone torture or ill-treatment, thereby creating hundreds of thousands of victims.[19]

Despite its prohibition under the Universal Declaration of Human Rights and the Geneva Conventions, torture remains a concomitant of armed conflicts. The French, for example, systematically tortured opponents during the eight-year Algerian War.[20] Evidence now compiled on the practice of torture during the Vietnam War clearly indicates that all parties involved used it.[21] According to well-documented reports, security forces in El Savador and Guatemala have routinely tortured captured guerillas and their sympathizers.[22] In 1982, Indonesian troops in East Timor were reportedly issued a secret military manual permitting the use of torture against members of the East Timor Resistance Movement, Fretlin.[23] The manual instructs soldiers to avoid the use of force in the presence of local witnesses during interrogation sessions so as not to arouse "the antipathy of the people." The manual also warns soldiers not to photograph prisoners being stripped naked and tortured with electric shocks.

The practice of torture today is not only used during conventional wars, it is also sanctioned by some governments, particularly military regimes, as a means of countering "subversion." Security forces throughout the world often see their major role less as fighting conventional war than as stopping the spread of insurgency or terrorism within their own countries.[24] As such, torture is said to expedite the extraction of information from real or imagined "subversives," so that others may be captured, and insurgency or peaceful opposition crushed.

Officially sanctioned torture often emerges and is combined with an erosion of the rule of law. Constitutional guarantees are cast aside, including the process of *habeas corpus* and other legal safeguards designed to acknowledge detention and to protect those in official custody. Martial law or a state of siege may be imposed, which allow governments to shift trials of political detainees from civilian to military courts and to suspend all constitutional rights. Strict press censorship inhibits the disclosure of torture to the public at large.[25] Finally, security operations using torture may be carried out by quasi-governmental, vigilante-type groups whose clandestine activities allow the country's rulers to deny all responsibility.[26]

Today, governments that routinely use torture generally deny that they do so. One way governments cover up torture is by using sophisticated psychological and pharmacological techniques that produce intense pain but leave few overt signs of physical trauma. Another way governments cover up torture is by making victims simply "disappear." A precursor to the current practice of "disappearance" was its use by the Nazis to smash resistance movements in occupied Europe. Under the *Nacht und Nebel* (Night and Fog) Decree, German officers were ordered to arrest, and often to torture, those suspected of "endangering German security" and to transfer them to Germany under "cover of night."[27] Twenty years later—in the 1960s—the word *"desaparecido"* was first used, by the Guatemalan press, to describe the presumed victims of political violence: persons who had simply vanished after being abducted by uniformed troops or death squads.[28] Between 1965 and 1984, independent human rights groups, journalists, and others reported that large numbers of people had been "disappeared" or had been massacred outright in Afghanistan, Argentina, Bolivia, Burundi, Cambodia, Central African Empire, Chile, East Timor, El Salvador, Ethiopia, Guatemala, Iran, Peru, the Philippines, Syria, and Uganda.[29] If the "disappeared" eventually

Ballad of the Spanish Civil Guard

Black are the horses
The horseshoes are black.
On the dark capes glisten
stains of ink and of wax.
Their skulls are leaden,
which is why they don't weep.
With their patent-leather souls
they come down the street.
Hunchbacked and nocturnal,
where they go, they command
silences of dark rubber
and fears like fine sand.
They pass where they want,
and they hide in their skulls
a vague astronomy
of shapeless pistols.

Federico García Lorca, *Selected Poems*. Copyright 1952 by New Directions Publishing Corporation. Reprinted by the permission of New Directions.

reappear, they are most often found, with signs of torture, murdered by the roadside or buried in shallow graves.

An alarming aspect of contemporary torture is the emergence of military or police training programs that instruct security personnel in interrogation techniques that amount to torture.[30] Torture trials held in Greece in the mid-1970s, for example, revealed that security personnel trained to torture under the military junta (1967–1974) underwent extensive ideological and psychological conditioning, including beating and being beaten by fellow conscripts, to prepare them for the task.[31] In Argentina, the Alfonsín government has found extensive evidence of the training and *modus operandi* of torturers and executioners, known as "task forces," who worked in hundreds of secret detention centers run by the military and police from 1976 to 1983.[32] Serious charges that US advisors working in Brazil and Uruguay in the late 1960s for the Office of Public Safety of the Agency for International Development (AID) had trained Brazilian and Uruguayan security personnel in "harsh interrogation techniques" prompted the US Congress to terminate the agency's Public Safety Program in 1975.[33] Although AID officials denied that US advisors had ever trained foreign policemen in "third-degree methods" of interrogation, they did concede that students at the Agency's International Police Academy (IPA) in Washington, D.C. were taught such interrogation techniques as making "emotional appeals," "exaggerating fears," and giving psychological "jolts." IPA officials contended that an integral part of the training program was to instruct foreign policemen that "a prisoner must be treated according to legal and humanitarian principles." However, many of the graduates' theses obtained from academy files by Senator James Abourezk and columnist Jack Anderson do not reflect the humanitarian aspects of their training. One student from Nepal wrote:

> With the failures of certain suspects and criminals to understand the
> implications and significance of their own answers to a certain
> question of the interrogator, I feel that the judicious use of threat
> and force to some extent . . . when other techniques have failed . . .
> is a practical necessity.

A Colombian student had this to say: "It is undeniable that in innumerable cases, the interrogator is forced to use systems of moral or physical coercion to obtain truth that the person knows. The practical problem is not in using, but in knowing how to use these systems."[34]

Torture and the Health Professions

One of the first recorded references to medical complicity in torture dates back to the Constitutio Criminalis Carolina of 1532. The penal code issued by Charles V, Holy Roman emperor from 1519 to 1556, specified that one of the physician's principal functions was to decide whether a defendant was strong enough to withstand torture.[35] However, other than anecdotal accounts by physicians themselves, little is known about the extent to which physicians participated in juristic torture.[36] In fact, it wasn't until World War II that medical complicity in torture gained public attention on a large scale.

During World War II, German and Japanese doctors performed some of the worst atrocities in the name of medical research, killing thousands of people. In a secret germ-warfare factory on the Manchurian Plain, for example, Japanese army doctors conducted experiments on captured Chinese and Korean soldiers, all of whom died. According to Seiichi Morimura and Masaki Shimozato, authors of *The Devil's Gluttony*, which documents these infamous experiments, doctors at the facility injected prisoners with bubonic plague, cholera, syphilis, and other deadly germs to compare the resistance of various nationalities and races to disease.[37]

In recent years, an increasing amount of anecdotal evidence indicates that many governments have called on health professionals to use their professional skills and expertise in the service of torture. However, it is often difficult to quantify the extent to which complicity takes place; this is particularly true while a repressive government is still in power. Information often is fragmentary, transmitted by word-of-mouth, and frequently comes initially from victims themselves. Information also comes from newspaper reports and, in some cases, from evidence revealed in judicial proceedings. Occasionally, torturers who confess to their crimes, as they have in Argentina, Greece, Uruguay, and Zimbabwe, reveal the names of other torturers and their accomplices, but this tends to be the exception rather than the rule.[38]

Evidence compiled by medical teams concerned about torture demonstrates that health professionals, particularly physicians, may be called on during and after torture

- to perform medical examinations on suspects before they are subjected to forms of interrogation—which might include torture;

- to attend torture sessions in order to intervene, as in a boxing ring, when the victim's life is in danger;

- to treat the direct physical effects of torture, and often to "patch up" a seriously injured torture victim temporarily so that later on the interrogation can be continued;

- to develop, by means of his own techniques, methods which produce the results desired by his superiors, as when psychiatric methods are used.[39]

Medical personnel have also inflicted punishment on prisoners serving sentences for political or criminal offenses and have provided information for nonmedical personnel to do the same. Since the introduction of Islamic *Shari'a* law in Mauritania in July 1980, for example, four men found guilty of theft have had their right hands amputated without general anaesthetic by doctors or medical auxiliaries, despite protests from the Mauritanian medical association.[40] A Sudanese official executioner and an assistant amputated the right hands of two prisoners convicted of theft in December 1983.[41] Prior to the amputation, the two officials received four days of training in a surgical theater at Khartoum Hospital. According to a bulletin issued by the news agency of the Sudanese government, "A doctor who was among the officials attending the amputation operation said each of the convicts was examined by doctors to see how fit they were for the operation, and that the convicts would also be seen immediately by doctors for quick treatment."[42] In Iran, medical personnel have reportedly drained blood from prisoners just prior to their executions so that it could be given to wounded soldiers fighting in the Iraq-Iran war.[43]

Each of the practices described in the examples above challenges the very tenets of medical ethics: Do no harm, give assistance to all in need, and render care with the consent of the patient. Yet, even though international standards of medical ethics strongly condemn professional participation in the punishment of prisoners through amputation or torture, individual health professionals confronted with these situations often face the dilemma of either complying with orders from their superiors or refusing, and by refusing, placing their jobs and their own lives or those of their families in jeopardy. Moreover, when prison medical personnel are called on to treat tortured prisoners, they may see their role as one of rendering care to keep the victim alive.

Such ethical considerations are not confined to situations involving torture. In the United States, for example, where most states have reinstated the death penalty since 1976, several states—among them Idaho, New Mexico, and Texas—have adopted legislation permitting a new method of capital punishment: death by drug injection.[44] This method entails injection of a lethal dosage of a drug prepared for that purpose and administered and monitored by medically trained personnel. Critics of execution by lethal injection charge that medical participation violates one of medicine's most fundamental ethical concepts, *primum non nocere* (above all do no harm). They also argue that laws that sanction death by drug injection set dangerous political precedents by involving medical personnel in state-ordered killings. In 1980, the American Medical Association declared medical participation in administering the drug directly or supervising its administration by other personnel to be unethical, regardless of the physician's personal views on the moral acceptability of capital punishment.

Long-term Effects of Torture on the Victim

History teaches that acts of violence, whether localized—such as murder or terrorist attack—or more widespread—such as mass killings or war—not only maim or destroy their intended victims but also undermine the emotional stability of the survivors. In recent decades, for example, many refugees who survived the Nazi concentration camps have developed a so-called post-concentration camp syndrome.[45] Psychiatrist Leo Eitinger's studies of concentration camp survivors in Norway and Israel, for example, show that many survivors suffer from "a significantly increased incidence of mortality and morbidity from a wide variety of medical illnesses."[46] Cambodian refugees who survived the death camps of the Khmer Rouge and who now live in the United States suffer from similar symptoms.[47] All of these studies imply that the emotional effects of internment in concentration camps can remain with the survivors, their families, and even those they interact with in daily life for many years after such events occurred.

After the second World War and the Korean War, medical scientists began studying the effects of interrogation and torture on former prisoners of war. More recently, medical teams in several countries have begun treating torture victims. Some of their findings are described in subsequent chapters. This research indicates that some torture victims suffer symptoms similar to those of concentration camp survivors and former prisoners of war: long-term physical and emotional trauma, including heightened anxiety, recurrent nightmares, and phobias, that, in some cases, require counseling or treatment. Equally apparent is the extent to which certain emotional problems increase once the torture victim takes refuge in another country and attempts to adapt to a new culture, find meaningful employment, and possibly learn a new language.[48]

Psychiatric Confinement for Political Reasons

In most countries, psychiatrists, like other medical personnel, may be called on to use their professional skills and expertise in the service of the state. A psychiatrist or a team of psychiatrists may be asked to examine persons suspected of being dangerous either to themselves or to others. If the psychiatrists find that such a person suffers from a temporary or permanent mental dysfunction, they are vested with the legal authority to have the person involuntarily confined in a psychiatric hospital for observation and treatment. Such a commitment is made on the understanding that it will protect the individual or the community from potential harm. Because involuntary commitment is similar in several respects to imprisonment (patients lose their liberty and many of their civil rights, and they are forced to adhere to institutional regulations), the psychiatrist is vested with exceptional responsibilities to society.

The World Psychiatric Association, recognizing these responsibilities, adopted a code of ethics in 1977 designed to guide psychiatrists when conflicting demands of allegiance force them into situations where the use of "psychiatric concepts, knowledge, and technology" may be applied "in actions contrary to the laws of humanity." Article 1 of the Declaration of

Hawaii sets out the basic aims of psychiatry:

> The aim of psychiatry is to promote health and personal autonomy and growth. To the best of his or her ability, consistent with accepted scientific and ethical principles, the psychiatrist shall serve the best interests of the patient and be also concerned for the common good and just allocation of health resources.[49]

Article 7 addresses the question of dual loyalty—namely, how psychiatrists should act in situations where the interests and the goals of the institutions in which they work conflict with the interests of patients whom they treat.

> The psychiatrist must never use his professional possibilities to violate the dignity or human rights of any individual or group and should never let inappropriate personal desires, feelings, prejudices or beliefs interfere with the treatment. The psychiatrist must on no account utilize the tools of his profession, once the absence of psychiatric illness has been established. If a patient or some third party demands actions contrary to scientific knowledge or ethical principles the psychiatrist must refuse to cooperate.[50]

For psychiatrists, the predicament of dual loyalty is a bedeviling and complex issue. On one hand, they must strive to practice their profession in an ethical manner, guided chiefly by the desire to serve the best interests and needs of the patient. On the other hand, society has vested them with the responsibility and legal authority to control, and if necessary modify, individual behavior that may threaten accepted societal mores.[51] Psychiatrists Frank Ochberg and John Gunn explain this dilemma:

> Mental illness is defined, by and large, in behavioral terms; there are few objective tests that a psychiatrist conducts that do not rely on behavior. Abnormal behavior is a subjective concept based on the mores of a particular group at a particular time. Thus, the psychiatrist has a dilemma. If he accepts society's definition of madness without using his own separate criteria, he becomes a depository for all sorts of problems unrelated to medicine and he risks becoming an agent of society for the enforcement of contemporary mores. On the other hand, if he takes the opposite view to extremes he ends up by refusing to treat any patient whose only symptoms are behavioral and who does not show organic changes.[52]

Given these vulnerabilities of psychiatry, it is not surprising that the very "nature of psychiatry is such that the potential for its improper use is greater than in any other field of medicine."[53] In fact, such problems are likely to be found in all countries, irrespective of political conditions or ideologies.

For example, in 1983, the International Association on the Political Use of Psychiatry found that, since 1980, six Romanian dissidents have been confined to psychiatric hospitals for political reasons.[54] In Hungary, a 58-year-old lawyer was detained in 1981 for going on a hunger strike to protest police harassment of Hungarian supporters of Poland's Solidarity union; he was interned in a mental hospital for several months and released in December 1982.[55]

Two former Uruguayan prisoners (one a physician), now living in Sweden, have charged that a psychologist and a psychiatrist working at Libertad prison, the main political prison for men in Uruguay, collaborated with prison officials "to bring about the depression and in many cases complete mental breakdowns" of certain prisoners.[56] Both prisoners suffered breakdowns in the prison and were forcibly administered Calmansial, a phenothiazine derivative which causes severe side effects such as swollen eyes and abnormal face and body movements.[57] A representative of the International Committee of the Red Cross who visited Libertad Prison in 1980 concluded that the prison administration was attempting, through long-term imprisonment, the administration of drugs, and social and sensory deprivation, to drive "prisoners through profound distress to suicide, homicide, or psychotic states."[58] These allegations prompted the Medical Convention of Uruguay, formed in July 1984, to open investigations into the role of medical personnel at Libertad Prison.

Since 1977, psychiatric care provided to South African blacks has been investigated for possible abuse by the World Health Organization, the American Psychiatric Association, the Royal College of Psychiatrists (London), and the UN Centre Against Apartheid.[59] Although the American delegation, which visited South Africa in 1978, did not find instances of confinement for political reasons, it did find "that the medical and psychiatric care provided blacks was grossly inferior to that provided whites," and that conditions were so bad it amounted to political abuse. They also found that the apartheid system "undermines blacks' mental health by proclaiming them inherently inferior and robbing them of individuality."[60]

In the United States, the Center for the Study of Psychiatry in Washington, D.C. has frequently charged that "psychiatric referrals in the military and the Federal government are sometimes used to punish people who simply have personality conflicts or disagreements with their superiors."[61] In an investigation of the center's claims, the CBS News program "60 Minutes" reported in January 1983 that Carl Mollnow, an Air Force officer, and Frank Alvarez, a Navy lieutenant, "were kept in locked mental wards" for brief periods during the 1970s, "even though no psychiatric illness or mental disease was ever diagnosed. After each was released, his military career was abruptly ended."[62] Mollnow claims that he was interned against his will because he had apparently embarrassed his commanding officers by persistently filing flight hazard reports that questioned the safety of C-141 missions over the Olympic Mountains. Alvarez maintains that he was involuntarily confined to a mental ward because his commanding officer objected to a technique he employed during race-relations seminars. Alvarez says his commanding officer told him to stop using the technique of verbal confrontation between blacks and whites, which is supposed to make them identify their latent prejudices. But when he insisted it was part of the program and persisted in using the technique, Alvarez was ordered to report to the psychiatric unit at the Naval hospital, where he was locked in a psychiatric ward for one week. Both officers have filed civil rights suits against their superior officers, claiming that they were imprisoned in psychiatric wards without due process.

The Japan Civil Liberties Union (JCLU) charged in 1984 that beating and drug deaths occur every year in Japan's private mental hospitals where the overwhelming majority of patients are forcibly confined for long periods of time with little or no judicial recourse for challenging these detentions.[63] The Japanese government has argued that such abuses are "extremely exceptional" and that the number of forced detentions is far lower than the JCLU has stated. However, in a September 1984 letter to Prime Minister Yasuhiro Nakasone, the International League for Human Rights in New York drew attention to data "on at least 13 hospital scandals, several involving the murder of patients."[64]

The overwhelming amount of documentation on psychiatric abuse, however, suggests that certain Soviet psychiatrists have exploited psychiatry as a punitive weapon of the state on an unprecedented scale. Evidence of such abuse includes hundreds of well-documented cases of Soviet citizens who, after expressing disagreement with their government, have been declared mentally ill and forcibly confined to psychiatric hospitals for indefinite periods of time. In March 1983, Amnesty International reported that nearly 200 persons were forcibly confined to Soviet psychiatric hospitals for political reasons since 1975 and that the real total was probably much higher.[65]

The Soviet Union's criteria for involuntary psychiatric confinement resemble such standards employed the world over: forcible commitment only if persons are dangerous to themselves or to others by reason of mental illness. However, family members and friends of dissidents committed to psychiatric hospitals in the Soviet Union, as well as international human rights organizations, claim that there is no evidence that these persons represented a danger to themselves or to others at the time of their confinement or before. Moreover, the examining psychiatrist did not attempt to prove that they posed such a threat. Rather, the dissidents were detained under Soviet civil and criminal statutes that allow involuntary confinement if there is evidence of the commission of a "socially dangerous act." Examples of "socially dangerous acts" that Soviet authorities use as grounds for psychiatric confinement include refusing to renounce religious beliefs, writing letters to Soviet authorities proposing economic reforms, distributing religious leaflets, and preaching Christianity to workmates.[66]

Examination of cases of forced psychiatric confinement in the Soviet Union also reveals that hospital authorities and psychiatrists have subjected dissidents to severe physical and mental pain as punishment. For example, sulfizine (a form of sulfur) is sometimes administered to dissidents, via daily injection, even though it is well known that this drug has no therapeutic value in the treatment of psychiatric disorders. Dissidents have also been treated with neuroleptics, despite the fact that they showed no evidence of massive agitation or violent behavior.[67] Moreover, several dissidents formerly held in Soviet psychiatric hospitals maintain that inherent in their "treatment" was the concept that, in order to "recuperate" and thus be released, they had to renounce their political or religious views.

Many persons consider the political misuse of psychiatry in the Soviet Union the most flagrant example of unethical medical practice in the world today. But, as the cases in this section show, it is not the only example. Furthermore, a perusal of Part II of this book will make it clear that psychiatrists in the USSR are caught in many of the same ethical binds as medical personnel everywhere.

Medical Responses to Human Rights Abuse

In June 1984, a team of forensic scientists assembled by the American Association for the Advancement of Science (AAAS), traveled to Argentina to assist the Argentine National Commission on the Disappearance of Persons in the identification of thousands of persons who had been abducted and killed during military rule in the 1970s. For the American scientists it was an emotional and sobering experience.[68] They had arrived at the end of the most tragic period of Argentina's history. Traveling to morgues and cemeteries throughout the country, the scientists were shown endless mounds of plastic bags containing the skeletal remains of persons exhumed in recent months from individual and mass graves. One mass grave contained 300 bodies, all of persons who were believed to have been "disappeared."

During their conversations with morgue employees, the American scientists were struck by the fact that many of their Argentine colleagues had been well aware of the atrocities being committed around them.[69] Some told of how army trucks arrived at morgues late at night, and of unloading bodies,

"I always had the fantasy of being able to find Noni because she had on a flowered black dress I'd lent her," said Dr. Laura Bonaparte, 59, as grave diggers uncovered a mass grave in a cemetery outside Buenos Aires. "We're about the same size. And she always wore a metal cross around her neck." On Christmas Eve 1976, Bonaparte, an Argentine psychoanalyst, got an anonymous call that her eldest daughter, who was teaching in a slum, had been taken away in an army jeep. Police claimed that Noni, then 24, died in a skirmish between terrorists and the military. "I demanded my daughter's body; I wanted an autopsy without a military doctor," remembers Bonaparte. "They brought me a jar with a hand in it." Authorities told her where Noni was buried in an unmarked grave. In February 1984, Bonaparte was given permission to exhume the body. Identification was impossible; hundreds of bones were wrapped in a plastic sheet and returned to their shallow grave.

(Margot Dougherty, LIFE Magazine © 1984 Time Inc/photograph AP/World Wide Photos.)

often mutilated and bearing signs of torture. Officers ordered the morgue workers not to perform autopsies, but simply to register the bodies as "unidentified" and to bury them in unmarked graves. One forensic pathologist asked, "What could we do? Some of us had families. And who could we have turned to for help? If we had protested, we, too, would have been detained and probably killed." Faced with complicity in covering up these atrocities, some morgue workers quietly left their jobs—one pathologist, it was learned, had suffered a nervous breakdown—while others reacted with indifference and went on with their work.

Argentina's tragedy, like those in Cambodia, Uganda, and several other countries, is not that country's alone; it has been acted out before and, if we are unable to confront the world with its own insanity, it will be acted out again. The health professions, with their constituency of millions of members worldwide, can do a great deal to end this heinous past. Already, health professionals are combining their professional skills with advocacy. Human rights networks, notably and most recently in the forensic sciences, have been formed to aid colleagues imprisoned for their peacefully held professional or political activities. Articles describing the effects of torture on victims, their families, and society have appeared in the world's most prestigious health journals. Professional organizations, such as the Chilean Medical Association, the Canadian Psychiatric Association, the American Public Health Association, and the many others described in Appendix B, maintain active ethics and human rights committees. Medical delegations have traveled to countries in support of their colleagues who have been subjected to government reprisals for documenting the use of torture or for offering treatment to victims.

Even with this substantial progress, the task of ending torture and psychiatric abuse remains considerable. There is no reason to expect these practices to decrease in the near future. It is our hope that health professionals and others will find this book useful to better understand some of the moral and ethical dilemmas inherent in the practice of medicine as well as the extent and nature of human rights abuse throughout the world. We also hope that this book will help all those concerned about the protection of human rights to recognize the potential effectiveness of their efforts to abolish torture and psychiatric abuse.

Notes and References

1. Jacobo Timerman, *Prisoner without a Name, Cell without a Number* (New York: Knopf, 1981), p. 54.

2. See references listed under the headings torture and medical studies in Appendix C.

3. See Amnesty International, *Torture in the Eighties* (London: Amnesty International, 1984).

4. "Ex-Deputy Tells Jury of Jail Water Torture," *Washington Post*, 1 September 1983.

5. Ibid.

6. The problem of defining torture is analyzed in Amnesty International, *Torture in the Eighties* (London: Amnesty International, 1984), pp. 13–17. For a better understanding of the concept of pain, see Richard A. Sternbach, ed., *The Psychology of Pain* (New York: Raven, 1978). Sternbach defines pain as "an abstract concept which refers to (1) a personal, private sensation of hurt; (2) a harm stimulus which signals current or impending tissue damage; (3) a pattern of responses which operate to protect the organism from harm."

7. Amnesty International, *Report on Torture* (New York: Farrar, Straus and Giroux, 1975), p. 35.

8. See "Declaration of Tokyo" by the World Medical Association in Appendix A.

9. See "Convention Against Torture and Other Cruel, Inhuman or Degrading Treatment or Punishment" adopted in 1984 by the United Nations General Assembly in Appendix A.

10. Amnesty International, *Report on Torture*, p. 34.

11. See commentary to Article 5 of the UN Code of Conduct for Law Enforcement Officials (1979) that is discussed, along with similar resolutions, in *United Nations Action in the Field of Human Rights* [New York: United Nations Publications (Sales No. E.79.XIV.6)], pp. 161–166.

12. Amnesty International, *Report on Torture*, pp. 39–40.

13. Jacobo Timerman, *Prisoner without a Name*, p. 34.

14. Amnesty International, *Torture in the Eighties*, p. 18.

15. *Encyclopedia Britannica*, s.v. "torture," 1965.

16. See Judith S. Koffler, "Torture and Mutilation in the Golden Age," *Human Rights Quarterly* 5, no. 2 (May 1983): 116–134.

17. There are numerous books on this subject, but in particular see Joel E. Dimsdale, ed., *Survivors, Victims, and Perpetrators: Essays on the Nazi Holocaust* (New York: Hemisphere Publishing Corporation, 1980) and Alexander Solzhenitsyn, *The Gulag Archipelago* (New York: Harper and Row, 1973).

18. See Ian Brownlie, ed., *Basic Documents on Human Rights* (Oxford: Clarendon, 1981), p. 23. For an examination of state obligations regarding torture, see Niall MacDermott, ed., *States of Emergency: Their Impact on Human Rights* (Geneva: International Commission of Jurists, 1983).

19. Amnesty International reports in *Torture in the Eighties* that, between mid–1974 and 1979, the organization interceded on behalf of 1,143 individuals in danger

of torture (excluding mass arrests) in 32 countries; between January 1980 and mid–1983, Amnesty International made similar urgent appeals on behalf of 2,687 individuals in 45 countries.

20. Office of the Governor-General, Civil Inspectorate-General in Algeria, *Wuillaume Report* (Algiers: 2 March 1955), report in Pierre Vidal Naquet, *Torture: Cancer of Democracy* (Middlesex: Penguin, 1963).

21. Amnesty International, *Report on Torture*, pp. 160–168.

22. *Report of a Medical Fact-Finding Mission to El Salvador from 11–15 January 1983*, American Association for the Advancement of Science, Washington, D.C., 1983. Mission cosponsors were the International League for Human Rights, Institute of Medicine of the National Academy of Sciences, New York Academy of Sciences, and the National Academy of Sciences. See also Americas Watch, *Free Fire: A Report on Human Rights in El Salvador*, August 1984, Washington, D.C. and Amnesty International, *Political Killings by Governments* (London: Amnesty International, 1983).

23. Amnesty International press statement, "Troops in East Timor Given Secret Manual Permitting Torture," 19 July 1983.

24. Amnesty International, *Torture in the Eighties*, pp. 10–12.

25. Ibid.

26. Ibid.

27. Walter Gorlitz, ed.,*The Memoirs of Field Marshal Keitel* (London: William Kimber, 1965), pp. 254–256.

28. Amnesty International, *"Disappearance": A Workbook* (New York: Amnesty International, 1981), p. 17; see also Amnesty International, *Political Killings*.

29. Ibid; see also *Report of the Working Group on Enforced or Involuntary Disappearances*, UN document E/Cn.4/1435 (26 January 1981).

30. See Matthew Lippman, "The Protection of Human Rights: The Problem of Torture," *Universal Human Rights* 1, no. 4(October–December 1979):32; Nancy Stein and Mike Klare, "Police Aid for Tyrants," in *The Trojan Horse*, edited by Steve Weissman (Palo Alto, Calif.: Ramparts Press, 1974), p. 22; Amnesty International, *International Mission to Argentina, 6–15 November 1976* (London: Amnesty International, 1977), pp. 56–59; A. J. Langguth, *Hidden Terrors* (New York: Pantheon, 1978).

31. Amnesty International, *Torture in Greece: The First Torturers' Trial 1975* (London: Amnesty International, 1977).

32. On 20 September 1984, the National Commission on the Disappearance of Persons, established by Argentine President Raúl Alfonsín in December 1983, completed its investigations into the fate of the "disappeared." The commission released a 26-page report to the press in September 1984: see *Clarín* (Buenos Aires) 21 September 1984. The complete report, consisting of 40,000 pages of testimonies given to the commission by family members and friends of the "disappeared," former detainees, and military and police personnnel, was

delivered to President Alfonsín in September and made public in November 1984.

33. See Langguth, *Hidden Terrors*; Michael T. Klare, *Supplying Repression*, The Field Foundation, December 1977; US House of Representatives, Committee on International Relations, *Torture and Repression in Brazil*, Hearing, 93rd Congress, 2d Session, 1974; "Death of a Policeman: Unanswered Questions About a Tragedy," *Commonweal*, 18 September 1970; US Senate, Committee on Foreign Relations, *Foreign Assistance Authorization, Fiscal Year 1975*, Hearings, 93rd Congress, 2d Session, 1974.

34. Letters dated 29 November and 27 December 1974 to Ned Schnurman, Associate Director, The National News Council, from Joseph C. Spear, an associate of columnist Jack Anderson. In 1974, Mr. Spear and Mr. Tom Daschle, an aide to Senator Abourezk (Democrat, South Dakota), visited the IPA, where they obtained copies of theses written by foreign policemen shortly before their graduation from the academy. See also Jack Nelson, "End Sought to U.S. Aid for Foreign Police," *Los Angeles Times*, 9 September 1979, and Jack Anderson, *Washington Post*, 8 October 1973 and 8 August 1974.

35. Jurgen Thorwald, *The Century of the Detective* (New York: Harcourt, Brace & World, 1965), p. 125.

36. Ibid.

37. Seiichi Morimura and Masaki Shimozato, *The Devil's Gluttony* (Tokyo: Banseisha, 1982).

38. For testimony by a former Uruguayan torturer, see Amnesty International, *Political Imprisonment in Uruguay* (London: Amnesty International, 1979).

39. Herman van Geuns, "The Responsibilities of the Medical Profession in Connection with Torture," in *Professional Codes of Ethics* by Alfred Heijder and Herman van Geuns (London: Amnesty International, 1976), p. 19.

40. Amnesty International, *Torture in the Eighties*, p. 120.

41. Amnesty International Newsletter, "Amputations in Sudan," February 1984. In October 1984, Amnesty International reported that the Decisive Justice Courts in Sudan had imposed 81 sentences of amputation and that, at that time, 56 amputations had been carried out. According to Amnesty International, amputations as a form of punishment also have taken place in Saudia Arabia since 1981.

42. Ibid.

43. "Iran Reportedly Draining Blood From Prisoners," *American Medical Association Newsletter*, 14 October 1983; see also Memorandum dated November 1983 from the World Medical Association to participants at the 35th World Medical Assembly held in Venice, Italy, October 1984 (SN. 2/83).

44. See Ward Casscells and William J. Curran, "Doctors, the Death Penalty, and Lethal Injections, *The New England Journal of Medicine* 307, no. 24, 9 December 1982: 1532; Alexander M. Capron, "Should Doctors Help Execute Prisoners?" *Washington Post*, 6 December 1984, p. A23.

45. Paul Thygesen, "The Concentration Camp Syndrome," *Danish Medical Bulletin* 27 (November 1980):224–228.

46. See Leo Eitinger, "The Concentration Camp Syndrome and Its Late Sequelae," in Dimsdale; *Survivors, Victims, and Perpetrators,* pp. 127–157.

47. See J. D. Kinzie, "Evaluation and Psychotherapy of Indochinese Refugee Patients," *American Journal of Psychotherapy* 35, no. 2 (April 1984):251–261 and J. D. Kinzie, "Posttraumatic Stress Disorders Among Survivors of Cambodian Concentration Camps," *American Journal of Psychiatry* 141, no. 5 (May 1984): 645–650.

48. See Chapters 2 and 4.

49. See "Declaration of Hawaii" adopted by the World Psychiatric Association in Appendix A.

50. Ibid.

51. See Walter Reich, "Psychiatric Diagnosis as an Ethical Problem," and Louis McGarry and Paul Chodoff, "The Ethics of Involuntary Hospitalization," in Sidney Bloch and Paul Chodoff, eds., *Psychiatric Ethics* (Oxford: Oxford University Press, 1981).

52. Frank M. Ochberg and John Gunn, "The Psychiatrist and the Policeman," *Psychiatric Annals* 10 (May 1980):35.

53. Sidney Bloch and Peter Reddaway, *Psychiatric Terror* (New York: Basic Books, 1977), p. 23; see also Nicolas Kittrie, *The Right to Be Different* (Baltimore: John Hopkins Press, 1976).

54. International Association on the Political Use of Psychiatry, "Information Bulletin No. 6," March 1983.

55. See Bloch and Reddaway, *Psychiatric Terror,* p. 465.

56. Amnesty International, *Mental Health Aspects of Political Imprisonment in Uruguay* (London: Amnesty International, 1983), p. 5.

57. Calmansial is the registered name of fluphenazine, which is a phenothiazine derivative used in the treatment of psychoses, such as schizophrenia. It has also been used for tranquilization in behavioral disturbances and (in conjunction with other drugs) for short-term treatment of severe anxiety. Its known side-effects include extrapyramidal symptoms (such as abnormal face and body movements, marked restlessness, and Parkinsonian symptoms), behavioral toxicity, autonomic effects, eye effects, and so forth.

58. Jean-Francois Labarthe, "In Libertad Prison," *New York Review of Books,* 19 November 1981, p. 39.

59. See World Health Organization, "Apartheid and Mental Health Care" (A report prepared for the United Nations Special Committee Against Apartheid), Geneva, 22 March 1977, pp. 3–25; Rachel Jewkes, "The Case for South Africa's Expulsion from International Psychiatry," United Nations Centre Against Apartheid, May 1984, Doc. 84-13687; Royal College of Psychiatrists, "Report of the Special (Political Abuse of Psychiatry) Committee

on South Africa," London 1983; American Psychiatric Association, "Report of the Committee to Visit South Africa," Washington, D.C., 15 May 1979. Members of the American delegation were Dr. Charles Pinderhughes, Dr. Jeanne Spurlock, Dr. Jack Weinberg (Observer-Participant), and Dr. Alan Stone.

60. Ibid.

61. Transcript of "Don't Make Waves" on *60 Minutes* (vol. 15, no. 20) as broadcast over the CBS Television Network on 30 January 1983.

62. Ibid.

63. See "Abuses in Japan's Mental Hospitals," *Human Rights Bulletin* of the International League for Human Rights, December 1984, p. 3.

64. Ibid.

65. Amnesty International, *Political Abuse of Psychiatry in the USSR* (London: Amnesty International, 1983).

66. Ibid.

67. Ibid.

68. Eric Stover organized the visit and traveled with the delegation of forensic scientists during their visit to Argentina. Members of the AAAS delegation were: Dr. Mary-Claire King, Dr. Lowell Levine, Dr. Leslie Lukash, Dr. Cristian Orrego, Dr. Clyde Snow, and Dr. Luke Tedeschi. For a report on their findings, see *The American Journal of Forensic Medicine and Pathology* 5, no. 4 (December 1984).

69. On 22 August 1984, the Supreme Court of Argentina opened an investigation into the role of forensic scientists working in the Judicial Morgue of Buenos Aires from 1976 to 1979. See "Una investigación en la Morgue Judicial pone al descubierto metedos irregulares en la represión antisubversiva," *La Razón* (Buenos Aires), 2 November 1984, p. 4.

Part I: Torture

Dr. Rieux resolved to compile this chronicle, so that he should not be one of those who hold their peace but should bear witness in favor of [the victims]; so that some memorial of the injustice and outrage done them might endure. . . .

. . . He knew that the tale he had to tell could not be one of a final victory. It could be only the record of what had had to be done, and what assuredly would have to be done again in the never ending fight against terror and its relentless onslaughts . . . by all who, while unable to be saints but refusing to bow down to pestilences, strive their utmost to be healers.

Albert Camus
The Plague

In what ways do health professionals participate in the practice of torture and is there any justification for their participation? How does torture affect the victims and their families? What is being done to treat and rehabilitate the victims? How can victims seek redress? What steps are health personnel and other people taking to abolish torture? These are the questions that the authors in Part I address.

Torture is almost universally condemned in public but often supported or apologized for in private. In the opening chapter, Albert Jonsen and Leonard Sagan trace the philosophical underpinnings of the defense of torture from both a historical and an analytical perspective. Some apologists for torture base their justifications on political expediency. According to such arguments, inflicting undesirable but "necessary" pain on a person or group of people is justified when it ultimately protects the greater good of a greater number of people. Thus it is argued that the use of torture in the interrogation of terrorists and revolutionaries can save innocent lives and preserve law and order. What the apologists for torture see as the "greater good," Jonsen and Sagan explain, is minified by the pernicious effects of torture on the victim, the victim's family, society at large, and, ultimately, our belief in human worth and dignity.

Accounts of torture victims remind us that brutality can never be comprehended or measured in the abstract. Cornelis Kolff and Roscius Doan present the testimonies of a husband and wife who were imprisoned from 1977 to 1979 and tortured by the Argentine military. These accounts reveal the devastating effects of torture not only on the victims themselves but also on their families. Kolff and Doan demonstrate how personal testimonies can be used to prevent torture and to assist in the rehabilitation of its victims.

Chapter 3 examines the diagnostic criteria medical teams in the United States and Canada use to detect the physical and psychological effects of torture. In some cases, medical examinations may be essential to treating and rehabilitating torture victims properly. The two studies described here suggest that the psychological effects of torture generally persist long after most of the physical effects have ceased to be troublesome. Their authors differ, however, on whether a specific "torture syndrome" can be distinguished from the group of post-traumatic stress disorders recognized by the American Psychiatric Association.

In many countries where torture is systematically used, victims and their families rarely receive restitution because judges are often afraid or unwilling to consider cases of such a politically sensitive nature. Richard Claude examines this problem in his study of Dr. Joel Filártiga and his family's struggle to gain legal redress for the 1976 torture-murder of their 17-year-old son at the hands of the Paraguayan police. The Filártigas' story illustrates the difficulties doctors and other persons encounter when they stand up for human rights, and it shows the effective role that medical experts can play in the struggle for human rights. The Filártigas' suit against a police official allegedly responsible for the crime who had traveled to New York led to a precedent-setting US court decision on torture.

In the final chapter of Part I, Eric Stover and Michael Nelson examine what national and international health organizations already do and consider what they could do to respond more effectively to torture and ill-treatment. The authors assess the actual effectiveness of medical codes of ethics in preventing the complicity of health professionals in the use of torture and suggest additional measures that should be taken to safeguard potential victims of abuse.

Chapter 1

Torture and the Ethics of Medicine

Albert R. Jonsen and Leonard A. Sagan

The participation of physicians in organized atrocities first came to world attention with the disclosure of practices in Nazi concentration camps. At the Nuremberg trials, testimony revealed that physicians had, for instance, placed prisoners in low-pressure tanks simulating high altitude, immersed them in near-freezing water, and injected them with live typhus organisms. Although only 21 German physicians were charged with medical crimes at Nuremberg, the evidence suggests that hundreds of physicians participated in these "experiments," conducting dozens of "tests" involving hundreds of prisoners. Mortality in many of these experiments was as high as 95 percent.

Nazi physicians presented themselves at the trials as scientists whose research was intended to benefit medicine, particularly military medicine. Their "experiments" nevertheless had the telling marks of torture: conscription of unwilling "patients" and subjection of them to great pain, injury, and death for no reasons beneficial to the victims. These "experiments" were not concealed from the German medical community nor were the even larger "euthanasia" programs for persons who were institutionalized because they were judged mentally retarded or otherwise incompetent. Torture, cruel and useless experimentation, and widespread murder of patients in mental institutions—all carried out by physicians—were widely known and tolerated by the German medical community.[1]

Disclosures during the Nuremberg trials prompted medical associations and other groups to declare the participation of health personnel in the administration of torture unethical. The World Medical Association, for instance, revised the Hippocratic Oath in 1948 to preclude a repetition of

Reprinted, in edited and updated form, with permission of the authors and publisher from *Man and Medicine* 3, no. 1 (1978).

Auschwitz and Buchenwald: "I will not permit considerations of race, religion, nationality, party politics, or social standing to intervene between my duty and my patient." The following year the World Assembly of the World Medical Association adopted the International Code of Medical Ethics, which contains the precept "Under no circumstances is a doctor permitted to do anything that would weaken the physical or mental resistance of a human being except from strictly therapeutic or prophylactic indications imposed in the interests of his patients." And in 1964, the World Medical Association adopted the Declaration of Helsinki, which instructs the physician to remain "the protector of the life and health" of human subjects of research and the investigator to respect the right of research subjects to safeguard their personal integrity.[2]

Forty years after Nuremberg, however, torture with no pretense of research has become, in many countries, a common instrument of government. Modern medical knowledge and techniques, and occasionally medical practitioners, are implicated in this "epidemic" of torture.[3] Because torture is applied to the body and ravages the physical and psychological constitution of its victims, people with special skills in affecting the body and mind may become accomplices in the spread of this malignancy. There are many levels of cooperation in torture: the unwilling participant can be duped or coerced to join in torture; the willing participant engages in torture quite deliberately.

Medical Cooperation in Torture

Medical practitioners may participate in torture at every level from unwilling accessory to willing agent. Some medical personnel participate simply by tolerating or, more seriously, by justifying acts of known torture. A distinguished Chilean physician, himself a prisoner, reports the reaction of fellow physicians who had been assigned as military doctors to his prison camp when he mentioned torture and the brutal way in which prisoners were treated:

> Most of the doctors were young and some had been my students.
> Several showed sympathy. . . . Others, perhaps the majority,
> pretended to ignore what they saw and appeared frightened to talk
> about it. A few justified what was happening on political grounds.
> One young doctor replied to me in an aggressive manner: "What do
> you expect? We are at war."[4]

Medical personnel may participate in torture more directly by providing torturers with assistance that appears to be within the scope of one's proper medical duties. This sort of participation is often unwitting, at least at the

31

beginning. For example, physicians employed to examine or treat prisoners may only slowly realize that they have become accessories to torture, if only by lending legitimacy to torture by their presence, by giving torturers information about the physical condition of their victims, or by resuscitating victims so that they may be tortured again. In an account of torture of Algerians by French authorities, a policeman tells the victim, "The chief wants you to talk. We have doctors here who can wake up the dead."[5]

Physicians may also indirectly cooperate in torture by failing to seek out or report evidence of torture found in medical examinations or autopsies. For example, during a libel suit brought against a Greek woman in the late-1960s for alleging that the plaintiff had tortured her husband, it was revealed that

> a doctor had presented a written deposition that there were no signs
> of torture on Professor Mangakis's body, but under cross-
> examination, he admitted that the examination had been very
> superficial; he had not even asked Professor Mangakis to take some
> of his clothes off. This was the same doctor who in the autopsy on
> Grigoris Lambrakis . . . claimed not to have seen a 20 centimeter leg
> wound, "having examined the body from the other side."[6]

Doctors who act as expert advisers on torture techniques are obviously directly implicated in the practice of torture. According to Amnesty International, since 1973 medical personnel working with the Chilean secret police have administered overdoses of cyclophosphamide to some detainees, resulting in hemorrhagic cystitis (the hemorrhaging of blood into the bladder) and death subsequent to the detainee's release from prison.[7] Several other forms of torture suggest that physicians have designed them. The efficient use of psychoactive drugs, such as the antipsychotics chlorpromazine and haloperidol, requires medical knowledge. Some knowledge of hemodynamics (the study of blood circulation) may also be necessary to keep victims alive while they are tortured by suspension in the air for long periods of time.

The most serious level of participation is acting as a torturer. Physicians tried at Nuremberg did just that, administering lethal drugs and performing lethal surgery. Today, however, evidence that physicians have acted as torturers is often difficult to obtain. Nonetheless, documented occurrences have been uncovered in a number of countries. In Portugal, soldiers raiding the Lisbon headquarters of the security police during the 1974 coup accidentally found evidence that in the Caxias Prison Complex on the outskirts of Lisbon a special hospital wing was reserved for torture victims.[8] There, several psychiatrists oversaw the application of the most refined methods of sensory and sleep deprivation. Many victims suffered hallucinations, anxiety, and nervous breakdowns.

Dr. Dimitrios Kofas, of the Greek military police, prescribed orange juice as medication for torture victims. (Courtesy of Amnesty International.)

In Greece, accounts of torture suffered before the 1974 collapse of the military junta also provide detailed evidence of physicians directly participating in torture. One such account relates events that took place in a military hospital:

> [I] awoke in a consulting room . . . the leather couch, the straps, all these people in white coats, the machine (for electric shock). . . . I couldn't understand what the whole business was about. . . . I thought they were making experiments.

The victim heard one of the white-coated torturers addressed as "Surgeon Colonel." "I held on to that—I wanted to find out his name. In ten days I learned it: he was Surgeon Colonel Karagounakis, General Director of General Military Hospital No. 401."[9] Another Greek physician, Dimitrios Kofas, was known as the "orange juice doctor" because he prescribed orange juice as a remedy for victims of torture. To one prisoner who had been severely tortured, for example, Kofas gave orange juice as a cure for hematuria, the presence of blood in the urine.[10]

Tom Murton, formerly warden of the Cummins Prison Farm in Arkansas, quotes the following report from Arkansas State Police files:

> [The prisoner] said that in June 1963, he got into a fight with a longline rider and was hit on the foot with a hoe. He had been hospitalized for three days when Mr. Bruton [the superintendent] came to see him and asked what happened. Mr. Bruton then had

33

him put on a table in the prison hospital, belted down with one strap across his chest and one across his legs. The inmate doctor wired him up on the "Tucker Telephone" with one wire to his penis and another to his big toe. The telephone was cranked five or six times. [An informant] stated this instrument was designed by Dr. Rollins (former prison doctor) and consisted of an electrical generator taken from a ring-type telephone, placed in sequence with two dry cell batteries, and attached to an undressed inmate on the treatment table at the Tucker Hospital by means of one electrode to a big toe and the second electrode to the penis, at which time a crank was turned sending an electrical charge into the body of the inmate. He stated that several charges were introduced into the inmates of a duration designed to stop just short of the inmate "passing out."[11]

Solzhenitsyn describes the role of the prison physician during his own imprisonment in the Soviet Union:

The prison doctor was the interrogator's and executioner's right-hand man. The beaten prisoner would come to on the floor only to hear the doctor's voice: "You can continue, the pulse is normal." After a prisoner's five days and nights in a punishment cell the doctor inspects the frozen, naked body and says: "You can continue." If a prisoner is beaten to death, he signs the death certificate: "Cirrhosis of the liver" or "Coronary occlusion." He gets an urgent call to a dying prisoner in a cell and he takes his time. And whoever behaves differently is not kept on in the prison.[12]

Torture instruments from the Cummins Prison Farm in Arkansas, including the "Tucker Telephone" (upper left), used in electric shock torture of inmates. (Reproduced by the permission of Grove Press, Inc.)

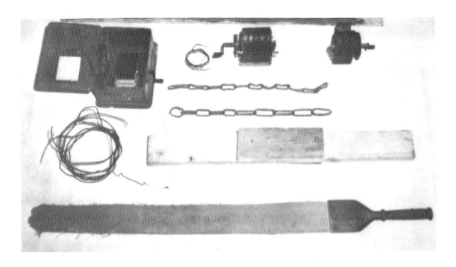

In our view, medical personnel directly participate in torture when they confine political dissenters in mental hospitals. Although some may deny that such a practice technically constitutes torture, it undoubtedly fulfills the definition of torture because it attempts to destroy the autonomy of the victim. To be considered and treated as if insane weakens the prisoner's fundamental power to resist. The aim of such treatment is to make the victim psychologically impotent. If involuntary commitment to mental hospitals is torture for the victim, then clearly the psychiatrist who authorizes commitment must be considered a party to torture.[13]

Although the collaboration of doctors in the practice of torture may sometimes be willing and eager, it is often the product of an agonizing moral dilemma. Military or prison physicians may be asked to perform a duty in accord with their professional responsibilities: provide medical care to a tortured person. At the same time, they know that the care they provide will improve the victim's condition so that the victim can be subjected to further abuse. Concerns about rank, status, and economic security, as well as fear of reprisal for refusal to cooperate, may pressure a physician or other medical personnel into grudging collusion.[14] The outright condemnation of torture and the moral dilemma of cooperation in its administration require a careful examination of the ethics of torture.

The Ethics of Torture

Torture is a topic seldom treated by modern moral philosophers or theologians. An extensive international bibliography on torture, for example, contains no titles under the rubric "ethics," and lists no well-known philosophers, with the exception of Hannah Arendt, as authors. The indices of some twenty current volumes on ethics reveals not a single reference to torture. Contemporary Western ethics is, of course, an offspring of the Enlightenment, and the philosophical battle against torture was fought by the great figures of that era: Montaigne, Voltaire, Bentham, Beccaria. Their arguments, articulating a swell of humanitarian sentiment, led to the abolition of judicial and penal torture in Europe during the late eighteenth and early nineteenth centuries.

Perhaps modern moral philosophers and theologians, satisfied that their enlightened predecessors had done their work well, find little interest in the grim subject. But the victories of the Enlightenment have been followed by an epidemic of state-sanctioned torture. New efforts must be made to expose and abolish the practice of torture. The arguments for and against torture now being heard are not new ones; many of them date from Roman times.

But these arguments appear in new guises, for the contemporary political crises—revolution and terrorism—set the old arguments in very different contexts. In addition, the new arguments in favor of torture must contend with a moral perception of human rights and dignity much different from that of our ancestors.

The participation of medical personnel in torture violates three basic tenets of medical ethics. First, the practitioner of medicine is enjoined to do no harm without the expectation of compensating benefit to the patient. Thus, medical intervention is ethical only when expected benefits outweigh the harm, pain, and risks attendant upon the procedure. Torture clearly harms without consequent benefit to the victim.

Second, medical intervention is justified not only by expected benefits but also by the willingness of the patient to undergo the procedure in order to attain the benefit. The patient, except when he or she is reasonably presumed to be mentally incapacitated, determines the acceptability of harm and risk and decides whether the expected benefits are worthwhile. Clearly, "informed consent" of the torture victim is of no interest to the torturer.

Finally, Western medical ethics dictate that treatment should be rendered to people in medical need, regardless of their social status, financial resources, or political beliefs. Although this principle is occasionally ignored by individual doctors and often vitiated by inequitable systems of health care, it remains vital to ethical medicine. Clearly, medical intervention for the sake of torture is a political act, performed for political purposes and at the behest of political authorities. Torture, then, is a radical violation of the three fundamental principles of ethical medicine. On these grounds, it deserves explicit condemnation by all persons and societies engaged in the art and science of medicine.

The incompatibility between the profession of medicine and the practice of torture seems clear. However, the tenets of medical ethics are not necessarily the last word in matters of human morality. One could argue, for instance, that torture, although a violation of medical ethics, is nevertheless justified because it could serve a higher purpose than the well-being of a given individual person. Can it be demonstrated that torture is incompatible not only with medical ethics but with the fundamental tenets of human morality? Most of the significant Western philosophical and theological theories of morality offered in the last few centuries do contain the elements of a *prima facie* case against torture. These theories, resting upon the principles of benevolence and justice and focusing on the dignity of the individual person, provide premises on which to demonstrate the immorality of torture.

Moral theories that are derived from Kant's categorical imperative—"act in such a way that you always treat humanity, whether in your own person or in the person of any other, never simply as a means, but always at the same time as an end"—make a strong case against torture.[15] Kant bases the concept of morality on the autonomy of the rational being. He argues that respect for the freedom of each person can generate moral rules that are absolute and universal. Torture, it would seem, is a violation not so much of a particular moral rule but of the fundamental principle of morality, because it repudiates the autonomy of the victim and reduces the victim to a mere means to the ends of others. Kant rejects utilitarian arguments that justify actions only in view of some greater good. In Kant's theory, acts are right to the extent that they reflect a universal respect for freedom. Torture is indefensible within such a theory.

Kantian philosophy is less in favor today than the utilitarianism Kant criticized. The fundamental principle of utilitarian moral theory is that those acts and practices are right which produce the greater good for the greater number of people. There are no absolute rules; every action or at least every rule must be tested against the good likely to come from its performance or observance. Modern moral philosophers have refined and reformulated this theory, but in general accept it as basically sound.[16]

Historically, utilitarian moralists helped to inspire important social reforms, including the abolition of judicial torture. But the theory has also been used to build an argument in defense of torture. British political author Brian Crozier states the utilitarian case for torture quite clearly.[17] He asserts that torture used in the interrogation of terrorists and revolutionaries has yielded invaluable information, leading to the protection of many innocent persons and to the restoration of social order. He cites as examples French torture of Algerian terrorists in 1957, British "depth interrogation" of Ulster detainees in 1971, suppression of the Turkish People's Liberation Army in 1971, and the action of the Uruguayan government against the Tupamaros in 1972. In each of these cases, Crozier states, the use of ruthless methods of interrogation quickly and effectively controlled activities that had terrorized many citizens.

Crozier argues that the outcome—restoration of order and protection of the innocent—justifies the use of ruthless methods in certain limited circumstances. Crozier, and other people who presumably agree with his argument, refer to desperate situations in which dedicated terrorists themselves employ torture and wanton murder and, when captured, adamantly resist all more civilized methods of interrogation. These proponents of torture suppose that information extracted through the use of torture will save many lives. Assume, they might say, that it is certain that a captured terrorist can reveal the placement of a bomb destined to destroy hundreds of unsuspecting people. Is not torture a legitimate means of pressuring the prisoner to speak?

This question is posed from a utilitarian viewpoint. A proper utilitarian response requires an inquiry into the effects of torture. What does torture do—or what is it intended to do—to the person tortured? What effects does torture have on society as a whole? Torture, a utilitarian might argue, would be a moral activity if it produces more good than evil.

Torture not only causes pain, it aims to destroy the ability of victims to defend themselves against unwanted intrusions into personal autonomy. One's personal autonomy—one's ability to determine what one will allow into one's life—is the center of selfhood and a vital ingredient in self-respect. The ultimate effect of torture is to damage and to destroy self-respect, the appreciation of being a person. Innumerable autobiographies of torture victims testify to this. In the words of Jean-Paul Sartre, "the purpose of torture is not only the extortion of confessions, of betrayal; the victim must disgrace himself, by his screams and his submission, like a human animal."[18]

Even a thoroughgoing utilitarian might hesitate to defend such an effect. As an ethical system, utilitarianism must presuppose that all moral action takes place between human persons. The reflective utilitarian may hesitate to approve an act intended to destroy the very characteristics of humanity: personal freedom, autonomy, and self-respect. Indeed, the classic utilitarians disapproved when they had to consider whether a person known to be innocent should be executed on the condition that a great good could be achieved or a great harm avoided by that death.[19]

Utilitarians have attempted to avoid the apparent moral incongruity of such cases by urging that it is the propriety of *rules* rather than particular *acts* that is determined by the principle of the greater good for the greater number. Rules that prohibit lying, deception, and violence, for instance, have been shown to promote the good of society, and it is the effect of observing such rules, rather than the consequences of individual actions, that the utilitarian principle addresses.[20] Thus, one should ask whether a rule allowing torture would effect a greater good in a society than the prohibition of torture. The rule that persons agreeing with Crozier might frame would probably be a very restricted one. For instance, it might state, "It is right to use torture in those very desperate situations where no milder means of interrogation seem likely to produce information that will, with high probability, save many lives." Could such a rule be admitted as a standard for action in a society?

The answer lies in an estimation of the range of effects that actions in accordance with such a rule might produce. First, it might be noted that "likely" and "with high probability" admit that the good effect which is sought is hardly certain. It is intended, at best. However, critics of torture, from the Roman jurist Ulpian through the Jesuit Spee to the Italian jurisprudent

The Cambodian Way of Death: 1975–1979

In the less than four years of Khmer Rouge rule, approximately two million people—about one-quarter of the Cambodian population—died as a direct or indirect result of the government's policies. The amount of deliberate killing under the Khmer Rouge rule was so great that it required a government bureaucracy to carry it out.

Although Cambodia was a largely peasant, non-literate society, the most important death squads kept meticulous written records of their work. The hub of a nationwide system of individual arrest, interrogation, torture, and execution was a former Phnom Penh secondary school, now called Toul Sleng. Extensive prison archives indicated that more than 15,000 persons brought to this prison, known as S-21 during Khmer Rouge rule, were executed ("smashed to bits" is the literal translation), usually after being tortured. Only seven survived—prisoners whose technical skills were useful in running the death camp.

Among the S-21 archives are formal notes that the interrogators used for "self-criticism" or "experience" sessions. In these records, the interrogators discuss such mundane problems as lying down on the job while questioning prisoners, not sharpening pencils, smudging papers, and the like. The major problem discussed in the interrogators' notes, however, was that prisoners were dying under torture ("croaking" is the exact translation, used in the Khmer language to refer to animal rather than human death) before their "confessions" were complete. Premature death (or prisoner suicide) was regarded as a "loss of mastery" by and a defeat for the Communist Party of Kampuchea.

The interrogators' notes also reveal that some of the country's remaining medical personnel—many, probably most, had been previously executed—participated in this macabre process. After one prisoner who was believed to have more to "confess" was inadvertently allowed by his guards to swallow nails, the author of one of the documents complains that

> . . . we expended the forces of two doctors all the time and expended good medicines to treat him. In the current situation our party is poor but the party needs the secrets that are in him. . . . Thus we, the children of the party, have such duties.

David Hawk

David Hawk is an associate at the Columbia University Center for the Study of Human Rights and the director of the Cambodia Documentation Commission. (Translation of prison documents by Stephen Heder.)

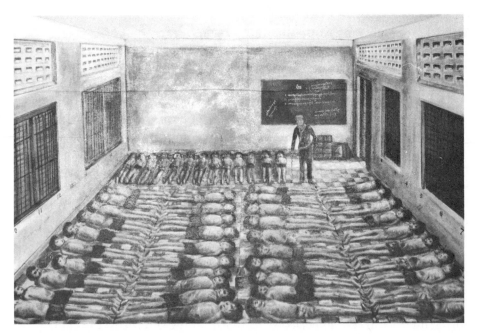

A photograph of a painting showing how prisoners held in the large cell-rooms were shackled by leg irons. This painting was done by one of the seven prisoners who survived S-21. (Courtesy of David Hawk.)

Beccaria, regularly remarked on its inefficiency and inefficacy.[21] Amnesty International, in its 1984 report *Torture in the Eighties*, argues that people who defend the use of torture often ignore "the fact that the majority of torture victims, even in countries beset by widespread civil conflict, have no security information about violent opposition groups to give away."[22]

Second, the scope of application of the rule is by no means clear. Information, contemporary apologists for torture argue, may be extracted from the perpetrators of a terrorist plot or from people who may know the perpetrators. But to whom should torture not be applied? The potential candidates ripple out into a society, including not only suspected terrorists but also their families, friends, and neighbors, and even strangers whose political views are remotely similar. In Argentina, for example, there is ample evidence that the majority of people detained and tortured by the military during the late 1970s had nothing whatsoever to do with terrorism. Many were kidnapped because of their affiliation with medical, political, student, trade union, or professional groups deemed subversive by the military; others were picked up because they were relatives or friends of suspected terrorists or simply because their names appeared in a suspect's address book.[23]

The collected remains from Tonle Bati mass grave, Cambodia 1982. (Courtesy of David Hawk.)

The very restrictive utilitarian rule is weakened by another consideration. Suppose torture proves effective in gaining vital information. Might it not then prove even more effective in discouraging interest in and support of revolutionary movements or, for that matter, any collective decision that a government believes to be disruptive, dangerous, or conspiratorial? Again, it would be not only the terrorists but also their sympathizers who could be deterred. Also, deterrence might be achieved by punishing people convicted of "subversive" crimes—and the more vigorous the punishment, the more effective the deterrence. Thus, the logic of the restricted rule moves torture out from the most plausible "just once" case to other cases that are initially less plausible but quite easily covered by the "effective for the greater good" argument.

One fault of the utilitarian argument in defense of torture lies in the narrowness with which its proponents state their typical case. It seems, both in logic and in actual practice, that state-sanctioned torture has a deeply destructive effect upon a society. The good that may be achieved is dwarfed by the evils that are imposed.

A utilitarian defense of torture, then, can be answered with a utilitarian argument to the contrary. A general defect in all utilitarian arguments, however, is their openness to the charge that the effects and consequences selected by supporters of one side of an issue are not the same or are not as important as those selected by supporters of the other side.[24] As a result, utilitarian debates have an air of inconclusiveness. One has the feeling that against even the best-made argument counterarguments can be made. In the matter of torture, calm arguments in favor of restricted or "humane" torture for some important social purpose may leave the reader with a feeling of horror. This is because, behind those calm arguments, looms the machinery for systematically demolishing a person's humanity.

We maintain that the professional ethics of medicine are based on fundamental principles and sound arguments of moral philosophy.[25] Because torture can so easily usurp medical science and because some medical practitioners have been drawn willingly or unwillingly, directly or indirectly, into the use of torture, we believe that physicians and other health professionals must taken an active stance against medical complicity in torture. In the United States, there has been little medical interest in these issues. Certainly many US military physicians in recent wars have encountered instances of brutality directed against prisoners. That must also be true of many police surgeons. Physicians serving in police or military organizations worldwide would certainly benefit from the establishment of clear ethical guidelines regarding their responsibilities. Together with a sufficient number of informed people in professional organizations, such guidelines, widely promulgated in medical school curricula, would be a powerful weapon against the epidemic of torture. It is unlikely that by exerting moral pressure and withholding their services physicians can eliminate torture. However, ethical guidelines might have a major effect on colleagues who find themselves entangled in these atrocious acts, and such guidelines would certainly lend these colleagues significant moral support.

It has always been appreciated that the "healing hand" can also be the "hurting hand." The Hippocratic physician swore never to provide anyone with a "deadly poison." In malicious hands, medical skills can be used with devastating effects on the spirit and the body. Such skills can revive an exhausted and battered prisoner for further torture; they can be withheld when a suffering prisoner cries out for help. Even when medical skills and personnel are not directly involved, the physical and psychological abuse of human beings should arouse, in anyone dedicated to promoting human well-being, the utmost disgust and anger. It is thus our obligation to protest in every effective way against torture as a means of political control or for any other reason.

Notes and References

1. A. Mitsherlich and F. Mielke, *Doctors of Infamy* (New York: Schuman, 1949).

2. All relevant codes are collected in H. Beecher, *Research and the Individual* (Boston: Little, Brown, 1970).

3. For a detailed analysis of the "new torture," see Matthew Lippman, "The Protection of Universal Human Rights: The Problem of Torture," *Universal Human Rights* 1, no. 4 (October–December 1979): 25–55.

4. A. Jadresic, "Doctors and Torture: An Experience as a Prisoner," *Journal of Medical Ethics* 6, no. 3 (September 1980): 124–128.

5. Anonymous, *The Gangrene* (New York: Lyle Stuart, 1960), p. 65.

6. *Workshop on Human Rights: Report and Recommendations* (London: Amnesty International, 1976), p. 8.

7. "Chile Is Killing People with Drugs," *The Observer*, 26 October 1975. A 1983 Amnesty International report cites eighteen cases in which medical personnel participated in torture of political prisoners in Chile since 1973. Torture appears to be a routine practice in detention centers run by the Chilean secret police.

8. *Manchester Guardian*, 3 May 1974.

9. P. Korovessis, *The Method* (London: Allison and Busby, 1970).

10. Amnesty International, *Torture in Greece: The First Torturers' Trial 1975* (London: Amnesty International, 1977).

11. Murton, T., "Prison Doctors," in *Human Perspectives in Medical Ethics*, edited by M. Visscher (Buffalo: Prometheus, 1972), p. 249.

12. A. Solzhenitsyn, *Gulag Archipelago* (New York: Harper & Row, 1973), p. 208.

13. See, for example, Z. Medvedev and R. Medvedev, *A Question of Madness* (New York: Vintage, 1971). See also *Prisoners of Conscience in the USSR* (London: Amnesty International, 1975).

14. S. A. Burges, "Doctors and Torture: The Police Surgeon," *Journal of Medical Ethics* 6, no. 3 (September 1980):120–124.

15. H. J. Paton ed., *Kant's Groundwork of the Metaphysic of Morals* (New York: Harper & Row, 1964), p. 96.

16. See D. Lyons, *The Forms and Limits of Utilitarianism* (Oxford: Clarendon Press, 1965).

17. B. Crozier, *A Theory of Conflict* (New York: Scribner, 1975), pp. 156–161. For a more recent utilitarian argument in favor of torture, see Michael Levin, "The Case for Torture," *Newsweek*, 7 June 1982, p. 13. See also the rebuttal to Levin's case made by Simon Leys, "The Case for Torture: A Rebuttal," *Newsweek*, 5 July 1982.

18. Cited in *Epidemic of Torture* (London: Amnesty International, 1974), p. 3.

19. See A. C. Ewing, *The Morality of Punishment* (London: Kegan Paul, 1929).

20. See R. Brandt, "Toward a Credible Form of Utilitarianism," in *Morality and the Language of Conduct*, edited by H. Casteneda and G. Nakhanian (Detroit: Wayne State University Press, 1965).

21. Ulpian wrote: "Torture is not to be regarded as wholly deserving or wholly undeserving of confidence: it is untrustworthy, perilous and deceptive. Most men, by patience or the severity of torture, come to despise it so that the truth cannot be elicited from them; others are so impatient that they will lie in any direction rather than suffer and so they depose to contradiction and accuse not only themselves but others" (*Digests* 48, 18, 23). Father Spee, who opposed the policy favoring torture adopted by his fellow Jesuits, wrote: "Under torture all of us, even the most innocent, would confess" (*Cautio Criminalis* [1613]). Beccaria, most influential critic of judicial torture and an early utilitarian, stated, "By this method, the robust escape and the feeble are condemned" (*Dei Delitti e delle Pene* [1764]).

22. Amnesty International, *Torture in the Eighties* (London: Amnesty International, 1984), p. 7.

23. See Edward Schumacher, "Argentina and Democracy," *Foreign Affairs* 62, no. 5 (Summer 1984):1071–1095.

24. G. Jones and P. F. Brownsley, "On the Permissibility of Torture," *Journal of Medical Ethics* 6, no. 1 (March 1980):11–15.

25. E. Pellegrino and D. Thomasma, *A Philosophical Basis of Medical Practice* (New York: Oxford University Press, 1981).

Chapter 2

Victims of Torture: Two Testimonies

Compiled by Cornelis A. Kolff and Roscius N. Doan

One afternoon in January 1977, Alicia Partnoy, a 21-year-old Argentine mother and student, answered her doorbell and found soldiers waiting for her. Terrified, she tried to escape with her 18-month-old daughter through a back entrance but was quickly captured. Fifteen blocks away, soldiers abducted her husband, Carlos Sanabria, from the tire factory where he worked as a salesman.

Alicia and Carlos were taken to a clandestine prison, tortured over the course of several months, and then held for nearly three years before being released. No criminal charges were ever filed against them, although Alicia believes that she was imprisoned because of her association with the Juventud Universitaria Peronista (University Peronist Youth Movement), a student group that supported President Isabel Perón until the military ousted her from power in March 1976.

Upon their release in late 1979, the couple left Argentina with their daughter and took up residence in Seattle, Washington. Once in a safe environment, Alicia and Carlos, encouraged by a medical committee of which the authors are members, told their story.

Testimony of Alicia Mabel Partnoy

On 12 January 1977 I was at home with my daughter, Ruth, when I heard the doorbell ring incessantly. It was noon. I walked down the hallway which separates the apartment from the main door. When I arrived, someone was kicking the door. I asked, "Who is it?" and they answered, "The army." At that instant, I recalled all the stories I had heard over the past year of people being tortured and disappearing after their abduction by the army. Out of fear, I ran through the hallway and climbed over the back wall. They began firing at me from one of the neighboring roofs. My daughter, who had followed me through the passageway to the door, burst into tears.

Outside in the yard, five soldiers grabbed me and forced me into an army truck. In response to my demands to know the whereabouts of my daughter, I only remember seeing the look of hate in the eyes of one of the officers who I assumed was in charge of the operation. I did not find out what had happened to Ruth until five months later.

Once I was inside the truck, my abductors headed toward the tire factory where my husband worked. They arrested him, taking us both to the headquarters of the Fifth Army Corps in Bahía Blanca. We remained there in separate cells until the afternoon. Then we were blindfolded and hand-cuffed and interrogated for several hours before being transferred to a detention center. When I stepped out of the vehicle, I was able to distinguish the facade of an old house through the corner of my blindfold. On the front of the house, I read in big black letters "A.A.A." (Alianza Anticommunista Argentina), the initials of a parapolice group responsible for numerous kidnappings and assassinations—a group with whom the army insisted they had no relations.

The soldiers took me inside the house and recorded what clothing I was wearing and stole my ring. I was then taken to a room and forced to lie down on a mattress. There, with hands tied behind my back, I listened all night long to the voices of men and women: "Sir, water," "Sir, I want to go to the bathroom," "Sir, bread." But no one responded. On several occasions, a guard would enter and hit someone or shout insults. I heard moans. I heard the screams of my husband being tortured. I learned later that they had tied him naked to a metallic bed and applied electric shocks to his temples, gums, chest, and testicles. In the morning, as I was being taken out of the room, I peered through the slit under my blindfold and saw my husband lying on the floor. There was also blood on the floor and they made me step in it.

I was taken to the kitchen to be interrogated by five or six men. At one point, one of the men put an electric prod against my head and shouted "Machine," which is what they call the electric shock torture. They also placed a gun barrel on my temple and pressed the trigger. Later they brought in my husband and told him to tell me of his torture. He could barely speak because his mouth was sore and his tongue hurt from biting it so often during the electric shocks. After beating me and threatening to make me into soap for being Jewish, I was taken back to the room where I had stayed the night before. They told me that they would return in two weeks and "kill me if I didn't remember things." I was terrified several times a day upon hearing the motor of the torturer's car; each time I thought they were coming to get me. However, the days passed and they did not return to interrogate me.

The old house where my husband and I were held is called *La Escuelita* (the Little School) and is located behind the headquarters of the Fifth Army Corps, not far from a motel named *Tú y Yo* (You and I) on the Carrindanga Road. It is near the railroad tracks, and one can hear the trains passing, shots from the army command's firing range, and the mooing of cows.

Prisoners were held in two rooms at *La Escuelita* and were constantly confined to their bunk beds or mattresses on the floor. When it rained, water streamed into the rooms and soaked us since we could not move. The floors

The layout of La Escuelita, *where Alicia Partnoy and her husband, Carlos Sanabria were held and tortured. (Courtesy of Holly Bishop/AAAS.)*

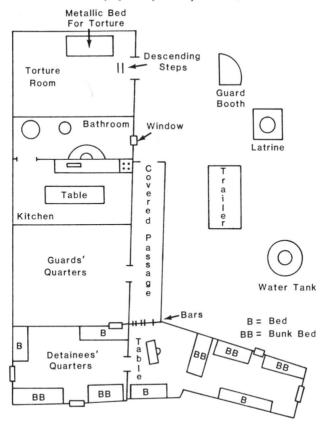

47

were wooden, with cracks and holes. . . . In the middle of these rooms was a hallway where a guard stood, making sure that we neither moved nor spoke. Bars closed off this part of the house from the rest.

At the other end of the passageway there was a room for the guards, a kitchen, and a bathroom where we could sometimes shower. A doorway led to the patio and beyond that to the torture room, the latrine, and a water tank that was used for torture. Outside and close by, there was a trailer where the guards slept. During my detention there, they added one or two trailers for more detainees.

Our guards were primarily personnel from the *Gendarme Nacional*, the army division responsible for border patrols. Twelve guards took custody of the detainees for two months and then a different group took over. Supervisors who were apparently officials toured the camp every day and a half. They were in charge of torture at the interrogations and also assisted in the kidnappings and transfers. Some guards who participated in the torture and kidnapping operations boasted about the activities, telling how they received extra money and shared in the booty. There were also two interrogators, intelligence personnel, who apparently supervised the shift bosses and visited the detention center without notice or when new detainees arrived. Only during the last few days at *La Escuelita* was a doctor or nurse present.

The guards ranged in ages from 18 to 40. I was able to see some of them by spying from under my blindfold. I glimpsed others when we took a shower because then the guards removed our blindfolds and covered their own faces with black hoods. They all called each other by nicknames.

Chiche was a shift supervisor in his early twenties, tall and thin. Once he ordered me to look at him without my blindfold so he could prove that he was not afraid of "subversives." I remember his self-assured tone and his slightly nasal voice.

Viejo was a small, thin man, about 40, who boasted about working at a concentration camp in Tucumán. . . . Peine said he was an electrician and a soldier. He was a *Gendarme* officer and almost always drunk. There were others: thin Bruja from Mendoza, mercenary Abuelo, and Chamame. Some talked about their wives and children. One, Heriberto Lebayen, talked about his mother who lived in Niniguau.

The uncertainty of our fate and our constant fear of death were prolonged for months and added to the misery caused by our severe deprivation and our physical abuse. Without a trial and with no charges against me, my recurrent question was: Will I ever get out of here? Being a "disappeared" person is, for the ones who detain you, being no person at all.

The guards forced us to remain in our beds, often immobile or face down for hours, with our eyes blindfolded and wrists tightly bound. The men prisoners were handcuffed. When the temperature fell below zero [Celsius], we were covered by thin, dirty blankets.

There were times when we were only allowed to relieve ourselves once a day, and only after asking permission for many hours. The guards took us to the bathroom, but the blows, shoves, and mistreatment we received on the way were so severe that we preferred not to go. On one of these trips to the bathroom they broke my tooth by pushing me into the grating that closed off the other rooms. Sometimes they made us form a little train. They entered the rooms yelling, beating us with rubber clubs, making us hurry to put on our shoes, which we had to grope for around the beds. Then the guards made us form lines of four or five, grabbing each other by our clothes. Other times we could hold hands to form the trains. The guards wanted to humiliate us, but they did not realize that the hand contact comforted us. The bathroom was a latrine without doors, out on the patio. While we relieved ourselves, we were watched by the guards who insulted us. Because we were so weak, we often fainted.

We were filthy. We bathed every twenty days and in between we were not allowed to wash our hands, even though we often ate with them because there were no utensils. The guards dusted us with toxic insecticide powder to ward off fleas and lice. While we bathed, we were watched by the hooded guards. After a bath, we put the same dirty clothes back on. Sometimes when guards ransacked houses they brought clothing to the camp. One time they made all the men dress in women's night gowns and dresses while their pants were being dried. The objective was to humiliate them. Once, on a very cold day, the guards hosed off the men on the patio, as if they were animals.

Our meals consisted of lunch at 1:00 P.M. and dinner at 7:00 P.M. , which meant that we didn't eat for eighteen consecutive hours. We were constantly hungry. I lost 20 pounds, until I weighed only 95 pounds even though I am five feet five inches tall. The constant state of stress that we were in made our bodies consume calories rapidly, and compounded our discomfort caused by meager food and a lack of sugar and fruits.

Talking was not allowed and was also punished by blows, punches, or removal of our mattresses. One time when the guards caught me talking they pushed me into the kitchen where I was made to undress and stand under drops of water leaking from the roof. I stood there for half an hour. Then they kicked me hard. On another occasion, they put me in the same room with my husband whom I had not seen for three months. After two days of trying to find a few moments alone to talk, we exchanged a few words, but the guards were listening. We were brutally beaten and then separated.

I will never forget my birthday, 7 February 1977. They allowed me to sit up in bed and gave me some cheese. I heard a radio playing loudly somewhere in the compound. I learned later that they were torturing two prisoners and were trying to drown out their screams with the blaring music. That same day they abducted a 17-year-old boy called Benja and brought him to *La Escuelita*. During the entire day he had been alternately hung by the arms, dunked in a well, and forced to stand in the sun. Then the guards brought him to our room. There they tied his hands to the legs of my bunk bed. I was in the top bunk. All night he remained standing, naked, receiving blows from the night guards, who entered every so often and who complained that they were bored and wanted to box a little. The guards punched Benja in the stomach and he fell, hanging from the bed by only his hands. They forced him to get up and then continued punching him. At one point, when the guards were out of the room I was able to pass him some pieces of cheese and bread under the blanket. I had to put them between my toes and reach for his hands, otherwise I would have been detected.

The atmosphere of violence was permanent at the camp. The guards threatened us constantly by placing guns to our heads or mouths and pretending to pull the trigger. Once a guard was standing in front of my bunk and he accidentally fired inside the room. It could have been fatal.

During my last days at *La Escuelita*, they brought in a so-called doctor, or male nurse, to ask us how we were. Because many of the women were not menstruating, he told us that he would give us an injection, but only "before going to the prison." I heard them say that they were going to inject Zulma Izurieta and Maria Elena Romero the night those two were removed. Secretly, Zulma passed me the earrings she was wearing. Minutes after the two women were injected, I overheard them speaking slowly, like people under the effects of anesthesia.

Maria Elena Romero was seventeen when she was arrested at home by heavily armed plainclothesmen. Her companion, Benja, was a high school student. They were both taken from *La Escuelita* in April 1977 and, according to the newspaper, shot.

Maria's sister, Graciela Romero de Metz, had been arrested in a town outside of Neuguén two months earlier with her husband, Raul Eugenio Metz. They were both at *La Escuelita* when I arrived. They had not heard about their 2-year-old daughter since their arrest. Graciela was five months pregnant at that time. During the transfer by truck to Neuguén, she was tortured with brutal blows and electric shocks to her stomach. Raul was taken away at the end of the month. His name is registered in Amnesty International's list of "disappeared."

Graciela remained at *La Escuelita* until the last month of her pregnancy, when she was allowed each day to walk ten times around a table, while holding onto its edge. They took Graciela to a trailer on the patio a few days before she delivered. She gave birth to a son without complications, but also without medical assistance. She was helped by the guards. Graciela was removed from the prison a short time later, and a guard told me the child was being adopted by another guard.

I spent five months as a "disappeared" person at *La Escuelita* before being transferred to a regular prison, where I was held for two and one-half years more. When the military finally acknowledged that I was a prisoner, I felt relieved. It eased, at least in part, the fear of being killed in the next hour or the following day. Besides, I was at last in touch with my family.

The day I was abducted, the neighbors took in Ruth and then gave her to my parents, who took care of her during my three years of imprisonment. Ruth was scared of noises after my abduction. She cried when the washing machine was on or when she saw masks and clothes resembling uniforms. After my husband and I were transferred from incommunicado detention to regular prisons, Ruth could at least visit us. That meant she had to travel hundreds of kilometers to the north to see me and that same distance south to see her father. Ruth couldn't touch me during her visits as we were separated by a glass window.

When Carlos and I were finally released and forced to leave the country, we brought Ruth with us. Even though she was with her parents, she missed her grandparents, friends, and her country. She often had nightmares and woke up crying that she wanted to go back to "Argentiníta," her Spanish word for little Argentina. I am lucky to have her with me now. Over a hundred and forty children are still "disappeared."

The first time I applied for a right of option to leave the country, it was denied. The second time, I obtained a US visa and my application was filed by coincidence during the visit to Argentina by the Inter-American Commission on Human Rights of the Organization of American States in 1979. International pressure on the government made them release some of the prisoners. I was among the lucky ones.

Now that I am free, I live constantly with another question: Where are the others . . . who were in *La Escuelita*, the child born to Graciela de Metz, the other thousands of "disappeared"? It is hard to be a survivor. It is hard to remember and tell this story over and over, but everyone should know. I reappeared because people worked on my behalf. Now I cannot let the others down.

Testimony of Carlos Sanabria

My name is Carlos Samuel Sanabria. I was born in a small Argentine city called Bahía Blanca. At the time of my abduction, I was 23 years old and in my fifth year of civil engineering studies. I also worked full-time as a tire salesman. I was also an active member of the Peronist Party, which was ousted from power during the military coup of 1976. I have never used violence to further my political beliefs, nor have I ever been charged with a crime.

I was attacked by a group of soldiers at noon while I was at work on 12 January 1977. I was hooded, beaten, thrown into a truck and taken away. . . .

Hours later, still blindfolded, and now naked with my arms tied to my back, I was sent to the torture chamber. At first the place was silent, but once on the metallic torture bed with electricity applied to my skin and genitals, electrodes on my head and scrotum, the shocks of the cattle prods running through my body, people screaming and beating me, the noise and pain were like hell. I was terrorized. I realized that pain can always increase without end. To have that feeling is devastating for the mind. There are not enough words to describe it. There was only one thing left: my mind and my will to live.

During my three months in the concentration camp, I was dirty, starved, and frequently tortured. For the entire three-and-a-half month period I was tied, blindfolded, and prohibited from talking with other prisoners. In that condition, one day felt like an eternity. There was nothing to hear, nothing to see, and no one to talk with. I lack the words to communicate how I felt. Absolute loneliness and endless time are abstract ideas that a human being can think about, but when experiencing them, the desperation is hard to describe. The pain in my shoulders caused by being in the same position on the floor with my arms tied to my back, the pain in each of my wounds, on the tongue, the nose, kidneys, eyes, seemed to be my only physical company. I was always waiting for another session of torture. Once in a room with another blindfolded prisoner, we secretly communicated by clicking fingernails. The communication had one single meaning: You are not alone.

As much as they tortured me, I still had the vision of my daughter and parents. I wanted to see them again. I frequently fell deep into terror and depression, but it was never enough to make me forget them. For others what motivated their survival may have been an ideology: their political or religious beliefs.

While at *La Escuelita* I received medical attention on two occasions. One time during a torture session and while still blindfolded, someone listened to my heart and lungs with a stethoscope. Later, samples of my urine were

Of all the dramatic situations I witnessed in clandestine prisons, nothing can compare to those family groups who were tortured often together, sometimes separately but in view of one another, or in different cells, while one was aware of the other being tortured. The entire affective world, constructed over the years with utmost difficulty, collapses with a kick in the father's genitals, a smack on the mother's face, an obscene insult to the sister, or the sexual violation of a daughter. Suddenly an entire culture based on familial love, devotion, the capacity for mutual sacrifice collapses. Nothing is possible in such a universe, and that is precisely what the torturers know.

Jacobo Timerman

collected because one of my kidneys had been injured. I felt like an animal in a laboratory experiment, with a professional taking care of my vital functions but not of me as a human being. Another prisoner told me that he knew the doctor. He had seen the doctor from underneath his blindfold and recognized him. I only remember that his last name was Germanic, and that he was a doctor in the Fifth Army Corps in Bahía Blanca.

After three and one-half months in the camp, I was sent to a jail, Unit Four of the Province of Buenos Aires. I was kept in isolation for an additional one and one-half months as a "disappeared" person until my name was published. I was then publicly acknowledged as a prisoner in administrative detention at the disposition of the executive branch. When I finally gained contact with other political prisoners, I felt the warmth of all the inmates who gave me the advice and consolation of brothers. The commitment of the prisoners to each other was very strong.

I was transferred to a prison in Rawson in the far south of Argentina two months later, on 22 August 1977. That jail was reserved for political prisoners only. There the reality of my situation was painful, and it seemed that it could last indefinitely. Although we knew that we were weaker than the prison regime, that it could kill any one of us alone, we sensed that we could do something about it through mutual support and sharing.

In the face of deprivation, we shared, even though it was forbidden. In the face of isolation, we developed new ways to communicate through Morse code and sign language. Prisoners collectively decided how many cigarettes each one would get based on the prisoner's previous smoking habits and need, not on the individual allowance of five cigarettes a day that the prison provided. In this way, sharing gave meaning to our existence.

One common discussion in the prison was: What would we do if we were the guards? The guards had weekly meetings and were constantly being pressured to dehumanize us. Their superiors told them that we did not love our families or homeland and that we were killers without souls. They were pressured to punish our smiles, our sharing, and talking. Few of the guards resisted that pressure. Their attitudes changed and they became more repressive as time went on. It was frightening to think that the difference between us was not genetic. Even though some were often drunk and others were sadistic, they were still human beings.

In that jail there were four male nurses, four doctors, one dentist, and one psychiatrist. One of the doctors, who was also a Protestant minister, always showed concern for our health. He visited each prisoner who required medical attention in his cell. He paid genuine attention to our problems. The other three would examine us from the other side of the bars of the cellblock. They showed complete indifference to us. Two of the male nurses were often drunk.

Finally, on 24 October 1979, I was taken by soldiers to the international airport in Buenos Aires, placed on a plane, and flown to exile in Seattle, Washington. Freedom was a shock. Initially, my main problem was lack of initiative. I was depressed about how difficult it was to restart my life. The language and cultural change were difficult. But the hardest part for me was to realize that the human warmth of fellow prisoners that I had experienced in jail was not always a part of the real world—the world outside. I encountered some loving people ready to accept me, but there were many more who did not care about anything other than themselves. These people were quick to think that those from other countries or races were different, and not their brothers and sisters. For me, my rehabilitation as a human being really began during my early days in the detention center when I recognized my need to relate to other human beings. The rehabilitation process continues now as I affirm my belief in love and support those dedicated to the cause of human rights.

Aftermath

Torture is such an overwhelming horror to contemplate that one may tend to forget that, for the victims who survive, its effects do not stop with release. People who have been tortured must learn to come to terms with their experience, and they face problems of reintegration with their families and society. In cases of exile, refugees must also learn to adapt to a new culture.

To help Carlos and Alicia (as well as other refugees) settle upon their

Alicia Partnoy, Carlos Sanabria, and their daughter, Ruth, upon arrival in the United States. (Courtesy of Alicia Partnoy.)

arrival in Seattle, the regional office of the International Rescue Committee and the locally organized South American Refugee Program (SARP) provided them with housing, clothing, language training, and other services.[1] To provide effective health care for the refugees, SARP's medical consultant formed a medical advisory committee of eight health professionals in the Seattle area.[2] As one of its activities, the committee conducted a study of Carlos, Alicia, and other torture victims in collaboration with Amnesty International.[3]

The study brought us in direct contact with several refugees who, until approached by committee members, had never received medical treatment for the torture they had suffered. Refugees in the study were asked to fill out a questionnaire, were interviewed by a psychologist, and were given a medical examination. Because the study helped to identify the common aftereffects of torture, it enabled community workers to recognize the problems that the victims faced and to provide the assistance that they required.

Our study revealed that torture victims and their families often face extensive problems. Family structures are often shaken as a result of the victim's sudden, violent arrest and indefinite detention; in many cases family members do not see their loved ones for several years. Wives often need to find employment if their husbands have been abducted. Splintered family groups often move to the homes of other family members or friends. Young children may suffer enormous mental strain caused by separation from one or both parents for extended periods of time.[4]

Prisoners who are eventually released often return to an altered family atmosphere. Physical and psychological changes in children, spouses, parents, and especially the victims of torture themselves place tremendous stress on the released prisoners. Many find it difficult to reestablish relations with their spouses or to discipline children, show affection, or make decisions. One woman who had been tortured while pregnant and had lost her baby while in detention, for example, found herself "with too many problems to try to be a mother again." For victims of torture, reunion with the family often coincides with exile, requiring adjustments to a new language and customs during a time of already great psychological stress and economic hardship. These victims encounter difficulties in obtaining jobs commensurate with their education and work experiences. The reactions of these victims, the course of their adjustment to new situations, and their methods of coping with their experience are similar to those of other exiled or displaced persons.[5]

Our study enabled us to identify many of these problems in victims of torture and to devise means of alleviating the effects of these problems on both the victims and their families. Community workers associated with the International Rescue Committee and SARP organized workshops on torture and exile for refugees with their American sponsors and church and human rights groups. They alerted local medical groups to typical problems so that the medical personnel could anticipate them. Television stations presented documentaries on refugees, victims of torture, and human rights so that the community at large would better understand their new neighbors.

In the course of rehabilitation, detailed testimonies such as those of Alicia and Carlos prove invaluable for the victims of torture themselves and for people working to prevent torture. Through the often difficult and painful reliving of past ordeals, victims confront the realities of the past and may learn to accept them. The recounting of past experiences also strengthens interpersonal bonds, which are so important during the rehabilitation process. Many torture victims have found some meaning in their suffering by using their testimonies to promote human rights issues. For example, Alicia's complete testimony, which contains the names of 50 other "disappeared" persons whom she met in *La Escuelita*, was given to President Alfonsín's special commission to investigate the "disappearance" of thousands of persons from 1976 to 1983. She has also contacted the families of several detainees at *La Escuelita* to help the families locate their missing relatives.

Finally, for people working to promote human rights, testimonies provide valuable records documenting torture as well as names, dates, and places for further investigation or intervention. For instance, during its investigation of past military abuses, staff members of Argentina's special human rights commission took testimony from hundreds of former prisoners who were tortured. On several occasions, torture victims accompanied commission members to former detention centers, where they described their imprisonment and ill treatment. Such accounts figure prominently in the commission's report detailing the activities of 340 former secret detention centers located throughout the country.

The elimination of torture and other forms of interpersonal violence requires, as a first step, that we acknowledge its presence. Accounts of torture by the victims themselves clearly demonstrate that the phenomenon of torture is not an abstraction but a succession of personal tragedies, disabling to individuals and destructive to humankind.

Notes and References

1. The International Rescue Committee, founded to aid refugees from Nazi Germany, now assists persons fleeing their countries because of political, racial, or religious repression. Pat Taran founded SARP with the support of the Church Council of Greater Seattle and a grant from the LeBrun Foundation.

2. As a member of the SARP board of directors, Cornelis Kolff reviewed programs and issues related to the resettlement and rehabilitation of refugees. The board included representatives from two major refugee organizations in the Seattle area, the Committee of Refugees from Chile, and the Committee of Solidarity for the People of Argentina.

3. Some of the findings of the study are presented in Chapter 3.

4. Amnesty International Seminar, Copenhagen, December 1979, in *Danish Medical Bulletin* 27, no. 5 (November 1980), pp. 213–252. See also Federico Allodi, "Acute Paranoid Reaction (Boufée Delirante) in Canada," *Canadian Journal of Psychiatry* 27, no. 5 (August 1982): 366–372.

5. See, for example: K. M. Lin et al., "Adaptational Problems of Vietnamese Refugees, Part I: Health and Mental Status," paper presented at the World Congress on Mental Health, Vancouver, B. C., 21–26 August 1977; R. D. Rambaut, "The Family in Exile, Cuban Expatriates in the United States," *American Journal of Psychiatrists* 133, no. 4 (1976), pp. 395–399; L. Tyhurst, "Displacement and Migration: A Study in Social Psychiatry," *American Journal of Psychiatrists* 107 (1971): 561–568.

Chapter 3

Physical and Psychiatric Effects of Torture: Two Medical Studies

Federico Allodi (Canadian study)
and
Glenn R. Randall, Ellen L. Lutz, José Quiroga, María Victoria Zunzunegui,
Cornelis A. Kolff, Ana Deutsch, and Roscius Doan (US study)

Each year a large number of people who have been tortured by their governments emigrate to the United States and Canada. They come from all parts of the world, including Central and South America, Indochina, the Middle East, and Africa. As a direct consequence of torture, these persons often suffer from devastating medical problems that require both immediate and long-term attention. In addition to physical impairments, torture victims often suffer from a wide variety of psychological disorders, including nightmares, memory loss, and anxiety, that persist for years and interfere with their daily lives.

An example of the problems encountered by torture victims even years after their torture makes clear the need to provide appropriate treatment.

> Mr. R. S., 37 years of age, married, with five children, was a professor in the Faculty of Arts at the University of San Salvador in the capital city of El Salvador.
>
> He came to Toronto in the spring of 1983, after harrowing experiences in Mexico. He had left El Salvador immediately after his release from a jail where he had been a prisoner for 18 months. Military authorities there had imprisoned him because of his university teaching practices. In prison, he was subjected to fifteen days of systematic torture, administered before interrogations in sessions lasting from six to ten hours. The torture included punching and kicking, threats and obscenities, beatings with wooden sticks, and

electrical currents applied to his mouth, ears, nipples, and genitals. In addition, he was hung from a swinging rope that was tied behind his back to his hands and feet. In every torture session, the victim was completely nude.

Mr. R. S. believes that the immediate precipitant of his arrest was an encounter he had with the cashier of the payroll office where he last worked. One day his regular paycheck was reduced by a considerable amount. When he demanded his regular pay in full, the man said sarcastically, "You must be one of those Communists who always protests," which under the prevailing circumstances in El Salvador meant a serious risk of jail or even death.

In Canada, while attending an English class provided by the government, he disagreed with some remarks that the teacher made in a conversation about Latin America. She said to him something like, "You seem to be a person who likes to protest and challenge other people's opinions." Although he had been a healthy and stable man until then, for the next three days he did not attend school, staying at home, mostly in bed, feeling depressed, agitated, and suffering from violent headaches. Unknowingly, the teacher's words had triggered in his mind the memory of his experience of torture.

Health professionals, employers, and other persons who interact with victims of torture need to be aware of and understand the consequences of torture on the life of victims. Without such understanding, victims of torture will continue to be victims—of misdiagnosis and inappropriate medical and psychiatric care, of preventable job stress and discrimination, of marital and family disruption, and of avoidable suicide.

To prevent subjecting torture victims to these potential tragedies, the signs and symptoms of torture must be recognized, and effective methods of treatment known. To evaluate any treatment, all available cases must be assessed and statistically analyzed so that generalizations applicable to new cases can be made. Anecdotal information, while interesting, is often of limited value, because circumstances and kind of torture vary, as do the experiences and physical and psychological makeup of each victim.

Presented here are the findings of two studies of refugees in North America who were tortured in Latin America. These studies describe the types of physical and psychological problems that health professionals and others may encounter in torture victims who are living in exile. The nature and extent of the problems that torture victims living in exile face are likely to be somewhat different from those facing victims who remain in their own countries because these victims had the ability to leave their country and must adapt to a new society.

The first study presented in this chapter gives the results of physical and psychological examinations of 44 torture victims who emigrated to the United

Torture victims, if they survive, often face problems locating their families and then rebuilding their lives. One of the happier stories is that of Rosemary Riveros, abducted and tortured by military personnel in Buenos Aires in December 1975. She lost contact with her daughter, Tamara, in June 1976 and continued to be held without charge or trial until May 1981, when she was released into exile after international appeals. Through the Grandmothers of the Plaza de Mayo, Riveros was finally able to find her child. They were reunited in Lima, Peru in July 1983. (Courtesy of Amnesty International.)

States. A group of health professionals associated with Amnesty International USA conducted the study. Since 1978 this organization has examined and arranged appropriate treatment for victims of torture who are living in the United States.

The second study, carried out in Toronto by a psychiatrist associated with Amnesty International, consisted of psychiatric examinations of 41 torture victims who had emigrated to Canada. Differences in methodology preclude comparing the two sets of findings directly, but their broad similarities permit a general discussion of the psychological effects of torture and approaches to treating torture victims.

The US Study
Methods

This study* was conducted in seven cities throughout the United States. The majority of participants (88 percent) were examined in Los Angeles, San Francisco, and Seattle—cities where large numbers of torture victims have resettled. Subjects were recruited through refugee organizations and by word of mouth and were examined by teams of physicians, psychologists, and psychiatrists using standard research protocols developed by physicians associated with Amnesty International USA. Each study participant gave informed consent in writing.

Subjects completed a questionnaire on their detention and torture, which included items on the circumstances and reason for their arrest, the duration and conditions of their imprisonment, and all episodes of abuse or torture. Information was gathered on the extent and type of torture and on the duration and intensity of immediate and later symptoms that developed. The family medical history and personal health status before and after torture were also recorded.

A physician performed a physical examination of each study participant, obtaining additional consultation and laboratory tests where indicated. A psychologist or a psychiatrist fluent in the participant's native language carried out a psychological examination, which included an evaluation of mental status. In some cases, multiple examinations were made either for more thorough investigation or for the convenience of the subject. Seven (16 percent) of the 44 subjects refused the psychological examination.

* The authors wish to acknowledge the assistance of Dr. Sedgwick Mead, Dr. Michael Nelson, Dr. Sandy Lawrence, Ms. Ana María Rodriguez, Dr. Dean Echenberg, Dr. Kevin O'Grady, and La Clínica de la Raza. This study was supported by a grant from the Le Brun Foundation.

Study Population

Thirty-seven males and seven females participated in the study, and all but four persons were under 40 years of age. Most study participants were from Chile (25) and Argentina (10), and most (38) were tortured in these two countries. Other Latin American countries accounted for about one-fifth (9) of the cases. Most of the participants stated that that had been detained and tortured between 1973 and 1976, several years before the examination. Four of the participants, however, stated that they had been tortured less than one year before the time of the examination.

Methods of Torture

Table 1 lists the methods of torture used and their distribution among the victims. All participants were subjected to more than one form of torture. Thirty-eight of the 44 were beaten, two-thirds were subjected to electric

Table 1 US Study: Reported Methods of Torture ($n = 44$)

Method	n	%
Beating	38	85
Electric torture	29	66
Parilla	7	16
Stretching	5	11
Submarino	12	27
Burns	9	20
Suspension	9	20
Sexual torture	5[a]	11
Rape	1	2
Other	4	9
Teléfono	7	16
Plantón	8	18
Asphyxiation	5	11

Note: Parilla is a form of electrical torture whereby the victim is strapped to a metal bed or bedsprings, often with strips of wet cloth, and electric currents are sent through the victim's body. *Submarino* is forced submersion of the victim into a tub of water, often filled with vomit, blood, urine, and/or feces, until the victim is nearly asphyxiated. *Teléfono* is a form of torture whereby the victim is boxed with cupped hands on the ear. *Plantón* is forced standing for hours or days at a time, often with arms outstretched and/or holding weights.

[a] 4 females and 1 male.

Table 2 US Study: Reported Psychological Abuse ($n = 37$)

Method	n	%
Isolation (>72 h)	25	68
Induced debility or exhaustion		
Food deprivation (>72 h)	24	65
Water deprivation (>48 h)	23	62
Sleep deprivation (>24 h)	20	54
Conditions of extreme heat or cold	14	38
Cold showers	9	24
Monopolization of perception		
Restricted movement	17	46
Blindfolding	34	92
Bright lights	6	16
Loud music	9	24
Threats		
Threats of death	23	62
Threats against family	8	22
Threats of further torture	9	24
Sham executions	17	46
Witnessing torture	24	65
Degradation		
Personal hygiene prevented	37	100
Denial of privacy	37	100
Verbal abuse (insults)	37	100
Overcrowding	12	32
Excrement in food	3	8
Infected surroundings (lice)	5	13
Nakedness	27	73
Occasional indulgence		
Fluctuation of interrogator's attitude	7	19
Pharmacologic manipulation		
Intravenous, sodium pentothal	4	11
Intravenous, unknown drug	2	5
Oral	3	8
Hypnosis	3	8

Note: This chart represents a modified version of the Biderman Chart of Coercion.

shock, and a substantial minority received burns or were suspended or submerged in water. Almost all were blindfolded or hooded during the early part of their detention. The movements of these victims were severely restricted, often by chains or manacles attached to a chair, bed, or wall or by confinement in cells too small to permit sitting or lying down. Deprivation of food (for at least 72 hours), water (for at least 48 hours), and sleep (for at least 24 hours) were common. All victims were denied privacy for personal hygiene, and most were forced to undress for interrogation sessions.

Victims or their families frequently received death threats, and 17 (46 percent) underwent sham executions. Drugs, probably sedatives or hypnotics, were administered to 9 subjects, in 6 cases by intravenous injection. All of the subjects suffered psychological abuse. Table 2 describes the types of psychological abuse that were inflicted.

Effects of Torture

Of the physical effects, signs on the skin were the most evident. At the time of examination, nine victims, including four who had been tortured within one year of examination, had visible injuries. Among these were the characteristic scars associated with cigarette burns or electric shock torture. Participants reported that superficial thermal or electrical burns often healed without leaving scars.

Obstetric and gynecological problems were common among the seven women. One, who was pregnant before detention, was subjected to intravaginal electric shock. She subsequently aborted and then suffered three months of vaginal bleeding, for which she received infrequent and offensive medical attention. Another woman was raped during detention and delivered a child after release. Since that time she has suffered several spontaneous abortions. Three other women were sexually abused during detention. Three women stopped menstruating during detention, and two more stopped following detention. Painful menstruation developed as a new problem in three of the seven women.

Three-quarters of the victims of *teléfono*—violent boxing of the ears—reported hearing loss at the time of examination. Two-thirds of the participants who were suspended by their arms suffered from persistent upper back pain.

Recently tortured victims generally had the greatest number of specific physical signs and symptoms of torture, as one might expect. Especially noticeable were orthopedic problems, extensive bruises from beatings, marks or wounds from burns, and abrasions from shackling or tying.

One common somatic complaint that could not be correlated directly to any specific method of torture was lower back pain. At the time of examination, this condition was noted in 20 percent of the subjects, although none had had lower back pain prior to torture. In addition, 55 percent of the victims complained of headaches during the period immediately following torture. The frequency of this complaint decreased to 30 percent at the time of the examination.

Although the physical symptoms of torture tended to decrease or become less troublesome over time, the psychological symptoms persisted and caused great distress in most of the study participants years after the episode of torture. Because the victims were subjected to many forms of physical and psychological torture, the psychological complaints could not be correlated with specific forms.

Most participants reported suffering from anxiety. Many had recurrent nightmares about their torture or were reminded of it by ordinary stimuli. Many experienced a diminished responsiveness to the external world. Table 3 lists the psychological consequences of torture reported by the participants at the time of the examination.

Thirty-eight percent of the study participants (17 out of 44) met all the criteria for the diagnosis of post-traumatic stress disorder, as described by

Table 3 US Study: Psychological Symptoms at the Time of Examination ($n = 37$)

Psychological symptom	*n*	%
Established by history		
Difficulty in establishing new relationships	12	32
Intrusive recollections of events	15	41
Inability to trust other individuals	14	38
Increased attachment to other individuals	7	19
Withdrawal from other people	7	19
Affective		
Anxious mood		
Anxiety	14	38
Irritability	12	32
Lability of affect	10	27
Tension		
Inability to relax	16	43
Phobias	15	41
Depressed mood		
Inability to enjoy life	9	24
Apathy	8	22
Difficulty with feeling emotions	10	27
Difficulty with sleep	23	62
Easily tired	16	43
Intellectual		
Decrease in ability to concentrate	22	59
Decrease in memory	22	59
Somatoform		
Conversion disorder (psychosomatic symptoms)	11	30

Note: The symptoms in this chart are grouped according to the divisions of the Mental Status Examination.

the Diagnostic and Statistical Manual III (DSM-III) of the American Psychiatric Association. The characteristic symptoms of this disorder are "re-experiencing the traumatic event, numbing of responsiveness to or reduced involvement with the external world, and a variety of autonomic, dysphoric [an abnormal feeling of anxiety, discontent, or physical discomfort] or cognitive symptoms." As the DSM-III notes, the disorder is apparently more severe and longer lasting when the stressor is of human design rather than of natural origin. For example, torture victims may be subjected to sham executions. They may be placed before a firing squad, hear shots fired, and see many of those standing with them killed. The survivors may then be returned to their cells, only to be brought before the firing squad again and again on subsequent days. The above example contrasts to cases in which persons are victims of a natural disaster, such as an earthquake or a flood, where the stress is not deliberately caused by human beings.

Even though less than 50 percent of the study participants met all the criteria for post-traumatic stress disorder, the examiners felt that the prevalence may be much higher. The research protocol in the study was not designed to evaluate each diagnostic criterion of post-traumatic stress disorder. Therefore, questions that might have confirmed a diagnosis of the disorder were not always asked.

The Canadian Study

Method

This study, reported in greater detail elsewhere,[1] presents the findings of the psychiatric examination of 41 victims of torture. Family physicians or lawyers had referred these victims for consultation or treatment to the Transcultural Psychiatry Unit of a university teaching hospital in Toronto. Subjects came from three Latin American countries, the large majority from Chile; the time of the torture incident varied from six years to a few months prior to examination.

A psychiatrist fluent in Spanish interviewed the patients. Information collected included the subject's demographic and social characteristics, year of arrival in Canada, and conditions of arrest, detention, and ill-treatment or torture. The psychiatrist recorded the methods of torture, both physical and psychological, and the victim's overt physical signs as well as symptoms of torture. Somatic, affective, and mental symptoms were examined, and changes in mental function and personality were estimated based on a history of each subject. Medical care after the episode of torture and the behavior of the doctor toward the victim were also noted.

Study Population

As in the US study, most of the torture victims in the Canadian study were male (33 out of 41), young (less than 30 years old), and fairly well educated. All had arrived in Canada between 1977 and 1979.

Almost all of the subjects had been violently and arbitrarily apprehended by the military, often in the middle of the night. The victim's home and possessions were frequently damaged or destroyed, and family members, including children, were menaced or molested. The most common reasons given for the arrest were political involvement of the victims themselves (36 cases) or of their families (10 cases). In two instances the reason was more tenuous. One person was maltreated because someone in the same building possessed political pamphlets, another because he had the same name as a person already wanted by the authorities.

Two women were maltreated but not imprisoned. The remaining 39 subjects experienced a total of 112 incarcerations. One person was imprisoned 11 times in five years, but most (31) were imprisoned from one to three times, usually for periods ranging from seven days to one year, the longest being five years.

Methods of Torture

After arrest, victims were usually blindfolded and taken to a military prison, where conditions were extremely unsanitary and the food poor. All were subjected to physical abuse and almost all to psychological abuse (see Table 4). The majority were slapped, kicked, and punched or beaten with a variety of weapons, including rifle butts, truncheons, whips, and heavy sticks wrapped in wet cloths to minimize visible damage. Eleven victims had had bones broken during interrogation. Almost two-thirds (27) of the victims underwent electric shock torture, either directly, with electrodes attached to the fingers, toes, head, and genitals, or by lying on the *parilla*, an electrified metal bedspring. Sexual molestation, including attempted rape, and stripping and pawing were experienced by almost one-half of the men and women in the group. Other forms of torture included subjection to bright lights for long periods of time, enclosure of the prisoner's head in a plastic bag, and extraction of fingernails and toenails. Five persons reported being burned with cigarettes, boiling water, burning sticks, or chemicals. Starvation (deprivation of food or water for more than 48 hours) was also common.

Effects of Torture

All but three of the victims displayed somatic symptoms resulting from the torture. (See Table 5.) The majority complained of severe nervousness or

67

Table 4 Canadian Study: Reported Methods of Torture ($n = 41$)

Method	n	%
Deprivation		
Food deprivation	12	29
Water deprivation	15	37
Food and water deprivation	16	39
Sensory deprivation	12	29
Overstimulation		
Bright lights, etc.	12	29
Physical torture		
Beating	40	98
Slapping, kicking, punching, *teléfono*	40	98
Striking with rifle butt	32	78
Striking with heavy whip, baton, or torch	25	61
Burns from cigarette, chemicals, hot water, electricity	5	12
Electric shock, *parilla*	27	66
Suspension, hanging by fingers	12	29
Cold water, showers, submersion	15	37
Other physical torture (nail removal, asphyxiation, etc.)	12	29
Psychological torture		
Verbal abuse	32	78
False accusations	35	85
Threats of death, execution	31	76
Threats against self, further torture	23	56
Threats against family and friends	13	32
Sham executions	12	29
Rape	6	15
Other sexual molestation or torture	14	34
Other psychological torture (degradation, excrement in food, etc.)	12	29

Note: *Teléfono* is a form of torture whereby the victim is boxed with cupped hands on the ear. *Parilla* is a form of electrical torture whereby the victim is strapped to a metal bed or bedsprings, often with strips of wet cloth, and electric currents are sent through the victim's body.

insomnia with recurrent nightmares. Many suffered from anxiety (36), depression (29), or unspecified, deep-seated fears (12). Thirty-one people showed objective evidence of physical damage, including scarring from lacerations or burning (21), deafness or blurred vision (5), weight loss (10), and evidence of fractures (8). Half of the victims mentioned behavioral and personality changes, mainly irritable outbursts, impulsive behavior, or social withdrawal. Four people attempted suicide. Eighteen of the victims reported changes in mental functioning; of these, 13 reported loss of concentration

Table 5 Canadian Study: Long-term Effects of Torture ($n = 41$)

Effect	n	%
Physical		
Scars, burns	21	51
Fractures	8	20
Deafness, blurred vision	5	12
Weight loss	10	24
Psychosomatic		
Pains, headaches	22	54
Nervousness	33	80
Nightmares, night panic	14	34
Insomnia	28	68
Tremors, weakness, dizziness, fainting, diarrhea, sweating	26	63
Affective		
Depression	29	71
Anxiety	36	88
Fears, phobias	12	29
Behavioral		
Withdrawal, irritability, aggressiveness, impulsivity	13	32
Sexual dysfunction, severe	5	12
Suicide attempt	4	10
Intellectual and mental		
Confusion, disorientation	5	12
Memory loss	12	29
Loss of concentration	13	32

or attention and blocking of the flow of thought. Twelve persons reported difficulty in remembering, and 5 persons reported episodes of confusion and disorientation.

Medical Care Following Torture

More than half the group received no or insufficient medical care during their imprisonment because it was either withheld or unavailable. For example, medical care for seven victims who needed it urgently because of fractures or large lacerations was withheld for 48 hours.

Physicians treating the victims of torture during their imprisonment ranged from passive accomplices, who determined how much torture victims could withstand without dying, to compassionate providers of care. Passive accomplices clearly violated medical ethics, although they may have felt themselves forced to do so by their superiors. The few who provided comfort and care behaved according to internationally established codes of medical ethics. In one case, for instance, a surgeon refused to allow soldiers to remove his patient from her hospital bed. Most physicians, however, remained detached from the situation, thus violating medical ethics. Such behavior by colleagues is a cause for concern for physicians worldwide.

Discussion

The broad findings of these two studies agree with each other and with findings of similar research conducted in Canada,[2] Denmark,[3] and Ireland[4] on persons tortured in Latin America and Western Europe. All of these studies reported similar forms of physical and psychological torture and the same range of aftereffects. It would be helpful in rehabilitating all torture victims if conclusions drawn from these studies could lead to effective treatment.

But before the findings of the US and Canadian studies presented here can be generalized to a wider population, several research constraints must be noted. First, unlike some victims of torture all of the participants in these studies survived their torture, were able to leave their countries, and satisfied the immigration requirements of the country in which they resettled. Second, neither group was randomly selected; in the US study all of the subjects were volunteers and were therefore self-selected, and participants in the Canadian study were seeking or referred for psychiatric care. Finally, the interval between torture and the time of examination was not controlled in either study.

Can the findings of these studies be applied to victims of torture who are still living in the countries where they were tortured? A recent study undertaken in Chile suggests that they can.[5] The study was conducted as part of a mental health program set up after the 1973 military coup to provide psychotherapeutic assistance to those persecuted by the military government. Thirty-nine persons were treated in the program, 15 of whom had been tortured and 2 of whom had survived execution attempts allegedly carried out by government agents. The Chilean study did not contain any statistics on the effects of torture; however, it did indicate that the predominant symptomatology presented by torture victims included "helplessness, anxiety, sleeplessness, feelings of disintegration, inability to concentrate, impaired memory, specific or generalized fear, social withdrawal, irritability, loss of appetite, and a variety of psychosomatic symptoms." All of these problems appeared frequently among the subjects in the studies reported here.

Another question is whether the psychological symptoms that the studies suggest are associated with torture are caused or aggravated by the psycho-social, linguistic, and cultural stresses of being a refugee. Recent evidence indicates that violent political persecution, including torture, is a major and significant cause of severe psychological stress that is independent of exile or immigration. This evidence comes from the only study of the medical effects of torture that included a control group of people who were not tortured but who did share nationality, political beliefs, socioeconomic status, problems of exile, and other potentially confounding variables with torture victims.[6]

Post-traumatic Stress Disorder and the "Torture Syndrome"

Researchers in other studies of torture and its aftereffects (sequelae) have referred to a "torture syndrome"—Is there a predictable cluster of sequelae that results from torture? For example, two Danish researchers, Rasmussen and Lunde, suggested that although their results did not permit them to describe a specific torture syndrome, future research might provide the basis for doing so.[7] Canadian researchers Allodi and Cowgill described a torture syndrome that includes torture as the stressor, any physical sequelae of torture, and the psychological sequelae of "severe anxiety, insomnia with nightmares about persecution, violence or other torture experiences, somatic symptoms of anxiety, phobias, suspiciousness, and fearfulness."[8]

Allodi and Cowgill believe that the torture syndrome represents a clinical pattern recognized for the past thirty years, either implicitly in the national and international systems of classifying disease or more generally in standard textbooks of psychiatry and specialized works on the subject. Generally, in international and US professional diagnostic classification systems it is generally included in the group of stress response syndromes, gross stress reactions, or post-traumatic stress disorders.*

A recognizable stress and the symptoms of anxiety, hyperalertness, disturbances in concentration and memory, and a tendency to reexperience the

---

* The *Diagnostic and Statistical Manual* of the American Psychiatric Association of 1968 and 1980 (DSM-II and DSM-III) included the torture syndrome under the general category of "transient situational disturbances" (DSM-II, code no. 307) and "post-traumatic stress disorder, acute, chronic or delayed" (DSM-III, code nos. 308 and 309). The ninth revision of the *Manual of the International Classification of Diseases* [ICD 9] of the World Health Organization provides for similar categories.[9]

trauma in dreams and thoughts are components of both the torture syndrome and other stress and post-traumatic disorders. However, a specific criterion of the torture syndrome is that the person affected lacks any apparent predisposition to mental disorder.

At this time, the US researchers do not think that their data are sufficient to establish a specific torture syndrome distinct from post-traumatic stress disorder. However, they also believe that the diagnosis of post-traumatic stress disorder should be modified to distinguish torture-induced stress from other severe natural and human-induced stresses, such as rape or assault. This could be accomplished by creating subcategories of the post-traumatic stress disorder according to etiology.

An argument for establishing specific diagnostic criteria for a torture syndrome is that many victims of torture are at risk of developing, or do develop, psychological symptoms that could benefit from treatment. However, because these people do not satisfy the strict criteria for post-traumatic stress disorder, their needs can be overlooked. Recognizing a torture syndrome would establish more flexible criteria and, without compromising specificity, make it easier to diagnose the psychological difficulties associated with torture and administer appropriate care to the victims.

Treatment Implications (Based on the Canadian Study)

Although neither of the studies described in this chapter was designed to evaluate specific modes of treatment, Allodi believes that his findings and clinical impressions have direct implications for treatment. He found that few of the physical problems suffered by the torture victims in his study required special treatment, and few were directly traceable to torture methods especially if a year or more had passed since the episode of torture. Because the physical methods of torture were either traumatic or deprivational, generally accepted methods of treating the resultant injuries were usually successful, and no specific, torture-related treatments were needed. For example, scarring from thermal burns or deformed fingers from previous fractures were treated by surgery, as other traumatic sequelae would be.

In contrast, the psychological effects of torture usually persisted long after most of the physical effects had disappeared. Consequently, health professionals working with torture victims frequently encounter psychological effects and should be prepared to treat patients so afflicted. Thus, recognizing the need for specific treatments for psychological, but not necessarily physical, sequelae of torture is useful in treating victims and in training mental health professionals.

The primary need for a victim of persecution is a safe environment. This is common sense, and it was also the consensus of a group of health professionals who, under the sponsorship of the World Health Organization and the Dutch government, met in The Hague in 1981 to discuss the psychosocial effects of violence.[10] Even after a refugee's safety is ensured, usually in another country, psychiatric help is generally not an immediate need. Only the most severely disturbed victims seek immediate attention either in the country where the torture took place or in the country to which they emigrate.

The torture victim's cultural background as well as the availability of relevant and affordable mental health services generally determines whether he or she seeks out psychiatric care. Once economic and language barriers are overcome, medical, psychological, social, and legal services are more likely to be used effectively if the various agencies integrate their services, collaborate among themselves, and create a climate empathetic to the torture victim.

For example, a torture victim may perceive psychiatric services offered independently of other services as irrelevant and thus underutilize them. Groups helping refugees in Holland, Chile, and Canada have designed programs to assist refugees, and these are good examples of how services can be integrated to meet the needs of torture victims. (Stover and Nelson describe these programs further in Chapter 5.)

Allodi maintains that when a torture victim begins psychiatric treatment, psychiatrists and other health professionals should be aware of the following issues:

1. *Trust.* The patient should perceive the physician or therapist as part of a secure environment. Without trust the so-called therapeutic alliance, a basic element in effective psychotherapy, cannot take place. Empathy and trust are often ensured by the fact that most physicians and health professionals working with refugees and victims of persecution volunteer and thus are especially motivated. In addition, group therapy for torture victims has the initial advantage of creating an atmosphere of mutual trust and acceptance among the participants.[11]

2. *Catharsis and regression.* The first interviews should be conducted in the quiet and safety of the consulting room, because the retelling of past experiences is invariably accompanied by an outpouring of emotions. The physiological concomitants of such emotions indicate the intensity of the emotional reaction. Not even a consummate actor could produce at will the flowing of tears, heavy perspiration, accelerated pulse rate, and elevated blood pressure that attend a torture victim's recounting of his or her

experience. Regression to the time of the torture is temporary, and the pressures of reality maintain the focus on the here and now.

3. *Feelings of guilt.* Only two of the patients in the Canadian study reported feelings of guilt—sentiments clearly related to trauma. In one case, a young man, who was a university student and politically active, had persuaded his father to participate in a community-based distribution program of food and clothing administered by the previous government. The new rulers put the father and son in jail and tortured them. The son came out 5 months later, but the father died in prison after five years. The son, with great remorse, felt that if he had not asked his father to get involved in politics, his father would still have been alive.

In the other case, a young woman, who previously had been raped repeatedly by soldiers while imprisoned in a soccer stadium, was trying to hide at home when the soldiers came to pay a regular check-up visit. Her 15-year-old sister opened the door and said that she was alone. The soldiers then began to make sexual advances toward her. When the older sister came out to defend her, the soldiers raped the 15-year-old as "punishment for having lied." The patient felt guilty for having asked her sister to lie in order to protect her.

Much has been written about survivors' guilt, the feeling that some victims of persecution or torture develop when they realize that they have survived while others, generally friends or loved ones, have perished. Rather than attributing their survival to external or to fortuitous circumstances, they attribute it to a personal act of commission or omission. Two types of guilt feelings should be distinguished: situational, or realistic, guilt and pervasive, or existential, guilt. In situational guilt, the guilty feelings of the survivors seem to be commensurate to the circumstances they believe led to their survival and to the deaths of others. Situational guilt as an initial or transient reaction is very common; it is often detected during the first interviews with survivors. Based on experience with survivors of political persecutions in Latin America in the last decade, situational guilt generally has a good prognosis and is easily dispelled with psychotherapeutic discussions and reassurances.

On the other hand, the guilt reactions fequently found among survivors of the Holocaust who emigrated to North America have a pervasive or an existential quality that might have resulted from the different experiences of those victims. The guilty feelings of these survivors tend to be quite unrelated to any of their acts of commission or omission, and no reassurance seems to dispell these feelings.

The psychoanalytic literature in North America reports that such severe and long-lasting feelings of guilt were common among Holocaust survivors. Eitinger, however, who conducted the best documented and most reliable epidemiological studies on the psychiatric morbidity of survivors of the Holocaust in Norway and Israel, did not find such feelings of guilt to be very prominent.[12]

To avoid confusion, reports of guilt among refugees should be accompanied by careful descriptions of this sentiment. In a sense, guilt is rage directed inward and treatment helps to expiate it without prolonged self-punishment. To blame someone is a psychological necessity; it is a search for both cause and meaning. Blaming serves as a symbolic retribution or compensation for suffering or loss, even though the loss cannot be fully compensated. Blaming others also helps victims to deal with their feelings of unforgiving rage toward the perpetrators. Experiencing restitution, whether real or symbolic, and punishment of the responsible agents afford victims a measure of protection and psychological stability.[13]

Many study participants asked how there could be so much evil in the world. Being told that torture was illegal everywhere and that their tormentors were wrong appeared to help them cope with this concern. Paradoxically, victims may find victory in their defeat and humiliation. This may explain why many torture victims become active in human rights campaigns. By doing so, they can tell the world that repressive governments are unjust. As a result, they gain a certain kind of retribution for what they have suffered. In his work with Nazi concentration camp survivors, Lifton called this process the survivor's "struggle for meaning." He found that concentration camp survivors often "seek something beyond economic or social restitution—something closer to acknowledgement of crimes committed against them and punishment of those responsible—in order to reestablish at least the semblance of a moral universe.[14]

4. *The new self and the continuation of a dialogue with society.* To achieve a favorable psychotherapeutic outcome, the torture victim must have an acceptable self-concept and see the world as a fairly secure and predictable place. However, exile or immigration may complicate the victim's rehabilitation because of the need to establish new relationships in a new community while still retaining a sense of continuity between the past and future. Daly notes that torture victims who leave their country of origin often feel "rejected and expect to be rejected."[15] They may be depressed and "not prone to good self care or to reaching out in social contacts with others in their new surroundings. Thus social skills training can be very important to their rehabilitation." Finally, in the process of therapy, the patient has to find some meaning and personal satisfaction in his or her role in the traumatic

experience. After such reconciliation has taken place, the patient can go on trusting and living.

A good example of a person attempting to come to terms with his experience of torture and his survival is provided by a 42-year-old Argentine schoolteacher. He spent five years in jail and then came directly to Canada in 1979 as part of a program sponsored by the Canadian government. He described his views of his past and present in this fashion:

> Politically there were errors, poor performance. . . . I blame myself and I blame others for that, but on matters of principle and reasons for participating I feel very comfortable. . . . The system that oppressed me and tortured me is not society, it was a group of society, a phenomenon of a moment of transition in the history of my country . . . . The problem of torture and repression is not only limited to my country, it is global. . . . The task [of mastering my experiences] is not complete. I still have memories and thoughts that unsettle me. The business of being alive is related to the necessity of overcoming those experiences. . . . In my poetry I deal with the ambivalence of reconciliation with the past and hope as primary goals. I would like to forget, but I can't. I have been marked for life. I don't have the right to forget my disappeared friends. I'm damned not to forget, to hope, which is not a passive but a very active state of being. [He continues:] when I returned to Argentina last year after the election of a democratic government, I felt very ashamed. It is sheer luck that I am alive. I don't torture myself but it is as if I felt guilty.

Conclusion

Although the studies described in this chapter contribute to our knowledge about the aftereffects of torture and provide some guidance in approaches to treatment, there is still much to be learned about the best ways to help victims recover. Moreover, the difficulties of comparing the results of the two studies emphasize the need for further research. Standard terminology and appropriate research instruments, such as questionnaires and scales specifically designed for evaluating victims from any country, need to be developed. Treatment protocols must be designed and evaluated to assess the role and effectiveness of support groups and networks, social activity in exile, and psychiatric intervention. The development of sequelae of torture over time also requires careful study.

Research along these lines should lead to the development of interventions that help in restoring physical and mental health to victims of torture. There is much that physicians can do, alone and with others, to prevent abuse.

Physicians, backed by internationally agreed upon codes of ethics, should refuse to participate actively or passively in torture. They should also make their views known to the international community and, if possible, contribute to treatment and rehabilitation of torture victims and their families. The ultimate aim, of course, is to prevent all torture. This can be done only if physicians and health workers work together with legal, governmental, religious, and humanitarian groups and agencies to stop this inhuman practice.

Notes and References

1. F. Allodi and G. Cowgill, "Ethical and Psychiatric Aspects of Torture: A Canadian Study," *Canadian Journal of Psychiatry* 27(1982):98–102.

2. L. M. Cathcart, P. Berger, and B. Knazan, "Medical Examination of Torture Victims Applying for Refugee Status," *Canadian Medical Association Journal* 121(1979):179–184.

3. Danish Medical Group of Amnesty International, *Results of Examinations of 14 Argentine Victims of Torture* (London: Amnesty International, 1980); O. V. Rasmussen, A. M. Dam, and I. L. Nielsen, "Torture: A Study of Chilean and Greek Victims," in *Evidence of Torture: Studies by the Amnesty International Danish Medical Group* (London: Amnesty International, 1977); O. V. Rasmussen and I. Lunde, "Evaluation of Investigation of 200 Torture Victims," *Danish Medical Bulletin* 27(1980):241–243.

4. R. Daly, "Psychiatric After Effects of Irish Prisoners Subjected to Ill-treatment and Torture," *New Scientist* 5(August 1976):272–273.

5. A. J. Cienfuegos and C. Monelli, "The Testimony of Repression as a Therapeutic Instrument," *American Journal of Orthopsychiatry* 53, no. 1(1983):43–51.

6. F. Allodi and A. Rojas, "The Health and Adaptation of Victims of Political Violence in Latin America: Psychiatric Effects of Torture and Disappearance," paper no. 104 presented at the World Congress on Psychiatry, Vienna, July 1983.

7. Rasmussen and Lunde, "200 Torture Victims."

8. Allodi and Cowgill, "A Canadian Study."

9. *Manual of the International Statistical Classification of Diseases, Injuries and Causes of Death (ICD 9)*, vol. 1 (Geneva: World Health Organization, 1977), pp. 204–205.

10. *Helping Victims of Violence: Proceedings of a Working Group on the Psychosocial Consequences of Violence* (The Hague: Ministry of Welfare, Health, and Cultural Affairs, Dutch Government Printing Office, 1983).

11. Danish Medical Group, *Results of Examinations.*

12. L. Eitinger, "Rehabilitation of Concentration Camp Survivors Following Concentration Camp Trauma," *Psychotherapy and Psychosomatics* 17(1969)42–49.

13. P. Aziz, *Doctors of Death* (Geneva: Ferni Publications, 1976).

14. R. J. Lifton, "The Concept of the Survivor," in J. Dimsdale, ed., *Survivors, Victims, and Perpetrators: Essays on the Nazi Holocaust* (Washington, D.C.: Hemisphere Publications, 1980), p. 123.

15. R. J. Daly, "Torture and Other Forms of Inhuman and Degrading Treatment," in *Helping Victims of Violence*, p. 64.

Chapter 4

Torture on Trial:
The Case of Joelito Filártiga
and the Clinic of Hope

Richard Pierre Claude

*The dead count only when
they leave a testimony.*
Joel Filártiga

On a summer's eve in 1976, Joelito Filártiga, the seventeen-year-old son of a noted medical doctor and artist, was taken from his home by the Paraguayan police, tortured, and murdered. Since that time, Dr. Filártiga and his family have attempted to bring to the world's attention the truth about Joelito's death and the conditions in Paraguay that led to it. Their story is testimony to the devastating effects of torture on the victim's family, and to the value of international pressure to abolish torture. The Filártigas were able to trace one of the policemen believed responsible for the murder to New York. Their suit against him led to a landmark US court decision on the liability of torturers for their crimes in other countries.

The story of Joelito's death and the work of Dr. Filártiga reveal the climate of political repression in which torture thrives and the dangers faced by health professionals such as Dr. Filártiga who attempt to focus public attention on human rights violations. In order to understand the circumstances that led to Joelito's death and the chain of events that led to the US court decision, it is important first to know something of recent conditions in Paraguay.

The preparation of this essay was supported by a General Research Board Grant from the University of Maryland, College Park.

Joelito Filártiga. (Courtesy of Amnesty International.)

The Political Economy of Fear

Politically independent since 1811, Paraguay is a small, landlocked South American country of three million inhabitants, the vast majority of whom are of Spanish and Guaraní Indian ancestry. Agriculture is the mainstay of the economy, employing over half of the country's labor force and accounting for nine-tenths of all officially recorded exports. In addition to the typical economic problems that confront developing countries, Paraguay faces such particular problems as a lack of known mineral resources, a small domestic market, and poorly developed transportation and communication systems.

Although inadequate transportation facilities have hampered the growth of the Paraguayan economy, air access to the capital city of Asunción makes possible a large trade in contraband goods—drugs, whiskey, and cigarettes. A tobacco exporter, Paraguay nevertheless imports more US-manufactured cigarettes than any other country. Cigarettes from the United States, along with transistors from the Orient, perfumes from France, and narcotics and hard drugs are transshipped abroad, where they are often sold illegally. Smuggling is so financially important that it affects the whole political economy. Illegal trade, the evidence suggests, comprises over one-half of Paraguay's trade with its neighbors and appears to be strictly controlled by the military.[1]

People who participate in and benefit from the smuggling trade often ascend to elite positions in Paraguayan society. They maintain their power through "disappearing," incarcerating, killing, torturing, and terrorizing others. Corruption is a cause of egregious human rights crimes in Paraguay, according to a 1978 Amnesty International report: "There is widespread corruption (contraband, drug traffic, etc.) which itself leads to favouritism and violence in the interests of self-protection. . . . Failure to comply with these procedures [i.e., to distribute the fruits of smuggling through backdoor channels] is punishable through extra-judicial action."[2] Ultimately, the structure of corruption is maintained by the dictatorship of President Alfredo Stroessner, who has demonstrated a preoccupation with internal order at the expense of economic development.[3]

Except for the Catholic hierarchy, which has emerged as an important voice of opposition,[4] groups within Paraguay that attempt to criticize social and political conditions generally face threats and harassment.[5] In February 1979, for example, the government moved to silence the Paraguayan Commission for the Defense of Human Rights by placing its president under investigation for illegally incorporating a civic association and illegally establishing international affiliations. The dictatorship also curtails freedom of expression and association by restricting academic and trade union activity by exercising continuous press censorship, and by enforcing Law 209, a special powers act. Law 209 calls for the imprisonment or expulsion of "those who form part of an illegal association of three or more persons for the purpose of committing crime." According to the International League for Human Rights, the government uses the statute to prevent opposing political groups from organizing.[6]

The 1967 constitution includes classic safeguards against violations of human rights.[7] Such guarantees, however, have been routinely sabotaged by Stroessner, who has proclaimed a state of siege every three months since he assumed power in 1954.[8] Under state-of-seige conditions, citizens can be detained without the place of imprisonment, the arresting official, or the authority ordering the arrest being identified. Medical examinations are not required at the time of detention or on release, and the accused has no rights of court protection or *habeas corpus*. In addition, anyone who tries to obtain legal vindication is likely to encounter judges beholden to the government, many of whom the Archbishop of Asunción termed "corrupt and immoral."[9]

Reliable legal safeguards for human rights do not exist in Paraguay because the power structure does not allow them, according to David Helfeld and William Wipfler, who authored the report of the Third Commission of Enquiry of the International League for Human Rights.[10] They argue that the many human rights violations that were documented in Paraguay in the late 1970s grew out of and were perpetuated by a dual system of political authority. The first system consists of the constitution, together with the codes, laws, and administrative regulations that make up the official legal structure of Paraguay. The second and more important system is an uncodified hierarchy of power. In the indigenous Guaraní language, this second system bears the name *mbareté*, which means "superior power over others," or "clout." Helfed and Wipfler conclude that when the code of *mbareté* clashes with the legal system, it is the latter that gives way.[11] With President Stroessner at the pinnacle of this system of clout, *mbareté* applies to officeholders in all echelons of the government and military down to the lowest officials, who may exercise their power over uninfluential citizens.[12]

According to Helfeld and Wipfler, the corrupting effects of *mbareté* are pervasive and deep-seated. *Mbareté* creates the sense of immunity that police officials feel when they violate basic human rights and that prosecutors or judges feel when they subvert the law. These officials know that they are secure as long as they act according to the code of *mbareté* and do not challenge its essential tenets.[13] The result is what Paraguayan bishops have characterized as "all kinds of robbery and fraud in public life."[14]

The death of Joelito Filártiga on a summer night in March 1976 reflected all the characteristics of the *mbareté* system of power. This death under torture was directly linked to the professional activities of his father, activities that clashed with the authoritarian dictates of *mbareté*.

The Politics of Public Health in Paraguay

"My clinic is called the 'Clinic of Hope,' and our praxis is hope," Dr. Joel Filártiga stated in 1982. He was referring to El Sanatorio la Esperanza, which he founded in 1960 and has operated ever since. It is the largest private health clinic for the poor in Paraguay, serving between 32,000 and 37,000 *campesinos* (peasants) in the central valley and mountains surrounding Ybycuí. Dr. Filártiga says the facility "has become my life, an expression of my philosophy. I believe that all people have a basic human right to medical care and, given the reality that all but a handful of doctors refuse to leave the comforts of the cities to practice medicine in the countryside, it was the only decision I could make and still retain my integrity."[15]

Dr. Filártiga's views of service to the poor are not typical of the view of most health professionals in Paraguay. Although the capital city of Asunción contains only 16.5 percent of the population, more than 75 percent of all health professionals are located there. The government does not encourage rural health care, and the availability of health services in rural Paraguay is very limited. Whether in the city or countryside, there are few health facilities for the poor.[16]

The main health problems in Paraguay are undernourishment; a high incidence of parasitic, infectious, and communicable diseases; diseases preventable by vaccination; tuberculosis; Chagas' disease; leprosy; and accidents and violent acts—maladies resulting primarily from extreme poverty and inadequate sanitation.[17] By any measure, the health situation in Paraguay is unsatisfactory because public financing of health services does not meet current needs and because existing health establishments and personnel are insufficient to treat the total population.

Against such odds, the conscientious work of health professionals such as Dr. Filártiga is praiseworthy. La Esperanza receives no government aid. It operates through Dr. Filártiga's mostly voluntary work, with the assistance of his wife, Nidia, who acts as nurse, and the part-time help of their daughters. Until his death in 1976, Joel, Jr., who was then a high school student, acted as the clinic's driver and handyman. Patients often pay for medical services by stacking wood or giving such goods as vegetables or chickens.

Because the clinic's income does not cover its expenses, Dr. Filártiga raises funds for the clinic through international exhibitions and sales of his artwork. His art combines expressionism and surrealism in the manner of the Mexican muralists Orozco and Siqueiros. Because the theme of Filártiga's art is the poverty and powerlessness of the peasants, expressed through such symbols as prison bars, ballot boxes with no slots, broken guitars, and suffering faces, government elites view it as subversive.

In early 1976, Dr. Filártiga traveled to Central and North America on a tour to lecture and exhibit his art. While he was away from Paraguay, an event occurred that would prove fateful for his family. A group of Paraguayan

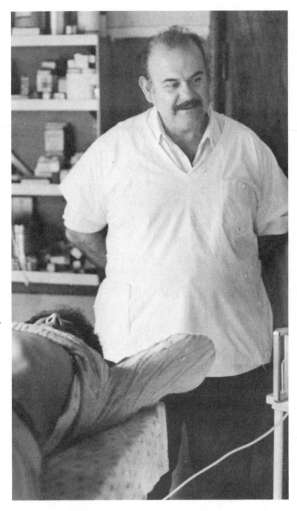

Dr. Joel Filártiga in his clinic, La Esperanza. (Courtesy of Richard Alan White.)

guerrillas first organized in Argentina, the *Organización Politico-Militar* (OPM), surprised authorities by successfully infiltrating the country through the border town of Posadas, Argentina. In March and April, confrontations between OPM guerrillas and the Paraguayan police led to deaths on both sides. In the wave of harsh repression that followed, government officials arrested hundreds of people for their supposed involvement with the OPM, stepped up a campaign against politically progressive sectors within the Catholic Church, and expelled eight Jesuits from the country.[18] After six members of a *campesino* project were arrested, the administrative head of the Protestant Friendship Mission (Disciples of Christ) complained, "Apparently the government's objective is to suppress any person or organization that strives to help those who live in miserable poverty."[19]

The Killing of Joelito

When a society such as Paraguay becomes politicized, all public activity is seen as either pro- or antigovernment. Thus Dr. Joel Filártiga's artwork, his clinic, his lecture tours, his work with the poor—all became suspect. Dr. Filártiga's frequent trips in the past to visit his mother-in-law in Posadas, Argentina—the site of the guerrillas' reported infiltration—only fueled the government's suspicion that he was an accomplice of the OPM.[20] Américo Peña-Irala, a neighbor of the Filártigas and the police inspector of Asunción, took action. Whether Peña was cleared by the chief of the secret police, Pastor Coronel, and the Paraguayan minister of the interior, Sabino Agosto Mantanaro, to kidnap the son of Dr. Filártiga remains a disputed matter. In any event, the kidnapping of Joelito in Asunción was planned to take place while his parents were 80 miles away at the clinic in Ybycuí. Supposedly the plan was intended to obtain from Joelito information about Dr. Filártiga in order to convict the physician on a count of sedition.[21]

During the night of 29 March 1976, Américo Peña and three other police officials kidnapped Joelito from the Filártiga home in Asunción and took him to the police station. There, they tortured Joelito for one and one-half hours while questioning him about his father's activities. The entire torture and interrogation session was tape-recorded. However, no evidence against Dr. Filártiga was obtained; instead, the recording carried Joelito's voice pleading, "I do not know anything. Why are you doing this to me?"

Peña and the three other policemen beat and whipped the youth severely over his entire body. They also sent high-voltage electric shocks through his fingertips and through a wire inserted in his penis. Ultimately, the frequency and intensity of the electric shocks were increased so much that Joelito died of cardiac arrest. In the face of his unexpected death, Peña and the other officers panicked. They attempted to cover up their deed by severing Joelito's major arteries so that the body could not be embalmed and thus would require quick burial.

Paraguayan law excuses from punishment a "crime of passion" by a husband who kills another man caught in adultery with his wife. To take advantage of this statute, the four policemen took Joelito's body to Peña's own house, two doors from the Filártiga residence in Asunción. Under the

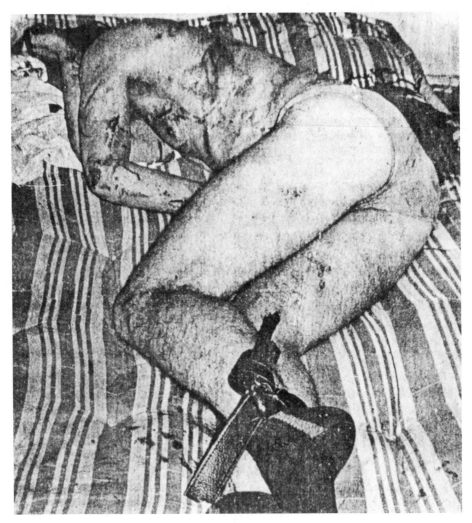

The body of Joelito Filártiga immediately after his torture-murder in March 1976. This photograph appeared in the Asunción newspaper, Hoy.

police inspector's supervision, the corpse was placed in the bed of Rosario Villalba, the 17-year-old daughter of Peña's mistress, Juana B. Villalba. Peña then contacted Rosario's husband, Hugo Duarte, and told him to come to the Peña residence immediately. Pleading a toothache, Duarte left his work as a night clerk and arrived at the Peña home only to be beaten by Peña and the other police. He was forced to agree to the fabricated story that he had found Joelito in bed with his wife and had killed him in a fit of passion.

Duarte was then arrested, and Dr. Hernan Molines, the coroner, made out a false medical report supporting the crime-of-passion theory. Judge Diogenes Martínez, who was later assigned to try the case, arrived at the house and legalized the falsified death certificate.

Four hours after Joelito had been kidnapped, his 20-year-old sister, Dolly, was awakened at her home by two uniformed police officers. They took her to Peña's house and showed her the mutilated corpse of her brother. In Dolly's testimony, she said:

> They told me to be as quiet as possible because it was dawn. They also asked me to take away the body of my brother as soon as possible and bury it. To which I answered them that they should let me think; that I didn't know what to do. In my desperation, I ran to the street, and I met Peña in the hall of the house. I asked him, "Sir, what have you done to my brother?" He answered me, "Shut up. Here you have what you have been looking for and deserved."[22]

Rosario, the supposed adultress, was arrested as a material witness but released on 7 April 1976. She then sent a note to Dr. Filártiga, saying that she wished to speak to him. Before they were able to meet, however, she disappeared and has not been found since. A Filártiga cousin, Juan Alberto Filártiga, attempted to locate her, but he, too, has disappeared.

Dr. Joel Filártiga requested and obtained an independent autopsy by three prominent Paraguayan physicians. They concluded that Joelito had been whipped and beaten and that he had died of cardiac arrest caused by electric shocks.

Paraguayan law allows a private party, on leave of the court, to proceed with a criminal suit in conjunction with the state but with the party's own lawyer and witnesses. The Filártigas brought such a suit to challenge the government's version of Joelito's death. However, when Dr. Filártiga's attorney, Horacio Galeano Peronne, asked that key police officers be summoned, he was arrested, taken to police headquarters, and shackled to a wall.[23] Inspector Peña visited him there on 30 September and threatened to kill Galeano as well as members and friends of the Filártiga family if they continued to press the lawsuit against him. In the days that followed, Dr. Filártiga was threatened with the loss of his medical license, the Filártiga family received frequent and frightening anonymous phone calls, and Mrs. Filártiga and Dolly were each detained in jail for a day. Attorney Galeano was disbarred. Finally, a Paraguayan court denied the Filártiga request to file the suit.

Even though the Filártigas' initial legal effort failed, their attempts to affect public opinion did not.[24] There was an outpouring of sympathy for the Filártigas, and two thousand people attended the funeral. Five thousand color duplicates of a photograph of Joelito's tortured corpse were circulated in Paraguay and abroad, and pictures and documentation of the crime were sent to Amnesty International in London. Human rights groups worldwide took an interest in the case. The US embassy sponsored a widely publicized exhibition of Dr. Filártiga's art, dedicated to the memory of his son.

The Filártigas' Search for Justice

By late 1977, the torture and murder of Joelito Filártiga had become a major international human rights issue. Under a barrage of criticism about human rights violations in Paraguay, which was reinforced by suspension of international loans to the country and protests by US Ambassador Robert White, General Stroessner "retired" Inspector Peña from the police. Shortly thereafter, on 21 July 1978, Peña, his mistress Juana B. Villalba, their son, and her niece, using their real names, entered the United States. They claimed to be tourists en route to Disney world, but instead they went to Brooklyn, New York, where they resided until exiled Paraguayans and human rights groups, primarily the Council of Hemispheric Affairs, discovered their whereabouts. The US Immigration and Naturalization Service then arrested Peña and his group, charging them with overstaying their three-month visa.

Upon arraignment the day after their arrest, Peña and his party requested immediate voluntary deportation, and they were ordered deported within five days. However, at the request of Dolly Filártiga and her father, who were in the United States at the time, district court judge Eugene H. Nickerson issued a temporary stay of the deportation order to allow the defendants time to secure an attorney, to permit questioning by the Filártigas, and to give the Immigration and Naturalization Service an opportunity to review the circumstances surrounding Peña's entry to the United States.

The Filártigas sought legal representation from Michael Maggio, an immigration attorney in Washington who worked in conjunction with the Center for Constitutional Rights in New York. The legal strategy was developed by center lawyers Peter Weiss, Rhonda Copelon, and José Antonio Lugo. They intervened in the deportation proceeding to file a $10 million civil suit against Américo Peña under the terms of a little-used provision of the Judiciary Act of 1789. That law, the Alien Tort Statute, now codified as Title 28 of the *United States Code*, Section 1350, provides: "The district courts shall have original jurisdiction of any civil action by an alien for a tort [personal wrong] only, committed in violation of the law of nations or a treaty of the United States."[25]

Peña's lawyers filed a motion to dismiss the Filártigas' alien tort action, denying that torture is a tort in violation of the law of nations (international law). Peña claimed that the proper forum for such a hearing was Paraguay and described as "mind boggling" the notion that in the name of human rights a US court could hold an alien in custody on a civil matter. Peña's attorney, Murray D. Brochin, argued that there were no grounds on which to detain his client further and that the suit was simply an attempt to "propagandize against conditions in Paraguay."

After Judge Nickerson granted the stay, a flurry of newspaper articles publicized the case.[26] Some journalists questioned Américo Peña's connections in the United States and Paraguay. The *New York Times*, for example, reported on Paraguayan government activities in the United States, as alleged by a Paraguayan refugee in New York.[27] The refugee, Gilberto Olmedo-Sanchez, claimed that Paraguayan government agents in New York, angered by his role in identifying Peña in Brooklyn, had threatened his life. The Council on Hemispheric Affairs issued a press release calling for an investigation of the US consul officer apparently responsible for issuing the visa.[28] The *Atlanta Constitution*[29] and the *Los Angeles Times* focused on questionable activity by US officials in Paraguay. For example, Richard Alan White, a historian of Paraguay, presented this argument in the *Times:*

> Peña is a suspected figure in a prostitution ring operating in the New York area. During the past several years, hundreds of young females, the majority from the rural Paraguayan town of Caraguatay, have entered the United States under visas that may have been obtained illegally from the U.S. consulate in Asunción. . . . These women are induced into prostitution upon their arrival in New York by the Paraguayan ringleaders. In Paraguay, it is generally understood that Peña was among the privileged officials who shared in the profits from international prostitution and narcotics smuggling.[30]

Judge Nickerson ruled in Peña's favor, however.[31] He held that precedent constrained him to interpret the jurisdiction provisions of the Alien Tort Statute so as to preclude consideration of a foreign country's treatment of its own citizens. The ruling rested on recent cases dealing not with human rights but with unrelated claims.[32] Judge Nickerson granted the motion to dismiss the case on 14 May 1979, acknowledging the strength of Peña's argument but leaving the door open for appeal. The Filártigas then filed notice that they would seek a review of Judge Nickerson's decision in the Second Circuit Court of Appeals.

Political scientists in the United States long ago accepted the notion that the judicial process is sometimes influenced by politics.[33] Although the charge is seldom heard in the United States, as it is in Paraguay, that the judiciary lacks independence, it is generally conceded that in the United States subtler political considerations often influence decisions. For example, the litigant in civil suits in the United States who enjoys the assistance (in the form of *amicus curiae* briefs) of government and private groups has a significant advantage. Because of international concern for the plight of the Filártigas, numerous briefs were filed by agencies of government, prestigious human rights groups, and respected scholars. As appellants, the Filártigas were aided by an impressive arsenal of attorneys from the Center for Constitutional Rights, the Department of Justice, the Department of State, Amnesty International USA, the International Human Rights Law Group, the Council on Hemispheric Affairs, the Washington Office on Latin America, the International League of Human Rights, and the Lawyers Committee for International Human Rights.

Moreover, the Filártigas submitted to the court of appeals the affidavits of several legal scholars supporting the view that the law of nations prohibits torture. Richard Falk of Princeton University noted that "it is now beyond reasonable doubt that torture of a person held in detention that results in severe harm or death is a violation of the law of nations." Thomas Franck of New York University argued that virtually all nations have banned torture and that it should therefore be viewed as a "violation of international law." Myres McDougal of Yale University stated that it has long been recognized that such internationally defined offenses as torture "virtually affect relations between states."[34]

Argument in *Filártiga v. Peña* took place before Chief Judge Feinberg and circuit judges Kaufman and Kearse. Their historic decision came down on 30 June 1980. They unanimously held that officially sanctioned torture violates international law. They therefore found that the Alien Tort Statute provided a basis for the exercise of US jurisdiction in the wrongful death action brought by the Filártigas.

Because Judge Nickerson had dismissed the Filártiga suit in the trial court for lack of subject matter jurisdiction, the court of appeals had to decide whether the conduct alleged by the appellants violated the law of nations.[35] In his opinion, Judge Kaufman noted that torture has been consistently condemned by numerous international treaties,[36] including the American Convention of Human Rights,[37] the International Covenant on Civil and Political Rights,[38] and the Universal Declaration of Human Rights.[39] Torture is also renounced as an inhuman act in the UN Declaration on the Protection of All Persons from Being Subject to Torture.[40] The UN declaration calls for redress and compensation for torture victims "in accordance with national law." Judge Kaufman noted that these declarations thus specify the obligations of member nations under the charter of the United Nations.[41]

"From the ashes of the Second World War arose the United Nations Organization, amid hopes that an era of peace and cooperation had at last begun. Though many of these aspirations have remained elusive goals, that circumstance cannot diminish the true progress that has been made. In the modern age, humanitarian and practical considerations have combined to lead the nations of the world to recognize that respect for fundamental human rights is in their individual and collective interest. Among the rights universally proclaimed by all nations . . . is the right to be free of physical torture. Indeed, for purposes of civil liability, the torturer has become—like the pirate and slave trader before him—*hostis humani generis,* an enemy of all mankind."

> Judge Irving Kaufman
> *Filártiga v. Pena-Irala*
> 630 F.2d 876, 890 (2d CIR. 1980).

Although both the United States and Paraguay adhere to the UN charter,[42] the court did not rely on the charter to bring the Filártiga complaint under the treaty provision of the Alien Tort Statute. Rather, the court relied on the charter and clarifying declarations as evidence of an expression of the evolving law of nations.[43] The court acknowledged that although "there is no universal agreement as to the precise extent of the 'human rights and fundamental freedoms' guaranteed to all by the Charter, . . . there is at present no dissent from the view that the guarantees include, at a bare minimum, the right to be free from torture." The court ruled further: "This prohibition has become part of customary international law, as evidenced and defined by the Universal Declaration of Human Rights."[44] Having found human rights in customary international law, the court was positioned to broaden the reading previously given to the Alien Tort Statute in cases concerning a state's treatment of its own citizens.[45]

Because the court of appeals found that it could assert jurisdiction over the Filártigas' claim, the action was remanded for further proceedings to the district court. However, the defendant did not appear in court, and Peña's New York lawyers withdrew when their legal bills remained unpaid.[46] In June 1981, Judge Nickerson entered a default judgment for the Filártigas. In February 1982, hearings to assess damages and to examine the $10 million claim of the Filártigas were held before Magistrate John Caden.

In these hearings, several physicians and psychologists presented affidavits on the effects of torture on family survivors. For example, Dr. Federico

Allodi, an authority on the long-term psychological problems faced by torture victims and their families,[47] testified that both Dolly and Dr. Joel Filártiga manifested psychological and psychosomatic disturbances which would probably affect them for years, that their symptoms were similar to those suffered by other persons in Latin America subjected to similar experiences, and that their disturbances were "intimately and causally related to the experiences they both underwent as close relatives of a victim of violence and as subjects of the profoundly distressing involvement in a police and legal investigation of the death of their relative, Joel Filártiga."[48] Damages awarded to Dolly and Dr. Joel Filártiga could not "make the victims whole," Dr. Allodi concluded, but "symbolic and material compensation will help to return to them a sense of trust in the justice and safety of the world, self-esteem and internal calm that is essential for the amelioration of the . . . symptoms of physical and psychological ill health."[49] Similar conclusions were presented by Dr. Ana Deutsch, an Argentine political exile and a member of a medical group investigating the medical and psychological consequences of torture.[50]

Two other medical doctors, Glenn Randall and José Quiroga, gave testimony regarding the medical effects of torture. They concluded:

> It is evident that members of the Filártiga family are also victims of Joelito's torture and have suffered heavily. . . . From what we know, the suffering is characterized by recollection of traumatic events, disintegration of family ties, both geographically and emotionally, feelings of guilt, . . . reduced involvement with the external world, feelings of estrangement with other people, loss of interest in previously enjoyed social activities, sleep disorders, and nightmares. These symptoms present in multiple members of the Filártiga family constitute the psychiatric diagnosis of Post-traumatic Stress Disorder.[51]

In the 1982 hearings, Jacobo Timerman, author of *Prisoner without a Name, Cell without a Number*,[52] and Robert White, former US ambassador to Paraguay, set the experiences of the Filártigas in their larger social context. Timerman said that in the Filártiga case, "torture is on trial," and testified about its effects on the victim and society at large. Timerman argued that once a person has been tortured, torture is with that person forever and that there is nothing that the person can do about it: "The moment you are tortured, and the days after torture, and the years after torture, they have changed your human condition. It is a biological change. . . . Your feelings are different." The wrong done is the most destructive imaginable, because "in the loneliness of the tortured man, . . . there is nothing, nothing is left to you; not your body, not your mind, not your imagination, and not your dreams, absolutely nothing." When torture is incorporated into a society,

Timerman argued, "you haven't changed society, you have changed . . . civilization."

Former US Ambassador Robert White testified that political torture is so "institutionalized" in Paraguay that "perfectly normal people get up and go to their jobs and their work is torture." Asked whether the Filártigas could get justice in Paraguay, the former ambassador answered simply, "No, it's impossible." In reply to the question of whether international opinion provided the Filártigas some protection in Paraguay, he said, "The only thing Paraguay responds to are international pressures." When asked "what role do you think the existence of civil remedies for the victims of torture, as we are here in this court for, might play in the overall effort to stop torture?" White said:

> I think one example might illustrate this. After the case was decided in favor of Dr. Filártiga [by the court of appeals], one of the people closest to General Stroessner told me that I just had to do everyting possible to get this decision reversed. They don't really understand the independence of our court system here. And he stressed to me that no Paraguayan government figure would feel free to travel to the United States if this judgment was upheld because, you know, they would feel that they would be liable to arrest for just being in any state in the United States.[53]

The US magistrate issued his damage award recommendation on 13 May 1983, subject to *pro forma* approval by the district court: $200,000 to Joelito's father and $175,000 to Joelito's sister for their injuries resulting from Peña's torturing Joelito to death. In Paraguayan currency, this is 90 million guaraní, which lawyers at the Center for Constitutional Rights believe to be the largest damage amount ever exacted from a Paraguayan national.[54]

In subsequent proceedings, the Filártigas noted that the award was calculated on the basis of standards found in the *Paraguayan Civil Code* regarding compensable "moral injuries." According to Paraguayan law, which guided Magistrate Caden's recommendation of 13 May 1983, such moral injuries include emotional pain and suffering, loss of companionship, and disruption of family life.[55] Paraguayan law, however, does not specify the granting of "punitive damages," and such an award was not included in Caden's recommendation. Upon considering this situation, Judge Eugene H. Nickerson ruled that, because Paraguay "will not undertake to prosecute Peña for his acts, the objective of the international law making torture punishable as a crime can only be vindicated by imposing punitive damages."[56]

On 12 January 1984, Judge Nickerson announced a total judgment for the Filártiga plaintiffs of $10,385,364. The court reasoned that Peña's behavior was marked by malice and that the nature of the wrongful action was important to take into account.[57] Judge Nickerson rested his enlarged award on the theory that punitive damages are designed not merely to teach a defendant not to repeat his conduct, "but to deter others from following his example." To deter inhuman abuse, the judge said, "this court must make clear the depth of the international revulsion against torture and measure the award in accordance with the enormity of the offense. Thereby the judgment may perhaps have some deterrent effect."[58]

Conclusion

The Filártiga episode in Paraguay and later litigation in the United States are important for many reasons. First, the example of the Filártiga family in undertaking humanitarian efforts on behalf of the poor and their health needs has had a salutory effect upon the Ybycuí peasantry. They and the residents of Asunción have learned from the example of Dr. Filártiga and his family about their human rights and the prospects for their solidarity. After Joelito died, a peasant told Dr. Filártiga: "You may not understand, Doctor, what is happening to you, because you are too close to it. But we do understand. Your son was killed, not because he was the son of Filártiga, but because he was the son of one serving us, the poor people. The punishment is not just for you, but it is also for us, the poor."[59]

Second, the example of the Filártiga family in "telling the world" of their human rights violation demonstrates the power of international public opinion. The work of diverse human rights groups helped to rouse the conscience of people throughout the world. Reports of these organizations, according to Dr. Filártiga, have impressed upon Paraguayans the lesson that the torturers are seen as criminals who have been publicly judged.

Third, the court of appeals decision represents a victory not only for the Filártiga family but also for the many governmental and nongovernmental organizations that offered their fact-finding skills so that the problem of institutionalized torture in Paraguay and elsewhere could be scrutinized. Several groups joined efforts in submitting the *amicus curiae* briefs, which presented research and analysis that clearly influenced the court's judgment.

Fourth, the ruling in *Filártiga v. Peña* "that deliberate torture perpetrated under color of official authority violates universally accepted norms of the international law of human rights regardless of the nationality of the parties" is a significant contribution to the growing authority of international standards of human rights. In this effort, the United States is by no means alone. From 1948 to 1973, the constitutions and laws of over 75 states either expressly referred to or clearly borrowed from the Universal Declaration of

Human Rights. The declaration has also been involved in a number of cases in domestic courts of various nations. In *Filártiga v. Peña,* the United States joined a growing number of countries whose courts have recognized that international law transcends sovereign boundaries to protect persons from their own government officials.[60]

On Human Rights Day, 10 December 1984, an important new step was made toward the abolition of torture worldwide. On that day, the General Assembly of the United Nations adopted by consensus an "International Convention Against Torture" (see Appendix A). The convention will take effect after it is ratified by twenty nations. It obliges states to prevent torture within their jurisdictions and to make torture a punishable offense. It provides for the extradition of torturers and the compensation of victims. It also commits states to ensure that education and information regarding the ban on torture be included in the training of law enforcement and medical personnel and other persons who may be involved in the custody, interrogation, or treatment of any person subject to arrest, detention, or imprisonment. The convention also sets up a committee of ten human rights experts who will monitor the implementation of the convention and investigate charges of torture by governments.[61]

Finally, *Filártiga v. Peña* should improve the enforcement of international human rights. Compliance with international law is the result of any given state's internal motivation, desire for accommodation, need for reciprocity with other states, and, in the words of Thomas Jefferson, its "decent respect for the opinion of mankind." In the United States, the *Filártiga* ruling means that officials who flagrantly disregard internationally accepted norms of human rights should not expect refuge from justice in the United States and that, in appropriate cases, the doors of US courts are open to the persecuted who find themselves shut out of their homeland. This development cannot help but encourage people such as Dr. Filártiga who courageously reject establishment-serving myths and frauds, and organizations such as human rights groups that seek to protect people against the abuse of power. The *Filártiga v. Peña* decision, Judge Kaufman noted, "is a small but important step in the fulfillment of the ageless dream to free all people from brutal violence."[62]

Notes and References

1. *Bulletin of the Paraguay Committee for Human Rights* (London: Paraguay Committee for Human Rights, 1978). Contraband commerce, accounting for 5 percent of the gross national product, forms an integral part of the political and eonomic system of Paraguay. Separate from contraband trade and

operating without official clearance are "unregistered shipments," which are protected by the authorities. In 1981, the Carteira de Comercio Exterior (Brazil) reported $411.5 million in exports to Paraguay and $188 million in imports from Paraguay. The corresponding figures from the Paraguayan Central Bank were $131.3 million and $54.1 million, 32 percent and 28.7 percent, respectively, of the Brazilian figures (Paraguayan daily *Ultima Hora,* 6 February 1982). For 1981, the Instituto de Estadística y Censo (Argentina) reported combined import and export values in trade with Paraguay at 362 percent of the figure noted by the Paraguayan Central Bank (the Asunción *ABC Color,* 21 February 1982). In short, illegal trade comprises over half of Paraguay's trade with its neighbors, and according to *Paraguay Watch* 2 (Washington, D.C.: Paraguay Watch, July 1979), "the percentage is rising."

2. Amnesty International, *Paraguay,* Briefing Paper No. 4 (London: Amnesty International, 1978), p. 3.

3. See Paul H. Lewis, *Paraguay under Stroessner* (Chapel Hill: University of North Carolina Press, 1980); Penny Lernoux, *1984 Revisited: Welcome to Paraguay* (New York: Alicia Patterson Foundation, 1976). For an important source of bibliographical information on Paraguay, see Richard Greenfield, "The Human Rights Literature of Latin America II," *Human Rights Quarterly* 4 (Fall 1982):515–517.

4. Pastoral Letter of the Paraguayan Episcopal Conference, "Between the Persecution of the World and the Comfort of God."

5. *Paraguay Watch* 2 (Washington, D.C.: Paraguay Watch, July 1979), p. 4. See also *Plan de Pastoral Orgánica* (Asunción: Paraguayan Episcopal Conference, 1981).

6. *Human Rights Bulletin,* May 1979, pp. 1, 3. See also Ben S. Stephansky and Robert J. Alexander, *Report of the First Commission of Inquiry into Human Rights in Paraguay* (New York: International League for Human Rights, September 1976); Ben S. Stephansky and David N. Helfeld, *Denial of Human Rights in Paraguay: Report of the Second Commission of Inquiry of the International League for Human Rights (New York: International League for Human Rights, 1977);* David N. Helfeld and William L. Wipfler, *Mbareté: The Higher Law of Paraguay* (New York: International League for Human Rights, 1980); International League for Human Rights with the assistance of Ligia Boliver, *Mbareté: Two Years Later, May 1980–May 1982* (New York: International League for Human Rights, 1982).

7. Individual freedom is broadly affirmed in the 1967 Constitution of the Republic of Paraguay, Article 50; Article 59 prohibits detention without charge for more than 24 hours. Article 65 explicitly bans torture and maltreatment; Article 76 guarantees freedom of association; Article 78 authorizes the writ of *habeas corpus* to ensure personal liberty. See *Report on Human Rights Practices in Countries Receiving U.S. Aid, 1979* (Washington, D.C.: US Department of State), pp. 316–323. In 1978, Amnesty International reported that *habeas corpus* was often ignored in 1977. Either judicial authorities did not pursue the writs in cases described by the authorities as political, or the head of the police station

or military barracks simply denied holding the prisoner; see Amnesty International, *Deaths under Torture and Disappearances of Political Prisoners in Paraguay* (New York: Amnesty International, 1977), p. 6.

8. Inter-American Commission on Human Rights, *Report on the Situation of Human Rights in Paraguay* (Washington, D.C.: General Secretariat, Organization of American States, 1978); OAS document OEA/Ser.L/V/II.43, doc. 13, corr. 1.

9. *Ladoc, Pastoral Communiques,* Keyhole Series Nos. 15 and 16 (Washington, D.C.: Latin American Documentation, 1978). On the role of the Church in Paraguay, see Kenneth Westhues, "The Established Church as an Agent of Change," *Sociological Analysis* 34 (1973):106–123.

10. Helfeld and Wipfler, *Mbareté: The Higher Law.*

11. Ibid., p. 155.

12. Ibid, p. 156.

13. Ibid., pp. 157–158.

14. *Ladoc, Pastoral Communiques.*

15. Quoted by Michele Burgess, "Physician Artist Is the Schweitzer of Paraguay," *Maryknoll,* September 1978, p. 9.

16. *ABC Color,* 15, 20, 21, 22, 26, and 30 December 1977. *Paraguay Watch* 5 (Washington, D.C.: Paraguay Watch, 1982) estimated in 1982 that over half of all Paraguayan-trained physicians practice medicine outside the country.

17. Pan American Health Organization, *Health Conditions in the Americas, 1977– 1980* (Washington, D.C.: Pan American Health Organization 1982); Table 11-2 (pp. 192–193) in *Health Conditions* itemizes the number of deaths from specific causes for Paraguay. These causes include such high-ranking categories as: enteritis and other diarrheal diseases, tuberculosis, parasitic diseases, cerebrovascular disease, pneumonia, other respiratory diseases, birth injury and other cases of perinatal mortality, and homicide and legal intervention; cf. p. 204. See also Pan American Health Organization, *1982–1983 Budget* (Washington, D.C.: Pan American Health Organization, 1981), pp. 333–338; Pan American Health Organization, *Report of the Director, Quadrennial 1978– 1981 Annual 1981* (Washington, D.C.: Pan American Health Organization, 1982).

18. *Latin America* 10 (7 May 1976):143

19. *Ladoc, Latin American Press* (12 August 1976), No. 70 (September–October 1976), p. 12.

20. See Alberto Cabral, "Political Murder in Paraguay," *America,* 23 April 1977.

21. The facts are set out in the Inter-American Commission, *Human Rights in Paraguay,* p. 26; the files on case no. 2158 of the Inter-American Commission on Human Rights, Washington, D.C.; and *Filártiga v. Peña-Irala* 630 F.2d 876 (2d Cir. 1980).

22. Transcript of hearings before Magistrate John L. Caden, 12, at 15–16, February 1982, *Filártiga v. Peña,* 577 F.Supp. 860 (1984).

23. Helfeld and Wipfler, *Mbareté: The Higher Law,* pp. 133–135.

24. Cabral, "Political Murder," pp. 376–377.

25. 28 *U.S.C.* 1350 (1976).

26. Lee Lescaze, "Paraguayan Police Figure Is Arrested in New York," *Washington Post,* 5 April 1979, p. A17; Selwyn Raab, "Paraguay Alien Tied to Murders in Native Land," *New York Times,* 5 April 1979, p. B1.

27. Selwyn Raab, "Death Threats Cited by Refugee, Informer in Paraguayan Case," *New York Times,* 15 May 1979, p. B4.

28. "The Strange Case of Américo Peña, Paraguayan Torturer," press release of the Council on Hemispheric Affairs, Washington, D.C., 17 April 1979.

29. Jeff Nesmith, "U.S. Probe of Visas Resisted," *Atlanta Constitution,* 9 April 1979, p. 1-A.

30. Richard Alan White, "In New York a Key Paraguayan Murder Suspect Faces U.S. Justice," *Los Angeles Times,* 15 April 1979, p. V-3.

31. Memorandum and order, *Filártiga v. Peña,* Civil case no. 79-917 (E.D.N.Y., 15 May 1979).

32. *Dreyfus v. Von Finck,* 534 F.2d 24 (2d Cir. 1976), cert. den., 429 U.S. 835; *I.I.T. v. Vencap, Ltd.,* 519 F.2d 1001 (2d Cir. 1975).

33. Samuel Krislov, "The Amicus Brief: From Friendship to Advocacy," 72 *Yale Law Journal* 694 (1963); David Weissbrodt, "U.S. Court of Appeals Rules in Peña Case," *Matchbox* (Amnesty International USA), November 1980, p. 2.

34. Affidavits of Richard Anderson Falk, Thomas M. Franck, Richard B. Lillich, and Myres S. McDougal, relied on in the Brief Amicus Curiae for the United States, at 19–20.

35. *Filártiga,* 630 F.2d 880. The opinion of the court stated:

> We conclude that official torture is now prohibited by the law of nations. The prohibition is clear and unambiguous, and admits of no distinction between treatment of aliens and citizens. . . . International law confers fundamental rights upon all people vis-à-vis their own governments. While the ultimate scope of those rights will be subject for continuing refinement and elaboration, we hold that the right to be free from torture is now among them.

36. Ibid. at 883. The court included Article 55 of the UN charter in its analysis of treaties. The charter is described by Judge Kaufman as a treaty binding the United States; it provides:

> With a view to the creation of conditions of stability and well-being which are necessary for peaceful and friendly relations among nations . . . the United Nations shall promote . . . universal respect for, and observance of human rights and fundamental freedoms for all without distinctions as to race, sex, language or religion.

According to Article 56, all members of the United Nations "pledge themselves to take joint and separate action in cooperation with the Organization for the achievement of the purposes set forth in Article 55."

37. Article 5; signed 22 November 1969, entered into force 18 July 1979; OAS Treaty Series No. 36 at 1; OAS document OEA/Ser.K/XV1/1.1, doc. 65, rev. 1, corr. 1 (1970); reprinted in Inter-American Commission on Human Rights, *Handbook of Existing Rules Pertaining to Human Rights*, OAS document OEA/Ser.L/V/11.50, doc. 6 at 27 (1980).

38. Opened for signature 19 December 1966, entered into force 23 March 1976; GA Res. 2200 A (XXI), 21 UN GAOR Supp. No. 16 at 52, UN Doc. A/6316 (1966).

39. Adopted 10 December 1948; GA Res. 217 A (III), UN document A/810 (1948).

40. Adopted 9 December 1975; GA Res. 3452 (XXX), 30 UN GAOR Supp. No. 34, UN document A/1034 (1975).

41. *Filártiga*, 630 F.2d 883.

42. In addition to human rights commitments made in accordance with principles of the UN charter, both the United States and Paraguay claim to eschew torture by virture of constitutional law; for example, the Constitution, Amendment VIII, forbids "cruel and unusual punishment," and the constitution of Paraguay, Article 65, prohibits the use of "the death penalty . . . applied for political reasons" and states, "No one shall be subjected to torture or to cruel or inhuman treatment."

43. UN GA Res. 2625 (XXV), UN document A/8082 (1970).

44. *Filártiga*, 630 F.2d 882.

45. For example, in *Dreyfus v. Von Finck* (see note 32), the tort alleged was that the defendants unlawfully took advantage of the plaintiff by buying his property at well below market prices when he was forced to emigrate from Nazi Germany. The court held that this kind of swindle did not violate the law of nations, noting that "violations of international law do not occur when the aggrieved parties are nationals of the acting state"; 534 F.2d 24 (2d Cir. 1976) at 31. But in *Filártiga*, the latter statement was repudiated as "clearly out of tune with current usage and practice of international law"; *Filártiga*, 630 F.2d 884.

46. "Torture on Trial in Landmark International Human Rights Case," press release of the Center for Constitutional Rights, New York, 12 February 1982.

47. Federico Allodi, "The Psychiatric Effects in Children and Families of Victims of Political Persecution and Torture," *Danish Medical Bulletin* 27 (November 1980):229–232.

48. Affidavit of Dr. Federico Allodi, *Filártiga v. Peña*, civil case no. 79-917 (E.D.N.Y. 1982) at 2.

49. Ibid.

50. Affidavit of Dr. Ana Deutsch, *Filártiga v. Peña*, civil case no. 79-917 (E.D.N.Y. 1982).

51. Affidavits of Dr. Glenn Randall and Dr. José Quiroga, *Filártiga v. Peña*, civil case no. 79-917 (E.D.N.Y. 1982) at 8.

52. Jacobo Timerman, *Prisoner without a Name, Cell without a Number* (New York: Knopf, 1981).

53. Transcript of Hearing, at 78–79.

54. Telephone interview with David Lerner, attorney at the Center for Constitutional Rights, 16 May 1983.

55. *Paraguayan Civil Code*, Articles 1102, 1103, 1112.

56. *Filártiga v. Peña*, 577 F.Supp. 860 at 864 (1984).

57. Ibid., 866, citing transcript at 16.

58. Ibid. There is precedent for the award of punitive damages both against individuals, such as Américo Peña, and against governments, such as Chile and Argentina. In *de Letelier v. Republic of Chile,* a US federal district court awarded $2,000,000 against the Chilean government to the survivors of the former ambassador to the United States and Ronnie Moffit, a passenger in de Letelier's automobile. Both were killed in Washington, D.C. by the explosion of a bomb arranged by Chilean operatives in violation of international law; 502 F.Supp. 259 (D. D.C. 1980). Likewise, in 1984, Judge Robert Takasugi relied on the Alien Tort Statute and the *Filártiga* precedent to award $2,707,515 in punitive damages to Mr. Siderman de Blake. In 1976, he was kidnapped by machine-gun-wielding soldiers on the night the military junta overthrew the government of President María Estela Martínez de Perón. Siderman de Blake was terrorized, tortured for seven days, and expelled from his country; *Siderman de Blake v. Republic of Argentina*, CV 82-1772-RMT (MCx).

59. Interview of Dr. Joel Filártiga by Richard Pierre Claude, Washington, D.C., 19 March 1982.

60. See *United Nations Action in the Field of Human Rights* (New York: United Nations, 1980), pp. 20–22.

61. Commission on Human Rights, United Nations Economic and Social Council, "Draft Convention Against Torture and Other Cruel, Inhuman, or Degrading Treatment or Punishment," E/CN.4/1984/72. See "Panel at U.N. Condemns Torture," *New York Times*, 6 December 1984, p. A4.

Chapter 5

Medical Action Against Torture

Eric Stover and Michael Nelson

In nations where state-sanctioned torture becomes routine, it develops into a malignancy of the body politic, prompted and sustained by the actions of people in many sectors of society. Although military and police personnel are its usual agents, politicians, civil servants, lawyers, judges, and health professionals act in attendance. Politicians may condone torture as a means of maintaining power, civil servants may officially deny the use of torture, lawyers and judges may prosecute or sentence prisoners on the basis of confessions extorted under torture, and health professionals may design methods of torture or monitor its victims so that they do not die unexpectedly.

Why do these persons participate in or condone the use of torture? In particular, why do health professionals, who have been trained to heal, yield to pressures and contribute to the horrors of torture? Understanding how this occurs is crucial to ending—or at least abating—the complicity of health professionals in the practice of torture. Removing health personnel from the torture room will not abolish torture, which is the ultimate goal, but it may make the performance of torture more difficult and eventually more reprehensible to people who would use it as a means of political control.

To understand torture, particularly state-sanctioned torture, one must know how the political conditions that foster its development and the processes by which individual persons are coopted as its agents. The political conditions that seem to contribute to the institutional (rather than random) use of torture include:

- institutional concentration of power with few, if any, effective alternative power bases;

- few, if any, effective institutional checks and balances;

- few, if any, ways to resolve conflicts nonviolently;

- few, if any, means for the orderly transfer of power; and

- state control of the dissemination of information, both within and outside of state boundaries.

These conditions prevail under military and one-party governments and police states. Democracies have occasionally practiced torture, despite the presence of an independent judiciary, freedom of the press, multiple sources of power, and civilian control of the armed forces. This has been particularly true during wartime. The French, for example, used torture during their eight-year war in Algeria.[1]

Torture was also a standard part of the Central Intelligence Agency's (CIA's) Operation Phoenix program in Vietnam, according to the congressional testimony of several US officials. In the program, which was terminated by the US Congress in 1973, CIA operatives recruited and trained hundreds of South Vietnamese military and police personnel in "counterterror techniques" designed to root out and imprison or assassinate Viet Cong leaders.[2] Democratic states may also use torture in domestic conflicts. British troops, for instance, have used sensory deprivation techniques to interrogate and punish members of the Irish Republican Army.[3] The same is true in Spain, where more than 100 detainees, mostly Basques, held under that country's antiterrorist laws have been tortured since 1980.[4]

However, what distinguishes torture practiced by democratic governments from that by authoritarian or totalitarian governments is that concerned sectors of a democratic society can respond quickly to such abuse and, through sustained political pressure, prevent it from spreading. Nowhere has this been more evident in recent years than in countries where freely elected governments have moved swiftly to dismantle the repressive policies of their military predecessors. When the civilian government headed by Raúl Alfonsín came to power in Argentina in December 1983, for instance, it began to take steps to punish people responsible for the deaths, often by torture, of thousands of persons during the previous seven years of military rule.[5]

Although human rights groups have criticized the Alfonsín government for not punishing hundreds of middle- and high-ranking officers for past abuses, the government has taken several steps to reduce the military's authority over civilian affairs. Two weeks after coming to power, the Alfonsín government abrogated the amnesty law introduced by the military government, a law which would have granted complete immunity from prosecution to all members of the police and security forces for past human rights violations. Since then, Alfonsín has appointed several leading human rights advocates to key government positions in an effort to thwart future abuses, and the Argentine congress has passed a series of laws that limit the use of pretrial detention (the period when torture or "disappearances" most frequently occur) and that stiffen penalties for persons convicted of ordering or carrying out illegal arrests or mistreating detainees.[6]

In Argentina, as well as in other countries of the world, both democratic and undemocratic, what actions there have been to prevent torture can usually be traced to the efforts of national and international groups. These groups usually act by working through domestic courts (applying for writs of *habeas corpus* when a person is detained or "disappeared," for example), by mobilizing public opinion against abuses of rights, and by collecting evidence on individual cases of torture.

Because they can focus international attention on issues that affect human welfare, individual health professionals and their national and international organizations can significantly contribute to efforts to abolish torture. Effective actions would include establishing and enforcing antitorture codes of conduct, systematically gathering and publicizing information on the epidemiology of torture, treating and rehabilitating torture victims, mobilizing support defending health professionals persecuted for upholding standards of ethical behavior, and supporting international measures designed to end torture.

Why Antitorture Codes Are Necessary

The fundamental challenge that health professionals face in their efforts to abolish torture is to make colleagues and governments recognize that professional complicity in torture, while not only morally wrong, is also a serious breach of medical ethics. In addition, health professionals must acknowledge that it is their duty to refuse to participate in acts that constitute or serve to cover up torture.

Alfred Heijder, professor of criminal law at Amsterdam University, argues that four main forces regulate the behavior of professionals.[7] First, professional groups and their members are influenced by the values, goals, and accepted means of the *political system* of their countries. Second, professionals are influenced by the values and norms of the *organizational* or *functional units* in which they receive their professional training. In effect, when making a decision, a professional considers what colleagues would do in the same situation. Third, *public opinion* plays a role in regulating conduct: Professionals are aware of the degree to which the general public would either condone or condemn them for their activities. Finally, Heijder believes behavior is influenced by a professional's own *individual values*.

The political system, the professional group, public opinion, and individual values often support the same rules of conduct. When the norms of these forces conflict, however, professionals must choose what norms to ignore. Thus, health professionals who are called on to participate in state-sanctioned torture confront a dilemma. Although they may be told that complicity is in the best interests of the state, such activity violates their professional duty to defend human lives and human rights, regardless of the issue of security. Health professionals called on to participate in torture face other issues as well. Wouldn't their presence during torture prevent permanent physical or mental damage or even death? Moreover, if they refuse to participate, will they be dismissed from their posts or face worse reprisals? Alternatively, what will their families or colleagues think if they do participate? Finally, when a state acts illegally, what is the health professional's role as a state employee? Is it better to seek reform from within or to create pressure from without?

The fact that professionals sometimes face such dilemmas underscores the importance of developing ethical standards in certain professions. This is particularly so in professions such as medicine and law, in which the professionals hold great power over patients or clients. The lawyer can affect whether a client lives or dies, goes free or is imprisoned, benefits financially or is ruined. The doctor can also ultimately determine whether a patient lives or dies.

In the practice of medicine, the Hippocratic oath and modern codes of ethics are testaments to the long-standing concern for standards of conduct within the profession. Medical standards have not come from professionals alone, however. Other sectors of society have been equally important in encouraging the development of medical ethics. In medieval times, for example, Christian teaching rejected the Greek practice of reserving the best medical services for the elite and supported equal treatment for all patients, regardless of their ability to pay or their social status. In modern times health professionals and the public alike have advocated various standards for the care of the dying and the handicapped, medical participation in capital punishment by lethal injections, euthanasia, eugenics, triage, and the cost-effectiveness of medical procedures.[8]

Among these issues, torture has become a focus of attention in the past decade, primarily because of its growing incidence on the one hand and the work of human rights groups in combatting it on the other. In the forefront of such groups is Amnesty International, whose members oppose the use of torture under any circumstances. For the past twelve years, Amnesty International has worked closely with health, legal, and police associations in drafting codes of conduct designed to prevent their members from complicity in torture.

In 1973, a group of physicians and nurses attending an Amnesty International conference in Paris reviewed existing principles and international codes of medical ethics.[9] What these codes lacked, they argued, were specific guidelines for health professionals working in state institutions who encounter conflicting demands in their work. For these professionals, the conference participants drew up the following set of principles for incorporation in any code of medical ethics:

- Medical and associated personnel shall refuse to allow their professional or research skills to be used in any way for the purpose of torture, interrogation or punishment, nor shall they participate in the training of others for such purposes.

- Physicians should diligently avoid abuse of their special power to commit persons to mental hospitals as a means of avoiding due process of law.

- Medical personnel should remain scrupulously vigilant of the possibility that their research may be used for purposes contrary to the original intent of the investigation and should avoid involvement in any work which seems likely to be so abused.

- Medical personnel working in prisons or security camps should insist that they be employed by and responsible to an authority independent from that of the confining institution.

- Medical personnel who have knowledge of instances of torture or plans for such are under the obligation to report this information to the appropriate authorities.

- Medical experimentation in whatever institutions, but particularly where persons are held against their will, should be carried out only with the strict observance of the Helsinki Rules of Conduct for human experimentation.

- Prisoners and others held against their will shall have the right of free access to physicians of their own choosing.

- Members of the medical profession shall give all possible support to colleagues who are penalized for abiding by this code of ethics.[10]

Since the 1973 Amnesty International conference on torture, several

Principles of Medical Ethics Relevant to the Role of Health Personnel, Particularly Physicians, in the Protection of Prisoners and Detainees against Torture, and Other Cruel, Inhuman or Degrading Treatment or Punishment (Adopted by the UN General Assembly, 18 December 1982)

Principle 1   Health personnel, particularly physicians, charged with the medical care of prisoners and detainees, have a duty to provide them with protection of their physical and mental health and treatment of disease of the same quality and standard as is afforded to those who are not imprisoned or detained.

Principle 2   It is a gross contravention of medical ethics as well as an offence under applicable interntional instruments, for health personnel, particularly physicians, to engage, actively or passively, in acts which constitute participation in, complicity in, incitement to or attempts to commit torture or other cruel, inhuman or degrading treatment or punishment.

Principle 3   It is a contravention of medical ethics for health personnel, particularly physicians, to be involved in any professional relationships with prisoners or detainees the purpose of which is not solely to evaluate, protect or improve their physical and mental health.

Principle 4   It is a contravention of medical ethics for health personnel, particularly physicians:

(a)   to apply their knowledge and skills in order to assist in the interrogation of prisoners and detainees in a manner that may adversely affect the physical or mental health or condition of such prisoners or detainees and which is not in accordance with the relevant international instruments;

(b)   to certify, or to participate in the certification of the fitness of prisoners or detainees for any form of treatment or punishment that may adversely affect their physical or mental health which is not in accordance with the relevant international instruments, or to participate in any way the infliction of any such treatment or punishment which is not in accordance with the relevant international instruments.

Principle 5   It is a contravention of medical ethics for health personnel, particularly physicians, to participate in any procedure for restraining a prisoner or detainee unless such a procedure is determined in accordance with purely medical criteria as being necessary for the protection of the physical or mental health or the safety of the prisoner or detainees himself, of his fellow prisoners or detainees or of his guardians and it presents no hazard to his physical or mental health.

Principle 6   There may be no derogation from the foregoing principles on any ground whatsoever, including public emergency.

health organizations have established standards of conduct for their members who treat detainees and prisoners. (The codes of ethics referred to in this chapter are presented in Appendix A.) The 1975 Declaration of Tokyo of the World Medical Association (WMA) prohibits physicians from participating in the practice of torture in "all situations." The 1977 Declaration of Hawaii of the World Psychiatric Association condemns the use of "compulsory psychiatric treatment in absence of psychiatric illness." Likewise, the 1975 Resolution of Singapore of the International Council of Nurses prohibits its members from participating in any "procedures harmful to the mental and physical health of prisoners and detainees." These declarations maintain that medical personnel have professional, ethical, and social responsibilities that transcend national and political loyalties.

In 1979, on the heels of these resolutions by nongovernmental organizations, the World Health Organization (WHO) drafted a similar set of guidelines for health personnel confronted with cases of torture or ill-treatment.[11] After three years of debate and revision, the UN General Assembly adopted the guidelines in December 1982. On several occasions it appeared as if the proposed code would never reach a final assembly vote. The WMA and several governments, notably the Dutch, objected to a provision in the original draft which stated that, in certain situations, health personnel "may be compelled under duress" to administer medical care to victims during torture, and in such cases "their actions should be determined by the will to protect the prisoner or detainee."[12] The Dutch contended that there was "a serious risk that physicians, when placed under duress to lend their assistance to [torture,] might too easily find an excuse for yielding to such pressure in the thought that by doing so they would be in a position to minimize noxious effects."[13]

What emerged from the United Nations was a set of six principles of medical ethics designed to stop professional complicity in torture. The UN member states struck out the controversial duress clause and explicitly prohibited medical participation in abusive acts under any circumstances. In effect, governments had recognized that it was an offence under international human rights agreements to order health personnel to engage actively or passively in torture.

Codes of Ethics in Practice

Establishing Codes of ethics are unique attempts to employ the prestige and moral influence of professional associations against the use of torture. But how useful are such codes in practice in identifying and preventing professional complicity in the use of torture? The answer depends on how local professional associations interpret these codes and sets of principles, how these associations enforce the codes, and what opposition the associations encounter from government officials.

Among professional groups, opinions vary as to whether a code of ethics should be viewed as a general statement of ideal behavior or as a quasi-legal guide for the adjudication of complaints and the censure of members.[14] This ambiguity is evident in the previously described codes against torture adopted by the United Nations and international health associations. For example, none of these declarations established measures for censuring members who violate ethical standards. Although the nursing and medical associations have supplemented their codes with provisions that oblige members to make public any activities that contravene ethical behavior, the World Psychiatric Association and UN statements contain no such provisions. Thus the burden of monitoring and enforcing codes of ethics is left to the discretion of each national society affiliated with the international association.

In enforcing ethical codes, professional associations also face more immediate problems, primarily political ones. Association members may fear that censure or criticism of their colleagues will unduly politicize the organization, divide the membership, and expose innocent members suspected of wrongdoing to harmful publicity. Furthermore, by disciplining members who participate in or cover up torture, professional associations may be seen as publicly opposing government policies. Finally, individual professionals may believe that loyalty to the state should take precedence over their professional obligations.

Several incidents in which national medical associations have either failed to uphold ethical standards because of internal pressures or have faced government opposition to their efforts illustrate these problems of enforcement.

South Africa

On 12 September 1977, the jailed black opposition leader Steve Biko, a founding member of the outlawed Black Consciousness Movement, died of head injuries while in police custody in Pretoria.[15] During the official inquest into Biko's death, held in Pretoria two months later, three physicians admitted that they had examined Biko at the request of security police in Port Elizabeth, where he had been detained without charge under South Africa's internal security laws. The police had called on the doctors to certify that Biko was fit for travel to Pretoria following an alleged scuffle between the activist and his six interrogators. The doctors testified that Biko had sustained severe head injuries as a result of the incident. Biko's family, however, claimed that he had nearly been beaten to death by his interrogators and that the doctors were called in to cover up the incident.[16]

The official inquest found that Biko's death could not be attributed to any one person, and the South African authorities brought no charges against any of the police officers involved in the incident. The presiding magistrate, however, referred the matter of the "Biko doctors" to the South African Medical and Dental Council in 1980. The council's political head is the minister of health; the government appoints two-thirds of the council's membership, and the medical profession one-third. Although the council had held open disciplinary hearings since 1928, it decided to examine the Biko case behind closed doors.[17] In April 1980, the council's executive committee declared "that there was no evidence of improper or disgraceful conduct on the part of the doctors" and closed the case.[18] Later that year the Medical Association of South Africa (MASA) also issued a statement exonerating the three doctors, although it did note that "the inadequate treatment received by Biko would probably have been different had the patient not been a detainee under the security act."[19]

Angered by the findings of the medical council and MASA, several South African private physicians and members of university medical faculties resigned from MASA and later formed an alternative medical association. The professional standards committee of the University of Cape Town's medical faculty in addition issued a statement in 1982 listing conditions that should be met in the medical treatment of South Africa's prisoners and detainees.[20] That same year, MASA responded by recommending that legally binding regulations governing prison health care be established and that the association be responsible for ensuring not only that adequate medical treatment is given detainees but that all possible measures are taken to safeguard them from torture and ill-treatment.[21]

Brazil

By 1980, several regional medical councils in Brazil had begun investigating the activities of ten physicians who, directly or indirectly, participated in torture during the early 1970s.[22] In October 1980, the São Paulo State Medical Council unanimously voted to remove Dr. Harry Shibata, the head of the São Paulo Forensic Medical Institute, from the medical register for falsifying medical certificates of two prisoners tortured while in military custody.

Fueron abatidos cinco extremistas

Fuerzas de Seguridad atacaron con armas largas, morteros y bazookas una casa de San Isidro. Otros 3 en S. M. de Tucumán

Early one September morning in 1976, Argentine soldiers arrived at the Lanuscou's home in San Isidro, a suburb of Buenos Aires. The soldiers opened fire and stormed in, neighbors recall. More gunshots from inside were heard, and as the soldiers left, the sound of a baby crying.

The next day, a local newspaper carried photographs of the bullet-ridden house and an official statement that the army had killed five "extremists"—three women and two men—in a shoot-out. The newspaper account made no mention of the Lanuscou couple or their three children, aged 6, 4, and 6 months. Despite appeals by the family's relatives and friends, the government failed to investigate the incident until 1983, when the military left power.

Court investigators then discovered that the day after the raid a police doctor, Roberto Bettale, had issued death certificates for five persons unknown, each bearing a physical description that matched that of a different member of the Lanuscou family, including one for the 6-month-old baby, Matilde. According to the cemetery's log, the five bodies had been brought to the cemetery from the Lanuscou residence and had been buried in separate caskets in a common grave.

In early 1984, Juan Ramos Padilla, an Argentine judge, ordered the graves of the Lanuscou family opened. To their surprise, the gravediggers found that only four of the caskets contained human remains; the smallest one was empty save for a baby's blanket, jumper, a pair of socks, and a pacifier. What had happened to Matilde?

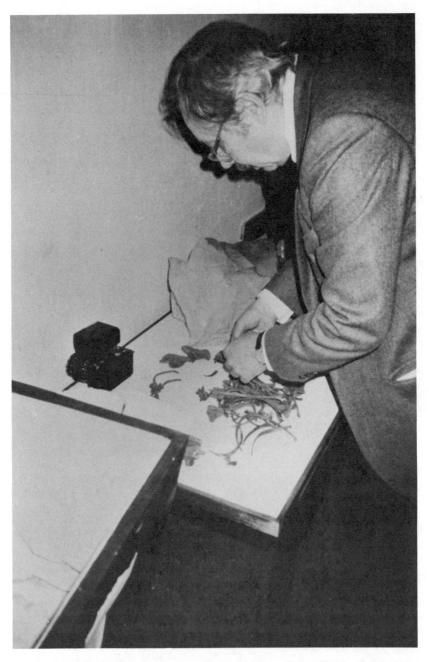

Dr. Clyde Snow, a US forensic anthropologist, may have an answer. Since June 1984, he and other forensic scientists from the United States and West Germany have been helping to investigate the "disappearance" of at least 10,000 persons during the seven years of military rule that ended with the election of Raúl Alfonsín.

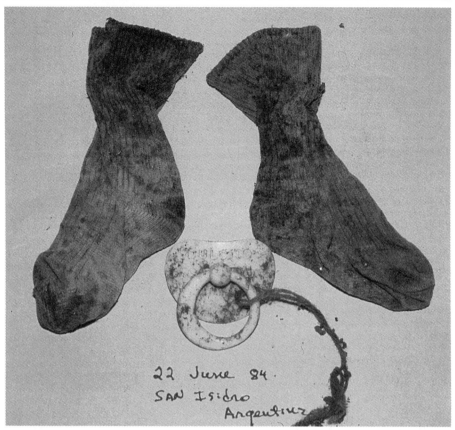

22 June 84.
SAN Isidro
Argentina

Snow found none of Matilde's remains among those of her relatives, even after X rays were taken of the baby's clothing and the lining of the casket. He concluded that Matilde had never been in the casket. A month later, in July 1984, a former collaborator with a Navy abduction team told a government commission that a nurse working in a Naval hospital was given custody of Matilde after the raid on the Lanuscou house and was requested to arrange for Matilde's adoption by a military family.

Since 1977, a local human rights group, the Grandmothers of the Plaza de Mayo, has been searching for at least 145 children who, like Matilde, were abducted with their parents or born in detention and later separated from their mothers. Many of these children, the Grandmothers believe, are now living with families of the same military personnel responsible for the "disappearance" of their parents.

Should Matilde be located, scientists using genetic screening techniques for determining grandpaternity may be able to confirm her identity. A judge ordered in December 1984 that custody of an eight-year-old girl living with a police officer and his family be given to her biological grandparents. The judge's decision to return the girl was based on genetic tests that showed a 99.9 percent certainty that she was a descendant of the grandparents who claimed her.

Photographs courtesy of Clyde Snow, the Abuelas de la Plaza de Mayo, and Lowell Levine; parts of text reprinted courtesy of *New Scientist*.

The first certificate was for a well-known Brazilian journalist, Vladimir Herzog, who, according to Brazilian military intelligence, hanged himself by his belt in his cell on 25 October 1975 after confessing to being a member of the Communist party. Shibata signed an autopsy report to this effect, and the security police returned Herzog's body to his family in a sealed coffin. Public outrage over the incident was widespread. Hundreds of journalists and the Brazilian Bar Association (Ordem dos Advogados do Brasil) circulated petitions protesting Herzog's death and demanded a full inquiry. A São Paulo federal judge later ruled that the Brazilian government was responsible for Herzog's death on the basis of such evidence as police photographs showing signs of torture on Herzog's body and testimony by a fellow prisoner.

In the case of the second falsified certificate, a former member of parliament, Marco Antonio Tavares Coelho, accused Shibata of signing a medical certificate which stated that Coelho had had no signs of torture on his body after he was subjected to prolonged interrogation at military intelligence headquarters in São Paulo in 1975. Doctors appointed by the army later examined Coelho and confirmed the existence of injuries on his body. In September 1975 Coelho showed a court marks of beatings, burns on his left arm, and bruises on his legs and calves.

Although the censure of Shibata demonstrates that Brazilian medical councils are seriously pursuing enforcement on a state level, their investigations into unethical behavior are held in secret, and no one other than those people involved are told of the date of any hearing. Moreover, the present Brazilian government has stated on several occasions that it does not intend to bring to court or to punish those people who participated in torture or repression during the years of military rule.[23]

Chile

In 1974 Amnesty International released a report alleging that since the 1973 military coup in Chile, "leading members of the medical profession [in Chile] have been aware that torture of political prisoners has taken place within the military hospital itself, and have at times had the opportunity to visit those prisoners who had been subject to torture."[24] Eight years later, in mid-1982, a team of physicians affiliated with Amnesty International traveled to Chile to examine a group of former detainees who alleged that they had been tortured while in official custody.[25] Fifteen of the eighteen individuals examined claimed that they had been in contact with someone whom they took to be a doctor while being held in detention centers and that they had been medically examined just before torture and again afterward. Six of

A judge's clerk takes notes during an exhumation in an Argentine cemetery. (Courtesy of Clyde Snow.)

those interviewed said that they had been given nontherapeutic medicine—medicine given for a purpose other than to treat illness.

When confronted with this information, the president of the Chilean Medical Association (Colegio Médico de Chile), Dr. Juan Luís Gonzalez, told the Amnesty International delegation that "his association was aware that doctors had been accused of taking part in torture and had condemned such participation—but it had not been possible to identify the doctors allegedly involved."

Since the delegation's visit, the association has investigated five physicians alleged to have taken part in torture.[26] However, the association's disciplinary committee has been hesitant to rule on the charges of unethical behavior. Dr. Carlos Trejo, chairman of the association's ethics committee, maintains that committee members are "extremely apprehensive" about making judgments in haste "lest the wrong physicians be implicated."[27] Furthermore, in 1981 the Chilean government revoked the medical association's power to set professional standards. Consequently, even if the association expels those doctors who are found to have participated in torture, it has no legal authority to stop them from practicing.

Nevertheless, the Chilean Medical Association and several of its regional councils have actively campaigned against torture in Chile. In late 1983, the association issued a public statement calling on the government to end torture and warning that the association "would not be turned into a haven and bastion for people who transgress professional ethics."[28] In November 1983, representatives of the association presented the president of the Chilean supreme court with documentary evidence of torture cases and expressed their concern over the continuing practice of torture. Seven months later, Drs. Gonzalez and Trejo traveled to the United States to testify before the US Congress about the Chilean Medical Association's efforts to stop professional complicity in torture.[29]

Uruguay

With the return of civilian rule in Uruguay in 1984, physicians there have begun to investigate the role of prison doctors in torture.[30] The newly formed National Medical Convention agreed in July 1984 to establish an ethics panel to probe the activities of five physicians and a psychologist who attended to political detainees held in military detention camps and prisons. The move was prompted by the death of Vladimir Roslik, a physician, who died in April 1984, less than 24 hours after being taken to military barracks for questioning.[31]

When Roslik's family and colleagues pressed the military authorities for an explanation, they produced a death certificate signed by a physician giving the cause of death as cardiac and respiratory failure. However, a second autopsy, carried out at the family's request, revealed that Roslik's lungs contained excessive amounts of water, suggesting that he had been subjected to submarine torture. In this method, the victim's head is held in a bucket of water for long periods of time. The examining physicians concluded that Roslik had died from suffocation as a result of this treatment.[32]

The two officers responsible for Roslick's detention were convicted of "involuntary manslaughter," and the regional medical union suspended the doctor who initially signed Roslik's death certificate for a period of 90 days.

These incidents in South Africa, Brazil, Chile, and Uruguay depict the problems and the advantages of implementing international codes of ethics in countries where torture has been or continues to be practiced. Although many of the problems appear insurmountable, it also seems that international and national health associations could strengthen antitorture codes by insisting that medical personnel responsible for the health of detainees be responsible to an authority other than the security force or prison adminis-tration.[33] Further safeguards include making the medical personnel's clinical independence legally binding and allowing them to have free access, without prior police authorization, to detainees at all times. According to Amnesty International, such a procedure could be governed by the following guide-lines:

- the offer of an examination on arrival at a detention centre, before interrogation begins;

- the offer of an examination every subsequent 24 hours while under interrogation and immediately prior to transfer or release;

- these offers to be made personally by the medical officer on duty, who would explain the importance of having complete records of the detainee's condition in detention;

- detainees to be informed in the written notice of their rights about the importance of these examinations;

- all examinations to be conducted in private by medical personnel only;

- any refusal by a detainee to have any of these examinations to be witnessed in writing by the medical officer;

- daily visits to each detainee by a medical officer, and access by the detainee to the medical officer on duty at any time on reasonable request;

- detailed record-keeping by medical personnel of such matters as the weight of the detainee, marks on the body, psychological state and complaints related to health or treatment;

- these records to be treated as confidential, as in any doctor-patient relationship, but capable of being communicated at the detianee's request to his or her family;

- examination by the detainee's own doctor at the request of the detainee or of his or her family, not in the presence of prison guards.[34]

In countries where national health associations face government opposition to efforts to promote ethical standards, the international association could send a delegation to discuss these concerns with government officials. If these initiatives fail, a national association might submit a complaint to the United Nations or to other international or regional bodies. Of course, such initiatives would require an investment of resources, but this investment would demonstrate to association members the commitment of their organization to ethical standards.

Gathering, Studying, and Publicizing Information on Torture

In order to prevent torture, it is necessary to establish a means for rapidly communicating information about incidents of torture to international and regional groups that monitor and respond to violations of human rights. Such a process already exists in the field of medical epidemiology, and it could be extended to include torture. Medical epidemiologists working with the Violence Epidemiology Branch of the Centers for Disease Control in the United States, for instance, have set up a national communication and data collection network for the study of the social "causation" and medicosocial implications of murder.[35] This approach has already increased the understanding of the incidence of murder, thus aiding in identifying and implementing social policies that may reduce the murder rate.

If an epidemiological approach is extended to include torture, participating health professionals and other volunteers would need to be geographically dispersed, sufficiently numerous, and safe to pursue their work. This could be assured if the project was affiliated with an international governmental body such as the World Health Organization or the United Nations Educational, Scientific, and Cultural Organization (UNESCO). Participants would need to obtain the relevant information and be trained to use a simple reporting mechanism. A central reporting center and data bank might be established, or existing international agencies could be used to establish a communications system. With an efficient information system, international standards designed to prevent torture would be much more effective. Health professionals, particularly forensic medical examiners, would clearly play a key role in such a reporting system, because they are often the first to

118

investigate complaints of torture or to be approached by torture victims seeking medical treatment.

A striking example of how forensic examiners can inhibit the abuse of detainees took place in Northern Ireland between 1977 and 1979.[36] In January 1976, the European Commission of Human Rights concluded that the British government and Northern Ireland authorities were responsible in the early 1970s for torturing and ill-treating persons held for interrogation purposes by the police.[37] Despite the British government's assurances to Parliament in 1972 and the European Court of Human Rights in 1977 that such abuses would cease, complaints of assault during interrogation were common until 1979.[38]

A prominent factor in the continued abuse of detainees, primarily by the Royal Ulster Constabulary (RUC), appears to have been the British government's policy of protecting "police discretion to question a suspect in private for extensive periods without the intrusion of the courts, laywers or any other independent person."[39] This policy, which gave the police the authority to hold suspects incommunicado for up to seven days, was accompanied by a relaxation of the rules governing the admissibility of confessions in court.[40] Moreover, government ministers and senior RUC officers failed to investigate and discipline interrogators who used assault and illegal coercion, thus setting a poor example for security personnel.

In March 1977 the Forensic Medical Officers Association, working with doctors employed in detention facilities, began a series of actions to prevent torture and ill-treatment in Northern Ireland.[41] At first the doctors quietly directed their appeals to the authorities, shunning publicity of any kind. The doctors, through the association's secretary, Dr. Robert Irwin, informed the RUC of their concern about the increasing number of injuries suffered by prisoners examined by police surgeons, and they requested a meeting with senior officials. Their request was ignored, and six months later the association's executive committee made a public statement to this effect. In November, doctors at the Castlereagh and Gough police stations threatened to resign unless actions were taken to stop the abuse of detainees.

A year passed before the RUC informed the government that the doctors had noted another rash of injuries and that resignations might soon follow. Finally, on 20 April 1978, Dr. Irwin, who had himself seen 150 injured detainees, and two other police surgeons held a meeting with the chief constable at the Gough Barracks interrogation center to air their concerns. The day after the meeting, the chief constable, at the doctors' suggestion, ordered that "spy holes" be installed in the doors of interview rooms at the barracks so that senior officers could monitor interrogations. The doctors also suggested that closed-circuit television cameras be installed in interrogation rooms for monitoring purposes. Over the next five months complaints of assaults at the barracks came to a virtual halt.

As a result of the actions of Dr. Irwin and his colleagues, a committee of inquiry (known as the Bennett committee) was eventually set up to investigate police procedures. In turn, the committee's report led to the implementation of administrative safeguards to protect detainees, and the number of complaints of ill-treatment gradually fell. In addition, the duties of police surgeons were extended to include the authority to gain access to detainees at all reasonable times, as well as to make use of newly installed spy holes.

The police surgeons in Northern Ireland were successful in decreasing the incidence of torture and ill-treatment in Irish prisons because they were willing to go public, at considerable professional and personal risk, to denounce abuses after they failed to persuade prison officials of needed improvements. Their suggestions for improvements—and certainly their actions—should serve as models for health professionals working in detention centers and prisons in other countries. The Medical Association of South Africa (MASA), for instance, made an encouraging move in this direction in 1983 when it drew up a series of recommendations designed to protect detainees from abuse. "When a detainee is interrogated," the association said, "this should be done in circumstances where there are always at least two persons present, with closed-circuit televison."[42] The association further recommended that district surgeons be given the statutory right "to have free access, without prior Police authorization, to a detainee at all times."

Recognition and Treatment of Torture

As torture victims and their families increasingly seek redress and compensation through the courts, medical testimony will be critical to verifying evidence of torture and determining the long-term physiological and psychological effects of torture on the victim and family members. The Filártigas' New York legal case (described in Chapter 4) demonstrates the importance of such testimony. In addition, medical verification of torture can help host governments determine if refugees will face persecution if they are returned to their countries of origin.

Physicians and psychiatrists need to become familiar with the immediate and long-term physical and psychological stigmata of torture for the purposes of diagnosis and treatment. There is a growing literature on the subject of the torture syndrome and elements of the post-traumatic stress disorder are well documented from the literature on the "concentration camp syndrome." The clinical studies presented in Chapter 3 demonstrate that medical teams in Canada and the United States have already developed protocols for verifying evidence of torture and treating torture victims. (Medical teams in Denmark and Chile have made similar progress.) This research has revealed that there is a high incidence of late physical and neuropsychiatric sequelae among torture victims. For example, in December 1982, a group of Danish doctors reported that five previously healthy and skilled men who were severely tortured six years before doctors examined them had experienced some form of brain atrophy.[43] On the basis of their findings, the doctors suggested that "torture victims should be offered appropriate medical and social aid and followed carefully in an attempt to avoid the sad consequences of possible premature cerebral aging, as observed among the victims of World War II."

In an attempt to meet the needs of torture victims, the United Nations established in 1981 a voluntary fund for victims of torture.[44] The fund, which has received donations from several countries, provides "humanitarian, legal, and financial aid to individuals . . . and their families" who have suffered as a result of torture. In addition to providing funds for medical treatment and psychological counseling, the fund enables relatives of victims who die while in detention to obtain independent forensic and legal experts to help establish the cause of death and, if possible, to obtain compensation. Forensic scientists and their associations could play a critical role in implementing some of the fund's objectives. They could begin by establishing international standards to assure that forensic scientists maintain independence from other authorities while they carry out death investigations and issue death certificates. In addition, members could travel to different countries as impartial observers of autopsies on prisoners who have died in detention.

Human Rights Violations Directed at Health Professionals

A vital component in the health professions' efforts to stop torture must be the defense of colleagues who may be imprisoned or harrassed by their governments for upholding ethical standards or for treating torture victims. Several scientific and medical associations, such as the American Association for the Advancement of Science (AAAS) and the World Medical Association, have already developed programs to respond quickly and effectively to reports of human rights abuses directed at scientists and health professionals abroad.[45] The AAAS has found that missions to countries where scientists and health personnel face persecution have proven effective means of demonstrating collegial support and putting pressure on the offending government. Since 1981 the AAAS has sent missions to Chile, Guatemala, El Salvador, and the Philippines in response to reports that health professionals had "disappeared" or were in incommunicado detention as a result of professional activities.[46]

Following the abductions of three Chilean physicians in June 1981, the AAAS, in conjunction with the American Public Health Association and other scientific societies, dispatched two American physicians to investigate.[47] By the time the delegation arrived in Santiago, the Chilean Medical Association and the Catholic Church had already filed writs of *hapeas corpus* on behalf of the jailed doctors; family members and medical colleagues had made personal appeals to government officials. Several physicians, including the distinguished Chilean neurophysiologist Joaquin Luco, publicly questioned the government's motives in the case.[48]

What motivated the secret police to detain the three physicians still remains unclear. However, there is good reason to believe that the secret police were angered by the fact that the doctors, along with human rights groups, were submitting complaints of torture to the Chilean courts and international human rights organizations. These testimonies contained detailed descriptions of the torture centers run by the secret police and in some cases testified to the presence of health personnel at the centers.

Three weeks after their abductions, the three physicians appeared in a public prison in the port town of Valparaíso. Eventually the military judge handling the case granted the two American physicians permission to see their Chilean colleagues. Visibly shaken by the ordeal, the Chileans recounted how they had been held for three weeks, most of the time with their eyes taped shut, without access to family or legal counsel. Besieged by hundreds of letters and telegrams from around the world, the Chilean authorities eventually released the three doctors and dismissed the charges against them.

Although the Chilean mission is an example of one strategy of aiding colleagues, there are certainly other strategies that can be adopted. University medical departments, for example, could work on behalf of persecuted colleagues or they could extend invitations or formal offers to scientists and health professionals in other countries who have been persecuted. Medical societies as yet uncommitted to any strategy could begin by sponsoring roundtable discussions or symposia at their annual meetings to increase awareness of torture among their members and to explore possible actions.

After years of relying on the World Medical Association to attend to human rights concerns, the American Medical Association has finally begun to take action on its own.[49] At the association's annual meeting in 1983, it adopted a resolution opposing "the use of medicine to suppress political dissent." In an adjoining resolution, the association also committed itself to raising concerns "about the disappearance of physicians, medical students, and other health care professionals with resulting inadequate care to the sick and injured of countries in turmoil." In 1983 the American College of Physicians formed a committee to defend physicians who face persecution abroad. The Institute of Medicine of the National Academy of Sciences and the American Public Health Association regularly write to governments to inquire about the physical integrity and legal status of health professionals reported to be detained without proper legal safeguards. Other medical groups should follow these examples of increasing professional and public awareness of the problem.

Conclusion

Codes of medical ethics forbid professional members from participating in torture and impose upon them—and their associations—the duty to work actively for the abolition of torture. It is not enough merely to condemn medical and health practitioners who take part in torture. Health associations nationally and internationally must act together to support those doctors and other persons who refuse to remain silent when torture takes place. Concerted action and publicity increase the chances that governments will listen to and heed such protests. Improved means of gathering accurate information on torture, as well as improved treatment methods and facilities for torture victims, need to be established. Equally important is the need for lawyers and human rights experts to share their knowledge and expertise with medical groups so that, collectively, they can propose measures for safeguarding potential victims from abuse.

The responsibility for ending torture rests with all of us. And it is a responsibility we can hardly ignore. For if we are unable to renew constantly our faith in the concept that "humanity can control what humanity creates," we surely run the danger of facing even more pervasive forms of human destruction in the future.

Notes and References

1. See Office of the Governor-General, Civil Inspectorate-General in Algeria, *Wuillaume Report* (Algiers: 2 March 1955), report in Pierre Vidal Naquet, *Torture: Cancer in Democracy* (Middlesex: Penguin, 1963).

2. See the testimony of K. Barton Osborn in US Senate, Committee on Armed Services, *Hearings on the Nomination of William E. Colby*, 93rd Cong., 1st sess., 1973, pp. 101–117; the testimony of former Agency for International Development official Theodore Jacqueney in US House of Representatives,

Committee on Government Operations, *Hearings on U.S. Assistance Programs in Vietnam*, 92nd Cong., 1st sess., 1971; and the interview with former Phoenix adviser Jeffrey Smith in "From the Ashes, Phoenix," *Commonweal*, 20 April 1973, pp. 154–159.

3. See Robert Daly, "Psychiatric After-Effects of Irish Prisoners Subjected to Ill-Treatment and Torture," *New Scientist*, 5 August 1976, pp. 272–273. Also see *Report of the Enquiry into Allegations against the Security Forces of Physical Brutality in Northern Ireland* (London: HM Stationary Office, 1971), also known as the "Compton Report"; *Ireland v. United Kingdom, Yearbook of the European Convention on Human Rights* 20 (1976): 348–362.

4. See Amnesty International, *Torture in the Eighties* (London: Amnesty International, 1984), pp. 214–217.

5. See Richard Pierre Claude, "Argentina's Return to Democracy," *America*, 17 December 1983, pp. 385–389; Eduard Schumacher, "Argentina and Democracy," *Foreign Affairs* (Summer 1984):1070–1095.

6. Among the executive orders and laws pretaining to human rights passed by the Argentine government since the inauguration of President Raúl Alfonsín on 10 December 1983 are: "Establishment of the National Commission on the Disappearance of Persons" (Executive Order No. 187, 15 December 1983); "Court Martial of the First Three Military Juntas and the Former Chief of Police of the Province of Buenos Aires" (Executive Order No. 158, 13 December 1983); "Prosecution of the Leaders of Terrorist Organizations" (Executive Order No. 152, 13 December 1983); "Repeal of the Military Government's Amnesty Law" (Law No. 23.040, 22 December 1983); "Reconsideration of Sentences Passed on Civilians by Military Courts" (Law No. 23.042, 11 January 1984); "Amendments to the Military Code" (Law No. 23.049, 9 February 1984).

7. Alfred Heijder, "Professional Codes of Ethics against Torture," in *Professional Codes of Ethics* (London: Amnesty International, 1976), pp. 9–10.

8. See Stanley Joel Reiser, Arthur J. Dyck, and William J. Curran, eds., *Ethics in Medicine: Historical Perspectives and Contemporary Concerns* (Cambridge, Mass.; MIT Press, 1977).

9. *Workshop on Human Rights: Report and Recommendations* (London: Amnesty International, 1976), p. 8.

10. Ibid.

11. See "Changes Sought in Proposed U.N. Code on Torture," in *Clearinghouse Report on Science and Human Rights* (Washington, D.C.: American Association for the Advancement of Science, December 1981).

12. *World Medical Journal* 28, no. 2 (March–April 1981):29–31.

13. *Report of the Secretary-General on a Draft Code of Medical Ethics*, UN document A/35/372/Add.1 (Geneva: United Nations Information Office, 1980), p. 7.

14. See R. Chalk, M. Frankel, and S. Chafer, *AAAS Professional Ethics Project: Professional Ethics Activities in the Scientific and Engineering Societies* (Washington,

D.C.: American Association for the Advancement of Science, 1980), pp. 99–101. This study concluded that such codes serve two purposes:

> They may provide both a forum for professionals to examine the range of values associated with their discipline in an impartial fashion and also a means for professions to instill in their members basic values intended to influence their professional behavior.

The study also concluded that many of the distinctions between general principles and rules of conduct formulated by the scientific and engineering associations surveyed were unclear. "The situation," the authors said, "might be characterized as one of 'laissez-faire ethics,' where scientists and engineers are commonly left to decide for themselves—or to be guided by rules developed by groups outside the profession—what set of values should influence the development and application of their professional knowledge."

15. "New Biko Protest," *Washington Post*, 14 November 1980, p. 9; for a more extensive report, see "South African Doctors Protest Biko Ruling," *Clearinghouse Report on Science and Human Rights*, December 1980, p. 1.

16. For an account of the Biko inquest, see Donald Woods, *Biko* (New York: Random House, 1979).

17. Quoted from Phillip V. Tokia, dean of the Medical School, University of Witwatersrand in a letter to *Nature*, 17 July 1980.

18. Associated Press report, 14 November 1980, Johannesburg.

19. Ibid.; Tokia, letter to *Nature*.

20. Tokia, letter to *Nature*.

21. Statement issued by the executive committee of the federal council of the Medical Association of South Africa, Johannesburg, 12 February 1982.

22. See "Record on Torture Victims Falsified," *Amnesty International Newsletter*, July 1980, pp. 4–6.

23. See Alan Riding, "Brazil's Rulers Await Defeat in Vote," *New York Times*, 10 December 1984, p. A3.

24. Amnesty International, *Chile* (London: Amnesty International, 1974), p. 63.

25. Amnesty International, *Chile: Evidence of Torture* (London: Amnesty International, 1983), p. 3.

26. "Doctors Who Make Pain," *Newsweek*, 1 August 1983, p. 25.

27. Ibid.

28. See "Médicos Piden Termino de Apremios Ilegítimos," *El Mercurio*, 25 November 1983. Also see "Declaración del Colegio Médico de Chile A.G.," dated 23 November 1983, which is available by writing to the Colegio Médico de Chile A.G., Esmeralda 678, Casilla 639, Santiago, Chile.

29. Testimony of Juan Luís Gonzalez Reyes, president of the Chilean Medical Association, in US House of Representatives, Committee on Foreign Affairs, *Hearings on the Phenomenon of Torture*, 98th Cong., 1st sess., 1984.

30. See Tom Harpur, "Uruguayan Doctors Accused of Torture," *Toronto Star*, 3 August 1984, p. A20.

31. "Caso Roslik: Médicos Juzgan la Conducta Del Dr. Eduardo Saiz," *El Día* (Montevideo), 24 July 1984.

32. See "Roslik Fue Ahogado En El 'Submarino,'" (Montevideo), *Mayoría* 3 May 1984, pp. 6–7; Martin Anderson, "Uruguay's Army Hunts Communists in Small Town Settled by Russians," *Washington Post*, 9 November 1984, p. E1.

33. Amnesty International, *Torture in the Eighties*, pp. 82—83.

34. Ibid.

35. Nikki Meredith, "The Murder Epidemic," *Science 84* 5, no. 10 (December 1984), pp. 42–48.

36. See Amnesty International, *Torture in the Eightees*, pp. 50–61.

37. European Commission of Human Rights, *Report of the Commission on Application No. 5310/71, Ireland against the United Kingdom of Great Britain and Northern Ireland*, adopted 26 January 1976, pp. 402, 468. The European Court of Human Rights, in their judgment on this case in January 1978, modified the commission's findings, omitting the word *torture* but confirming that there had been an "administrative practice" of inhuman and degrading treatment in breach of Article 3.

38. According to calculations based on data given in the *Report of the Committee of Inquiry into Police Interrogation Procedures in Northern Ireland* (known as the Bennett Report) (London: HM Stationery Office, March 1979, paragraph 44 and Appendix 2), between 1976 and 1978, one in eleven detainees arrested under emergency legislation in Northern Ireland filed official complaints of assault by the Royal Ulster Constabulary.

39. Amnesty International, *Torture in the Eighties*, p. 53.

40. The Bennett Report, paragraph 30, reports that during the first half of 1978, between 75 and 80 percent of all convictions for politically motivated offences were based solely or mainly on confessions.

41. The role of the Forensic Medical Officers Association in preventing torture and ill-treatment is documented in Amnesty International, *Torture in the Eighties*, pp. 57–60.

42. *Medical Care of Prisoners and Detainees*, Report of the Ad Hoc Committee of the Medical Association of South Africa to Institute an Inquiry into the Medical Care of Prisoners and Detainees, adopted by the Federal Council of the Medical Association of South Africa, Johannesburg, 10 May 1983.

43. Troels Staehelin Jensen et al., "Cerebral Atrophy in Young Torture Victims," *New England Journal of Medicine* 307, no. 21 (18 November 1982):1341.

44. The General Assembly of the United Nations established the fund through GA Resolution 36/151 on 16 December 1981. The United Nations has appealed to all governments to contribute to the fund if requested.

45. See listing under Clearinghouse on Science and Human Rights in Appendix B.

46. Information on missions carried out under AAAS sponsorship is available by writing Eric Stover, AAAS Committee on Scientific Freedom and Responsibility, 1515 Massachusetts Avenue, N.W., Washington, D.C. 20005.

47. See Nicolas Wade, "Chilean Doctors and AAAS Mission," *Science*, 24 July 1981, p. 421. For Chilean press coverage of the incident, see Patricia Verdugo, "Viaje al Puerto," *Hoy*, 17 June 1981; Alejandro Gonzalez, "Disposición Vigesimocuarta Transitoria," *Mensage*, July 1981, p. 320.

48. "Doctor Luco se refiere a los médicos detenidos," *La Segunda*, 9 June 1981.

49. Resolutions 127 and 133 were adopted by the American Medical Association at their annual meeting in June 1983. The full texts of the resolutions can be found in *American Medical News*, 1–8 July 1983, p. 10.

Part II
Psychiatric Abuse

Our professional duty demands of us that we care for others. I appeal to you, my colleagues, not for a moment to forget those who are now condemned to spend years in the nightmarish world of psychiatric wards, exhausting themselves in a debilitating struggle to preserve their psyches, a struggle against torturers armed with drugs—all because they have stood up for the rights and freedoms people need. To remember them and to do everything possible for their release is our obligation. Their fate is a reproach to our conscience, a challenge to honor, a test of our commitment to compassion. We must brand, brand with shame, those who out of self-interest or anti-humanitarian motives trample on the ideals of justice and on the doctor's sacred oath.*

Dr. Anatoly Koryagin

* Reprinted with the permission of the New York Review of Books, copyright 1982 Nyrev, Inc.

A major feature of the nightmarish anti-utopias of George Orwell's *1984* and Aldous Huxley's *Brave New World* is the state's ability to maintain power by controlling the thoughts and actions of its citizens. The state quickly quashes political protest in these novels. Both in books and in the real world, at times methods are brutal. But the methods may also take subtler forms. For instance, the state may interpret a person's intentions and actions in such a way as to undermine the legitimacy of the individual's political dissent. Manipulated in this manner, political protest turns into a psychiatric issue.

Psychiatry is always vulnerable to co-optation by the state, since state officials can call on psychiatrists to label political and social reformers mentally ill and pronounce them in need of confinement for psychiatric care. The state, with the aid of psychiatrists, can thus discredit and effectively silence people who oppose its policies. State manipulation of psychiatry for political ends is a reality in the Soviet Union and, to a lesser extent, in other countries (e.g., Yugoslavia and Romania). Critics have charged that psychiatrists in Western countries have also occasionally used their professional skills and expertise to look after the state's interests rather than the patient's.

Medical personnel play a central role in psychiatric abuse. Without the participation of psychiatrists, the definition of political dissent as insanity would have little credence. Dissidents languishing in a psychiatric hospital also face the danger of being tortured physically or psychologically. Torture is used to force them to recant their political views. As in other settings where torture is used, medical personnel usually play a supportive rather than a central role.

The authors in Part II explore psychiatric abuse, particularly in the Soviet Union, and describe what measures have been taken to end it. In Chapter 6, Sidney Bloch and Peter Reddaway trace the development of psychiatric abuse for political purposes in the Soviet Union from the first documented case in the early nineteenth century to the present day. In this context, they then analyze the diagnostic methods used to incarcerate dissidents and the extent of psychiatrists' complicity in, or resistance to, abusive practice.

In the first part of Chapter 7, Kevin Klose describes the misfortune that befell two Soviet citizens—Alexei Nikitin, a mining engineer, and Anatoly Koryagin, a psychiatrist. Nikitin was confined to a psychiatric hospital and subjected to painful and prolonged drug treatment because he had persistently criticized the safety of the coal mines where he worked; Koryagin came to Nikitin's defense, and was later incarcerated in Chistopol prison for "anti-Soviet activities." Before his arrest and imprisonment, Koryagin served as chief psychiatric consultant for a human rights group, the Working Commission to Investigate the Use of Psychiatry for Political Purposes.

Formed in 1977, the commission campaigned for the release of dissidents in psychiatric hospitals, visited the dissidents, and provided their families with moral and material support. During the group's four-year existence, Koryagin and another psychiatrist, Alexander Voloshanovich, examined 55 dissidents who had been released from mental hospitals or who were in danger of being detained and sent to psychiatric hospitals. They concluded that, as in the case of Alexei Nikitin, there was no medical justification for the forcible confinement or treatment of these people. The doctors found that some hospitalized dissidents had been subjected to beatings, disorienting and pain-causing drugs, insulin shock therapy, and isolation for prolonged periods of time. Frequently harassed for his work, Voloshanovich emigrated from the Soviet Union in 1980. Within a year, all six remaining members of the group, including Koryagin, were imprisoned or exiled.

Prior to imprisonment, Koryagin smuggled the article that forms the second part of Chapter 7 to the West. It describes dissidents' paths to imprisonment in special psychiatric hospitals, and his view of Soviet psychiatrists' role in these matters.

In 1978 a panel of American psychiatrists had the opportunity of examining the well-known dissident Pyotr Grigorenko after he arrived in the West. Walter Reich details the panel's findings in Chapter 8. For most of his life, Grigorenko had pursued a distinguished military career, but by 1962 his faith in the Soviet system had begun to waver; in 1964 he was arrested for "anti-Soviet activities," declared mentally ill, and committed to a hospital for the criminally insane. Over the next ten years, he spent two periods in forced psychiatric confinement. Grigorenko claims that the hospital treatment he received was designed to make him recant his dissident views.

In Chapter 9, Walter Reich examines the present state of Soviet psychiatry, emphasizing the psychiatric concepts that underlie the diagnosis of dissidents. He challenges the commonly held belief that Soviet psychiatrists who diagnose dissidents as mentally ill are simply acting on orders from the KGB. Based on interviews with Soviet dissidents and psychiatrists, Reich argues that the process leading to the misdiagnosis of dissidents is much more complex. The theories of Soviet psychiatry, the characteristics of the dissidents, the nature of Soviet life, Reich suggests, all must be considered in order to understand and respond effectively to psychiatric abuse in the Soviet Union.

The response of the World Psychiatric Association and the American Psychiatric Association to reports of psychiatric abuse in the Soviet Union and elsewhere is examined in the final chapter of Part II, written by Paul Chodoff and Ellen Mercer.

Chapter 6

Psychiatrists and Dissenters in the Soviet Union

Sidney Bloch and Peter Reddaway

In this chapter we examine the role of the psychiatrist in a particular misuse of professional skills and expertise that is prevalent in the Soviet Union—labeling sane dissenters as mentally ill and in need of compulsory hospitalization and treatment. Although this form of misuse has occurred elsewhere, in no other country, to our knowledge, has it become widespread and systematic, part of a deliberate governmental policy.

As Soviet citizens have developed various modes of dissent since the 1960s, reports have emerged that substantial numbers of human rights activists, nationalists, religious believers, and would-be emigrants—almost all mentally healthy in the eyes of families and friends—have been declared insane by psychiatrists and compulsorily confined to psychiatric hospitals for indeterminate periods. Rather than receiving appropriate care there, the dissenters have encountered brutal and punitive "treatment," apparently in an effort to stamp out their nonconformist behavior.

Who is responsible for the misuse of psychiatry in the Soviet Union? Is it perpetrated by the entire psychiatric profession or just a minority? What factors underlie the participation of psychiatrists? Is it fear, obedience to the authorities, corruption, ignorance of ethical issues? Are the diagnoses given to dissenters clinically reasonable? Would they be acceptable to psychiatrists outside the Soviet Union, or are they shaped to fit the requirements of the regime? Before attempting to answer these questions, we first look at how the problem has developed.

Reprinted in edited and updated form with permission from the authors and Basic Books, Inc., Publishers, New York, from *Psychiatric Terror: How Soviet Psychiatry is Used to Suppress Dissent*, 1977.

Development of Psychiatric Abuse

The first recorded instance in which psychiatric means were used in Russia to repress dissent was in the case of the philosopher Pyotr Chaadayev (1793–1856) in 1836. After returning home from service in the czar's army in western Europe, Chaadayev wrote a "philosophical letter" critical of the regime of Nicholas I. The letter, published in the Moscow journal *Telescope*, was promptly denounced at the instigation of the chief of the czar's secret police. Nicholas himself ordered the *Telescope*'s publisher into exile and officially declared Chaadayev insane. Disguising his repressive motives under a mask of benevolent paternalism, Nicholas proclaimed:

> I consider this to be a farrago of insolent nonsense worthy of a lunatic. . . . The essay of P. Y. Chaadayev . . . and the thoughts expressed in it have aroused feelings of anger and repugnance in all Russians without exception. But the horror quickly turned to sympathy when they learned that their unhappy compatriot, the author of the article, suffers from derangement and insanity. Taking into consideration the unwell state of this unfortunate person, the government in its solicitude and fatherly concern for its subject, forbids him to leave the house and will provide free medical care with a special doctor to be appointed by the local authorities from among those under their jurisdiction.[1]

Why Nicholas I chose a procedure so unusual for the times is not fully clear, but it did serve to discredit Chaadayev's reformist ideas. When Chaadayev was released from house arrest a year later, he resumed his literary and political activities, but no more of his philosophical letters were published in Russia during his lifetime.

Political use of psychiatric diagnoses was only occasional and localized during czarist times. It was also rare in the years immediately after the 1917 revolution. On several occasions, the then shaky Bolshevik government attempted to defuse the political potency of persons viewed as threatening by labeling them mentally ill, but with little success.

The Stalin Period

The scanty evidence available suggests that the policy of systematically interning dissenters in mental hospitals began during Stalin's rule in the late 1930s. Between 1936 and 1938 Andrei Vyshinsky, a subordinate of the head of the secret police, initiated the practice of confining dissenters in prison psychiatric hospitals. Since that time these hospitals, later renamed special psychiatric hospitals (SPHs)*, have remained under the control of the Ministry of Internal Affairs—the ministry that also directs the operations of the politce, prisons, and labor camps.

A psychiatrist who emigrated to the United States soon after World War II gave an illuminating account of this period in a series of four letters published in the *American Journal of Psychiatry*.[2] In 1941 the psychiatrist had joined the staff of a 400-bed mental institution in Kazan that was used exclusively for treating politicals from the entire country. The mental institution was on the grounds of an ordinary mental hospital but was run independently under the direction of the secret police.

The psychiatrist differentiated two types of political inmates at Kazan. Inmates of the first type, the majority, were indeed mentally ill. People in this category had been sent to Kazan because their delusions and other psychological abnormalities had a political content. One schizophrenic patient, for instance, had the delusion that he was Trotsky. Another patient believed that Judaism had the power to destroy the world.

Political inmates of the second type, the minority, were sane people confined for political reasons. One "patient" was a Moscow factory worker who said that he had been too poor to contribute a month's salary to the war effort, a "voluntary" state requirement of all workers and farmers. Steadfast in his refusal, he had been arrested, detained in Moscow's Lubyanka prison, and there diagnosed as schizophrenic. He was then transferred to the Kazan hospital and again diagnosed as a schizophrenic.

The autobiography of Ilya Yarkov, published in *samizdat*† and smuggled out to the West, provides a glimpse of the experience of one political prisoner ruled insane during the regime of Stalin.[3] In 1948 the authorities decided to rearrest those people who had served sentences as political dissenters in the 1920s and 1930s. Yarkov fell into this category and was arrested in 1951, charged with being a dangerous leader of a sectarian group. Eventually Yarkov was examined by a psychiatrist at the Kuibyshev Medical Institute in the presence of his police investigator and duly ruled not responsible for his actions.

---

* The "purest" sort of SPH is a self-contained institution that holds only inmates sent there under criminal commitment by decision of a court. There are also psychiatric sections in the hospitals of certain prisons. These sections are used to hold (apart from temporarily ill inmates from the attached prison) remand prisoners who are either undergoing psychiatric assessment or are awaiting trial after assessment, or prisoners already ruled not responsible by a court and awaiting assignment to an SPH proper.

† A *Samizdat* is a system by which manuscripts denied publication in the Soviet Union are circulated clandestinely in typescript or in mimeograph form, or are smuggled out for publication abroad.

The psychiatrists whom Yarkov met in the three hospitals during his three years of confinement varied considerably. The head of the psychiatric section of the prison hospital in Gorky, for instance, was described as a perfect example of a person uniting the roles of doctor and police officer, yet a very pleasant man. Another Gorky psychiatrist was decent and cordial. The opposite could be said of an elderly psychiatrist on the Kazan staff, who often humiliated and punished her patients. Her favorite form of punishment was the "roll-up" treatment. Sheets of wet canvas were rolled around the patient's body. As the canvas dried, it shrank, making it progressively more difficult for the patient to breathe. The degree of tightness and the duration of a roll-up were varied depending on how much punishment was prescribed.

The commissions that visited the hospitals about twice a year from Moscow were usually chaired by a secret police doctor, who often had the rank of general. Yarkov and his friends believed that the decision to recommend an inmate's release depended on the highly secret term of imprisonment that the authorities had prescribed for each inmate. This view sounds plausible enough, because nowhere does Yarkov mention recantation—one's "admission" that one's anti-Soviet acts were the result of mental illness, accompanied by a statement of gratitude to the doctors for the cure. Neither the hospital staff nor the visiting commissions, it appears, were obliged to persuade inmates to take such a course of action. However, this task was soon given to them.

Attempts at Reform After Stalin

After the death of Stalin, several party officials attempted to end psychiatric abuse. An important early figure in these attempts was Sergei Pisarev,[4] a longtime party official who had been arrested in 1953, soon after submitting a report to Stalin criticizing the secret police for its fabrication of a nonexistent "Doctors' Plot" to poison leading political figures. Pisarev spent his first seven weeks of detention in the Serbsky Institute for Forensic Psychiatry. Then, having been diagnosed as schizophrenic, he was confined in the psychiatric ward of Moscow's Butyrka prison for four months and in the Leningrad Prison Psychiatric Hospital for nearly a year and a half. Three times during his Leningrad hospitalization Pisarev learned that even his psychiatrist had reported that he was "healthy and fully capable of accepting responsibility for his actions."

After his release in 1955, Pisarev mounted a campaign to combat psychiatric misuse, particularly at the Serbsky. He presented evidence to the party's Central Committee of numerous instances when mentally healthy scholars, writers, artists, and party workers had been labeled insane by the Serbsky and hospitalized along with genuine patients for several years. The Central Committee responded by appointing a commission headed by a senior party official, A. I. Kuznetsov, and comprising eminent professors of psychiatry and directors of important psychiatric institutions. The commission conducted a thorough investigation of the Serbsky Institute, visited the prison psychiatric hospitals at Kazan and Leningrad, and recommended reforms at these hospitals and the transfer of their supervision from the Ministry of Internal Affairs to the Ministry of Health.

The commission's carefully prepared report, however, was never considered by those officials who had ordered it. For two years it was carefully concealed from the Central Committee by the responsible official, who then discreetly consigned it to the archives. Nevertheless, some reforms were instituted in both the Leningrad and Kazan hospitals, Pisarev reported. Conditions for both political and genuinely ill patients improved, and the psychiatrists, many of whom were new, more frequently repudiated the Serbsky Institute's unjustified diagnoses.

Despite Pisarev's initiative and the work of the investigating commission in 1955–56, the practice of interning sane dissenters in mental hospitals continued. New hospitals similar to those in Leningrad and Kazan were set up in other cities. An important reason was probably the implicit support that Mr. Krushchev gave to equating social deviance with insanity. The party leader was keen to convince both domestic and foreign opinion that his regime had put the Stalin era behind it and no longer held any political prisoners.

In 1956, the same year that Krushchev denounced the excesses that Stalin committed in his later years, Nikolai Samsonov, a noted geophysicist, was arrested. He was charged with counterrevolutionary crimes after submitting a treatise to the party's Central Committee critical of the erosion of Leninist principles.[5] During the criminal investigation that followed, Samsonov underwent a psychiatric examination. The examining commission, headed by Professor Torubarov of the Serbsky Institute, concluded that Samsonov was mentally ill and not responsible. The court accepted the commission's conclusions and ordered his transfer to the Leningrad Special Psychiatric Hospital, where he remained until September 1964—one of the longest periods of confinement of a dissenter whose case is well documented.

Samsonov's hospital psychiatrists considered him mentally well according to the *Chronicle of Current Events*, a clandestine journal put out by Soviet human rights activists. However, psychiatrists advised him to concede that he had been of unsound mind when he wrote his heterodox document. Such an admission, they argued, would "testify to his recovery." After two years

of internment, during which time he persistently refused to acknowledge
that he had been mentally disturbed when he wrote his treatise, Samsonov
was threatened with injections of chlorpromazine, a tranquilizer in wide use
in the West for treating certain severe mental illnesses. These threats did
not undermine Samsonov's determination. Only in 1964, after he had actually
received chlorpromazine injections and his general health was failing, did
Samsonov sign a declaration to the effect that he had been mentally ill. On
his release from the hospital, he received a pension and worked for two
months of each year at a geophysics research institute until his death in
1971.

In all likelihood the cases of Yarkov, Pisarev, and Samsonov are representative of a sizable group—one cannot even guess its numbers—of Soviet
citizens who, during the 1950s and early 1960s, were charged with political
offenses, diagnosed as mentally ill, declared not responsible, and transferred
to mental hospitals for indefinite periods of internment.

The Tarsis Case: First International Awareness

Public awareness in the West that Soviet psychiatry was possibly being used
for political purposes first became widespread in 1965, when *Ward 7* by
Valery Tarsis was published in Britain.[6] The book was serialized in the
Observer (London) and reached a wide audience.[7] *Ward 7* is an autibiography
superficially disguised as a novel. It records the plight of a writer, Valentine
Almazov (representing Tarsis), who is forcibly interned in a mental hospital
for writing and distributing anti-Soviet literature.

Ward 7 is a chilling account of sane people in insane places. Tarsis himself
was actually a patient for seven months in the Kashchenko Psychiatric

Hospital, one of Moscow's largest. It is clearly to this hospital that the novel's protagonist, Almazov, is committed by order of the chief city psychiatrist, acting under pressure from party officials.

Almazov soon realizes that he is being hospitalized neither because he has a severe mental illness nor because he constitutes a physical danger to himself or society. Rather it is because of the imminent publication of his manuscript in the West, an act construed by the authorities as "anti-Soviet."

As the novel unfolds, the reader's suspicion is aroused that something is terribly amiss in Ward 7, not just for Almazov but for all but one of the inmates. Almazov's revelations about the "patients" he meets and the nature of their medical treatment leads the reader to conclude with the hero that only 1 patient of the 150 in the ward is mentally ill. "No one in it except Karen was the victim of anything except his lot as a Soviet citizen." He identifies three groups of inmates. First, the failed suicides—mainly young people. They have attempted suicide because of their dissatisfaction with society, although the official psychiatric and ideological view is that anyone attempting suicide* because of such dissatisfaction must be abnormal—no one could possibly be unhappy living under the Soviet system. The second group consists of people who have sought information about emigration from a foreign embassy or who have actually applied for an exit visa. The third group comprises young people who have rejected the values and standards of Soviet society. They have manifested their dissatisfaction and rejection in diverse ways, often by not adhering to conventional norms.

In a fictionalized autobiography it is difficult to tease out fact from fiction, but material in *Ward 7* is both consistent and coherent enough to persuade us that in 1962–63 the Kashchenko Psychiatric Hospital contained several people who were there for their political beliefs rather than for medical reasons. Our impression is confirmed by a report that Tarsis submitted to Amnesty International in 1966.[8] In any case, regardless of how accurately *Ward 7* reflected events in the early 1960s, it made Western observers realize that the Chaadayev episode had a counterpart, and a more alarming one, in contemporary Soviet society.

The case of Alexander Volpin best reflects the practice of curbing dissent through psychiatric means during the 1950s and 1960s. Volpin was interned in psychiatric hospitals on five occasions over a nineteen-year period.[9]

Born in 1924 to the celebrated Russian poet Esenin, Volpin graduated

---

* The notion of suicide as a reflection of mental illness is shrouded with controversy and complexity. Indubitably, many suicides and attempted suicides are symptomatic of serious mental illness. Other suicides are committed with rational insight. In such cases, value-laden judgments abound as to whether such a profound act can be interpreted as normal.

from Moscow University in 1946 and received his doctoral degree in mathematical logic in 1949. That same year he was arrested for writing poems regarded by the authorities as anti-Soviet. Volpin was initially interrogated in Lubyanka prison and then transferred to the Serbsky Institute, where he was declared insane and not responsible. The court accepted the Serbsky's recommendations, and Volpin was incarcerated for a year in the Leningrad Special Psychiatric Hospital.

During Krushchev's regime, Volpin was forcibly hospitalized on three occasions: in 1957 for three weeks in an ordinary psychiatric hospital in Moscow, for twelve months in 1959–60 in the Leningrad special hospital, and for four months in 1962–63, again in an ordinary mental hospital. On the occasion when he was confined in special hospital, the procedure followed was that of criminal commitment—a criminal charge of a political kind was made, a psychiatric examination conducted, and a court order issued stating that Volpin was not responsible and in need of compulsory treatment in a hospital.

Political factors also appeared to be important in the three confinements based on civil commitment. Volpin details the reason for each of these commitments: "once for advising a French woman against accepting Soviet citizenship, once for failure to inform on an acquaintance who had allegedly engaged in treasonable activities, and once for my refusal to denounce the American publication of my book *A Leaf of Spring* and my assertion of the right of everyone to leave any country."[10] Volpin's final hospitalization, in 1968, was also based on a civil commitment, this time probably prompted by his having applied for a visa in order to participate in a scientific conference held in the United States.

Volpin ascertained that the diagnoses of his condition made during his hospitalizations had repeatedly been a "simple form of schizophrenia." Not all the diagnoses were identical, but three findings were in each: He was "psychotically disturbed," his condition was regarded as "incurable," and between attacks he was "in a state of temporary remission only." Despite these clinical conclusions, Volpin was never seriously treated for mental illness. During his 1960 detention, he received small amounts of reserpine, a drug then used as a tranquilizer. At another time a psychiatrist, who Volpin viewed as sympathetic, helped him avoid treatment with haloperidol, a potent tranquilizer used for some major psychiatric disorders.

Opposition Within the Soviet Union to Psychiatric Abuse

When Volpin was last interned, in February 1968, he was released after three months, undoubtedly because of the large-scale protest that his detention provoked both in the Soviet Union and abroad. A petition by 99 Soviet mathematicians and scientists was especially effective in securing his release. The petition within the Soviet Union was in fact the first of its kind in a case of the psychiatric internment of a dissenter. Volpin's colleagues protested to the authorities asserting that his forced confinement was a "flagrant violation of medical and legal norms."[11] Later, some of the signatories were themselves penalized for their outspokenness, and 12 others withdrew their signatures under pressure. Virtually all were denied the right to travel abroad to attend conferences, and some were actually dismissed from their posts or demoted.

As the petition gained attention at home, a group of Soviet human rights activists called on participants attending a conference of Communist parties, then meeting in Budapest, "to consider the peril caused by the trampling on human rights" in the Soviet Union.[12] Dissenters, they said, had been victimized in many ways: unjust dismissal from jobs, summonses from the KGB, threats of arrest, and "finally—the most shocking form of reprisal— forcible confinement in a mental hospital." Ironically, one of the signatories, Major General Pyotr Grigorenko, who had himself spent a year in the Leningrad special hospital in 1964, would again encounter "the most shocking form of reprisal" in 1969. (His case is discussed in Chapter 8.)

Some of the signatories of the Budapest appeal later became founding members of the first formally constituted group of dissenters, the Action Group for the Defense of Human Rights, established in May 1969. The group's first act was to submit an appeal to the UN Commission on Human Rights in May 1969. The group requested that the commission investigate violations in the Soviet Union of the citizen's basic right to hold and express independent convictions. The group also referred to "a particularly inhuman form of persecution: the placing of normal people in psychiatric hospitals for their political convictions."[13] This was the first explicit mention of the practice in an appeal from a Soviet dissenting group to an international organization.

Four members of the action group were later subjected to the very practice that they had protested. Natalya Gorbanevskaya was confined to a psychiatric hospital for a few days in February 1968, but was destined for a much lengthier internment later. Vladimir Borisov, a Leningrad electrician, was arrested less than a month after the group's first letter to the United Nations and sent for psychiatric examination. Declared insane, he spent nearly five years in the Leningrad special hospital. Yury Maltsev, a translator, was forced to undergo a psychiatric examination and committed to the Kashchenko hospital, where he spent a month. Leonid Plyushch, a mathematician from Kiev, was arrested in January 1972 for alleged anti-Soviet activities and eventually sent to the Dnepropetrovsk Special Psychiatric Hospital for compulsory treatment.

In 1970 three events brought the abuse by Soviet psychiatry into dramatic international focus. The first was the publication in the West of General Grigorenko's account of his psychiatric examinations. The second was the nineteen-day involuntary hospitalization of internationally respected biologist Zhores Medvedev, prominently reported in leading Western newspapers.

The third event to attract widespread attention was the television interview by an American journalist of Vladimir Bukovsky, at that time aged 28, who had devoted all his adult years to the struggle for human rights in the Soviet Union. The interview was filmed in Moscow and then broadcast over the CBS network in the United States on 28 July 1970. Broadcasts followed in other Western countries. The same Bukovsky who a few months later would send to the West copies of the psychiatric case reports of several dissenters interned in mental hospitals, related in the interview his own experiences with Soviet mental hospitals and the political use of psychiatry. He recounted how at the age of 21, in 1963, he was arrested and charged with anti-Soviet agitation. After several months in prison, he was transferred to the Serbsky Institute, where he was declared insane, not responsible, and in need of compulsory treatment. He landed in the special hospital in Leningrad, where he spent over a year.

On his release Bukovsky plunged straight back into human rights work, only to be arrested some months later for helping to organize a demonstration. Again, he was interned in a mental hospital, this time for most of an eight-month period in the Serbsky Institute. He was released without explanation, and the charges against him were dropped. A representative of Amnesty International visited Serbsky and talked to its director, Dr. G. Morozov, during Bukovsky's stay there, which may have been a factor prompting Bukovsky's release. However, after a year of freedom Bukovsky was again arrested and charged with slander against the state. On this occasion he actually stood trial for the first time and was sentenced to three years of corrective labor.

The allegations of psychiatric abuse, which have been widely publicized in the West since 1970, were exceptionally grave and constituted a major attack on the Soviet psychiatric profession. Nevertheless, the suppression of dissent by psychiatric means continued until the time of writing. In *Soviet Psychiatric Abuse: The Shadow over World Psychiatry*,[14] we were able to document the cases of nearly 500 dissenters forcibly hospitalized over the previous two decades. The number of internments had fluctuated during this time, apparently dependent on external factors, particularly the international pressure placed on the Soviet Union to end the abuse. For instance, between

1980 and 1983, the incidence of psychiatric internment decreased, a change that can almost certainly be ascribed to Western psychiatric associations, which had increasingly called for the explusion of the Soviet Psychiatric Society from membership in the World Psychiatric Association.

Soviet Methods of Diagnosis

The Soviet approach to psychiatric diagnosis, particularly the concept of schizophrenia, is a critical factor in labeling dissent as mental illness. We shall focus on schizophrenia, for it is this diagnosis that has usually been applied. Psychopathy, particularly of the paranoid type, is the other diagnosis used to pigeonhole dissenters, but its use is less frequent.

What Is Schizophrenia?

Psychiatrists in most countries have used the term *schizophrenia* since it was first introduced by Eugen Bleuler in 1911. There is little agreement among psychiatrists about its meaning, however. This is not surprising if one considers the vague and ill-defined symptoms commonly held to constitute the disorder. The greatest difficulty in diagnosing schizophrenia stems from a lack of objective criteria. Thus far, no tests have been developed that allow a definitive diagnosis to be made. Moreover, the cause of schizophrenia, despite an avalanche of research findings, remains obscure. Given these limitations, schizophrenia is generally defined in terms of its clinical features.

Kraepelin, a German psychiatrist, made a pioneering attempt at the turn of the century to classify the major psychotic mental illnesses. The term *psychotic* is a controversial one but is used in this context to indicate a person's loss of contact with reality. The symptoms Kraepelin regarded as characteristic included hallucinations (perception of stimuli not actually present), most commonly auditory or tactile; unusual and illogical associations of thought resulting in incoherent speech; delusions (false beliefs held with conviction); lack of insight into the illness; withdrawal from the real world; blunting of the emotions; and stereotypical patterns of behavior.[15]

Although the German psychiatrist Kurt Schneider[16] and others have attempted to develop a disciplined method for diagnosing schizophrenia, other psychiatrists have moved in the opposite direction. Hoch and Polatin, for instance, introduced the concept of pseudoneurotic schizophrenia, a disorder characterized by multiple neurotic symptoms—anxiety, phobias, obsessions, and a tendency to withdraw from reality—but not necessarily overt psychotic features, such as delusions and hallucinations.[17] The diagnostic manual used in Britain includes a category of latent schizophrenia "to designate those abnormal states in which, in the absence of obvious schizophrenic symptoms, the suspicion is strong that the condition is in fact a schizophrenia. Eccentric, purposeless behaviour and emotional anomalies could be the basis of the suspicion."[18]

A Danish psychiatrist, Erik Strömgren, comments on the rapidity with which psychiatric terms and concepts change from time to time.[19] He also points to the danger of using terms without concepts behind them. He argues that confusion may arise in applying terms with imprecise definitions and changing connotations. "Borderline psychosis" and "latent psychosis", for example, have both been introduced as diagnostic categories but are commonly applied to patients "where examination and consideration have not given sufficient evidence for making a diagnosis at all."

Some of Strömgren's points were well illustrated by a series of studies undertaken in the 1960s to investigate methods of diagnosis. One group of researchers compared the diagnoses made by American and British psychiatrists and demonstrated major discrepancies between them, particularly regarding schizophrenia.[20] Despite comparable groups of patients, schizophrenia was diagnosed twice as often in New York as in London; patients termed schizophrenic in New York would have been considered in London to be suffering from depression, neurosis, and personality disorders.[21]

The World Health Organization, aware of the low level of agreement among psychiatrists in diagnosing schizophrenia, initiated the International Pilot Study of Schizophrenia, a large-scale, cross-cultural investigation involving 1,200 patients in cities representing nine countries.[22] The study showed that differences in diagnosis were minimal in cases where a relatively narrow definition of schizophrenia was applied; however, differences became obvious when a broader definition was used. Moscow and Washington, D.C., diverged from the other seven centers in using the diagnosis more broadly and to cover other psychiatric illnesses. The wider limits were found in the two centers despite their differing theoretical approaches. Let us now look more closely at the Soviet concept of schizophrenia.

The Soviet Approach to Schizophrenia

The World Health Organization study showed that psychiatrists in the Moscow research center had not only a broader concept of schizophrenia but also a unique system for categorizing it. The creator of this system is Professor Snezhnevsky, who was helped by his associates at the Institute of

Psychiatry.[23] They recognize three forms of the condition: periodic, shiftlike, and continuous, with several subtypes for each form. Although the clinical features of each form differ, the final criterion for distinguishing among them is the course of illness. What category a patient is assigned to depends on a review of the patient's life history: the nature of his or her personality before the onset of the illness, the age at onset, previous episodes of mental illness, social functioning during periods of apparent health, and the rate of progression of the illness.

The periodic form accounts for 30 to 35 percent of diagnosed schizophrenias. It has the best prognosis because typically the patient's premorbid personality is normal, and the illness consists only of attacks of delusions and abnormal changes in mood, between which the patient functions normally. A mild abnormal personality change may take place after several years.

The prognosis for shiftlike schizophrenia, comprising 40 percent of all cases, is held to be intermediate between that for periodic and continuous schizophrenia. The course is progressive, as in the continuous form, but attacks of the disorder are followed by remissions (i.e., recovery) as in the periodic form. The remission is not complete, however, and the patient never returns to his or her previous level of functioning.

In the continuous form, which accounts for the remaining 25 to 30 percent of the schizophrenias diagnosed, the patient typically deteriorates progressively with no remissions. Initially, subtle personality changes occur, referred to as "secondary" symptoms—withdrawal, apathy, and diminished interests. The development of symptoms may be so gradual that no actual attack of the disease is observable. The secondary symptoms are followed by the development of "positive" or psychotic symptoms such as delusions and hallucinations. Subtypes of the continuous form reflect the rate of progression of the disease: "rapid" (or malignant), "moderate," and "sluggish" (mild). In the malignant course, the symptoms are severe and easily discernible. The moderate course is characterized by slowly evolving paranoid features (ideas of persecution).

In the sluggish type—the most frequent diagnosis for dissenters—an almost unimpaired ability to function socially is retained; the symptoms can resemble those of a neurosis and include obsessional, hysterical, or hypochondriacal features or take on a psychopathic or paranoid character. Patients developing paranoid symptoms are usually middle-aged, retain some insight into their condition, but overvalue their own importance and may have grandiose ideas of reforming the world or offering new inventions of outstanding significance. Despite the mild nature of the sluggish type, the clinical course is still progressive, and the chance of improvement is minimal.

The Snezhnevsky school postulates that although the three main forms of schizophrenia are clinically distinguishable and the prognosis for each is predictable, all schizophrenias are genetic in origin. Also, patients tend to belong to one form only, although they may shift from one subtype to another within that form. The emphasis on genetic factors is seen in Soviet studies of schizophrenia, most of which search for a genetic cause. Environmental factors are believed to exert only a minor influence, as a trigger or precipitant of the illness.

Once patients are diagnosed as schizophrenic, they are always considered schizophrenic thereafter, even if they return to a normal state, as in the case of the periodic form. A diagnosis of early schizophrenia may be applied to persons who manifest personality changes of the "secondary" kind, even though no psychotic features are present. Mild states of the illness are assumed to be genetically associated with more severe states and therefore are often viewed as a prelude to the latter.

The Soviet view of schizophrenia as an irreversible, deep-seated illness with extremely broad diagnostic criteria has serious consequences for the large number of people who are labeled schizophrenic. For example, they are liable to be deprived of their driving licenses, rejected for jobs, and barred from places of higher education.

Forensic Implications of Schizophrenia

The forensic (legal) implications of the Soviet view of schizophrenia are also far-reaching. Dr. Morozov states that "schizophrenia is a disease in which patients are, with rare exceptions, deemed not responsible."[24] This doctrinaire position matches the absence in Soviet law of any provision for determinating a defendant's diminished or partial responsibility. The law explicitly calls for a definitive evaluation from the psychiatrist: was the defendant ill or not at the time of committing the offense? (In recent years, however, a few defendants have been sent to an SPH for treatment; in such cases the court specifies that the defendants should be given a full-scale trial upon their recovery.)

Consider now the case of a person charged with a criminal offense in which mental illness is suspected. Because of the extremely broad conception of schizophrenia, the diagnosis may be pinned to the defendant on the most tenuous of grounds. And with the diagnosis comes the automatic declaration of nonresponsibility. Morozov concedes that "forensic psychiatrists often experience difficulties when psychopathological symptoms are mild and the presence or absence of schizophrenia must be established, or when it is a

> A person shall not be subjected to criminal responsibility who at the time of committing a socially dangerous act is in a state of non-responsibility, that is, cannot realize the significance of his actions or control them because of a chronic mental illness, temporary mental derangement, mental deficiency or other condition of illness. Compulsory measures of a medical character may be applied to such a person by order of the court.
>
> Article II,
> Criminal Code of the
> Russian Republic (RSFSR)

question of differential diagnosis or an evaluation of remissions."[25] The diagnosis may be based on a history of psychiatric symptoms long before the offense was committed and without any symptoms at the time of the offense. The defendant may appear normal during the examination, but, according to Soviet concepts, still harbor the illness.

These concepts are well illustrated in the trials of several dessenters. In Gorbanevskaya's trial a psychiatrist at the Serbsky Institute, Prof. Daniil Lunts, defended his diagnosis of sluggish schizophrenia. In this illness, he contended, well-defined psychotic phenomena such as delusions and hallucinations are not characteristically present; indeed, this form of schizophrenia "has no clear symptoms." But mental changes superficially resembling improvement cannot be viewed as such from "the theoretical point of view."[26] Lunts thus called for the acceptance of a concept that a disease like schizophrenia is "theoretically", but not clinically, present in the patient.

Schizophrenia and the Dissenter

In view of psychiatry's lack of objective criteria for diagnosing schizophrenia, it is irrational to argue that the Soviet concept of schizophrenia is incorrect. Many differing theories exist, and none can yet be regarded with certainty as being more valid than the rest. Nevertheless, there is good reason to be partially skeptical of three basic features of the Soviet model: the breadth of its diagnostic criteria, the extreme schematism of its classification, and the overwhelming pessimism of its prognosis. Furthermore, even within the context of the model, the application of the diagnosis to dissenters appears completely unwarranted, at least to those whose detailed case histories Bukovsky sent to the West.

The phrases most frequently used by Soviet forensic psychiatrists for the diagnosis in dissenters are "paranoid reformist delusional ideas" (a variant includes "paranoid delusions of reforming society or reorganization of the state apparatus"), "uncritical attitude towards his abnormal condition" (or "situation"), "moralizes" (or "opinions have moralizing character"), "overestimation of his own personality" (or "overinflation of his capabilities"), and "poor adaptation to the social environment."

These evaluations are contained in the case reports of three persons who were separately interned in SPHs for their dissident activities in the late 1960s. A criterion emphasized in all three reports is the dissenter's conviction that society, the state, or Marxism-Leninism must be changed. The psychiatrists arbitrarily label this "reformism" as delusional in character—that is, the dissenter manifests false beliefs and holds on to them with unshakable tenacity. Yet it is patently clear that the dissenter's social and political beliefs, while deemed delusional, only involve criticism of specific acts and policies of the Soviet government, such as violations of the constitution, the lack of rights of minority groups, and the 1968 invasion of Czechoslovakia.

The case reports show no evidence that the psychiatrists seriously examined the dissenters' criticisms to determine whether they were delusional. Rather, the psychiatrists frequently twist and distort the dissenters' views to make them appear symptomatic of illness. Thus one dissenters' belief that supporters in the West would speak up in his defense is transmogrified by the examining psychiatrist as delusions of grandeur. Similarly, in Grigorenko's case report, his views on human rights are distorted and parodied and made to appear grandiose: "All his energy and activity were 'devoted' to the fight for 'truth' and the creation of conditions which would exclude injustice from the life of the community."[27]

The dissenters whose cases are well documented have not advocated some extraordinary scheme for changing the entire society but have been operating within an internationally recognized movement to promote human rights for Soviet citizens. These are not the bizarre, confused thoughts of madmen, but rather the political and social views of people extremely aware of the realities of their society.

Not only is there no evidence of "reformist delusions" in the thinking of these dissenters, there is also no basis for concluding that they commonly suffer an "overestimation" of their own personalities. We know of no dissenter diagnosed as mentally ill who has believed that he or she alone could or would alter Soviet society or that the Soviet regime would instantly heed his or her words. On the contrary, many dissenters clearly believe that their campaign to achieve basic human rights for Soviet citizens will necessarily be protracted and frustrating. They understand well that their movement is small and subject to constant erosion through arrest, exile, and compulsory hospitalization.

"Poor adaptation to the social environment" is another commonly cited criterion in the diagnosis of schizophrenia in dissenters. Adjustment to society is widely regarded throughout the world as a criterion of mental health. Although a vague concept, most psychiatrists accept maladjustment as a feature of psychiatric disturbance. Consider a person who devotes all his energy to disseminating his ideas about a "unique system" for reorganizing society and at the same time neglects the needs of his family and himself, loses his means of livelihood, and is hostile to people who refuse to support his views. Without question, this person's adaptation to society would be regarded as quite poor. The Soviet dissenters, however, rather than withdraw from reality wage a campaign within the boundaries of Soviet law, calling on the regime to respect the fundamental rights of citizens as stated in the Soviet constitution. Their campaign is not an exclusive preoccupation; they continue to work as physicists, electricians, mathematicians, writers, artists, and bricklayers (unless arbitrarily dismissed from their posts as a means of punishment).

It is also interesting to note that many of the dissenters who were interned and later emigrated have adapted quickly and successfully to life in their new countries. Similarly, none of the families or friends of the dissenters whom we interviewed regarded tham as mentally abnormal or in need of treatment. None of these people, who have lived closely with the dissenters, have submitted complaints to the authorities about the strangeness of the dissenters' behavior. On the contrary, they have invariably insisted that their relatives and friends are mentally well. It is only the officials and psychiatrists who have maintained otherwise.

Who Participates in Psychiatric Abuse?

We believe that Soviet psychiatrists' participation in the misuse of the discipline can be evaluated along a continuum—a small core group at one end, an even smaller dissenting group at the other, and the vast majority of average psychiatrists between them. These three groups differ markedly in their characteristics, and the core and average psychiatrists probably examine a dissenter with different motives.

The Core Psychiatrist

The core group includes Prof. Andrei Snezhnevsky, director of the Institue of Psychiatry of the Academy of Medical Sciences (AMS); Dr. Georgy Morozov, director of the Serbsky Research Institute for Forensic Psychiatry;

The Serbsky Institute of Forensic Psychiatry. (Courtesy of Aid to Russian Christians.)

Prof. Ruben Nadzharov, deputy director of the Institute of Psychiatry; and, until his death in 1977, Prof. Daniil Lunts, head of the Serbsky's special diagnostic section.

Dr. Snezhnevsky, born in 1904, is without doubt the most influential figure in contemporary Soviet psychiatry. Along with only a handful of other psychiatrists, he is a full member of the AMS, thus holding the prestigious title of academician. As director of the Institute of Psychiatry, he plays a significant advisory role to the Ministry of Health on many matters pertinent to psychiatry. His influence is further expanded by his editorship of the Soviet psychiatric journal (the *Korsakov Journal of Neurology and Psychiatry*), by his membership in the presidia of the AMS and the All-Union Society of Neurologists and Psychiatrists, and by his central role in the foreign relations of Soviet psychiatry. During the special joint session of the AMS and the Academy of Sciences in 1950, Pavlov's ideas were used to form the foundations of Soviet psychiatry. This was a period of intense politico-ideological upheaval. The Pavlov-oriented psychiatrists, with Dr. Snezhnevsky at the helm, triumphed then and have retained control of Soviet psychiatry since.

Shortly thereafter, Snezhnevsky published his theories on schizophrenia. In essence, Snezhnevsky's ideas broadened the concept of schizophrenia and encouraged the view of dissent as a symptom of severe mental illness. Snezhnevsky's view of schizophrenia led to a protracted battle with other schools of psychiatry, mainly those centered in Leningrad and Kiev, both of which adamantly opposed the wider and much more frequent application of the diagnosis. For example, in the 1950s the dissenter Viktor Rafalsky was ruled sane three times in Leningrad and ruled a schizophrenic three times in the Serbsky. However, by the late 1950s, the Snezhnevsky orientation, with strong official support, had come to dominate the theory and practice of psychiatry in the Soviet Union, a dominance that has endured to the present day. Vocal opponents were transferred to less influential positions, often in provinces.

Since attaining almost complete power in his profession, Snezhnevsky has become the chief defender of Soviet psychiatry against charges that it has been compromised for political reasons. He vehemently denied the allegations of Soviet abuse of psychiatry by critics at the 1971 congress of the World Psychiatric Association in Mexico City; he has continued to argue that the criticism is nothing more than a "malicious concoction."[28]

Snezhnevsky has participated, either as a member of a commission or as an adviser, in several well-known cases of dissenters who have undergone psychiatric examination. For example, he chaired a commission that examined the mathematician Leonid Plyushch in 1972, diagnosed him as a schizophrenic, and recommended compulsory hospitalization.[29] After almost two years of treatment and a marked deterioration in Plyushch's health, his wife, in the company of a family friend, managed to visit Snezhnevsky in his home. The friend, Prof. Yury Orlov, described the tense conversation that ensued and their astonishment when Snezhnevsky said, "Would it really have been better for [Plyushch] to have got seven years in strict-regime camps?"[30]

Although Snezhnevsky had no part in the 1970 detention and diagnosis of biologist Zhores Medvedev, quite clearly he played a role behind the scenes. In their account of the episode, Zhores and Roy Medvedev graphically describe that role. A friend of the Medvedev family gained access to Snezhnevsky and was told that Zhores was a psychopathic personality with an exaggerated opinion of himself, but that this diagnosis did not warrant compulsory treatment, only supervision of Zhores in an outpatient clinic. The following day Academician Andrei Sakharov met with a group of doctors, including Snezhnevsky, at the Ministry of Health. On this occasion, after praising the Soviet psychiatric profession, Snezhnevsky conceded that mistakes were made, particularly in the provinces, where standards were occasionally low. If Medvedev's doctors erred, he explained, a directive from the Ministry of Health could rectify this. Public protest was only liable to damage the reputation that psychiatry enjoyed.[31]

Several days earlier, however, Snezhnevsky had participated in a meeting of high-ranking functionaries in the Ministry of Health to discuss the Medvedev affair. By then, international protests were pouring in against his commitment. Snezhevsky took the opportunity to point out that if internment continued, it would be acutely embarrassing for the Soviet delegation to the World Psychiatric Association's congress in Mexico a year hence. On this occasion he apparently argued for Medvedev's release; Dr. Boris Petrovsky, the minister of health, and Dr. Zoya Serebryakova, then the chief psychiatrist in the ministry and a woman with considerable influence because of her position, opposed his advice and decided that Medvedev should remain in the hospital indefinitely.

This episode reveals one of Snezhnevsky's prominent qualities, that of political pragmatism. Aware that Medvedev had been committed inappropriately, his concern was for the image of his profession rather than for the welfare of the patient. Presumably he had calculated that it was best to release Medvedev in the light of the stormy protests and the forthcoming international congress, but nonetheless he acquiesced to his political superiors at the Ministry of Health.

Georgy Morozov, born in 1920, has since 1957 directed the Serbsky Institute, where many dissenters have undergone psychiatric examination. Since 1974 he has been a full member of the AMS, and since 1975 the chairman of the presidium of the All-Union Society (a position comparable to the presidency of the Royal College of Psychiatrists or the American Psychiatric Association). He exerts a marked influence on forensic psychiatry throughout the Soviet Union by virtue of his Serbsky position and his coeditorship of the authoritative Soviet textbook on forensic psychiatry.[32]

Morozov's name has cropped up regularly in discussions of the political use of psychiatry. He has served on commissions, often as chairman, investigating several cases of dissenters (they include Grigorenko, Gorbanevskaya, Medvedev, and Plyushch), and he rebuts the charges of unethical practice brought against him and his colleagues.

Dr. Ruben Nadzharov, deputy director of the Institute of Psychiatry, wields considerable power and influence like his superior, Snezhnevsky. He has been a member of several commissions that have examined dissenters and has also defended his profession against Western criticism. For instance, Nadzharov participated in the examination that found Medvedev to be suffering from sluggish schizophrenia. Nadzharov's defense of his profession is typified by an interview that he gave to a Soviet journalist in 1973.[33] In it he berated his critics, asserting that they were motivated only by "unseemly political aims" and actively engaged in anti-Soviet slander.

The psychiatrist viewed by the dissenting movement as one of the most notorious was Prof. Daniil Lunts, who died in 1977.[34] He was born into a well-established family: His father was an esteemed pediatrician, his mother a professor at the Moscow Conservatory. After working in the mid-1930s as a psychiatrist in the hospital portion of the main prison in Gorky, he moved to the Serbsky Institute, where in 1940 he became a senior associate and earned the Soviet equivalent of a doctorate. At the end of the decade he lectured at the college of the Ministry of State Security, the predecessor of the KGB.

Lunts tended to introversion, suspiciousness, and dogmatism. His family life was marred by tragedy: In the mid-1960s his wife and daughter died. Lunts, a Jew, survived the anti-Semitic purge that affected the Serbsky and other medical institutions in the early 1950s, and he also remained after the special investigation of forensic psychiatry by the party's Central Committee. However, his position was apparently tenuous until Georgy Morozov assumed the directorship in 1957. Lunts headed the special diagnostic section, which assessed political offenders, from at least the early 1960s until his death.

Lunt's notoriety derives principally from his clinical approach: applying the diagnosis of schizophrenia in an extremely loose and broad way. He also worked closely with the KGB, which regularly referred dissenters to his section. For instance, in 1968, Lunts ruled as sane two dissenters who he had previously ruled not responsible, explaining that his earlier diagnoses had been wrong and that his criteria for nonresponsibility had become more strict. This ruling was essential to the KGB, because the KGB had pressured one of the two men to give false evidence of the type it needed at the trial. After the trial Lunts reverted at once to his broad definition of schizophrenia and ruled a succession of dissenters not responsible.[35]

Less information is available on other psychiatrists who clearly belong to the core group. We have mentioned the role played by Dr. Serebryakova, who was chief psychiatrist in the Ministry of Health at the time of the Medvedev confinement, and she probably played a significant part in the misuse of psychiatry. In May 1981, however, she and others presented a paper at the seventh All-Union Congress of Psychiatrists in Moscow. The paper stated that 1.2 percent of the patients admitted to Moscow Ordinary Psychiatric Hospital were hospitalized—implicitly, by force—in connection with visits to state agencies to present groundless complaints and slanderous statements. Cautious extrapolation of these figures suggests that perhaps about 6,000 inmates of Soviet mental hospitals may be held on nonmedical grounds.

In addition, we know of some 50 other psychiatrists who participated in commissions leading to the internment of dissenters. Some, like Drs. Viktor Morozov and Yakov Landau, have been members of several such commissions, and additional evidence leads us to place them in the core group. Information on most of the others is too sketchy to assign them with any certainty to the core or the average group.

Motives of the Core Psychiatrist

What motivates core psychiatrists to collude with the state in declaring healthy dissenters mentally ill? The pattern of behavior in these psychiatrists is too complex to be explained by any one factor. More likely several operate in various ways according to the specific situation.

There is almost certainly an ideological factor that motivates core psychiatrists—they adhere, whether sincerely or opportunistically, to the view that the party knows best and that whoever questions or criticizes the party and fails to recgonize his or her error must be mentally disturbed and poorly adapted to his environment. We suspect, however, that the ideology serves as a rationalization, conscious or unconscious, to justify these psychiatrists' misuse of their profession. Whatever the case, the clinical approach of doctors like Morozov and Lunts is determined by their consistent contention that those who dissent by propounding ideas on how to change the state are indeed suffering from delusions of reformism.

Even if we were to accept that the core psychiatrists genuinely believe that dissenters are mentally ill, their recommendations for treatment strongly suggest that they knowingly misuse their profession. The treatment commonly recommended in an SPH strikes us as entirely inappropriate for the illness diagnosed and the needs of the patient.

Dr. Boris Zoubok, a psychiatrist now settled in the United States, formerly worked at the Kashchenko hospital under Snezhnevsky. Zoubok feels that Snezhnevsky and his colleagues genuinely believe in their method of diagnosis and in dissent being a form of mental illness. Although sharply disagreeing with them, Zoubok grants them the right to their opinion: After all, there are many conflicting theories about the diagnosis of mental illness. What is wholly indefensible, in his view, is the core psychiatrists' customary recommendation for SPH internment, when these psychiatrists know what the patient will encounter there.

If we extend Zoubok's arguments, two facts are noteworthy. First, the SPH is primarily designed for mentally ill offenders who have committed violent crimes and who are a danger to society. Yet no dissenter discussed here had ever committed a crime even bordering on violence or manifested any intent to do so. Second, in many cases commissions made diagnoses of sluggish schizophrenia. For such a relatively mild form of this illness, one would expect an ordinary psychiatric hospital (OPH) to be more suitable and therapeutic.

In addition to a diagnostic method strongly influenced by ideology, we surmise that the core psychiatrists are also influenced by the desire to rise to high professional positions. With such a position come many rewards: the exercise of power, the satisfaction of ambition, and the more tangible privileges.

A professional person wishing to rise up the adiministrative ladder must have political qualifications, a fact attested to by the high proportion of party members in positions of authority in the health service. Almost certainly, most if not all the core psychiatrists belong to the party, and their subordination to its direction is axiomatic. Clearly psychiatrists like Lunts, Snezhnevsky, and Morozov have attained top administrative positions in large measure because of their political qualifications, which have facilited their active connivance with the party authorities and permitted the misuse of psychiatry to become a systematic and state-directed policy. In this connivance core psychiatrists are secure in the knowledge that the party will not allow their victims to call them to account in a court of law or in any other way. In a political system where power is undivided and the expression of protest is strictly controlled, the party can guarantee them this security without difficulty.

The rewards of the good life include access to a variety of privileges and benefits not available to ordinary Soviet citizens. The core psychiatrist is likely to travel abroad, as a tourist or as an attendant at a conference, to have access to stores selling luxury goods at moderate prices, to have a country cottage, and to take vacations at special sanatoria. Their salaries are about three times higher in real terms than those of ordinary psychiatrists. Rewards are maintained and safeguarded so long as the "contract" between donor and recipient remains undisturbed and respected. The continuation of the reward is the quid pro quo for each act of collaboration.

The Average Psychiatrist

Thus far we have discussed the parts played by a few powerful psychiatrists. What of attitudes among the rank and file? Interviews with emigré psychiatrists in Britain, Israel, and North America lead us to believe that the average psychiatrist has had limited knowledge of the political use of the discipline, at least until recently. This is not surprising. Many of the misdiagnoses are concentrated in one institution, the Serbsky, and only a small minority of Soviet psychiatrists work in the SPHs to which most well-known dissenters have been sent for treatment (by far the majority work in psychiatric clinics or OPHs). Access to evidence of the abuse is denied.

Since autumn 1971, however, the average psychiatrist has been able to read in the Soviet press a number of rebuttals of Western allegations by his authoritative colleagues. One psychiatrist whom we spoke to in Israel first became aware of something being amiss in his profession only in 1970. He then heard about the Grigorenko case in a broadcast over the Voice of America. Another psychiatrist, now in the United States, learned of malpractices in 1972, when an article published in France was broadcast on Radio Liberty.[36]

Dr. Marina Voikhanskaya, formerly a psychiatrist in a Leningrad OPH, described to us how her suspicions that psychiatric abuse existed were confirmed in 1974. On learning that an artist, Yury Ivanov, was a patient in the hospital but seemed healthy, Voikhanskaya began to visit him regularly and satisfied herself that he was indeed sane and that his internment was unjustified. At first she thought that this might be an isolated case of abuse, but soon she found evidence that convinced her that it was part of something much wider.

We believe, then, that the average psychiatrist is relatively ignorant of the abuses and, when better informed, generally passive. What accounts for this passivity? Probably the most cogent factor is conformism typical of Soviet society. The psychiatrist, like everyone else, observes the conventions and practices that are prescribed by the state and does so largely out of fear and habit. Take a single deviant step and the results will almost certainly be dire. This was the thought behind the advice given to us in Moscow by friends of a psychiatrist who was strongly, but only privately, critical of the abuses. They felt a meeting with us be too hazardous for her: If the meeting became known to the authorities, her carrer might well be at risk. We received similar advice in Leningrad concerning another psychiatrist.

Noncompliance with the demands of the state obviously entails considerable risk and may be tantamount to professional suicide. How, then, can the average psychiatrist be sure that he or she will comply with these demands when encountering a dissenter for examination? Does the psychiatrist have instructions and guidelines to turn to? Yes and no. The Soviet citizen learns at an early age how to "understand." As one emigré psychiatrist said to us, the Soviet Union is a country of "perfect understanding." Like the core psychiatrist, the average colleague usually senses without specific instructions what is expected of him in various situations.

When, for example, he learns that a prospective examinee is a political offender, he immediately recalls the nature of his unwritten contract: The KGB usually tranfers such cases for examination when it wishes the psychiatrists to affix a label of nonresponsibility and to recommend compulsory treatment. Similarly, he understands what is expected of him when, as in the case of Medvedev, he is informed that there are good grounds to suspect the sanity of a citizen, the citizen has a record of dissent, and the referral agency is an authority such as the local town council.

Yet with the average psychiatrist's understanding often comes apprehension and ambivalence. All the emigré psychiatrists whom we interviewed have emphasized two tactics that many average psychiatrists resort to: if possible, avoidance of the whole task; otherwise, as prompt an exit from the case as is feasible. Such tactics are characteristics of the Soviet bureaucracy—to which psychiatrists belong. If action is required in an unusual situation where precedent is vague and guidelines nebulous or nonexistent, the bureaucrat tends to evade responsibility in whatever way possible. If evasion is impossible, he avoids taking risks, performing the task in the manner understood to fulfill the wishes of his superiors.

For a Kiev forensic psychiatrist with whom we discussed the question, this generally meant referring complicated cases to the Serbsky Institute for a more authoritative opinion, thus sparing the Kiev staff of making the decision on diagnosis and treatment. According to another psychiatrist, the most useful strategy is to act naively with the hope of eluding responsibility for any unusual matter.

Evasion and retreat are not always feasible. Additional maneuvers must then be undertaken, of which moral evasion is among the most helpful. The average psychiatrist cannot afford even to begin pondering whether the action of labeling dissent as illness is unethical. Such a process would entail soul-searching and inevitably pave the way for distressing reactions of guilt and frustration. Further, if the psychiatrist disclosed his uneasiness to colleagues, he could not be sure that one of them might not inform on him and thus render his professional position insecure. Accoring to all the emigré psychiatrists whom we have interviewed except one (Dr. Voikhanskaya), they and their colleagues at no point discussed their attitudes and feelings with colleagues because of the dangers posed by self-exposure. Even when psychiatrists suspected malpractice regarding dissenters, the issue was not broached.

We may have conveyed the impression that all average psychiatrists act in a similar fashion—as frightened, retreating conformists, attempting at all costs to elude the dissenter as examinee. But exceptions do exist. For instance, a commission chaired by Professor Detengof in Tashkent apparently failed to conform to the party line when it declared Grigorenko sane and responsible in 1969. Indeed, the commission underlined its conclusion by stating that there were "no doubts concerning Grigorenko's health" and that "in-patient investigation ... would complicate a diagnosis."[37] As a result, the KGB referred the case to more trustworthy psychiatrists at the Serbsky. Predictably, these professionals fulfilled their contract and reversed the conclusions of their Tashkent colleagues.

Once committed to a hospital, a dissenter may face a variety of attitudes in the psychiatric staff. Several dissenters claim that psychiatrists treated them harshly. By contrast, a few doctors showed compassion for the dissenter to the extent of assisting him in various ways and even recommending his release after the minimal period that they had calculated would satisfy the authorities.

An illustrative case is that of Ilya Rips, who spent eighteen relatively comfortable months in an OPH in Riga. He was well cared for by his doctors, who spared him the rigors of drugs and other psychiatric treatments. Even in the SPH we know of cases where doctors helped their dissenter-patients by, for example, smuggling out letters and materials for *samizdat* circulation. We cannot name these doctors, since publicizing such acts could lead to severe reprisals against them even now.

However, the compassion of a psychiatrist for a dissenter does not normally involve direct collusion of this sort. Usually it is expressed within limits that are set to protect the psychiatrist. The average psychiatrist dare not articulate his collusion, for he cannot afford even to hint to the patient that he considers the patient's commitment unjustified.

Another factor that may influence the average psychiatrist involved in the forensic assessment of a dissenter is his rationale that a year or two in a mental hospital under reasonable conditions may be considerably less traumatic and punitive than a long term of imprisonment. This rationale, however, is probably ill conceived, certainly as regards the SPH, which is in several respects worse than a prison or camp.[38]

The Dissenting Psychiatrist

Many psychiatrists act with implicit benevolence toward the dissenter-patient and therefore, in their way, express passive, veiled dissent from the misuse of their profession. We know of half a dozen Soviet psychiatrists, however, who have publicly displayed their opposition. A few others have expressed criticism, too, but anonymously.

The first of this minute group to be active was Dr. Semyon Gluzman. He was born in 1946, the son of a professor of medicine in the Kiev medical school. After obtaining his doctorate in 1969, Gluzman commenced psychiatric training, working for two years in regional Ukranian hospitals. He was then offered a post at the Dnepropetrovsk SPH but declined it because he knew that the hospital was being used to intern dissenters and that he would be compelled to practice unethically. Gluzman embarked on a frustrating job hunt, ultimately taking a post at a first aid station in Kiev.

In March 1972 his home was searched, and two months later he was arrested for purportedly reading and circulating *samizdat* material. At his trial, from which his parents and friends were barred, the charges revolved chiefly around the fact that he had given someone Solzhenitsyn's novel *Cancer Ward*. The result was a sentence of seven years in a strict-regime labor camp, followed by three years of exile. This was inexplicably savage, since the formal charges did not include Gluzman's composition of any documents and since it was a first offense that would normally incur no more than a three-year term.

Almost certainly the real reason for punishing Gluzman so harshly was the detailed document that he and two colleagues anonymously prepared on the diagnosis of Grigorenko, and his steadfast refusal to reveal the identity of these colleagues to the KGB. Entitled "An In Absentia Forensic-Psychiatric Report on P. G. Grigorenko," the document began circulation in *samizdat* form in 1971.[39] Gluzman and his fellow psychiatrists analyzed the reports of the two commissions that examined Grigorenko in 1969 and leveled detailed criticism at the members of the Serbsky team. The authors also contended that, based on Grigorenko's own writings and the reports of the commissions in both Tashkent and the Serbsky, they were able to conduct their own forensic examination of the case.

Gluzman and his colleagues suggested that the Serbsky experts who diagnosed Grigorenko as not responsible (they name two of them—G. Morozov and Lunts) were either professionally incompetent or deliberately wrote false statements into their report. If the latter case was true, they recommended that legal action be brought against the Serbsky psychiatrists.

This explicit criticism could not be brooked by the authorities. Although the indictment did not state that Gluzman was one of the authors of the critical document, his severe punishment was undoubtedly intended to deter other psychiatrists who might also feel the impulse to protest publicly against abuse.

Most of Gluzman's energies during the first four years of his incarceration were devoted to a campaign for the rights of his fellow prisoners. He took part in several hunger strikes to protest conditions in the prison, and in November 1974 he suffered serious heart problems as a result.

That same year Gluzman wrote with Vladimir Bukovsky a *Manual on Psychiatry for Dissenters*. Because of his activities, Gluzman was informed in September 1975 that a second case had been initiated against him. He was to be charged as a recidivist with new acts of "anti-Soviet agitation and propaganda." The KGB's official at his Perm camp detailed the charges:

sending out information about the collective 1974 hunger strike in which he participated, writing an article on Grigorenko, and preparing the manual with Bukovsky.[40]

In March 1976 Gluzman was tranferred to a prison in Perm, where the KGB again warned him about the new case being prepared against him. The warning failed to silence Gluzman, however, and he was returned to the camp a month later.[41] After his exile ended in May 1982, Gluzman continued to express a desire to emigrate, but KGB officials told him that he would not be granted a visa.

Marina Voikhanskaya and Anatoly Koryagin (see Chapter 7) are among the very few other Soviet psychiatrists who have defiantly opposed the abuse of their profession while still in the Soviet Union. Voikhanskaya has given us a vivid and informative account of her colleagues' reactions to the attention that she paid to the dissenter-artist Yury Ivanov, whom she tried to support during his internment in her OPH. After hearing that Ivanov was in one of the wards, Voikhanskaya asked her psychiatrist for a report on his clinical state. She was astounded by her colleague's reply that Ivanov was perfectly normal and that she should keep this knowledge completely secret.

Voikhanskaya began to visit Ivanov regularly, bringing him books and cigarettes. Colleagues started to shun her. After a superior had forbidden her visits for both the dissenter's and her own good, she saw the artist on Sundays as an ordinary visitor. Consistent pressure by fellow psychiatrists to stop her visits failed to deter her. The hospital director finally threatened her with dismissal. During this ordeal she was progressively ostracized and ultimately lost the friendship of most of her colleagues; only a few remained loyal to her and then only in private.

Before long Voikhanskaya actively intervened in the case of Viktor Fainberg, who had been interned in her hospital after issuing a militant statement in support of Bukovsky and other political prisoners. When she learned that Fainberg was being threatened with forcible injections and had stated that he would commit suicide in protest, she successfully dissuaded a colleague from proceeding.

In addition to these interventions, Voikhanskaya became active in the human rights movement and soon attracted the attention of the KGB. In April 1975 she emigrated, although her young son was denied permission to join her until 1979.[42]

Conclusion

We have often been asked how sincere or insincere Soviet psychiatrists are when dealing with dissenters. Do they really believe that dissent is a form of illness? Because one cannot see into men's souls, the question is a difficult one. Nonetheless, we believe that most of these psychiatrists do not so believe. Bukovsky told us that in his opinion the great majority of the psychiatrists in the Leningrad SPH in the mid-1960s did not in fact regard the political prisoners as ill. Two of the psychiatrists, Drs. Kalinin and Kelchevskaya, considered Nikolai Samsonov to be mentally healthy, but "advised him to admit in writing that he had been ill when he composed his letter to the central committee. Such an admission, they told him, would testify to his 'recovery.'"[43] Grigorenko's and Fainberg's psychiatrists in Chernyakhovsk and Leningrad likewise hinted that they would be satisfied with formal recantations. Only Plyushch seems to have run up against a psychiatrist, Lydia Lyubarskaya, who genuinely believed that he was ill.

By contrast, some psychiatrists have been openly cynical. According to Dr. Voikhanskaya, Dr. V. M. Morozov likes to say, "It's no secret to anyone that you can have schizophrenia without schizophrenia." The doctors in an Ashkabad OPH told the poet Annasoltan Kekilova that she was "in good health" but that "if you don't give us a signed statement that you wrote to the Central Committee because you were in a nervous condition, you'll stay in hospital forever."[44] Finally, Dr. V. V. Kokorev, head of the psychiatric section of the Mordovian camps' hospital, told a dissenter's parents that "in his opinion their son was mentally healthy, but he refused to guarantee that this would be the diagnosis, and referred to some special instructions he had regarding political prisoners."[45]

In light of the foregoing discussion, it is perhaps no surprise that in recent years hundreds of dissenters have been labeled as mentally ill. First, the authorities can rely on the core psychiatrist to cooperate fully, while the average psychiatrist is too conformist to refuse to participate when called upon. Second, the Soviet approach to the diagnosis of mental illness, particularly the Snezhnevsky model of schizophrenia, lends itself more than conveniently to a view of dissent as a kind of illness.

Notes and References

1. Quoted in Z. Medvedev and R. Medvedev, *A Question of Madness* (New York: Macmillan, 1971), pp. 196–197.

2. Letters in *American Journal of Psychiatry* 126: 1327–1328; 127: 842–843; 127: 1575–1576; 131: 474. The identity of the psychiatrist has never been disclosed and was withheld at his request at the time of publication. The journal's editor commented, however, that he was satisfied with the credentials of the writer, who had been a member of the American Psychiatric Association for many years.

3. I. P. Yarkov, "Reconvicted: 1951–1954," *Arkhiv Samizdata* manuscript dated 27 May 1967. *Arkhiv Samizdota* is the Samizdat Archive of Radio Liberty in Munich, which assigns numbers to all documents that it receives. Copies of all volumes are deposited in the U.S. Library of Congress and elsewhere. Yarkov's document, his autobiography, was dated 27 May 1967.

4. S. P. Pisarev, "Soviet Mental Prisons," *Survey*, no. 77, pp. 175–180.

5. *Chronicle of Current Events* 18. The *Chronicle* is a journal produced in typescript every two to four months in Moscow by an anonymous and changing group of human rights activists.

6. V. Y. Tarsis, *Ward 7* (London: Collins/Harvill, 1965).

7. The book was serialized in the *Observer* on 2, 9, and 16 May 1966.

8. V. Y. Tarsis, unpublished report for Amnesty International, 1966.

9. Sidney Bloch interviewed Volpin in Boston (where he is now a professor of mathematics) in September 1975. The author was impressed with Volpin's vitality, lack of bitterness, sense of humor, and honesty. The author concludes that Volpin was mentally healthy and that there was no reason to believe he had been mentally ill in the past. Volpin gave testimony to the U.S. Congress in 1975. See *Abuse of Psychiatry for Political Purposes* (New York: Arno Press, 1973), pp. 2–16. The book is the same document as U.S. Senate, *Hearing before the Subcommittee to Investigate the Administration of the Internal Security Act and Other Internal Security Laws of the Committee on the Judiciary*, 92nd Cong., 2nd sess, 26 September 1972. Published first by the US Government Printing Office, (Washington, D.C.: 1972), then by Arno Press (New York: 1973).

10. *The New York Times*, 12 September 1972.

11. *Abuse of Psychiatry*, p. 4.

12. P. Reddaway, *Uncensored Russia* (London: Cape, 1972), pp. 86–87.

13. Ibid., pp. 150–151.

14. See Sidney Bloch and Peter Reddaway, *Soviet Psychiatric Abuse: The Shadow over World Psychiatry* (London: Gollancz, 1984).

15. E. Kraepelin, *Dementia Praecox and Paraphrenia* (Edinburgh: Livingstone, 1919).

16. K. Schneider, *Clinical Psychopathology* (New York: Grune & Stratton, 1959).

17. P. Hoch and P. Polatin, "Pseudoneurotic Schizophrenia," *Psychiatric Quarterly* 23 (1949): 248–276.

18. *A Glossary of Mental Disorders* (London: H. M. Stationery Office, 1968).

19. E. Strömgren, "Uses and Abuses of Concepts in Psychiatry," 126(1969): 777–788.

20. R. E. Kendell, "Diagnostic Criteria of American and British Psychiatrists," *Archives of General Psychiatry* 24(1971): 123–130.

21. For more information on differences in psychiatric diagnoses between the United States and the United Kingdom, see J. E. Cooper, R. E. Kendell, B. J.

Gurland, et al., *Psychiatric Diagnosis in New York and London,* Maudsley Monograh No. 20 (London: Oxford University Press, 1972).

22. *The International Pilot Study of Schizophrenia,* vol. 1 (Geneva: World Health Organization, 1973).

23. We are indebted to Dr. J. Holland of the Albert Einstein College of Medicine, New York, for her invaluable help in clarifying the Soviet model of schizophrenia. She worked in Professor Snezhnevsky's Institute of Psychiatry on an exchange program in 1972–73 for eight months with Prof. R. Nadzharov and others, and has made a significant contribution to understanding Soviet concepts. See her "Schizoprenia in the Soviet Union" in R. Cancro, ed., *Annual Review of Research in Schizophrenia,* vol. 6.

24. Morozov and Kalashnik, p. 221.

25. Ibid., p. 222.

26. *Chronicle of Current Events* 15.

27. *Abuse of Psychiatry,* p. 69.

28. *Manchester Guardian,* 29 September 1973.

29. *Chronicle of Current Events* 29.

30. Appeal by Yury Orlov dated 22 April 1975, *Arkhiv Samizdata* 2165.

31. Medvedev and Medvedev, *Questions of Madness,* pp. 129–130.

32. G. V. Morozov and I. M. Kalashnik, eds., *Forensic Psychiatry* (New York: International Arts and Science Press, 1970).

33. *Izvestia,* 10 August 1973.

34. We have received information on Professor Lunts from dissenters who have been his "patients"—Viktor Fainberg, Alexander Volpin, Natalya Gorbanevskaya, and Yury Shikhanovich—as well as Alexander Lunts, a distant relative now living in Israel, and a Moscow dissenter who has asked to remain anonymous.

35. See entires on Galanskov and Dobrovolsky in *Kaznimye sumasshestviem* (Frankfurt: Possev, 1971).

36. Personal communication, 27 September 1975. Both psychiatrists wish to remain anonymous.

37. *Abuse of Psychiatry,* p. 64.

38. Ibid., p. 110.

39. "An In Absentia Forensic-Psychiatric Report on P. G. Grigorenko," circulated in samizdat in 1971. Published in Russian in *Russkaya mysl,* Paris, 12 April 1973; also see *Arkhiv Samizdata* 1243.

40. *Chronicle of Current Events* 38.

41. Ibid., p. 40.

42. *The Times* (London), 30 August 1976.

43. *Chronicle of Current Events* 18.

44. *Chronicle of Current Events* 21.

45. The dissenter was Igor Ogurtsov. See *A Chronicle of Human Rights in the USSR* 10 (1974).

Chapter 7

A Question of Conscience

Kevin Klose:
The Cases of Alexei Nikitin
and Anatoly Koryagin

Anatoly Koryagin:
Unwilling Patients

In the first section of this chapter, *Washington Post* correspondent Kevin Klose describes how the fates of two Soviet citizens—Alexei Nikitin, a mining engineer from the Donetsk region, and Anatoly Koryagin, a young psychiatrist from Siberia—became inextricably intwined because they believed that certain injustices within the Soviet system needed to be corrected. In the second section, Anatoly Koryagin describes his interviews with several dissidents, including Nikitin, who were confined to psychiatric hospitals for political reasons. (Editors)

The Cases of Alexei Nikitin and Anatoly Koryagin*

Alexei Nikitin

Alexei Nikitin spent most of his working life at the Butovka works, one of 49 coal mines in Donetsk, an eastern Ukrainian city of one million. A blocky, baldish man with a hearty, forthright, and rough-and-ready manner, he was an unlikely candidate for a Kafkaesque odyssey through modern Russia.

Nikitin's early biography might have been written by a party propagandist. The tenth and last child of a peasant farmer of the V. I. Lenin Collective

---

* Kevin Klose's case studies are based on detailed interviews that he conducted with Nikitin and Koryagin while on assignment for the *Post* in the Soviet Union. Unless otherwise noted, quotations in the first part of this chapter are from the interviews.

Farm in the hamlet of Fedorovsky, 250 miles west of Moscow, Alexei grew up in the rural poverty of Russia's heartland. German armies swept through the area in World War II, but the family survived. After the peace, Alexei went off to a local school, where he quickly bobbed to the top of his class, getting high marks and displaying a gift for leadership. He eagerly joined the stream of youth organizations that can lead to party membership: He became a Young Oktobrist, a Young Pioneer, and a Komsomol leader. He graduated and was drafted, spending two years with the Soviet Navy in the far north. He then returned to Donetsk and obtained a degree in electro-mechanical engineering from the best local school, the Donetsk Polytechnic Institute. He found a job at the Butovka mine, married the daughter of a family of party members, and soon fathered a daughter, Irina.

"I was raised on the idea that the party really senses people in the best spirit," he said many years later in an interview with me and my colleague, David Satter, of the *London Financial Times*, during a visit to Donetsk in December 1980. "I never listened to foreign radio stations; I read Soviet newspapers and assumed they were truthful."

By the mid-1960's, Nikitin had become a trade union activist at the mine and an energetic party worker who seemed headed for a share of some of the privileges and power available to successful party *apparatchiki*. But life was not nearly as satisfying to him as he had hoped, and there were disturbing facts that he could not overlook: Party meetings seemed devoid of meaning, and workers' concerns or complaints of unfair treatment were deflected by crude ridicule and jokes or simply shoved aside by the mine directorate. "I began to understand that all questions were decided in advance," he recalled.

His work repairing, adjusting, and installing electric equipment took him to every nook and cranny of the mine's network of shafts and tunnels, and he began to see that the rules for storing dynamite, providing ventilation, and shoring up the tunnel roofs were being violated. He voiced his worries about the danger of explosions and accidents in the mine at a series of open party sessions, but each time the mine leaders rebuffed him, talking only of the requirement to fulfill production norms. When he took his case to the Donetsk party committee itself, he was told: "How could you, a simple engineer, predict an explosion? We sent experienced safety engineers to the mine and we trust them."

In June 1969 Nikitin's frustrations centered on the complaints of nineteen Butovka miners who had not been paid for overtime. Alexei headed the group in a showdown session with Butokva director Viktor P. Savitch, an in-law of the top party official in the Donetsk region. Savitch threw the petitioners out of his office; Nikitin retaliated by gathering 129 signatures on a collective letter that he sent to the Communist Party Central Committee in Moscow. In the letter he complained of how he and the larger group of miners whose long-standing complaints had not been heeded were treated. Within weeks the Central Committee responded: Nikitin was fired from his job and dismissed from the party.

In tens of thousands of similar cases, this was the kind of intimidation and ostracism that paid off: The recalcitrant person caved in. Not Alexei. He took odd jobs—as a carpenter, painter, collective farmer—and during his spare time went repeatedly to Moscow, where he attempted to petition the Soviet Supreme Court, the national legislature, and the Central Committee. He spent hours in waiting lines, was rebuffed repeatedly by indifferent functionaries, and sent back to Donetsk, or to another Moscow office, only to be told to "take this up with local authorities." In these endless, shuffling queues of disgruntled petitioners, under tight surveillance from uniformed police and plainclothesmen, Nikitin joined the army of dissatisfied petitioners who have thronged the Russian seat of power since czarist times.

Once, he was allowed to present his case to the highest party review board, the Party Control Commission. There, he came face-to-face with Arvid Pel'she, then 71, a gaunt Latvian whose immobile face had been a fixture of Politburo meetings since the 1960s. For twenty minutes Nikitin presented his story. Pel'she remained silent; his severe expression, Nikitin thought, "betrayed a desire to punish." Nikitin had barely completed his tale when an aide blustered: "Your appeal is not satisfied! Next case."

During this time Nikitin's marriage disintegrated under the pressure, and one day his wife disappeared with his daughter. He never attempted to find them for fear it would only bring trouble to the child.

Nonetheless, Nikitin fought on. Certain that he could get a response somewhere, he took an extraordinary step: He went to Moscow, and after some time watching how the police guarded foreign embassies, slipped into the Norwegian embassy. He pressed the startled and nonplussed diplomats to accept some written appeals; they soon ushered him out of the building.

"I am a Russian and I was raised in a patriotic family," Alexei told us. "I deeply love my people, our land, our folk songs. But I began to believe that to live in this country is impossible. There is unlimited control by the authorities, without any law. This happened to me because I started to defend workers without official permission." A short time after he slipped out of the embassy, he was intercepted by Moscow police and sent to City Psychiatric Hospital No. 14 for a few days. The intention, he said, "was to frighten me." Nikitin did not frighten.

Late in December 1971, Nikitin's troubles suddenly took a turn for the worse. Several miles from where he lay sleeping early one morning, the weary night shift at the Butovka mine was slowly emerging from the pit.

Alexei Vasilyevich Nikitin. (Courtesy of Kevin Klose.)

The morning crews had not yet descended. Suddenly, a powerful blast shook the mine, and acrid, dense smoke poured out of the shafts. Families and friends rushed to the pithead. KGB cars poured onto the mine territory, and agents jostled into the fierce crowd, yelling at them to disperse. Tense moments followed, but the furious and frightened workers disbanded. Seven had been killed in the explosion and more than a hundred injured; the toll would have been much higher if the shifts had not been changing. There is no known public mention of the mishap in the Soviet media.

When Butovka workers began seeking out Alexei to tell him that he had been right and the mine chiefs wrong, he knew his own days of freedom were numbered. On 13 January 1972, KGB agents and police broke into the apartment where he was sleeping and hauled him off to Donetsk jail. The charge: disseminating anti-Soviet propaganda.

Nikitin sat unnoticed for six months; it is unclear why. However, the inactivity came to an abrupt end on 19 June 1972. On that day, Nikitin was taken by train and *voronka* (police van) from Donetsk to the neighboring city of Dnepropetrovsk, which unlike Donetsk is closed to non-Soviets. In 1968 the Ministry of Internal Affairs had opened a new facility there of which Nikitin and most other Soviet citizens were totally unaware. Nikitin was taken to this secret place. He found himself inside a double-walled fortress surrounded by watchtowers manned by uniformed guards carrying automatic weapons. This strange and forbidding prison was called the Dnepropetrovsk Special Psychiatric Hospital for the Criminally Insane.

Nikitin spent four years there. The most dreaded treatment administered in the hospital was injection of sulfizine, a form of purified sulphur that was shown several decades ago to have no therapeutic effect.[1] The drug brings on intense fever, excruciating pain, convulsions, and disorientation. Recalled Nikitin: "If they torture you and break your arms, there is a certain specific pain and you can somehow stand it. But sulfizine is like a drill boring into your body that gets worse and worse until it's more than you can stand—it's impossible to endure."

In addition to sulfizine, Nikitin described a number of other drugs that were used at the prison to control and disorient patients in his ward of 30 men. He was forced to take Aminazin (chlorpromazine) and haloperidol, both of which are commonly used for treating severe schizophrenia and other extreme mental disorders. Because the drugs disrupt normal body movement, in the West other medicines are used with them to suppress the side effects, which resemble Parkinson's disease. But this was not practiced at Dnepropetrovsk. Nikitin said the prison staff, from doctors to orderlies (most of whom were prisoners who had been convicted of nonpolitical crimes), frequently threatened to inject these drugs into patients caught talking politics quietly among themselves.

Nikitin estimated that up to 85 percent of all the inmates at Dnepropetrovsk were sane. Many were convicted murderers, he said. But he also met Ukrainian nationalists, Baptists who had circulated religious tracts, and several men who had tried to escape by walking or swimming across the country's closed borders. He also found other worker-activists like himself who had been adjudged deranged because they defended their colleagues from exploitation by the state. One of these was Vladimir Klebanov, also a Donetsk miner, who had been incarcerated for defending workers' rights and who would surface a year later to announce formation of the first independent trade union in modern Soviet times. Klebanov was isolated thereafter in psychiatric wards.

In March 1976, as suddenly as he had been imprisoned, Nikitin was released. He returned to Donetsk, but his troubles continued. When he tried to have himself classified as an invalid, entitled to a state pension because of his drug treatments, authorities refused to acknowledge that he had ever spent time in Dnepropetrovsk or even that such a facility existed.

Frustrated once more, Nikitin returned to the Norwegian embassy in February 1977 and asked for political asylum. The diplomats again turned him away. He was then arrested, sent to Dnepropetrovsk, and later transferred to a psychiatric hospital in Donetsk. Three years later—in May 1980—he was again set free.

Once again, Alexei Nikitin made his way to Moscow. This time he went to the apartment of Feliks Serebrov, one of the few members of the unofficial Working Commission to Investigate the Use of Psychiatry for Political Purposes who was not in prison or in exile. Founded in early 1977 largely through the inspiration of a young medical worker named Alexander Podrabinek, the commission had publicized nearly 200 cases like Nikitin's of state abuse of psychiatry.[2] Later that year, on 6 September 1980, Serebrov arranged for Nikitin to be interviewed by Anatoly Koryagin, a psychiatrist and consultant to the commission.

Anatoly Koryagin

Like Nikitin, Koryagin had begun to question his government's principles. Ultimately, he actively opposed several aspects of the Soviet system. He would later pay dearly for those acts of conscience.

Born on 9 September 1938 in the peaceful Siberian backwater town of Kansk, Koryagin's early years were shadowed by World War II. His father was killed at the front, and a sister died from starvation brought on by the war. He and his childhood friends, he later wrote, grew up "accustomed to hunger and unheated huts, and the tears of widowed mothers." In the presence of misfortune, people consoled themselves with the reassuring thought that "the party and government existed to overcome such problems."

Koryagin attended local schools, deciding early on to become a physician because he regarded medicine as a profession of the highest calling. He wanted a better material life for himself, he also wanted much more from life: "I felt that spirit, intellect, ideas and knowledge were more significant for man than any fancies of material possessions." His search to understand the human interior led him to psychiatry.

His first post following graduation was in the remote region of Khakass, in the highlands of south central Siberia. He was the first resident psychiatrist ever to serve the population of some half million miners, farmers, and

Dr. Anatoly Koryagin. (Courtesy of Aid to Russian Christians.)

bureaucrats. He worked in a mental health clinic, which was housed in an old *izba* (timber house) that was heated with a stove. The clinic had small cells equipped with barred, padlocked doors in which violent or psychotic patients were occasionally confined. The staff had little medical training; most were tough peasant wives from the collective farms who sought to supplement their tiny pensions with nightwork at the clinic. They used their fists to pacify patients. Koryagin was appalled by the conditions at the mental health clinic; but he found himself confronted by indifferent superiors chiefly interested in making sure that no one rocked the boat. It took him four years to get the doors removed from the cells, which he had to do himself.

Koryagin eventually left Siberia and found a research position at the Research Institute for Neurology and Psychiatry in the Ukrainian city of Kharkov. Within a few months, he discovered that this position, too, could not satisfy his yearning to dedicate himself to humanity. The academics around him were chiefly accomplished at "driving off able graduates and surrounding themselves with toadies so that against such a background they would appear to be the most imposing figures."

He came to believe that it was the state, not the physicians, who were to blame for the poor quality of psychiatric care in the Soviet Union. "The state needs healthy, hardworking members of society, but mental illness most often limits or eliminates from people the ability to work hard. . . . The psychiatric service cannot effectively restore a patient's full health, so what use is it to the State? Surgery, for example, is an entirely different matter: the result of an operation is apparent—either into a box or back to the work-bench. But when a person gets mentally ill, he is sitting on the State's back from sick pay to pension."

In 1979, Koryagin became psychiatric consultant to Podrabinek's commission against psychiatric abuse, succeeding Dr. Alexander Voloshanovich. Examining persons interned in psychiatric institutions for political purposes, Anatoly Koryagin at last had found the useful work that he had yearned for. In an account written sometime later, he said that "all the people I examined had joined,the ranks of the mentally ill because they did or said things which in our country are considered 'anti-Soviet.'"

At the meeting at Feliks Serebrov's apartment on 6 September 1980, Koryagin interviewed Alexei Nikitin to see if he exhibited any of the symptoms of "psychopathology-simple form" that the prison doctors at Dnepropetrovsk had eventually decided was Nikitin's affliction. The two men talked, Nikitin explaining his history and Koryagin taking notes. The hours passed, and Koryagin finally jotted down his findings:

> [Nikitin's] judgment is sound, thinking quick, logical and coherent.
> Critical abilities are well developed. He shows tolerance to the
> opinions that differ from his own and is capable of accepting them
> when presented with sufficient evidence. Firm in his own beliefs,
> determined in his statements and actions. Memory good, emotional
> reactions are adequate to the stimuli, vivid, accompanied by changes
> in facial expression. No psychopathological symptoms elicited.

He reached this conclusion: "On the basis of personal history and examination, . . . Alexei V. Nikitin suffers no psychiatric illness or character disorders, and there is no evidence that he has ever had either of those conditions. His admissions to the special psychiatric hospital in 1972 and 1977 should be considered totally unjustified."

Three months after the meeting between Koryagin and Nikitin, David Satter and I journeyed to Donetsk with Nikitin to see for ourselves how Soviet coal miners lived and to interview any who cared to speak with us about how they viewed their world and their own conditions. We visited a succession of living quarters, sat over hot tea and cookies with miners' families, and heard story after story of how the Donetsk workers eke out a living. The miners told us of their daily battles to receive extra pay for which they had toiled, or to get the private apartment that they were promised years earlier, or to keep clear of stool pigeons and agents ready to report a disgruntled worker to his superiors. These random meetings allowed us to see the actual conditions of Soviet workers, and we owed this to Nikitin. But the authorities were not to let Nikitin's courage go unpunished.

Five days after David and I left Donetsk, police and KGB agents broke down the door to Nikitin's apartment, swept into the bedroom before he could escape, and punched a syringe of drugs into him. Within minutes Nikitin had passed out. He was then bundled into a heavy canvas and carried downstairs to a battered police-driven truck and driven off to the Dnepropetrovsk Special Psychiatric Hospital for the Criminally Insane. Some weeks later, relatives reported, he was being heavily drugged and appeared very disoriented. Still later they reported that the drug treatments seemed to have affected Alexei's eyesight: He was going blind. After this report reached Wetern correspondents, the Soviets shifted Nikitin to a psychiatric hospital located in Alma-Ata, the capital of distant Kazakhstan, apparently to prevent relatives from meeting with him.

Meanwhile, Koryagin continued his work for the commission. By early 1981 he had examined fifteen other political activists committed to psychiatric hospitals for the criminally insane, and although he assiduously kept his activities concealed, he did not hesitate to speak out publicly in defense of Nikitin. Shortly after David and another correspondent interviewed Koryagin in Kharkov, the psychiatrist was arrested and jailed on a charge of anti-Soviet activities.

His trial opened in Kharkov Regional Court on 3 June 1981 and lasted three days. The charge sheet accused the psychiatrist of being a "clear example" of an "ideologically unstable person" who had fallen under the "influence of enemies of Soviet power and the Party." These enemies, said the prosecutor, V. I. Popov, reach the Soviet Union through foreign radio broadcasts. "Radio Liberty, Radio Free Europe, the German Wave, Voice of America, the BBC, even the Voice of Israel regularly broadcast slanderous lies about our reality." According to the prosecutor, Koryagin had developed anti-Soviet ideas by listening to such broadcasts, by "reading anti-Soviet literature, and by associating with persons who had previously been convicted of anti-Soviet activities [and] . . . launched himself on the criminal road of activities harmful to Soviet power and the Party."

Koryagin was indicted on 20 counts of allegedly criminal antistate activity, plus a charge that he possessed an unlicensed handgun, which turned out to be a rusted souvenir that could not be fired. The prosecution charged that the psychiatrist had written anti-Soviet letters and articles, including an article on Soviet psychiatry published in the medical journal *Lancet*. He was also charged with having kept "foreign magazines" at home and having corresponded with a relative in the West. These acts were committed with "conscious criminal intent," charged the state. But as procurator Popov presented his evidence, gained from several searches of Koryagin's apartment and interrogation of friends and medical colleagues, it became clear that the physician's refusal to conform to the collective ways of his clinic and his stubborn independence were the issues on trial. Popov portrayed Koryagin as a loner, a person who would always be *chuzhoi*—an oddball, an outsider.

Procurator Popov never addressed Koryagin's work on behalf of dissidents confined to psychiatric hospitals for political reasons. In fact, the trial transcript, painstakingly reconstructed by the psychiatrist's supporters inside the Soviet Union and smuggled to the West, indicates that the prosecutor never even mentioned the existence of the Working Commission. However, Koryagin and his supporters little doubted that he was on trial because the state wanted to suppress the work of the commission.

In his closing remarks, Koryagin touched on this. "Not a single fact about dissemination of anti-Soviet materials has been proven either by the investigation or the trial," he said. "I know the sentence will be brutal. I don't ask anything of this court. . . . I declare I will never [denigrate] myself in view of the situation prevailing in our country, when mentally healthy people are confined to mental hospitals for trying to think independently."

The judge and his two lay assessors declared Koryagin to be "fully guilty . . . and subject to punishment." He was sentenced to a maximum term of seven years' imprisonment in a strict-regime labor camp with five additonal years of internal exile. In July 1982 the Soviet authorities transferred Koryagin from the camp to the still harsher Chistopol prison in Tatarstan, the main Soviet institution for political prisoners.

Some months later, worker-activist Alexei Nikitin was diagnosed as having contracted stomach cancer. Early in 1984 he was released from incarceration and allowed to return to his relatives in Donetsk. He died there in the spring of 1984, according to reliable sources.

As for Dr. Koryagin, the psychiatrist refused to give up his defense of the politically repressed, carrying his cause into Soviet labor camp. According to reliable sources inside the Soviet Union, Koryagin conducted several hunger strikes to protest inhuman conditions in the Urals labor camp and later in the Chistopol prison in East Central Russia, where he was transferred. The sources report that he suffered savage beatings and other reprisals and that his health began to fail. In the autumn of 1984, Amnesty International expressed grave concern for Dr. Koryagin and issued an urgent appeal to Soviet authorities for his immediate release from prison. The Soviet Union ignored the appeal.

Unwilling Patients*

In my capacity as consultant psychiatrist to the unofficial Working Commission to Investigate the Use of Psychiatry for Political Purposes, I examined a number of people who, on several occasions, had undergone compulsory treatment in ordinary and special (i.e., prison) psychiatric hospitals. . . . These people were involved with the psychiatric service, although when I examined them they showed no signs of psychiatric illness, psychic defects, or psychopathy. Furthermore, a study of their life histories leads to the conclusion that they had not previously shown any signs of mental disorder. Therefore, these people must be considered psychologically healthy.

My aim in this paper is to analyze the conditions under which healthy people in the Soviet Union are pronounced mentally ill and are condemned to exist as such. I can mention some people by name: Their cases illustrate what happens to the group as a whole. All the people I examined had joined the ranks of the mentally ill because they did or said thing which in our country are considered "anti-Soviet." Some had tried to leave the Soviet Union by crossing the frontier or asking for asylum at foreign embassies; some circulated leaflets with appeals or poems; others stated that they disagreed with the existing order in the country.

The life histories of these people present virtually no evidence of the characteristics embodied in the generally accepted psychiatric description "predisposition to morbidity"—when certain physical and psychological features in an individual's personality are likely to lead to mental illness. The overwhelming majority of them were noted from early childhood for qualities typical of strong personalities—energy, enterprise, a marked ability to

* The text of Anatoly Koryagin's article was smuggled out of the Soviet Union and published in the *Lancet* (vol. 1, no. 8224) on 11 April 1981. It is reprinted here in edited form by the permission of the publisher.

communicate, leadership, and good or excellent marks at school. They showed early signs of independent judgment and behavior and determination in overcoming difficulties and achieving their aims. Many of them quickly completed their secondary and higher education and became exemplary production workers, took an active part in voluntary activities, were active members of the Komsomol (some became party members) and doting parents. When I examined them, most of them exhibited a fairly wide range of interests, were knowledgeable on several subjects, were consistent in their reasoning, clear and logical in their judgments, and perfectly adequate in their emotional responses; they had firm convictions, clear aims, and realistic plans for the future. All these people were "positive" Soviet citizens with real prospects of succeeding in society—but all of them, eventually, came into conflict with that very society.

The moment these people came into conflict with the state, they were placed under the observation of psychiatrists who judged their behavior to be abnormal and assumed the clinical and social status of the mentally ill, with all its consequences: compulsory confinement and treatment in a hospital, a definitive diagnosis of psychiatric illness in some cases, and relegation to invalid status due to mental illness. The reasons for their internment varied. For example, Dr. A. Butko's psychiatric "odyssey" began when he attempted to swim to Turkey, that of engineer and former Communist L. Pribytkov when he renounced his Soviet citizenship, and that of engineer A. Paskauskiene when she circulated nationalist leaflets.

The Roads to Internment

A patient's first contact with a psychiatrist to a large extent determines his subsequent fate. Normally, such contact takes place at the patient's own request or at the request of his family when they notice abnormalities in the patient's speech and behavior. In cases of sudden manifestation of psychological disturbance (when the patient becomes "socially dangerous"), the patient is taken to a psychiatric hospital, usually under police escort. Nothing of this kind happened to the people I examined. None of them sought medical assistance, their families did not ask for psychiatric help, their speech and behavior posed no threat to anyone; nonetheless, they were all confined to psychiatric hospitals by force or by deception. The fate of these people depended on those who controlled their personal freedom: officials of the KGB, the Procuracy, and the Ministry of Internal Affairs. These officials stated that the people I examined behaved in a manner incompatible with mental health, and on this basis alone, they were forced to see the psychiatrists

If you say to the interrogator that there is no freedom of the press in the USSR, that means you are a slanderer, a criminal. If you say that same thing to a doctor-psychiatrist he says that this is delirium, a mental illness. . . . If you say to the interrogator that elections should be made elections and not just theatrical productions of unanimity, that means that you are a criminal, you are against the Soviet system, you are anti-Soviet. If you repeat the same thing to a psychiatrist he will ascribe to you "concepts of reformism". . . . And so you have a whole clump of symptoms of schizophrenia. In order to be cured of such "illnesses," you have to renounce your own convictions . . . . And if you are unwilling to thus recuperate, you will be subjected to an indefinitely long "treatment"— lifelong. This gives you something to think about. . . . The alternative— imprisonment for life—is terrifying.

Pytor Grigorenko
Memoirs

who became responsible for them. Many of those I examined have said they were initally presented with the following alternative: renunciation of their views and activities or internment in a psychiatric hospital.

The most widespread methods of confining dissenters to psychiatric hospitals in the Soviet Union are as follows:

1. The investigative organs bring charges against you under the "anti-Soviet" articles of the Criminal Code. At the investigator's order, you are subjected to a forensic psychiatric examination and pronounced mentally ill. The next stage is compulsory treatment in a special or an ordinary psychiatric hospital.

2. You are summoned to the Military Registration Office "for examination by a military commission." You arrive. And you are then escorted by a police officer to a psychiatric hospital "for observation." The role of the Military Registration Office is sometimes played by the executive committee of the district Soviet, the city Party committee, the police, or the State Motor Vehicle Inspectorate, where you are summoned on some pretext.

3. Due to circumstances over which you have no control, a brawl breaks out between you and your neighbors at home or between you and your colleagues at work. The police are called, but only you are taken to the police station and from there to a psychiatric

hospital. One individual I interviewed—Seventh-Day Adventist V. Kushkun—relates that he was beaten up by drunken colleagues at work who called him a "traitor" and a "spy." He was then arrested by police who took him to a psychiatric hospital without a psychiatrist's order.

4. You are in bed or doing something at home when a car draws up outside. Medical orderlies and KGB officials take you straight to a psychiatric hospital. This happens all the more unexpectedly if the order to commit you to hospital is issued by a psychiatrist in your absence. A. Roslan recounts that in 1978, S. Buknis, district psychiatrist in Mozheikov, Lithuania, issued an order for his admission to a psychiatric hospital without even having examined him.

The Second Confinement

The methods used to confine people to psychiatric hospitals a second time differ little from those used on the first occasion, although physical coercion is more common. The pretext for a second confinement to the hospital is always "deterioration in the patient's condition," which manifests itself in increased "anti-Soviet" activity. The KGB and the police take people straight to a psychiatric hospital from home, from work, or from the street, often in handcuffs.

Occasionally, a second admission to the hospital takes the form of a preventive measure. This happened, according to several of the people I examined, before President Nixon's visit to Moscow in 1972 and before the Olympic Games in 1980. S. Belov, who was confined to Ivanov Regional Psychiatric Hospital in June 1980 was told by his doctor that "they advised me to keep you" until the beginning of August. Such reports are confirmed by the fact that in towns where Olympic competitions were held and in districts through which the Olympic torch passed, doctors at psychiatric clinics received instructions from their superiors to admit to the hospital those patients who could present a danger to society—and especially those with "anti-Soviet tendencies"—for the duration of the Olympics.

Each time the people I examined were admitted to psychiatric hospitals, this was done forcibly and in contravention of an instruction issued by the USSR Ministry of Health in 1972. This instruction grants the health authorities the right to confine mentally ill persons to hospitals if they become socially dangerous and to summon the help of the authorities responsible for keeping public order. The clinical meaning of the term "socially dangerous" is that the person is in danger of committing acts which would endanger his own health or that of people around him (such as murder, suicide, and personal injury). However, the individuals I examined were not dangerous in this sense. It must be clearly stated that each time a decision was taken to hospitalize the people under discussion, the clinical meaning of "socially dangerous" was replaced by its judicial meaning, that is, that the patient was capable of harming the social system as a whole. The responsibility for this decision lies undoubtedly with the psychiatrists who issue confinement orders as well as with those who accept patients for treatment.

Diagnosis

With rare exceptions, the people I examined were aware of how their condition had been diagnosed. However careful doctors may be, any intelligent patient confined to a hospital for a long time will find an opportunity to get to know what is written in his case history.

On their first confinement, all the people I examined were diagnosed as either psychopaths (70 percent) or schizophrenics (30 percent). Moreover, several doctors, in different hospitals and at different times, diagnosed nearly all the people whom I examined as either psychopaths or schizophrenics. In most cases, the term *paranoid* was used in the diagnosis. Paranoid behavior generally refers to a disorder in the thought process that manifests itself in the formation of distorted or fantastic ideas.

One easily gains the impression that "paranoia" is an indubitable clinical sign of mental illness in all "anti-Soviet elements." All diagnostic problems disappear, however, when the psychiatrist adopts the attitude of Dr. A. P. Filatova. During a forensic psychiatric examination of A. Butko in Kursk, she stated that "no normal person can be opposed to the Worker's and Peasant's State."

Treatment

From what has been said by the people I examined, one may conclude that the nature, intensity, and duration of the treatment they received was not based upon their diagnosis, but depended solely on their behavior in the hospital and evaluation of what they had said and done in the past.

A. Butko, who was diagnosed as "schizophrenic" and subjected to compulsory treatment in Chernyakhovsk Special Psychiatric Hospital and Kharkov Regional Psychiatric Hospital from 1974 to 1978, reported that he was given no treatment, although treatment was prescribed in his medical notes. L. Pribytkov was also diagnosed as "schizophrenic" and confined to a psychiatric hospital every time he attempted to enter a foreign embassy. On several occasions he was discharged after a few days without treatment, but during his nine-month stay in Kazan Special Psychiatric Hospital, he was given an intensive course of insulin therapy just before his discharge. A. Roslan was diagnosed as "paranoid" and forcibly admitted to the New Vilnius Psychiatric Hospital in 1978. He spent six weeks there without any treatment and was then discharged. I. Koreisha was twice (in 1978 and 1979) admitted to Vitebsk Regional Psychiatric Hospital and was discharged after a few days each time without any treatment.

It seems that the main aim of these hospital confinements was to isolate the patient and not to treat mental illness—a fact well borne out in cases where psychopathy was diagnosed. It is not without reason, therefore, that the term *wall therapy* has become part of the terminology used by Soviet psychiatrists, as is described in detail by the well-known dissenter Y. Belov[3] in his book *Reflections on Sychevka*.

Patients' descriptions of their state of mind during their stay in psychiatric hospitals show no trace of any psychopathological symptoms. They all tried to make contact with "undamaged" patients like themselves, mixed with the medical staff (some of them even established personal relationships with doctors and nurses), and made every effort to obtain a speedy discharge. Their only symptoms were those very "anti-Soviet" attitudes, expressions, and actions—the degree of which directly influenced the medical staff's attitude towards them and also the treatment that they received.

According to the people I examined, the basic reason for giving them insulin comas and high doses of neuroleptic drugs and depriving them of the opportunity to work in the open air was not to increase their hallucinatory or confused experiences but rather to punish them for "breaking the rules." This included such actions as sending letters and complaints that bypassed the doctor's censorship, making remarks of an anti-Soviet nature, circulating news from foreign radio stations, not admitting that their former actions were wrong, or directly accusing the doctors of persecution and complicity with the KGB. In the case of I. Koreisha, for example, doctors at the Vitebsk Regional Psychiatric Hospital subjected him to a week-long intensive course of neuroleptic drugs after a foreign radion station had broadcast remarks about him. A. Paskauskiene states that at the age of 16 she was brought back to Kaunas Psychiatric Hospital after attempting to escape and that she was severely beaten by the medical staff there and subjected to treatment with neuroleptic drugs.

According to some of the people I examined, the KGB directly intervened to influence the conditions and length of their confinement, a fact which the doctors themselves did not conceal. For example, during this stay in Kharkov Regional Psychiatric Hospital, A. Butko was told by his doctor that after a call from the KGB, the chief doctor, A. Popov, had forbidden Butko to go out freely. For the same reason Butko was refused permission to go to his father's funeral.

The Criminal Code article under which dissenters are charged often determines the length of time they spend in psychiatric hospitals. This undoubtedly means that the patient's condition as a result of treatment bears no relation to when he is discharged.

Discharge and Aftercare

It is also incomprehensible from the point of view of medical logic that people who have been confined to psychiatric hospitals on several occasions and are finally given a definite diagnosis of mental illness can still be considered capable of military service. . . . A. Nikitin, for example, spent a total of about seven years in psychiatric hospitals, but was not granted invalid status. A. Roslan and S. Belov were deprived of their driving licenses after their discharge from psychiatric hospitals, but no note of their illness was made in their military registration cards.

All the people I examined were discharged from psychiatric hospitals without having fulfilled what is normally a fundamental requirement: that of having a critical attitude to their experiences during illness. None of them agreed with the doctor's assertions that their former opinions and behavior were the result of mental illness. Nevertheless, they were eventually discharged, with the warning: "Don't do it again." They all left the hospital unaided, without an escort, a totally arbitary and incomprehensible attitude on the part of their doctors to the concept of "social danger." The patient's condition does not change, but he is dangerous when admitted and not dangerous when he is discharged.

Once out of the hospital, these people took up their lives as before: They tried to obtain work according to their qualifications, went about their personal and family business, tried to have their diagnosis revoked, and stood by their beliefs and opinions. Aftercare for discharged psychiatric patients includes their attendance at a psychiatric clinic for observation and treatment; there are also a number of measures intended, in a broad sense, to help their rehabilitation at work and in society, so that "the patient may become as active in his work and social life as he is able." Let us see from their own accounts, how our patients experienced this "care."

Immediately after his discharge from a psychiatric hospital, Dr. A. Butko tried to find a job as a doctor. He wrote to the head of Donetsk Regional Health Authority and received the following reply: "I cannot give you even a temporary job because you have seriously discredited yourself." However, he did manage to get a job as a doctor in a village in another republic. Donetsk city police issued engineer A. Nikitin a passport and residence permit five months after his discharge from a psychiatric hospital, but he was still unable to get a job, despite his persistent visits to numerous factories. Until his subsequent arrest, this individual with a diploma from an institute of higher education survived by doing odd jobs. The only job S. Belov, a lawyer, was able to obtain was that of shipping clerk at a food depot. At the time of writing, agricultural worker I. Koreisha is still trying to obtain the right to work on a collective farm in his native village and because of this is constantly being threatened by police and KGB officials. After six weeks in a psychiatric hospital, A. Roslan was dismissed from his job "for failing to fulfil the plan as agreed" and was forced to go to court to get the job back.

The Psychiatrist's Role

Not one of these people has said that the health authorities or, more particularly, the doctors at psychiatric clinics have helped them in any way whatsoever. . . . The fact that most of them did not consider themselves ill and therefore did not attend their psychiatric clinic regularly obviously does not excuse the psychiatrists. A doctor is obliged to take an active interest in all the patients on his list, so that he may help them in legal and social, as well as medical, matters.

All that has been said concerning the group of people I examined leads to the conclusion that the criteria and instructions generally accepted in Soviet psychiatry were ignored by its officals in their attitude toward the admission of these people to hospitals, clinical appraisal of their condition, and treatment and help in social matters. Because of this unorthodox approach, these people found themselves treated as chronic psychiatric patients. Our observations show that the most influential factor determining the psychiatrist's attitude towards these patients was the label "anti-Soviet," which was commonly applied to representatives of this group.

Leaving to the doctors' own consciences their flagrant, almost criminal, disregard of professional duty, it is legitimate to pose the following question: How does it happen and who is responsible for the fact that in a country like the Soviet Union, were every aspect of economic, political, and social life is strictly controlled by the state, perfectly healthy people are treated as though they are mentally ill? There can be only one answer: These things are done by those who have the power and are in circumstances for which it is convenient to do so.

Notes and References

1. Sidney Bloch and Peter Reddaway, *Psychiatric Terror: How Soviet Psychiatry Is Used to Suppress Dissent* (New York: Basic Books, 1977).

2. Despite continued harassment and imprisonment of its members by the Soviet authorities, until April 1980 the Working Commission published more than twenty information bulletins on its investigations into individual cases of psychiatric abuse. The commission has campaigned for the release of those wrongly interned in psychiatric institutions, visited them in psychiatric hospitals, and provided moral and material support to their families. The work of the commission has come to a virtual halt because most of its members have been arrested in recent years.

3. Yury S. Belov, imprisoned in 1967 for writing a *samizdat* essay entitled "Report from the Darkness," was declared mentally ill in 1971. He spent the next six years in psychiatric hospitals, including three years in Sychevka Special Psychiatric Hospital in Smolensk. He was released in December 1977.

Chapter 8

The Case of
General Grigorenko:
A Second Opinion

Walter Reich

Pyotr Grigorievich Grigorenko was the perfect realization of the Bolshevik dream. Emerging from the humblest soil of czarist Russia, he rose to the highest precincts of Soviet power. An ardent patriot, a committed Communist, and an effective leader, he became a major general in the Red Army, exercised a deep and seminal influence on Soviet military theory, and was showered with medals, honors and promotions through five decades of his Soviet life.

In the early 1960s, at the height of his career, he turned dissident. He was twice arrested, twice declared mentally ill, and committed for almost five years to prison hospitals for the criminally insane. After he was allowed to reach the West, he asked for a second opinion on his psychiatric condition. This is my report on the examinations conducted as a result of his request and the findings they yielded. The findings are of some interest in General Grigorenko's case, but more important, the fact that the examinations were conducted and how they were conducted may offer a model for evaluating future cases of reported medical—and particularly psychiatric—abuse.

Introduction

On 23 January 1978 I was informed, through an intermediary, that P. G. Grigorenko, a prominent Soviet dissident visiting the United States, wanted

Reprinted in edited form with permission of the author and publisher from *Encounter*, vol. LIV, no. 4, April 1980.

a psychiatric examination. The intermediary, Dr. Marina Voikhanskaya, herself an emigré Soviet psychiatrist, explained that the former major general expected, upon the expiration of his six-month visa in May 1978, to return to the Soviet Union and to resume speaking his conscience in support of human rights. Because of his political dissidence, he anticipated official harassment, arrest, and possibly psychiatric examination and rehospitalization. His hope was that if he were indeed examined and found ill by a Soviet psychiatric commission, he or his supporters would be able to announce that a commission of American psychiatrists had found him to be psychiatrically well.

I had been approached to organize and carry out the examination because of an interest I had developed in Soviet psychiatry and in the question of Soviet psychiatric abuse. In 1971 I became aware of persistent reports about psychiatric abuse in the Soviet Union. In order to educate myself about the theories and practices of Soviet psychiatry, I began to interview a series of Soviet dissidents, both those who had been hospitalized and those who had not, as well as a number of emigré Soviet psychiatrists. I had come to feel that the experience of Soviet psychiatry had much to teach psychiatrists everywhere about the social functions of their profession as well as its special vulnerabilities, particularly in relation to diagnosis and the law.[1]

Although I appreciated the humanitarian basis for Grigorenko's request and recognized its unprecedented, historic nature, I felt somewhat uncomfortable about its political overtones. I was concerned that, in the service of humanitarianism, there might develop subtle pressures to slant a diagnosis in the direction of health. I had myself never examined the man, knew that a small minority of other hospitalized Soviet dissidents had some symptoms of genuine mental illness, and was worried that I would either be unable to carry out a truly objective examination or might, in the end, find myself issuing a diagnosis of illness that would harm him, perhaps irreparably.

In order to reassure myself on this matter, I met with Grigorenko for about four hours on 9 February 1978, both to discuss the matter more fully and to develop my own initial impression of the man. These discussions, as well as others through the intermediary psychiatrist, reassured me. What he wanted, he insisted, was the scientific, clinical truth. He had, he felt, nothing more to lose—after all, he said, he had already been labeled insane.

Before much could be done, however, I read in the *New York Times* that on 10 March 1978 the Supreme Soviet had published a special decree (signed by Leonid Brezhnev, dated 13 February) stripping Grigorenko of his citizenship and denying, in effect, his right to return home. A month later, Pyotr Grigorenko, together with his wife, Zinaida, and his stepson, Oleg, applied for asylum in the United States.[2]

Given this turn of events, I suspected that Grigorenko might no longer be interested in undergoing an American examination. During the following autumn, however, I was informed that Grigorenko still desired it. He said that he continued to feel himself to have been unjustly diagnosed in the Soviet Union and that he wanted to clear up any doubts about his psychiatric status in the minds of both Westerners and Soviet citizens.

Earlier I had discussed the matter of the examination, in confidence, with a number of psychiatric colleagues. One—Alan Stone, professor of law and psychiatry at Harvard—had been especially interested in participating in the project. In the summer of 1978 he had visited the Soviet Union and, as part of a research project on comparative practices of civil commitment for the mentally ill, had met with Andrei V. Snezhnevsky, the head of the Institute of Psychiatry of the USSR Academy of Medical Sciences and the chief defender of his profession against Western charges of Soviet psychiatric abuse. Dr. Stone (who had just become president-elect of the American Psychiatric Association) had asked Snezhnevsky directly what he thought about an American examination of Grigorenko. Snezhnevsky had answered that he would welcome it and that, in fact, an unbiased, direct examination by respected Western psychiatrists was exactly what was needed in order to clear up the charges of "abuse," which he considered to be spurious and based on irresponsible reports.

The Case of General Grigorenko

Snezhnevsky's invitation to Stone helped convince me that the examination project was worth undertaking. The project offered the conditions for a valid and unbiased second opinion on a man at the center of a psychiatric and international political controversy. In addition, it represented precisely the sort of exercise that the Soviets themselves had been requesting for some time. And it was, potentially at least, a humanitarian gesture. Because Grigorenko gave his examiners the right to publish any and all findings and gave up all his rights to confidentiality, the examination posed, for him, the danger of a public confirmation of his Soviet diagnoses. But it also offered him the hope that the psychiatric cloud enveloping him and his ideas for so long would be, at long last, blown away.

Accordingly, in December 1978 Dr. Stone and I made plans for a full-scale examination. Because the diagnoses he had received in the Soviet Union asserted the presence of a paranoid condition, we asked Dr. Irene Stiver (director of psychology at McLean Hospital near Boston and principal associate in psychiatry at the Harvard Medical School) to administer a battery

General Pyotr Grigorievich Grigorenko. (Courtesy of W. W. Norton and Company, copyright 1983.)

of psychological tests, including the kinds of interpretive, projective tests that would reveal any paranoid trends that might be present. Particularly because the Soviet diagnoses had repeatedly mentioned the existence of atherosclerotic brain disease, we asked for consultations with both Dr. Norman Geschwind (before his recent and untimely death the James Jackson Putnam Professor of Neurology at Harvard and a world authority on the behavioral effects of brain abnormalities) and Dr. Barbara Pendleton Jones (a neuropsychologist at the McLean Hospital and instructor in psychology at the Harvard Medical School).

Finally, we asked Dr. Lawrence C. Kolb (the author of a standard American textbook of psychiatry and formerly chairman of psychiatry at Columbia University, commissioner of mental hygiene of New York State, and director of the New York State Psychiatric Institute) to join Dr. Stone and me as the third psychiatric member of the U.S. examining commission. He agreed to the task, feeling that such an undertaking could serve as a model for future attempts at monitoring and resolving, within the profession, cross-national allegations of psychiatric abuse. Throughout, we were skillfully assisted by Dr. Boris Zoubok, who was then in the midst of his psychiatric residency at Columbia. Dr. Zoubok, who had received medical training in Moscow (part of it in Snezhnevsky's own institute and clinical facilities) and had emigrated from the Soviet Union in 1973, kept Grigorenko fully informed about the commission's procedures, advised me on special aspects of Soviet diagnostic definitions, and acted as translator.[3]

What follows is (1) an account of Mr. Grigorenko's personal and psychiatric history; (2) an elaboration of the Soviet psychiatrists' own theories regarding his psychiatric condition; (3) a formal examination of Mr. Grigorenko's psychiatric status; and (4) conclusions based on the examination and on the consultants' findings. This evaluation of P. G. Grigorenko is my own. As it happens, the other psychiatric examiners, Dr. Kolb and Dr. Stone, working separately, arrived at the same conclusions.[4]

The Man

Pyotr Grigorievich Grigorenko, the second of three sons, was born in 1907 to a peasant family in Borisovka, a village in the Ukraine. His mother died of typhus at the age of 25, when he was three. His father remarried three years later, in 1913, but the new wife abandoned the household within a year, soon after the father was called up to serve in World War I. The young Grigorenko was raised by his arthritic grandmother, with his uncle substituting for the father until the latter's return in 1918.

Grigorenko's earliest memories are of privation. The family's resources, meager under the best of circumstances, were strained to extremes under the conditions of revolution and civil war. Grigorenko shared in the farm work through his mid-teens, and in recalling those years speaks of the harshness of that rural life. The elder Grigorenko remarried again in 1922, but by then the boy was already 15 and had just left home to find work in Donetsk, a city in the Ukraine, as a locksmith and machinist.

Grigorenko had attended elementary school in his native village and was the first in Borisovka to join the Communist Youth League. Later, in Donetsk, he continued his schooling at night; in 1927, at the age of 20, he joined the Communist party. Two years later, having completed his secondary education, Grigorenko entered the Polytechnic Institute in Kharkov. Showing considerable academic promise, he was transferred during his third year upon party order to the Kuibyshev Military Engineering Academy, graduating with distinction in 1934. In the midst of his engineering education, in 1931, Grigorenko joined the Soviet armed forces, embarking on a military career that would continue without interruption until 1964, when he would be forcibly retired.

In 1939, after graduating from a course of advance study at the General Staff Military Academy, Grigorenko served in a number of units in the Red Army. He saw his first military action in 1939, as chief of an army brigade in the Khalkin-Gol campaign against the Japanese, where he sustained a back injury in a grenade explosion. Later, in fighting against the Germans, he was hurt twice, first in the ankle, which was permanently damaged and required a series of operations, and then in the head following an explosive shock wave, which resulted in a brief loss of consciousness but no hospitalization.

In 1945, after the war, Grigorenko joined the Frunze Military Academy, where he was appointed deputy chairman of the Department of Scientific Research in 1949 and then chairman of the Department of Cybernetics in 1958. While there he pursued graduate studies, receiving the degree of master of military sciences in 1949. At the same time, he studied history and philosophy; read widely in the works of Marx, Engels, Lenin, and Stalin; and pursued studies at the University of Marxism-Leninism. In 1959 Grigorenko achieved his highest military rank, major general. By the end of his military career five years later, he was the author of more than 60 articles on military science, most of them classified, and possessed numerous decorations, including the Order of Lenin, two Orders of the Red Banner, the Order of the Red Star, and the Order of the Second World War, as well as seven military medals.

Grigorenko's first marriage, begun in 1927, ended in divorce fifteen years later. Three sons from that marriage now live in the Soviet Union. His second marriage (to his current wife, Zinaida) resulted in the birth of one son, Andrei, who emigrated to the United States several years ago. Zinaida, who had also been divorced, has a son from a previous marriage. Grigorenko's relationship with his wife has been a strong and mutually devoted one, and it is no doubt primarily due to her years of energetic and persistent protests that his case ultimately gained world attention and prominence.

Grigorenko's medical history includes several bouts of typhus and malaria between 1918 and 1923; scarlet fever in 1936; pneumonia in 1943; coronary insufficiency in 1963; a probable small stroke in 1972, manifested by permanent partial blindness in his right eye and very mild signs of motor and sensory impairment on the left side of the body; a myocardial infarction in 1976, confirmed by electrocardiogram; and an adenoma of the prostate, removed in 1977. There is no evidence of a history of mental illness on either side of Mr. Grigorenko's family.

The Dissident

Grigorenko's first serious clash with Soviet authorities occurred in 1961. On 7 September, in a speech as a delegate to a party conference in Moscow, Grigorenko called for the democratization of party rules, including the rotation of elected officers and the imposition of a ceiling on the salaries of officeholders. At the time he was becoming increasingly concerned that the party, having begun the process of "de-Stalinization," was showing signs of a return to a "cult of personality" (this time focusing on Nikita Khrushchev), and that some Stalinists were beginning to regain their power and influence.

Grigorenko's speech caused consternation among the conference participants; as a result of a special vote, he was stripped of his delegate status. At about the same time, Grigorenko wrote an open letter to Moscow voters criticizing the "unreasonable and often harmful activities of Khrushchev and his team." Grigorenko immediately lost his position at the Frunze Military Academy and was then sent to the Soviet Far East as chief of the army operations headquarters.

While at his new post in Ussurisk, Grigorenko founded a thirteen-member "Union for the Revival of Leninism" in 1963, which included his sons and a nephew. Enlisting their aid, he distributed leaflets in November 1963 calling for "a return to Leninist tenets and principles."

A few months later, Grigorenko was arrested, charged under Article 70 of the Criminal Code, and sent to the Lubyanka prison in Moscow. While under investigation on that charge, he was subjected to his first psychiatric examination at the Serbsky Institute of Forensic Psychiatry. Psychiatrists found him to be mentally ill, not legally responsible for his actions, and in need of compulsory hospitalization at a special psychiatric hospital for the criminally insane. After some months in Moscow prison, Grigorenko was transferred to the Leningrad Special Psychiatric Hospital in August 1964. Following Khrushchev's fall, Grigorenko was reexamined and finally released from the hospital in May 1965.

After his release Grigorenko was unable to obtain any work in his field of knowledge and experience. Reduced to the ranks following his arrest and having lost his officer's pension, he was forced to find work as a porter and longshoreman.

During this period Grigorenko engaged in a number of activities that propelled him into open dissent. In 1966 he sent a letter to Premier Kosygin demanding that "distortions of Lenin's policy on nationalities" be discontinued. Receiving no reply, he wrote a letter to *Pravda* asking that Moscow citizens vote against Kosygin during the forthcoming elections. In 1968, following the publication of an article by him in an emigré journal, the KGB summoned Grigorenko for an interview. Later he sent a letter to Yuri V. Andropov, then chairman of the KGB, complaining about the interview. Some months after that he and the writer A. E. Kosterin again wrote to Andropov regarding KGB harassments. Throughout, he repeatedly complained, in writing, about the loss of his military rank and pension.

However, the activities that seem to have resulted in the most serious repercussions were Grigorenko's open demonstrations during dissident trials in the middle and late 1960s. In addition, he demonstrated outside the court building during the trial of dissidents protesting the Soviet invasion of Czechoslovakia.

Meanwhile, Grigorenko had taken up the cause of the Crimean Tatars, a nationality which, he felt, had suffered at the hands of the Soviets. In May 1969, in response to an appeal, he flew to Tashkent to be a witness for the defense in a trial of dissident Tatar leaders. Later he was charged with having committed a criminal offense, arrested, imprisoned, and, in August 1969, sent to a Tashkent psychiatric commission for examination. That commission found him healthy, legally responsible for any criminal acts he may have committed, and, by implication, capable of standing trial and participating in his own defense, as would have been his right under Soviet law.

However, in an unusual move, Grigorenko was transferred across the country to the Serbsky Institute in Moscow for a second examination. There he was found ill, legally not responsible for any criminal acts he may have committed, in need of compulsory treatment in a special psychiatric hospital for the criminally insane, not capable of taking part in his own defense at a trial, and therefore subject by law to being barred from such a trial. He was returned to prison in Tashkent in November 1969 and then sent to the Chernyakhovsk Special Psychiatric Hospital, where he was involuntarily held between May 1970 and October 1973. He was subsequently transferred to a general psychiatric hospital in Moscow (known as "Stolbovaya"), where he remained until his release in June 1974.

Following his final release, Grigorenko continued to engage in a variety of dissident activities. In November 1977 he was granted a six-month guest visa to visit his son in New York and to obtain medical treatment. Three months later his citizenship was revoked.

The Patient

In all, Grigorenko was committed by Soviet courts to two periods of compulsory hospitalization on the recommendations of two commissions of forensic psychiatrists, both from the Serbsky Institute in Moscow. In 1964 the first Serbsky commission found that Grigorenko "suffered from a mental illness in the form of a paranoid delusional (*bredevoi*) development of the personality combined with the first signs of arteriosclerosis of the brain." That commission concluded that, as a result of that illness or illnesses, Grigorenko had developed "reformist ideas," particularly regarding the reorganization of the state apparatus, and that those ideas were linked to an overestimation of his own personality, messianic notions, and paranoid interpretations of neutral facts. The commission found him unshakable in his ideas, which he set forth with great intensity.[5]

The second Serbsky commission, held in 1969, also found Grigorenko to be mentally ill. In the report, the Serbsky examiners concluded:

> Grigorenko is suffering from a mental illness in the form of a pathological (paranoid) development of the personality, with the presence of reformist ideas that have appeared in his personality, and with psychopathic features of the character and the first signs of cerebral arteriosclerosis.
>
> Confirmation of this can be seen in the psychotic condition present in 1964 which arose during an unfavorable situation which manifested itself in ideas, with strongly affective coloring, of reformism, and of persecution. Subsequently, as is evident from the documents of the criminal case and the data of the present clinical examination, the paranoid condition was not completely overcome. Reformist ideas have taken on an obstinate character and determine the conduct of the patient; in addition, the intensity of these ideas is increased in connection with various external circumstances which have no direct relation to him, and is accompanied by an uncritical attitude to his own utterances and acts. The abovementioned condition of mental illness excludes the possibility of his being responsible for his actions and controlling them: consequently the patient must be considered of unsound mind.

In support of this theory of Grigorenko's illness, the second Serbsky commission not only cited his dissident acts and theories, but also noted his general characteristics, which, it said, were consistent with the characteristics of someone suffering from his ascribed psychiatric condition. These included periods during which Grigorenko became "hasty-tempered and irritable, and could not bear contradiction." Similarly, the commission noted, Grigorenko's colleagues observed that while he was at his post in the Far East in 1964, Grigorenko suffered from "extreme conceit," "over-estimated his own knowledge and capabilities," and "was hasty-tempered, lacking in restraint, and not in self-command."

The second Serbsky commission further cited other people as believing that Grigorenko had "dictatorial ways" and that he tended to talk heatedly and at great length when he was trying to prove a point. Witnesses who saw Grigorenko demonstrating outside a courthouse during a political trial were quoted as saying that he "stood out" by his heated behavior, and "that he was active, gave loud voice to his opinions, was abusive, insulted the voluntary police, calling them fascists and Black-Hundreders, that he drew a crowd around him, to which he spoke about himself, shouting that he would fight for democracy and truth."

The diagnosis of arteriosclerosis of the blood vessels supplying the brain and, by implication, damage to areas of the brain affecting behavior or judgment arises several times in the Soviet psychiatric reports. Although the notion is offered that certain events in Grigorenko's environment may have served to worsen his illness and to precipitate his dissident acts, there are also some suggestions that that illness was somehow aggravated by arteriosclerosis. That this became an increasingly important element in the Serbsky theory of Grigorenko's mental condition is evident from the information provided to two Western psychiatrists who accepted an official invitation to visit him in his hospital in 1973. They were told by Soviet psychiatrists that Grigorenko had had at least one stroke in 1960–61 and that the arteriosclerotic brain disease which that stroke suggested had complicated and aggravated his persistent underlying paranoid condition.

The Psychiatric Problem

The essence of the Soviet case for Mr. Grigorenko's mental illness lies in the theory (1) that he had a condition that distorted his capacity to assess the world realistically, influenced his behavior beyond his control, and was evident not only in his behavior and thought but also in his temperament and other characteristics; and (2) that a paranoid condition caused him, during the early and mid-1960s, to make statements and commit acts that violated Soviet laws.

In order to evaluate Grigorenko's history and present psychiatric state, it is necessary to understand the meaning and implications of the Soviet theory of his illness. "Paranoid" conditions have always posed theoretical and clinical problems for psychiatrists everywhere. In general, the paranoid conditions align themselves along an extended clinical spectrum—beginning, near the normal end, with temporary suspiciousness and mistrust that can be based on misinterpretation of reality in reaction to certain circumstances, and ranging, in the direction of increasingly severe pathology, through paranoid personality, paranoia, paraphrenia or paranoid state, and paranoid schizophrenia.

These categories of paranoid psychopathology are somewhat arbitrarily defined and merge into each other, often imperceptibly, and the conditions probably have a variety of causes. Typically, in the conditions of paranoia that are more pathological than paranoid personality, the patient maintains delusional—which is to say, false and unalterable—beliefs about reality, either in general or with regard to specific concerns or situations. These beliefs become guiding themes in the person's life and tend to impair his or her capacity for discretion, judgment, and action. This becomes an increasingly dominant characteristic of the conditions arrayed along the paranoid spectrum the further one proceeds towards its highly pathological end.

The paranoid categories are somewhat arbitrarily defined, and a number of psychiatric theoreticians have proposed other names and typologies. The mildest clinical type of paranoia is probably *paranoid personality*, which, typically, is a condition that exhibits its first signs during youth, even childhood. The individual with a paranoid personality often lacks a sense of humor and tends to be egotistical, suspicious, resentful, meticulous, authoritarian, embittered, impatient, uncompromising, inflexible in his affairs and beliefs, highly argumentative, and, frequently, incapable of maintaining lasting relationships with others, whom he often distrusts. Such a person often seeks goals that are unrealizable and cannot tolerate criticism of his methods or stated beliefs. If he is a member of a group or an organization, he usually tries to dominate it, often in tyrannical ways.

These descriptions are essentially personality characteristics. There is usually no central, organized, delusional belief that is maintained at all costs. Because such a dominating belief is absent, it is an error to characterize a person with a paranoid personality as suffering from any psychosis. Therefore, such a person would ordinarily be considered legally responsible for any criminal acts that he might perform.

The border of psychosis probably exists at the arbitrary line between paranoid personality and *paranoia*, a condition first described by the German psychiatrist Emil Kraepelin (1856–1926). Kraepelin applied the term to persons with persistent, rigid, systematized delusions whose thinking is otherwise clear and well preserved. This condition, he said, is not characterized

193

by hallucinations. The individual may try to convince others to accept his delusional beliefs and may even attempt to hide the core of the delusion—which usually has to do with some organized attempt to persecute him—because he senses that others doubt it. He may try instead to engage others in some cause that is designed to counter the threat that is secretly feared.

Sometimes the delusional idea in paranoia may be one not of persecution but instead of grandiosity: The person may be convinced that he has remarkable, even superhuman powers. Such a person often feels aggrieved and finds ulterior motives in the actions or statements of others. In general, the characterological descriptions noted above for the paranoid personality are applicable in paranoia but may be more pronounced, at least in the arena related to the delusional idea.

Often, the person with paranoia is chronically sullen. He believes that a conspiracy is afoot, hints of which he finds everywhere. Such a person may eventually become depressed, even suicidal, if the feeling develops that there is an overwhelming threat from the outside and that it is impossible to overcome it. In general, such a person cannot evaluate the premises of his delusional system; he fastens upon minor details of an event or statement—details that he believes prove or in some other way bear upon his delusional system—and focuses upon those details or minor inferences, ignoring the context.

Kraepelin differentiated paranoia from the next, more serious condition on the paranoid spectrum, *paraphrenia*, in which the delusions are less well systemized and hallucinations occur. This condition is often, called "paranoid state." Finally, there is *paranoid schizophrenia*, which generally involves a disintegration of the personality, grossly inappropriate and bizarre responses to reality, and an active and unfettered external projection of thoughts that are experienced as hallucinations—voices, visions, or other false sensory experiences.

In the case of Grigorenko's two diagnoses of illness, it would appear on the basis of a simple inspection that by "paranoid development of the personality," the Serbsky psychiatrists were referring to what is described as paranoid personality. However, since that description applies to what is really a personality disorder and not a psychotic condition, it seems unlikely that that is quite the condition they meant. This assumption is supported by a recent Soviet textbook on forensic psychiatry, available in English and edited by two Serbsky psychiatrists—one of whom, G. V. Morozov, is now the director of the Serbsky Institute and was in 1969 one of Grigorenko's examiners. It contains a discussion of "psychopathy," a broadly defined category of mental illness which is said to be differentiable from the more serious mental illnesses primarily by the lack of psychotic symptoms. This category contains what are called in the United States "personality disorders" (such as paranoid personality) and neuroses. As the authors put it: "A distinguishing feature of psychopathy is its pronounced pathological nature, which hinders adaption of the person to his environment. . . . In the majority of cases, psychopaths are declared responsible (for criminal acts) and are subjected to the usual punitive measures."[6]

There are exceptions to this rule, to be sure, but only in the small minority of psychopaths who do have psychotic symptoms, such as delusions and hallucinations. By these Serbsky criteria, what has been described above as "paranoid personality" would probably not justify a finding of legal nonresponsibility, the kind of finding made in Grigorenko's case. Hence, Grigorenko seems to have been found to have a condition in the psychotic and paranoid range.

It seems likely that in their diagnoses the Soviets were referring, then, not to paranoid personality but rather to something akin to what is called in the West "paranoia." In part, this assumption is sustained by the first Serbsky diagnosis, which specifically noted the presence of "paranoid delusional [bredevoi] development of the personality." Presumably, bredevoi modified the diagnosis to indicate the presence of delusional—which is to say, psychotic— content. Certainly, in locating Grigorenko on the paranoid spectrum, they could not have gone beyond this category—into the realm of paraphrenia or paranoid schizophrenia—since there is no historical evidence of (nor any mention of the presence of) either hallucinations or any disintegration of the personality.

As it happens, true paranoia as a clinical category is said by almost all diagnosticians to be extremely rare. Nevertheless, it appears that this is the Western equivalent of the diagnostic category applied to Grigorenko by his Serbsky examiners.

In my own examination, I kept that category in mind in attempting to confirm or exclude the presence of mental illness at this time or at any previous time. However, in reviewing Grigorenko's history and in examining him directly, I also searched for characteristics of other, milder paranoid conditions and types, even the ones that are usually too mild to justify a finding of "legal nonresponsibility," either in the Soviet Union or elsewhere. In essence, I tried to give the Serbsky psychiatrists, the Soviet psychiatric system, and the Soviet forensic definitions the full benefit of the doubt. I was prepared to agree with a diagnosis of mental illness even if all I found was a condition or even a suggestion of a condition at the mild, nonpsychotic end of the paranoid range. And despite the evidence, I was prepared to accept that, in Soviet juridical and forensic practice, such mild conditions routinely constituted sufficient justification (1) for finding a defendant legally nonresponsible, (2) for barring him from participating in his defense at his own trial, and (3) for hospitalizing him involuntarily in an institution for the criminally insane.

The second condition that the Soviet psychiatrists in both Serbsky commissions had attributed to Grigorenko was arteriosclerosis, a term that is usually used interchangeably with atherosclerosis. It refers to the accumulation of fatty material on the interior walls of blood vessels causing a narrowing of the vessels and a reduction of blood flow to the organ served by the vessel, in this case the brain. The term "cerebral arteriosclerosis" is a diagnosis often given in cases where the intellectual capacity deteriorates with advancing age. This condition (generally called "senile dementia" by US neurologists) may have symptoms and signs of some of the paranoid conditions. In particular, delusions may arise, and there may be a certain amount of jealousy present. In addition, notions of grandeur may be observed, and there are often periods of confusion, restlessness, incoherence, headaches, and a clouding of consciousness. Besides these clinical features, which may or may not be present, there is usually some sign of a deterioration of intellectual function, which may become extremely pronounced. Characterologically, there may be signs (as in the paranoid conditions) of irritability, quarrelsomeness, obstinacy, and emotional instability. Usually the condition appears during the sixth or seventh decade of life.

The implication that must be drawn from the mention of arteriosclerosis in the two Serbsky reports is that this organic condition provoked or aggravated Grigorenko's underlying paranoid condition. Possibly, it is implied, the two conditions together resulted in a state in which Grigorenko was unable to make accurate judgments about reality and therefore could not control his behavior—in short, because of these conditions, he became psychotic and was therefore not legally responsible for his actions. Accordingly, in evaluating the Soviets' diagnostic theory, it would be necessary to look for medical and psychiatric signs and symptoms suggesting not only the presence of "cerebral arteriosclerosis" but, more specifically, a senile dementing process causing psychosis. As Dr. Norman Geschwind, the consulting neurologist, pointed out, confirmation of that diagnosis would require the finding of strong suggestions of intellectual deterioration, confusion, and other compromises of higher brain functioning resulting from damage to the brain. If the other meaning of "cerebral arteriosclerosis" is assumed—a condition of intellectual or emotional deterioration resulting from multiple strokes—then confirmation would require the finding of not only behavioral changes but also clear-cut evidence of brain damage caused by strokes.

Interviews, Examinations, and Findings

In my formal interview with Grigorenko, I tried as much as I could to resolve the question of his "paranoid traits." I paid special attention to the history, development, and nature of his oppositionist acts and theories, his motivations, and his sense of himself, his cause, his power, and his capacities. In asking my questions, I tried to bring into the open any paranoid, grandiose, or other pathological trends or characteristics, psychotic or not, that might be present. I wanted to clarify why he was willing to endanger himself; for which ideals he was willing to court punishment; under which conditions he felt it possible to speak out; whether he could assess the world around him and its possibilities for danger; his capacity to change his views and to distinguish between important struggles and less important ones; his ability to organize and concentrate his oppositionist energies; and his assessment of his role, his accomplishments, and his life.

Grigorenko is a large man of distinguished bearing with a shaven head and a slow, somewhat shuffling gait. Sitting down to face me after completing an earlier, two-hour psychiatric interview, he appeared tired but indicated an eagerness to answer all questions. In response to direct questions, he was able to retell aspects of his history with great precision, and he reacted to the content of his memories with a wide range of appropriate responses, ranging from sadness and regret to evident enjoyment, and from wistful reflection to obvious humor. He established a relationship with me quickly, easily, and fully and was able to share with me his most distressing concerns as well as his jokes about the reversals, triumphs, and ironies of his life. He was generous with me when I asked questions whose answers should have been self-evident, and at no time did he exhibit any sense of annoyance, distraction, impatience, or haughtiness.

Grigorenko took pains to answer questions fully and openly. In fact, he offered examples, reflections, concerns, and experiences that he obviously knew were somehow psychiatrically important—that could be construed, under particular circumstances, as symptoms or signs of certain psychiatric conditions, and that, in fact, had been so construed by his psychiatric examiners in the Soviet Union. Nevertheless, he ofered up such material freely and frequently.

In the main, Grigorenko spoke slowly, carefully, and thoughtfully; but the rapidity of his speech varied according to its content. Despite the stresses of the day, he appeared alert throughout the examination, and although he yawned from time to time, he responded to the questions put to him with understanding, perceptivity, and without undue delay. At no time was there evidence of any fluctuation of consciousness.

I discussed with Grigorenko his specific political views. In fact, my first challenge to him in the interview had to do with the content of his views during the mid-1960s, and that challenge provoked him to some spirited reflection on his former ideas about Leninism and his revisions of those ideas during his confinement in a psychiatric hospital in 1965. It appeared that the depth of his feeling in response to this subject had to do, at least in part, with the past insistence by Soviet psychiatrists that his political ideas were somehow inadequate or that he was characterologically unable to change or moderate them. When I reminded him of his Leninist position and of his change in that position in 1965, a change he had recorded in a memoir, he acknowledged that he had decided then that it was a fundamental error to rely on the dogma of Leninism. He said that in thinking about the matter during his hospitalization, he had decided that he had been naive. He said that it was necessary to take the present into account, that it would be impossible to go back 50 years. That revision, he added, represented a drastic change in his views. At that time, he explained, "I started to consider Leninism a delusion. . . . I left the hospital with the idea that one had to fight in the open and appeal to the laws. I gave up the conspirational, underground way of achieving change."

As Grigorenko spoke about that change in his views, he grew increasingly animated. Although I attempted to ask him about other matters, he continued to return to the topic. Clearly, it had affected him, and he felt the need for continued elaboration and clarification. However, there was no evidence of an inability to leave the subject of the discussion or of an obsessional, perseverative quality to his answer.

Much of the interview was taken up with an exploration of the motivations for Grigorenko's dissent and risk-taking acts, the clarity of his purpose, and the sense he has and has had of himself—the sense, that is, of his personal power and capacities.

Why [did you persist in your struggle]?
The Soviet psychiatrists asked me the same question. It's not a
personal cause. It's a social, communal cause. Someone always has to
start. I always like to repeat the verse by Yevtushenko written when
he was still a real poet. He wrote, "When lack of talent summons
itself to fight for truth, then talent, I am ashamed of you." . . . This
system of government should not be tolerated by people, but it never
happens that everyone rises against it. There always have to be
people who start—then others will follow. And those who start,
regardless of whether or not they are talented, or have special
abilities—they become a slogan, a banner, for those who follow. This
places a particular responsibility on them and they should not
abandon the cause. You are responsible not just for yourself, but also

for the cause in the eyes of those who follow. During my life, in my faithful service to Communism, I caused a lot of damage to my people, and I wanted, at least in my remaining days, to repair it. . . . What's the sense of living one extra year if you continue in the fraud of not facing things? It's better to live the rest of your life creatively so that you will not be ashamed in the eyes of your grandchildren. I have always considered the inner impulse to serve as a vocation inspired—instilled in my soul—by God.

Why in your soul? After all, only a few people did what you did.

No, this is not true. It's just that I became known. I just was lucky that I became known, mostly as a result of the campaign in my defense. There are many who did more than I did, but no one knows about them.

Did God put it in their souls, too?

I think so. I think that Providence plays a greater role in the lives of people than we think.

Do you think that you have some kind of special relationship with God?

No. Even though I firmly believe that God exists in the world, and that there is some Supreme Reason, I unfortunately cannot absorb myself fully in prayer. . . . Some people can detach themselves and allow themselves to be fully absorbed in prayer, but I can't. For example, I feel that I can't proselytize using the name of God—I can mention it in a private conversation, but I think that there are people chosen by God for that.

I questioned Grigorenko further in order to see if I could find any grandiose trends—any sense of himself as somehow superhuman, divine, possessed of extraordinary powers or knowledge, or being more important than he could possibly be. His answers, however, consistently suggested that his sense of himself was a modest one, that he viewed himself as relatively unimportant in the cosmic scheme of things, and that he felt that irony and chance rather than some special destiny had fashioned his prominence and his fate.

Finally, I attempted to gauge Grigorenko's capacity to assess reality, both now and in the past—his capacity to assess the nature of the historical moment and to respond to it, as well as his capacity to appreciate danger from without and to moderate his behavior in response to that danger. I again brought up the event that had precipitated his political troubles in 1961—the speech that he made as a Party delegate criticizing certain official Party policies.

In 1961, when you made that speech, it was after all, after the era of Stalin. The period of repression had eased; and while, obviously, it was dangerous to speak out, it was not a capital offense. Would you have said the same thing then years earlier, during Stalin's terror—during the late 1940s or early fifties? Or, to put it another way, what stopped you [from speaking out then]?

199

At that time I couldn't have made such a statement because I didn't measure up to it. I was a faithful Communist. The difference between 1951 and 1961 is not just a difference of ten years, but the fact that the Twentieth Party Congress took place in 1956, from which I learned that what I had considered to be local mistakes were really widespread perversions of the party line. And after 1956, I had another five years for observation and reflection. This is the way I was able to become worthy of making the statement that I made (in 1961). And as for what you said [that Grigorenko had organized his underground group in 1963 knowing that it was not then a capital crime], Dr. Reich, let me tell you that I was convinced then that if I was found out I would be killed.

So if your understanding had been the same in 1951 as it had been in 1961, would you have done what you did later: You would have done that under Stalin, too?

(Smiling) As an old historian, a military historian, I have to object to that question. One cannot say what would have happened if the past was other than the way it was. I was not different then. I was the way I was. And whether I could have been different under different circumstances is just a matter of speculation.

Throughout the interview, it was clear Grigorenko's cognitive capacities were fully intact. He was well oriented in all spheres, and his memory was exceptionally good about both the remote and recent past. At several points he corrected me on certain dates or events; those corrections were appropriate and sound. His fund of information, his intellectual resources, and his capacity to concentrate and to think abstractly were unflawed. His judgment regarding past events as well as his present situation was excellent. And his insight into his motivations was acute.

Conclusions

There is no evidence that Grigorenko is suffering from any significant mental illness or impairment of thinking or intellect at this time, and there is no good evidence that he has suffered from such illness or impairment at any time in the past. In particular, there is no evidence of any mental illness in the paranoid range, even of the mildest sort. Although there is evidence, on the basis of physical findings, of atherosclerotic disease, there is no sign that this condition has significantly compromised Grigorenko's intellectual or emotional capabilities, or that it has formed or determined his behavior or mood.

In reviewing Grigorenko's life prior to 1961 (the year in which he committed the political trespass that precipitated both his decline in the official world and his rise in the dissident one), a picture emerges of a proud, forceful, energetic, and achieving man who expected the most and the best not only of himself but also of everyone around him: those who worked for him, those for whom he worked, and the military and political figures who held the safety and fate of his country in their hands. He expressed those characteristics consistently and always within reason. Taking the theory of the Revolution and of his society seriously, he immersed himself in the classics of Marxism-Leninism and attempted to participate, in his role as a responsible Soviet citizen, in the development and strengthening of the country he loved. During his life he developed understandings of Communist ideology that were within the mainstream of the approaches used at various times by official Soviet ideologists. At no time, either before 1961 or after, was there any evidence of strange, bizarre, or reckless behavior associated with or driven by some idea concerning the reformation of society or related to a special role he felt for himself in such a reformation.

During the pre-1961 period, two events particularly stand out as fore-shadowing his tendency to defend and act upon his convictions and principles. The first took place in 1941, when he criticized Stalin's planning for the war. The second event, in 1949, was his confrontation with his academy over his implied criticisms contained in his master's thesis, of prominent military figures. In neither act did he behave recklessly. In the first, he had simply had a private conversation with someone whom he had assumed could be trusted, understanding the possible dangers of speaking out critically against the leader of the country on the first, disastrous day of World War II. In the second instance, he maintained an exchange of views with his thesis adviser, without making a public issue of it, until that adviser finally convinced him, through reasoning, that it was more important for him to get his degree than to make his admittedly valid point. This last experience illustrates Grigorenko's capacity for flexibility and compromise.

The events surrounding Grigorenko following his speech in 1961 can in large measure be understood in light of that speech and the circumstances that resulted from it. It seems clear that the speech itself was the result of Grigorenko's longstanding policy of speaking and acting according to his conscience. The conference was a closed one. He felt himself in the right in expressing his views within it, particularly since there had recently been revelations about massive deviations from stated Soviet principles under Stalin—revelations that had been made officially—and the development of a political "thaw" that permitted previously sensitive matters to be discussed. Grigorenko's presentation was probably forceful, experienced by others present as beyond the pale of acceptable criticism, and it presumably suggested to his listeners that he was somehow politically unreliable or even dangerous. Receiving an official reprimand—and, in effect, losing position and influence at the prime of his professional life by being transferred to the Soviet Far East—Grigorenko seems to have concluded, apparently correctly, that open criticism would not be tolerated and that he would inevitably suffer for it.

It was at that time that Grigorenko engaged in his first clandestine activity, forming his Union for the Revival of Leninism and distributing leaflets. He understood very clearly, he says, that this was an illegal, dangerous act. He fully expected that he would be punished for it, possibly by death. The leaflets contained information that was in no way bizarre or extreme. Following his arrest, investigation, and incarceration in a mental hospital during 1965 and the loss of his officer's pension, Grigorenko focused his substantial energies not only on the goals of social justice and democratization but also on the goals of personal justice and self-justification. The series of letters and demands about his lost pension and about the punishments he received, as well as his complaints about the hospitalization, can all be understood as reactions to the challenges arising from his environment.

Again, there is no delusional thread that can be seen to run through this period of Grigorenko's life or to extend from an earlier period. There is no evidence that his words and his acts were a result of some exalted sense of himself or his place in Soviet society or of some sense of unreal conspiracy. Nor is there any evidence that any of his words or acts were produced by someone who was incapable of adequately assessing reality or of controlling his thoughts or behavior.

In addition, there is no evidence of any mental changes, sudden or slow, that might have been caused by a cerebrovascular accident at any time. Even when a stroke probably did take place, in 1972, there is no evidence of any significant or lasting compromise of Grigorenko's intellectual or emotional functioning. The assertion, made to visiting Western psychiatrists in 1973, that Grigorenko had suffered from a stroke in 1950–51 could not be substantiated; but in any case there is no evidence of any characterological or behavioral change at that time that might have been caused by such a cerebral event.

In all of Grigorenko's history, there is no evidence of signs or symptoms of a schizophrenic disorder, paranoid or not, chronic or acute. In particular, Grigorenko never experienced hallucinations of any type, personality dis-organization, systematized or fragmented delusions, or any compromise in his capacity to relate to others in intimate or social ways. Although demanding the most from others, all evidence indicates that he has always been able to establish strong and warm relations with them. His behavior as a father and as a husband, which I witnessed in February 1978, exemplifies that of a devoted and loving parent and a faithful and caring spouse.

The consultants' findings confirm and strengthen these conclusions. In his full neurological examination, Professor Geschwind found that there was evidence of turbulent blood flow in Grigorenko's right internal carotid artery, a finding that almost certainly implies blockage of that particular blood vessel. He noted that in 1972 Grigorenko probably suffered a small stroke that caused a loss of vision in the right eye and some mild signs of weakness and sensory loss on the left side of the body. He stressed, however, that he found no evidence of intellectual or emotional changes as a result of this slight damage to the brain.

Professor Geschwind's neurological conclusions were supported by Dr. Jones's findings from neurospychological testing. After a very extensive battery of tests, Dr. Jones found Grigorenko to be an individual of superior intellectual capacities, with verbal intellectual abilities higher not only than those of his age but also of the population as a whole without reference to age. This superior function, she stressed, ranged across a variety of areas, including fund of information, verbal concept formation and abstraction ability, judgment, reasoning, and mental arithmetic. She also found his memory to be superior, and his capacity for verbal learning and retention "especially impressive." Dr. Jones did note that in one area, visuoperceptual and constructional functioning, it was possible that Grigorenko's capacities had diminished with age. She stressed, however, that in this realm his abilities and skills are fully average for his age level and that even here he does not display a clinical degree of impairment.

Finally, she pointed out that if Grigorenko had suffered any brain damage as a result of cerebrovascular disease, that damage was very minimal and probably not sustained earlier than 1971 or 1972—and, in that case, could not have been a basis for any behavioral changes attributed to that kind of damage during the periods under consideration in the Soviet diagnoses.

Irene Stiver, the consultant psychologist, supported and strengthened the overall findings through her psychiatric interview. After three hours of projective testing, Dr. Stiver was impressed by Grigorenko's full range of emotionality as well as his highly developed capacity for humor, laughter, and irony. She found him to be a man of superior intelligence, highly creative, and remarkably flexible in his thinking. She noted that he did have a heightened perceptiveness, but that, unlike the paranoid person, who is fixed in his interpretation of what he believes he perceives, Grigorenko had an ability to shift his point of view, an ability that protected him from distortions of perception. Overall, she found him to be an idealist, with a strong conscience, who feels responsible for others.

Finally, the biometrics research staff at the New York State Psychiatric Institute filled in the Psychiatric Status Schedule, a diagnostic questionnaire, on the basis of the interview videotapes. After applying their research diagnostic criteria, they concluded that although Grigorenko did display signs of mild depression, he did not suffer from a diagnosable mental illness.

The main task of the psychiatrists and consultants who examined Grigorenko was to look for signs of illness. What we found was a man who, ironically, reminded us in some ways of the patient in Soviet descriptions. But in our judgment, their version of Grigorenko was consistently askew. For where they claimed obsession, we found perserverance; where they cited delusion, we found rationality; where they identified psychotic recklessness, we found committed devotion; and where they diagnosed pathology, we found health.

Notes and References

1. In 1975 I published a study of the diagnostic implications of the dominant Soviet approach to schizophrenia ("The Spectrum Concept of Schizophrenia: Problems for Diagnostic Practice", *Archives of General Pschiatry* 32:489–498).

2. *New York Times*, 19 April 1978, p. A4.

3. The examinations themselves were held in several locations on four separate dates. Dr. Stone examined Mr. Grigorenko psychiatrically for about three hours in Cambridge, Massachusetts, on 11 December 1978; Dr. Geschwind neurologically in Boston on the same day for over two hours; Dr. Stiver psychologically in Belmont, Massachusetts, on 12 December for three hours; and Dr. Jones neuropsychologically, also in Belmont and also on the same day, for two more hours. Not having completed her examination, Dr. Jones administered six more hours of neuropsychological tests in New York City on 18 December. Finally, on 21 December, Dr. Kolb and I met with Mr. Grigorenko at the New York State Psychiatric Institute, where we spent over five hours with him, three of them videotaped. The use of the Psychiatric Institute's videotape laboratories was arranged by Dr. Kolb, who felt strongly that the actual interviews should be available for verification by any interested party, including any Soviet psychiatrist. Also seeking as much verification as possible in our own examinations procedures, Dr. Kolb based much of his own interview on the Psychiatric Status Schedule, a research diagnostic questionnaire designed to identify mental illness.

4. Walter Reich, "Grigorenko Gets a Second Opinion," *The New York Times Magazine*, 13 May 1979, pp. 18ff.

5. The conclusions of the 1964 Serbsky commission were noted in the psychiatric report of the 1969 Tashkent psychiatric commission, which was headed by Prof. Fyodor F. Detengoff and which found Grigorenko to be healthy. The entire report of that 1964 commission is not available in the West. The two reports that are available, apparently in full—the one by Detengoff's Tashkent commission and the one by the second (1969) Serbsky commission—were included as testimony before the US Senate's Subcommittee to Investigate the

Administration of the Internal Security Act and Other Internal Security Laws of the Committee on the Judiciary. The subcommittee, which held hearings on the abuse of Soviet psychiatry on 26 September 1972, issued a compendium of that testimony under the title *Abuse of Psychiatry for Political Repression in the USSR* (Washington, D.C.: U.S. Government Printing Office, 1972). The documents relating to Grigorenko, including the extant psychiatric commission reports, are on pp. 47–107 of that volume.

6. See *Forensic Psychiatry: A Translation of a Text Approved by the RSFSR Ministry of Higher and Secondary Specialized Education*, edited by G. V. Morozov and I. M. Kalashnik, with an introduction by David L. Bazelon (White Plains, N.Y.: International Arts and Sciences Press, 1970), pp. 393 and 412. The chapter on "Psychopathy," by O. V. Kerbikov and N. I. Felinskaia, is on pp. 393–413. The textbook was originally published in Russian as *Sudebnaia psikhiatriia* (Moscow: Juridical Literature Publishing House, 1967).

Chapter 9

The World of Soviet Psychiatry

Walter Reich

This chapter contains an account of a meeting between Walter Reich, an American psychiatrist, and the most important members of the Soviet psychiatric establishment. The meeting, which took place in Moscow at the Institute of Psychiatry of the Academy of Medical Sciences, touched upon the Soviet psychiatric response to dissent and the role that Soviet psychiatric theories have played in that response. It is significant that the originator of many of those theories—Andrei Snezhnevsky, who is not only the most powerful Soviet psychiatrist but also one of the persons most often criticized in the West for abusing psychiatry—was present at, and a prime actor in, the meeting.

The building in one of Moscow's older neighborhoods seemed ordinary enough to me, familiar in the drab way so many psychiatric hospitals are familiar, its grounds tended by patients and its gates manned by guards. Yet there was something special about this particular building, something that had drawn me to it from half a world away. It was the source of theories of mental illness that, since the late 1960s, had been applied to Soviet dissidents with results that shocked the West. And it was the headquarters of the author of those theories, whose life and work I had been studying for a decade. Waiting for me inside that building was the man in charge of the Soviet Union's psychiatric profession, Dr. Andrei V. Snezhnevsky.

I was hurried past a dark lobby, through long corridors, into a bright office. The white-coated man who stood up behind his ornate desk, smiling broadly, had not changed much from the last time I had seen him, five years

This article is printed here in edited and updated form with permission of the author and publisher from the *New York Times Magazine*, 30 January 1983.

earlier, at the 1977 congress of the World Psychiatric Association in Hawaii. He and his delegation had come under strong attack at that meeting, and the conference had voted to condemn "the systematic abuse of psychiatry for political purposes in the USSR." In the interim, Western concern over psychiatric abuse in the Soviet Union had only grown, and the Russians were in danger of being suspended or even expelled from the international psychiatric organization at its scheduled conference in Vienna in July 1983.

Snezhnevsky's deputy, Dr. Marat Vartanyan, entered the room briskly with two other psychiatrists. A robust man of about 50, Vartanyan looked younger than he did in Hawaii; he had slimmed down by at least 30 pounds, his movements were faster and surer, and he was dressed in a well-fitting pinstripe suit of Western cut. He had developed, in those five years, an appearance of prosperous success.

"You remember Dr. Reich," Vartanyan said to Snezhnevsky. "You met him in Honolulu."

Snezhnevsky acknowledged the memory. He arranged us around his elegant conference table. His secretary rushed in with a delicate china service.

Though 78 now, and heavier than the last time we met, Snezhnevsky still commanded the look his former students and colleagues had described to me as *sardonichesky*—scornful, derisive, sardonic. It was a look, I remembered, made up of a dismissive grin that would burst into a mocking laugh the moment he would hear something he didn't like.

The Soviet psychiatrists asked me about my own recent professional activities, and I told them of my work on a research conference on the effectiveness of psychotherapy. Vartanyan smiled tolerantly. Snezhnevsky guffawed: Psychotherapy—now there's something that needs some research!

There is, in fact, little of what Americans know as psychotherapy in Soviet psychiatry. Nor is that state of affairs accidental. Soviet distrust of psycho-therapy has been strong ever since the 1930s, when the ideas of Sigmund Freud, the originator of insight-oriented talk therapies, were declared inconsistent with Marxist science.

But there are other ways, too, in which Soviet psychiatry differs from its American counterpart. In the United States, psychiatric treatment has become acceptable enough during the last decades for people in emotional distress to seek it out. In the Soviet Union, the need for psychiatric care is more likely to be seen as a cause for shame. Treatment there emphasizes medication rather than talk.

The concepts of mental illness are, in some respects, similar in the two countries. The same illnesses exist in the two populations roughly with the same frequency. But their definitions differ, as do, sometimes, their presumed causes. While American practitioners, on the whole, tend to pay greater

Dr. Andrei V. Snezhnevsky, director of the Institute of Psychiatry of the USSR Academy of Medical Sciences in Moscow. (Courtesy of Walter Reich.)

attention to illnesses generally known as neuroses, their Soviet colleagues concern themselves to a greater extent with the more severe psychiatric conditions known as psychoses.

In recent years, Soviet psychiatry had devoted the greatest part of its energy to the most important and prevalent of the psychoses, schizophrenia. And, in large measure, it has been through his concept and definition of schizophrenia that Snezhnevsky has transformed the Soviet psychiatric profession—transformed it and taken ownership of it. He has managed to do so not because of a ukase from above but because his researchers, students, and followers, who together comprise what has come to be known as the

Moscow school of psychiatry, have spread his teachings into every corner of the country and have made them the standard and genuinely accepted Soviet approach to the understanding, diagnosis, and treatment of mental illness.

Coffee was served, the finest I had tasted in the Soviet Union. There were linen napkins, good brandy, black caviar. The large, high-ceilinged office was appointed with prerevolutionary antiques, oriental rugs, leather chairs, figurines. There were pictures of Snezhnevsky's Russian medical heroes on the wall. A large photo of Ernest Hemingway in a turtleneck sweater dominated the room. "My favorite writer," Snezhnevsky offered. "He's very popular in our country." A bust of Lenin watched from afar.

The meeting had been arranged for their sake as well as for mine.

The charge of psychiatric abuse was a long-standing one. For years, Soviet psychiatrists had been accused in the West of diagnosing as mentally ill political dissidents they knew to be mentally well. According to both Western critics and Soviet dissidents, the KGB—especially after it was taken over in 1967 by Yuri V. Andropov—had regularly referred dissidents to psychiatrists for such diagnoses in order to avoid embarrassing public trials and to discredit dissent as the product of sick minds. Once in psychiatric hospitals, usually special institutions for the criminally insane, the dissidents were said to be treated with particular cruelty—for example, given injections that caused abscesses, convulsions, and torpor, or wrapped in wet canvas that shrank tightly upon drying.

In 1971, at the World Psychiatric Association's fifth congress in Mexico City, Western psychiatrists made their first attempt to censure their Soviet colleagues. But the accusations of psychiatric abuse were new, the campaign was unorganized, and Snezhnevsky, who led the Soviet delegation, was unscathed. "The charges," he said in rebuttal, "were a Cold War maneuver carried out at the hands of experts."

At the 1977 world congress in Honolulu, Snezhnevsky again defended his country's psychiatric practices; but by then the accusations were familiar and the sentiments they aroused were strong, and the censure motion passed by a narrow majority. Snezhnevsky returned home wounded, with members of his delegation blaming their defeat on the "Zionists."[1]

An even greater setback seemed to await the Russians at the association's seventh congress in Vienna in July 1983. At the time of our meeting, in May 1982, there were strong indications that two resolutions would be presented before the World Psychiatric Association. One, then under discussion by members of the national psychiatric association of the United States, proposed that the Soviet association, the All-Union Society of Psychiatrists and Neuropathologists, be suspended. The second, offered by the psychiatric association of Britain, proposed that the Soviet association be expelled.

It was, I think, primarily because of the Soviet authorities' desire to avert such action that Snezhnevsky and Vartanyan agreed to meet with me. They knew, to be sure, that I had written critically of Soviet psychiatry. Nevertheless, with official scientific exchanges between the United States and the Soviet Union all but severed in the wake of the Soviet invasion of Afghanistan, any contact with an American psychiatrist—even one who had come to Moscow, as I had, on a private visit—would serve to demonstrate that Soviet psychiatrists were reasonable professionals willing to discuss differences and explain their views.

However, I also believe Snezhnevsky had his own reasons for wanting to see me. He had long been under attack in the West as an exemplar of psychiatric abuse in the Soviet Union. He had himself diagnosed or been involved in a number of famous dissident cases, including those of the mathematician Leonid Plyushch and the biologist Zhores Medvedev, and he had been accused of cynically devising a system of diagnoses that could be bent for political purposes. Seeing himself as a great clinician and theoretician, heir and contributor to a psychiatric tradition stretching back to nineteenth-century German medicine, Snezhnevsky had often complained bitterly about these accusations, which tarnished his prestige abroad and even among some of his Soviet colleagues. Moreover, he was facing the possibility of being stripped of his honorary fellowship in the American Psychiatric Association, conferred on him twelve years before, in better times.

But if the meeting was an opportunity for Soviet psychiatry and for Snezhnevsky, it was also one for me. I had been following reports of Soviet psychiatric abuse since the early 1970s, soon after they first reached the West. Disturbed by the news that fellow professionals were distorting their knowledge and their trust, and wanting to understand what had happened and why, I interviewed many of the dissidents who were then beginning to emigrate from the Soviet Union, including dissidents who had been diagnosed and hospitalized as mentally ill. In time, I met Soviet emigrés who were psychiatrists themselves—some of them dissidents escaping political trouble but most of them people who had simply wanted to leave. Among the latter, several had worked as scientists and clinicians at the heart of Soviet psychiatry, either in Snezhnevsky's institute or in other important research centers.

Soon enough, it became apparent that the experience of Soviet psychiatry had a lot to teach—not only about Soviet political repression but about the ways in which people who have spent their lives in the Soviet environment think, talk, and perceive each other. And, too, it had a lot to teach about the vulnerabilities of psychiatry to misuse wherever it is practiced. Some of the characteristics of Soviet psychiatry that have resulted in the misdiagnoses of dissidents were distortions of standard psychiatric logic, theory, and practice.

In short, the story of Soviet psychiatry was a case study in what could go wrong in a profession and in a society.

What emerged most forcefully from my interviews and research was that one factor—Snezhnevsky's theory of schizophrenia—accounted more than any other for the diagnoses and hospitalizations of Soviet political dissidents. It was that theory that I wanted to discuss with its author. In going to Moscow, my goal was to raise the questions about his approach that had troubled me ever since I began to study it and to see what he had to say in response.

I called Vartanayan from my room at the Intourist Hotel the morning after my arrival in Moscow.

"Yes, Dr. Reich," Vartanayan responded eagerly, in his fluent English. "Of course we should meet. I'll arrange it right away."

He said he had just returned from a trip, and only that morning had come across a month-old letter from a mutual acquaintance, an American, informing him that I would be arriving in Moscow and calling him.

The black Volga sedan he sent for me the following week waited outside my hotel. The chauffeur drove wordlessly, crossing the Moscow River into the old Zamoskvorechiye section of Moscow. Turning at a guardhouse, we passed through a gate and entered the precincts of the Kashchenko Psychiatric Hospital, on whose wooded grounds the Institute of Psychiatry of the Soviet Academy of Medical Sciences is situated. The driver stopped, and I found myself in front of the institute's main building, a building whose inhabitants I had been studying from afar for so many years.

I had not brought a tape recorder to the meeting, and none, so far as I could see, was used. The following account is based primarily on a summary that I set to paper immediately upon returning to my hotel. The quotations and paraphrased exchanges are as faithful to what was said as I could make them. Besides Snezhnevsky and Vartanyan, the meeting was attended by Dr. Ruben Nadzharov, Snezhnevsky's clinical deputy, and Dr. Andrei Pyatnitsky, who was in charge of the institute's international activities. In the main, I spoke in English, with Vartanyan translating. The first question I asked Snezhnevsky and Vartanyan had to do with an article that had appeared in *Pravda* a week before I left for the Soviet Union. The article reported that Snezhnevsky's institute was to be transformed into a much larger Center for Health and Psychiatry, which would contain three institutes, one of them devoted to the problem of preventive psychiatry.[2]

I asked my Soviet hosts which psychiatric illnesses they thought could be prevented. One set of preventable illnesses, they answered, is made up of "borderline" cases—persons whose illnesses were relatively mild, without the symptoms of a psychotic break with reality, such as hallucinations or delusions,

Features of the Snezhnevsky Course Forms

Course forms	Continous			Periodic	Shiftlike		
Subtypes	Sluggish (mild)	Paranoid (moderate)	Malignant (severe)		Mild	Moderate	Severe
Some characteristics	Neurotic: self-consciousness; introspectiveness; obsessive doubts; conflicts with parental and other authorities; "reformism"	Paranoid; delusions; hallucinations; "parasitic life style"	Early onset; unremitting; overwhelming	Acute attacks; fluctuations in mood; confusion	Neurotic, with affective coloring; social contentiousness; philosophical concerns; self-absorption	Acute paranoid	Catatonia; delusions; prominent mood changes

Adapted from Walter Reich, in *Psychiatric Ethics*, edited by S. Bloch and P. Chodoff. © 1981, Oxford University Press.

that are typical of what has been known for seven decades of schizophrenia. This gave me an opportunity to challenge Snezhnevsky's concept of that illness—or set of illnesses, since there may be several schizophrenic conditions that display similar symptoms but have separate (and, in large measure, unknown) causes, probably both biological and environmental.

Snezhnevsky has argued that there are three main forms of schizophrenia. In the "continuous" form, he has said, the illness grows progressively worse. In the "recurrent" or "periodic" form, there are acute episodes of illness but, after each episode, the patient returns to health. And in the "shiftlike" form, there are also acute episodes, but the patient usually emerges from each episode more damaged than before, and his condition progressively worsens. Each of these states of illness, according to Snezhnevsky, had a broad range of severity. Thus, a person could suffer from a "malignant" type of "continuous" schizophrenia, in which there is very rapid mental deterioration, or, at the opposite end of the clinical spectrum, from a very mild type, which Snezhnevsky has called "sluggish."

It is this category of "sluggish schizophrenia" that has been most prominently used in dissident cases. But it has been commonly employed in everyday Soviet psychiatric practice as well. What is most troubling about it is that, by Snezhnevsky's criteria, "sluggish schizophrenia" may be diagnosed as such on the basis of very mild, nonpsychotic characteristics of behavior—characteristics that would not fit into the West's definition of *psychotic* and could even be considered normal.

Also disquieting is the quality of the research that was carried out by the institute's staff after Snezhnevsky became its director in 1962, research designed to prove his theories valid. The researchers' strategy was to examine the relatives of schizophrenic patients to see if they, too, displayed any psychiatric abnormalities, particularly schizophrenic ones. If the researchers did find such abnormalities, they almost always concluded that the relatives either had the same Snezhnevskyan form of schizophrenia as the original patient or some milder version of it. In other words, if the original patient had been found to suffer from "shiftlike" schizophrenia, then, if he had schizophrenic relatives, those relatives would almost invariably be found to have the same "shiftlike" form of the illness. And if he had relatives who, though not schizophrenic, displayed certain psychopathological traits, those traits were found to be similar, in some sense, to the symptoms and other characteristics that, Snezhnevsky had taught, were typically displayed by shiftlike schizophrenics.

Hundreds of patients and thousands of relatives, including children of schizophrenic patients, were examined in these studies. Theoretically, the studies provided remarkable validation of Snezhnevsky's concepts, since they seemed to demonstrate to a very significant extent that the forms of schizophrenia he had described "bred true"—that is, were hereditarily (which is to say genetically, and therefore biologically) distinct.

If this were correct, it would represent a revolution in psychiatry. Many psychiatric theoreticians, particularly in Europe, have sought to classify different forms of schizophrenia on the basis of the patients' clinical characteristics—that is, on the basis of the way they talk and behave. Thus, in the most widely used classification scheme, paranoid schizophrenics are distinguished from, say, catatonic schizophrenics on the grounds that, while the two forms of the illness share certain characteristics, the first is characterized especially by one set of symptoms, such as hallucinations, extreme suspiciousness, and grandiosity, while the second is more classically characterized by pronounced stupor or excitement.

But it has never been possible to prove that those two forms of illness breed true. It has not been found that if, for instance, a paranoid schizophrenic has a schizophrenic cousin, that cousin will invariably be afflicted with the paranoid variety of the illness. Snezhnevsky's researchers, however, left the clear impression that their chief had discovered clinical principles in accordance with which any schizophrenic can be assigned to one of three categories of schizophrenia, each having a distinct genetic basis.

When my hosts began to describe the work on "borderline" conditions being planned for the new center—conditions that seemed to me to be indistinguishable from some of the mild types of schizophrenia in Snezhnevsky's classification scheme, particularly the "sluggish"—I saw the opportunity to challenge them about Snezhnevsky's theories and about the research that had been designed to prove those theories true.

I started with the research. As far as I was concerned, I said, their institute's studies were unacceptable: The results were too perfect and the methods too flawed. I pointed out that, in the family studies, the psychiatrists who had diagnosed the original patients were the same ones who diagnosed the relatives and knew who was related to whom. They were not, in other words, experimentally "blind," as they should have been by commonly accepted principles of research methodology. And, therefore, it was just too easy for them, even if they were honest, to be swayed by their mission to prove Snezhnevsky right—to be swayed enough, at any rate, to discern the same form of schizophrenia in both patient and relative.

After all, I pointed out, the researchers were testing their own director's theories, theories upon which he was staking his international reputation. Many of the studies were of Snezhnevsky's own design or had been developed at his direct inspiration. Some of the researchers were working toward advanced degrees, and getting those degrees depended on the success of their research. Others were just beginning their careers at the institute and wanted to stay on the permanent staff. A momentum of research findings developed, all moving in the same direction—that of "proving" Snezhnevsky's theories. In the midst of such a uniform and focused culture of validation, the pressure on researchers to prove yet another Snezhnevskyan category true must have been considerable. And that pressure could hardly have been eased by the fact that the *Korsakov Journal of Neuropathology and Psychiatry*, the only psychiatric periodical in the Soviet Union—the only such periodical in which they could publish their findings—happened to have as its editor none other than Andrei Snezhnevsky.

"Look," I said to Vartanyan, who, as I understood it, had not been personally involved in this research, "you're a scientist. You understand that the material of psychiatry can be very vague, and that even the most honest researcher's objectivity is stretched beyond acceptable limits if he's testing a hypothesis that was developed by his own director and that is the accepted and dominant hypothesis in his environment. You understand that, under such conditions, researchers have to protect their work against their own

Dr. Andrei V. Snezhnevsky (left) and Dr. Marat E. Vartanyan. (Courtesy of Walter Reich.)

biases in every way possible. But in these studies, no such protection was put into force."

Vartanyan shrugged. He said the studies I had described were over and done with and new studies, more sophisticated and reliable, and focusing on other matters, were under way.

I sat up. Vartanyan seemed to be distancing himself from his chief's theories. But his chief, unaware of this ripple in the conversation—since Vartanyan had not translated his own response to me—continued to maintain the sardonic smile that had animated his face for most of our talk. I smiled, too, but at Vartanyan, hoping to elicit from him some confirmation of subtle disloyalty. He did not smile back.

I went on to question the clinical usefulness of Snezhnevsky's ideas. Even if his diagnostic system were valid, I said, it would be too dangerous to use. It was too broad, too inclusive, too likely to result in the application of the schizophrenic label to persons with other illnesses, such as the "borderline" conditions his new prevention institute was planning to study.

Perhaps, I said, some relatives of schizophrenics exhibit mild symptoms because they have a mild version of the same illness. But what about the person walking down Gorky Street who exhibits the same mild symptoms but has no schizophrenic relatives? Why call him a schizophrenic? Maybe he's an eccentric artist. Maybe he had a difficult upbringing. Maybe he's under some kind of stress. It may well be, I told Snezhnevsky, that many or even most people with symptoms that satisfy his criteria for "sluggish schizophrenia" do not have that illness, never will, and exhibit the behavioral characteristics that ought to be considered instead, signs of a neurotic condition, of a personality disorder, or even of normality.

Snezhnevsky irately denied the importance of these diagnostic dangers. A good clinician, he insisted, should be able to distinguish between mild schizophrenia and a nonschizophrenic condition.

I disagreed. Relying on a diagnostician's acumen begs the question, I said, since clinical judgments are themselves determined, in great measure, by the diagnostician's theoretical orientation.

Vartanyan, I noticed, was making little effort to defend his boss. It occurred to me that this meeting was important to him, too, but for his own reasons.

For many years in Snezhnevsky's shadow, Vartanyan, an Armenian by nationality, was now developing what promised to be a spectacular career. Trained as a psychiatrist, he had specialized in biological research on mental illness, and for a long time had headed the main biological research laboratories at Snezhnevsky's institute. With Snezhnevsky moving toward retirement, Vartanyan was poised to inherit the older man's mantle of power as director of the grand new psychiatric center that *Pravda* had just announced.

There was, apparently, some opposition to Vartanyan in Moscow, led by his chief rival, Dr. Georgi V. Morozov, head of Moscow's Serbsky Institute of Forensic Psychiatry, where some of the most notorious dissident cases had been sent for diagnosis. Morozov, according to my informants, had supporters high in the KGB. Yet his name had become so widely linked to the worst cases of psychiatric abuse that his usefulness in the international arena was badly compromised, and, I was told, his opposition to Vartanyan's advancement stood little chance.

Already Vartanyan was beginning to take over as Soviet psychiatry's chief spokesman to the world. Meeting with me in advance of the international psychiatric congress in Vienna, scheduled for the following year, was almost surely seen by him as an opportunity to fulfill his new responsibility. The Soviet Union's suspension or expulsion would denote, in official Soviet eyes, a certain failure on his part in the exquisitely vital task of protecting Moscow's interests. Any possibility of averting such a catastrophe was, at the least, worth exploring.

And so it was Vartanyan, not Snezhnevsky or I, who brought up the matter of psychiatric abuse. Soviet dissidents, Vartanyan insisted, were not being misdiagnosed. "Too much has been made of the matter in the West," he said, "all of it for political purposes."

Soviet psychiatrists, he went on, were well acquainted with my own writings on the subject, including my report on the reexamination of General Pyotr Grigorenko (see Chapter 8).

The Grigorenko case was, of course, very much to the point. A Soviet Army war hero who joined the dissident movement in the 1960s and spoke up on behalf of the Crimean Tatars, a small ethnic group expelled by Stalin from the Crimea during World War II for disloyalty and resettled in Central Asia, Grigorenko was arrested, diagnosed as mentally ill (though not, as it happens, with any form of Snezhnevskyan schizophrenia), and committed twice to psychiatric hospitals and finally exiled. In 1978 he was reexamined in New York and Boston by a team of psychiatrists, psychologists, and other medical and mental health specialists from Columbia, Harvard, and Yale, myself among them. We concluded that Grigorenko was not mentally ill when we examined him, and had probably not been mentally ill when his Soviet examiners had said he was.

"Look," Vartanyan said, "Grigorenko, when he was here, was sick. He's a remarkable man, but he got involved with the Crimean Tatars—he just got fixed on them and on a few other causes. When you and the others reexamined him, he was in the States, away from that setting and that stress, and he was OK."

The same was true, Vartanyan said, of the dissident Vladimir Bukovsky, who had also been found ill in the Soviet Union and well in the West. "I'd like you to see his hospital records. If we sat down, four or five of us from our two countries, and looked at them, you'd see that he was sick."

I demurred. If Grigorenko and Bukovsky had really suffered from the illnesses that had been diagnosed in the Soviet Union, at least some signs of those illnesses should have been recognizable even after a long period of time and change in their social surroundings.

Vartanyan shifted his line of argument. To show up the absurdity, as he called it, of the West's accusations, he pointed out that some of the Western critics had gone so far as to say that Snezhnevsky had developed his concept of schizophrenia, including its mild, "sluggish" category, with the deliberate aim of providing the Soviet authorities with a diagnostic niche within which dissidents could easily be placed.

Snezhnevsky, with a laugh, expressed his contempt for that accusation.

I replied that, having studied the development of Snezhnevsky's theories, I agreed that this particular charge was probably untrue. Snezhnevsky's theories, I recognized, had emerged during the 1940s and 1950s under the influence of a number of his teachers, and had achieved mature form in his mind and in his writings during the late 1950s and early 1960s, well before the commitment of dissidents to psychiatric wards began to take place with any frequency. In short, I acknowledged, the theories had developed independent of their purported usefulness in the diagnosis of Soviet dissenters.

But that did not mean, I added, that Snezhnevsky's theories had nothing to do with such diagnoses. It was precisely the flaws in those theories that had resulted in their easy applicability to dissidents. Snezhnevsky's concepts, I said, were only part of the reason that dissidents were being diagnosed as mentally ill in the Soviet Union, but they were an important part.

It was my belief, I said, that, in some cases, dissidents were hospitalized as a result of deliberate misdiagnosis. I also suspected, I added, that some hospitalized dissidents were mentally ill. Dissent is, after all, a marginal activity in the Soviet Union, with its highly repressive political system, and the margins of any society contain a disproportionately high number of people with mental illnesses. But it seemed to me that most hospitalized Soviet dissidents were pronounced ill not because the KGB had ordered the psychiatrists to make that diagnosis and not because they were really ill, but for other reasons.

In the context of Soviet society, I reasoned, dissidents constitute a deviant element. They behave and speak in ways that are different from other Soviet citizens, and, for that reason, they come to be seen as strange. After all, I asked, isn't it strange when someone openly does and says things that, under the conditions of Soviet political life, everyone knows to be dangerous? In fact, there is good evidence, based on dissident accounts, that, upon encountering dissidents, many KGB and other Soviet officials are often struck by a sense of strangeness, a sense that is compounded when the dissidents start lecturing them about their rights under the Soviet Constitution. The sense that someone is strange is not infrequently followed by the suspicion that the strangeness may be due to mental illness. And as soon as that suspicion arises in the minds of Soviet authorities, they have powerful reasons to call upon psychiatrists to examine the dissidents.

First of all, the official Soviet code of criminal procedure requires that in all cases—not only political ones—psychiatrists be consulted if any doubt exists in the mind of an investigating official about the mental health of the accused. Given the bureaucratic nature of the Soviet legal system, an official would rather protect himself by requesting a psychiatric consultation than worry about being criticized someday for not having done so. Besides, the trial of a dissident who has been pronounced ill and in need of hospitalization is usually less demanding on the prosecutor than an ordinary trial, since the testimony comes mostly from the psychiatrists who diagnosed the alleged illness. That provides another reason for calling in the doctors if there is even the smallest doubt about the dissident's mental health.

My argument was turning into a lecture, to which my Soviet hosts were listening in silence, but I continued. The Soviet psychiatrists who are called upon to render their diagnostic judgments are themselves Soviet citizens. They grow up in the same culture, are affected by the same political realities, and develop the same social perceptions. And since the way in which a psychiatrist goes about determining whether a person is ill depends to a great extent on the psychiatrist's assumptions about what is usual and expected in his society, he may, upon coming into contact with the dissident, have the same sense of strangeness felt by the KGB agent—and may go on to suspect that the defendant may be ill.

Should such a suspicion develop in the psychiatrist's mind, it would not be hard for him to resolve his doubts by finding a category of illness to apply to the dissident. That category, I reminded Snezhnevsky, is most often his category of "sluggish schizophrenia." And this entire process could occur even without a conscious intent to misdiagnose.

Snezhnevsky was scowling; Vartanyan and the other two psychiatrists seemed no more pleased. Vartanyan had been nodding agreement during

219

the initial stages of my argument, when I talked about the way Soviet dissidents are seen in Soviet society, but stopped nodding when I brought the argument home.

My ideas, it seemed, were at once welcome and disturbing. Unlike most other Western critics, I was not saying that all diagnoses of mental illness in dissident cases were made by psychiatrists who knew that the dissidents were well. Some of these psychiatrists did know that dissidents they had diagnosed as ill were healthy—but, I believed, not all of them knew that; perhaps not even most. Nor was I saying that Snezhnevsky had deliberately created the tools that had made those misdiagnoses possible. I was saying that, because of the nature of political life in the Soviet Union and the social perceptions fashioned by that life, dissenting behavior really does seem strange there; and that, because of the nature of Snezhnevsky's diagnostic system, this strangeness has, in some cases, come to be called schizophrenia. In other words, I was saying that in many and perhaps most instances of such diagnoses, not only the KGB and other responsibie officials but the psychiatrists themselves really believed that the dissidents were ill.

This, I said, was even more frightening to me than the usual picture of Soviet psychiatric abuse, the monochromatic picture of the KGB ordering and the psychiatrists obeying. What does it mean, both about Soviet psychiatry and about Soviet society, that such a state of affairs could have developed?

My hosts were silent. Then Vartanyan spoke. "What we need," he said, "is to sit down and settle this matter. We should go over the cases and get some understanding. This shouldn't be used for political purposes."

"It hasn't just been a matter of taking political advantage," I returned. The fact that he thought the cases were being used in the West for purely political purposes was, I said, part of the problem. These charges of psychiatric abuse have not been raised as a convenient ploy but because psychiatrists and others in the West really believe that something terribly wrong has been happening in Soviet psychiatry.

"You can enter into a dialogue with us on this," I said, "only if you're willing to recognize that what the other side says, or at least some of what it says, *may* be correct. And if you're willing to recognize this and concede it, then, at the very least, you risk having to acknowledge mistakes."

"We're ready," Vartanyan replied.

He stood up and ate the last of the caviar. Snezhnevsky seemed tired. He allowed me to photograph him and the others, and Vartanyan took me on a tour of his laboratories.

What Vartanyan was ready for was still far from the exchange that the problem requires. The proposal he made to me was merely to go over case histories prepared by Soviet psychiatrists about persons identified in the

West as having been hospitalized for political reasons. But how can we be sure that the information in these documents represents a true account of a person's life and psychiatric symptoms? How can we even be sure that some tampering with the records has not taken place? A real discussion of the problem of psychiatric abuse would have to begin with nothing less than a reexamination, by Western specialists, of the hospitalized dissidents themselves—perhaps a systematic reexamination of a series of dissidents using the methods employed in the Grigorenko case. The dissidents to be studied would have to be chosen by the Western, not the Soviet, participants in this effort.

As it happens, Vartanyan's suggested project and the impending event whose prospect provoked the suggestion—the meeting of the World Psychiatric Association (WPA), at which a vote was to be held on the Soviets' expulsion from that organization—were rendered moot by subsequent events. In early February 1983, the All-Union Society of Psychiatrists and Neuropathologists announced that it was quitting the world body. There would be no Soviets in the WPA—and therefore no Soviets to expel from it. In one action, they pulled themselves out of reach of world criticism.

Since that withdrawal, little discussion has taken place between Western and Soviet psychiatrists on the subject of Soviet psychiatric abuse. The practice continues to be condemned in the West, both by private and governmental organizations, but no exchanges of any substance or consequence have taken place.

By most accounts, Soviet dissidents continue to find themselves in psychiatric hospitals, though the number of such occurrences remains obscure. As of this writing—early 1985—the issue remains unresolved, and there seems little likelihood that it will be resolved soon.

In many ways, both the Soviets and the West are losers in this process. For the Soviets, human rights violations continue to stain their history, and their psychiatric profession continues to be mired in a dark enterprise in ways and to a depth that even they do not fully understand. As for the West the persistence of these violations continues to raise anxieties about other Soviet behaviors of an even more distressing kind.

If the Soviets care so little about their own people, then is it not possible— some in the West believe—that, despite their repeated invocations of their terrible losses in World War II, and despite their frequent insistence that they seek only peace, they might be more willing to risk the lives of their people than we might be willing the lives of ours in the event of a looming nuclear confrontation?

My own belief is that the Soviets' fear of war, especially nuclear war, is genuine, and that they do not value the lives of their people so lightly that they would be willing to risk those lives significantly more easily than would we. Nevertheless, their treatment of those of their citizens who dissent is disconcerting, and can only continue to raise our anxieties, not only about those particular citizens, but also about all citizens—theirs, ours, and, ultimately, the world's.

Notes and References

1. For an American memoir of the effort to condemn the Soviets in Honolulu, see Walter Reich, "Soviet Psychiatry on Trial," *Commentary*, January 1978, pp. 40–48. For a contrasting account by Soviet psychiatrists, see *"VI vsemirnyi psikhiatricheskii kongress* [Sixth World Congress of Psychiatry]," *Zhurnal nevropatologii i psikhiatrii imeni S. S. Korsakova* 78 (1978): 607–624.

2. During my visit, Vartanyan was named the new institute's deputy director—in effect, its director-designate, since the 78-year-old Snezhnevsky, who was already in partial retirement, had been leaving the day-to-day running of the institute to Vartanyan for some time and would be retiring completely.

Chapter 10

Response to Psychiatric Abuse

Paul Chodoff and Ellen Mercer

Except in unusual circumstances professional organizations usually confine their nonscientific activities to their own countries. However, the profession at large must respond when its methods are misused and thus pose a threat to human rights.

The world psychiatric community faced such a situation in the early 1970s, when allegations of the misuse of psychiatry to suppress political dissent in the Soviet Union began to surface in the West. As the volume of reliable information on Soviet abuse increased, several national psychiatric associations set in motion a series of actions to bring professional and public attention to the issue. This chapter examines the efforts of the American Psychiatric Association (APA) to develop an effective means of responding to allegations of psychiatric abuse in the Soviet Union and elsewhere. For the most part, these efforts have focused on creating procedures within the World Psychiatric Association (WPA) designed to receive and investigate complaints of abuse and, if necessary, to seek remedies.

The APA, which represents some 28,000 psychiatrists from the United States and abroad, issued its first statement on psychiatric abuse in December 1971 by condemning "the misuse of psychiatric facilities for the detention of persons solely on the basis of their political dissent, no matter where it occurs." Later that month, several national psychiatric associations, including the APA, raised the issue at the WPA meeting in Mexico, but there was no official response. This lack of action prompted noted commentator I. F. Stone to publish a highly critical article in the *New York Review of Books*.[1]

Partly in response to Stone's blast, the APA called on the world psychiatric body to establish a mechanism for responding to complaints of political abuse of involuntary hospitalization. But the WPA leadership, fearful that such a move would be disruptive, pigeonholed the initiative. Meanwhile, within the APA itself, opinion on how to handle the issue of Soviet abuse was divided. Some members denied the importance or even the occurrence of Soviet abuse. Most of the membership, however, continued to pressure the APA to take effective measures. Accordingly, in conjunction with other national societies, particularly the British Royal College of Psychiatrists, plans were made to bring the issue of Soviet abuse before the Sixth International Congress of the World Psychiatric Association to be held in Honolulu in August 1977. Three significant events took place at that meeting.

First, the WPA delegates unanimously accepted a statement of ethical principles to guide psychiatrists in their professional work—the so-called Declaration of Hawaii. This work had been in preparation by a group of psychiatrists led by Dr. Clarence Blomquist of Sweden since the previous international congress in 1971.

Second, the congress adopted a resolution calling on WPA member societies to "renounce and expunge" psychiatric abuse for political purposes wherever it might occur and to "implement the resolution in the first instance with reference to the systematic abuse of psychiatry for political purposes in the USSR." That resolution, put forward by the Royal Australian and New Zealand College of Psychiatrists, sparked a firestorm of controversy among congress delegates. Soviet delegates, representing the All-Union Society of Neuropathologists and Psychiatrists of the Soviet Union, fought bitterly and tenaciously to block its passage. But in the final tally the resolution passed by a vote of 90 to 88. Ironically, the Soviet delegates lacked full voting strength because their society had failed to pay its WPA dues for a number of years. Had the dues been paid prior to the meeting, the resolution would have probably been defeated. Nonetheless, passage of the resolution marked the first time that an international body of psychiatrists had specifically criticized one of its own members—and a very powerful one—for the unethical use of professional knowledge and skills.

The third event at the congress was the passage of an APA resolution calling for the establishment of a committee—eventually called the Committee to Review Alleged Abuses of Psychiatry for Political Purposes (the Review Committee)—to investigate allegations of psychiatric abuse.[2] The committee, comprised of seven members from different parts of the world, began functioning in December 1978, despite opposition from the All-Union Society, which argued that the WPA lacked the legal authority to establish such a committee and that it constituted an infringement of national sovereignty.

Psychiatric Abuse in Yugoslavia

Yugoslavia's federal criminal code enables a court to impose "compulsory psychiatric treatment and confinement in a health institution" on an offender who, at the time of committing his offense, was not accountable for his acts and was "dangerous to his surroundings." The legislation is worded in such a way that the nonviolent expression of political opinion or religious beliefs may be treated as grounds for confinement or even as a symptom of mental illness sufficiently serious to require confinement. Of the nearly 2,600 political cases tried before Yugoslavian courts since 1981, several have resulted in involuntary hospitalization, according to Amnesty International.

The ordeal of 58-year-old Radomir Veljkovic is a case in point. In 1973 Veljkovic was detained and charged with "hostile propaganda" and "damaging the reputation of the state." The charges stemmed from letters that Veljkovic, a retired army officer, had written to President Tito years earlier and circulated to friends. In the letters, Veljkovic criticized abuses allegedly committed by members of the state security police. A Sarajevo court eventually found him guilty but unaccountable for his actions on the basis of a psychiatric diagnosis of insanity. He was sentenced to confinement in Belgrade's Prison Psychiatric Hospital. In an unsuccessful appeal of the court's decision, Veljkovic argued that the court neither explained how his actions were dangerous nor considered five earlier medical certificates diagnosing him as sane.

In recent years, groups of Yugoslav citizens have petitioned President Sergej Krajger on behalf of at least eight other persons whom they allege are being held involuntarily in psychiatric institutions for their nonviolent political views. The national newspaper, *Politika*, published one such appeal on 14 October 1983. Another appeal, sent to the UN Secretary General in March 1984, urged the United Nations and other organizations to request of the Yugloslavian government permission for an international group of psychiatrists to examine the dissidents confined to psychiatric hospitals in an effort to determine the veracity of the insanity rulings.

Yugoslav human rights activists, while foreseeing no immediate end to the political use of psychiatry in their country, find it encouraging that the state-controlled press has published their appeals and that the government has promised to investigate at least one of the cases. The Yugoslav government is sensitive about its image abroad, some activists say, and thus international pressure for improvements must be kept up.

Eric Stover

The Review Committee operates on a referrel basis. Upon receiving a complaint of psychiatric abuse from a WPA member society, the committee examines the documentation; if it feels a reply from the offending country is necessary, it then forwards the complaint to the national society in whose jurisdiction the alleged abuse took place. Theoretically that society is expected to respond to the Review Committee. What happens next, however, has not been tested, because the only complaints that have gone through this process have concerned persons in the Soviet Union. Since the accused society denied any wrongdoing, it is doubtful whether the WPA could have taken any effective steps. This lack of follow-up constitutes a major weakness. However, the procedure should not be considered entirely a charade. The Review Committee's public airing of cases does protect the victims somewhat and may also influence government agencies to think twice about their actions knowing that their abusive practices may be exposed.

In the United States, the APA has established a Committee on International Abuse of Psychiatry and Psychiatrists (APA Abuse Committee) to review complaints and, if worthy of investigation, to forward them to the WPA Review Committee. By December 1984 the APA Abuse Committee had reviewed nearly 100 complaints and referred twenty cases, all from the Soviet Union, to the WPA Review Committee. In the same month, the Abuse Committee sent a letter to the WPA raising its "concern about the increasing number of cases of alleged abuse of psychiatry [in Yugoslavia]," which the committee had received in recent years. The APA is also concerned about human rights issues in South Africa because of apartheid; however, an APA-sponsored visit to that country in September 1978 concluded that there was more reason to be concerned about the quality of psychiatric care for blacks than about the political abuse of psychiatry.

Another APA committee, the Task Force on Human Rights, reviews cases of alleged civil rights offenses that have psychological and psychiatric implications rather than cases involving the direct abuse of psychiatry. The task force also examines complaints of human rights abuses directed at individual psychiatrists. Instances of this kind have been reported in Argentina (between 1976 and 1983), Chile, and the Soviet Union.

The APA board of trustees passed a resolution in June 1982 stating that if the All-Union Society failed to respond by 1 April 1983 to the inquiries directed to it from the WPA Review Committee, it should be suspended from WPA membership until these abuses were terminated. Other psychiatric associations around the world passed similar resolutions. Although the Soviets finally responded to some of the cases (two in 1982 and five in 1983) brought to its attention by the Review Committee, it has now become moot whether the Soviet responses would have affected action on the suspension resolution.

Whether to avoid the confrontation scheduled to take place at the World Congress of Psychiatry in Vienna in July 1983 or in response to a political decision from the Soviet leadership, the All-Union Society withdrew from the WPA in late January 1983. The Czechslovakian, Bulgarian, and Cuban psychiatric societies also resigned, citing "politicalization" of the WPA. Although the congress delegates acknowledged these resignations, they also made it clear that the Soviets would not be welcomed back without "sincere cooperation and evidence beforehand of amelioration of the political abuse of psychiatry." The WPA delegates also bestowed honorary membership upon Soviet psychiatrist Dr. Anatoly Koryagin, presently imprisoned for his protests against psychiatric abuse. (See Chapter 7 and 8.)

What can be said about the APA's efforts, as well as those of other Western psychiatric groups, to put an end to the perversion of their profession taking place in the Soviet Union? The most obvious answer is that these efforts have failed. The Soviet practice of confining political and religious dissidents to psychiatric prisons on flimsy or nonexistent evidence of mental illness continues, although its frequency may have abated slightly. The Soviet withdrawal from the WPA has insulated Soviet psychiatrists from any influence that could be exerted through the WPA. It has also given ammunition to those APA members who advocate "quiet diplomacy" rather than direct protest. Furthermore, a chill has been placed on all collaborative efforts between American and Soviet psychiatrists.

Many Western psychiatrists, however, believe that no other course was open to them. They argue that the Soviets had been given an adequate chance to discuss Western concerns through various WPA complaint mechanisms but failed to do so. They point to Soviet refusals to allow foreign psychiatrists to enter Soviet special psychiatric hospitals to examine named dissenters. According to these psychiatrists, the Soviet failure to seize upon these opportunities and to correct past abuses amounts to an act of forfeiting their membership to an association dedicated to upholding the professional ethics of psychiatry throughout the world.

The campaign to end the political misuse of psychiatry in the Soviet Union and wherever else it may occur will continue. The WPA is not the only forum in which protests can be lodged and influence exerted. The APA actively publicizes events in the struggle not only to its own members but also to the public at large through articles, meetings, and press releases. The APA Abuse Committee continues to write letters of inquiry and protest to countries where political abuse is suspected. There has been collaboration between the APA and the UN Commission on Human Rights, where the US delegation is attempting to bring the whole matter of unjust psychiatric hospitalization before the General Assembly. The APA plans to sponsor an international conference on the "Problems of Psychiatric Hospitalization in the Modern World." Fact-finding missions on the model of the 1978 visit to South Africa are also possible.

Finally, are US psychiatrists clean enough in a moral sense to justify their taking such a strong position regarding activities in another country? Clearly problematic ethical issues exist in the United States, including such matters as the power exerted by psychiatrists over the lives of citizens, the fiasco of deinstitutionalization, and above all, the maldistribution of psychiatric services with the determining factor often being economics rather than need. These areas and other have to be a concern of US psychiatrists; if colleagues from other countries with different systems choose to take them up, they have a right to do so, and the APA needs to respond to them.

As for the issue of the deliberate, systematic misuse of psychiatry to suppress political and religious dissent, no strong case can be made that this is a problem in the United States. The case usually considered most relevant is that of the poet Ezra Pound.[3] Arrested at the end of World War II for his treasonous broadcasts from Italy, Pound was never tried but was found incapable of assisting in his defense by reason of mental illness. Later he was confined, under relatively comfortable conditions, at St. Elizabeth's Hospital in Washington, D.C. This judgment, largely the work of Dr. Winifred Overholser, superintendent of St. Elizabeth's Hospital, was made in spite of what seems to have been a lack of substantial clinical evidence of psychosis and the fact that Pound had written a lucid and detailed defense of himself to the US attorney general.

The Pound case appears to constitute a political subversion of psychiatry. But it should be noted that the action was taken in the primary interest of the accused person rather than that of the state, as is the case in the Soviet Union. Most important, it was an isolated example, and very few similar ones have taken place in the United States.

Thus, in spite of the mixed results, the response of psychiatrists in the United States and elsewhere to the misuse of their profession to attack rather than protect human rights seems to be morally appropriate and, in our view, should continue.

Notes and References

1. I. F. Stone, "Betrayal by Psychiatry," *New York Review of Books*, 10 February 1972, pp. 7–14.

2. The WPA delegates also voted to establish a Committee on Ethics to consider matters of ethical concern to psychiatrists in accordance with the Hawaii declaration.

3. E. Fuller Torrey, *The Roots of Treason: Ezra Pound and Saint Elizabeth's* (New York: Harcourt Brace Jovanovich, 1984).

Toward the Prevention of Torture and Psychiatric Abuse

Elena O. Nightingale and Eric Stover

My work in Hiroshima convinced me of the immorality of claiming professional neutrality in the face of ultimate forms of destruction. I was troubled during my Vietnam work by the extent to which American professionals, notably psychiatrists and chaplains, could inadvertently employ their spiritual counseling in ways that reinforced the atrocity-producing process. In reexamining the history of the concept of "profession," I was struck by the extent to which its early religious connotation (the profession of faith or of membership in a particular religious order) was transformed almost totally into a matter of technique (or professional skill).

We need a new model of the professional that balances technique with advocacy, skill with ethical commitments. That kind of model would serve us well in approaching . . . extreme forms of inhumanity . . .

For only by understanding more of what happens to victims and survivors, and of what motivates victimizers, can we begin to imagine the future holocausts that threaten us, and thereby take steps to avoid them.

Robert Jay Lifton[1]

For all the many words spoken, resolutions passed, and standards set, torture and psychiatric abuse remain two of the most abhorrent concomitants of political repression today. In the past four years alone, governments in one-third of the world's countries have systematically practiced or tacitly condoned torture or ill-treatment.[2] Security agents, specially trained interrogators, and sometimes health personnel use such techniques as prolonged beatings, electric shock, and mind-altering drugs, mostly in secret, to interrogate, punish, and intimidate political dissenters and social nonconformists. Apologists for torture openly, and with increasing frequency, justify its use as an undesirable but "necessary" means of stopping those who threaten the rule of law. These apologists put forth the "just once" argument for practicing torture to combat political violence, but that argument doesn't hold, for those who torture will go on using it, creating more and more victims.

In many parts of the world systematic brutality has developed into a social disease, debasing both its victims and its perpetrators. Judges and legislators in some countries have condemned torture and ill-treatment, and they have instituted administrative and legal safeguards to protect persons in official custody. But in countries where repression is pervasive, such primary means of prevention are often unattainable. Concerned citizens must, therefore, rely on secondary means of prevention: namely, documentation and subsequent international exposure and condemnation of ill-treatment. Tertiary prevention is also possible, but its aim is less to attack the causes of the problem than to treat and rehabilitate victims and their families.[3]

Given a situation so grave and a prognosis so guarded, what can be done to prevent political acts that destroy healthy minds and bodies? The major stumbling block is that those who have the power to prevent abuse believe they benefit from it. And those who would like to see it abolished often are not in political positions to do so. Preventive strategies, therefore, must be aimed at those in power. Human rights organizations have long recognized the effectiveness of this approach. The aim of Amnesty International, for instance, is to make governments—regardless of their ideology—accountable at home and abroad for their actions that violate internationally recognized human rights standards. In pursuing this mandate, the organization takes no sides in political or other conflicts "because human rights are absolute and the defence of such rights should not be dependent on political convenience."[4]

Traditionally many health professionals, particularly physicians, have been hesitant to take public positions on issues that they perceive to be political. Their reticence is understandable. The practice of medicine is based on the precept that the provision of medical care should be a neutral act, devoid of personal or political motives. Nearly every statement designed to guide professional activity, from the Hippocratic oath to the Geneva Conventions, reflects this view. The Hippocratic oath, for example, states that it is the physician's duty to render proper treatment only, to avoid taking advantage of the physician-patient relationship and, in particular, to respect the patient's right of privacy. To uphold and preserve these responsibilities, the medical profession has maintained a long tradition of professional self-regulation without outside interference. Such precepts imply that political considerations should play no part in the care and attention medical practitioners render to their patients.

To discuss the duties of health professionals without referring to society's needs and goals, however, is to ignore the actual political context in which medicine is practiced in the world today. The philosopher H. Tristram Engelhardt describes the relation of medicine to society this way:

> Medicine has become part of society's explicit political response to the general predicament of man. That is, society has begun to invest in and use medicine for the general political purposes of the community. Private individuals no longer provide the major support for medical research and education. Rather, medicine has become a social or civil instrument, and in this sense has become socialized. Medicine has been employed to affect the conditions of society, e.g., change infant mortality rates, enable a population explosion, provide contraception, make life in cities possible without frequent fatal epidemics, etc., and it has thereby become an instrument of society in the sense of a publicly supported means of effecting publicly chosen goals.[5]

Because medicine in some respects has become an instrument of society, and because the actions of medical professionals can have political consequences, medical personnel are often involved in politics. That is not to say that the principle of personal and political noninterference in clinical practice is no longer valid. But it does mean that the medical profession has a positive duty to take action when its members or other persons violate the ethical tenets of the profession.[6]

Awareness of the political contexts in which torture and psychiatric abuse take place and of the actions of medical personnel who assist in such practices has prompted the medical profession to clarify its position on complicity in ill-treatment. Knowledge that Nazi doctors carried out cruel and inhuman experiments on concentration camp prisoners led, first, to the Code of Nuremburg, which set out the rules for medical research that were subsequently incorporated in the Declaration of Helsinki. In 1948, the World Medical Association promulgated the Declaration of Geneva and, a year later, established the International Code of Medical Ethics as a model for national codes of ethics. More recently, several international health associations were instrumental in prompting the United Nations to adopt a set of principles making it an offense under international human rights agreements for governments to order health personnel to engage in torture or ill-treatment of prisoners or detainees.

Many health professionals throughout the world have played an important role in promoting the protection of human rights. In addition to encouraging

231

Dr. Bobby de la Paz was murdered in 1982 in his clinic in Catbalogan, the Philippines. Local military authorities, who have been implicated in the killing, were reportedly suspicious that Sylvia and Bobby de la Paz, rural health physicians, were treating suspected members of the New People's Army (NPA). Sylvia de la Paz did not deny that she and her husband might have treated suspected NPA members. However, she said that it was impossible not to because they treated anyone who approached them, rich and poor alike; the de la Paz couple were the only physicians for a rural community of 30,000 people. Dr. Sylvia de la Paz now works with the Medical Action Group, an organization of health professionals who report on human rights abuses against their colleagues and other people in the Philippines. (Courtesy of Medical Action Group, Inc.)

the adoption of codes of medical ethics aimed at preventing professional complicity in torture and ill-treatment, health professionals have, for example, been active in treating and rehabilitating victims of abuse. Health personnel in prisons have also on occasion reported incidents of torture to their medical societies, at considerable personal and professional risk. Such progress notwithstanding, large numbers of health professionals still remain relatively unaware of actions they could take which would greatly enhance those efforts to prevent abuse that are already underway.

Torture: The Shame of Exposure

Protection of human rights is based on three methods: pressure by the international community; actions by national judicial systems; and enforcement by international or regional bodies, such as the United Nations Commission on Human Rights and the Inter-American Court on Human Rights.[7] So far, health personnel and their professional associations have relied almost exclusively on international opinion to bring attention to the problem of torture. However, the other two methods of protection can prove equally effective in certain situations.

The most powerful weapon for preventing the use of torture is the mobilization of international opinion and pressure. It is the "shame of exposure" that governments fear most. For international pressure to be most effective, however, human rights organizations and other groups need to establish an information system which will ensure that allegations of torture become public knowledge both inside and outside the offending country.[8] Those in authority will then be challenged to develop their own means of stopping torture.

Argentina and Brazil offer recent examples of how international exposure and condemnation, coupled with information gathering by domestic groups, may help to eliminate, or at least to reduce, the use of torture. Argentine human rights groups, for instance, played a decisive role in documenting and quickly relaying abroad reports of torture and "disappearance" during the 1976–1983 period of repressive military rule in that country. This information prompted, in 1978, a worldwide Amnesty International campaign against torture and "disappearance" and later, in 1980, a highly critical report on Argentine military brutality issued by the Inter-American Commission on Human Rights of the Organization of American States.[9] By all accounts, these actions greatly embarrassed Argentina's military rulers and led, in 1982, to a significant drop in the number of complaints of torture and "disappearance."

In Brazil, torture had reached such epidemic proportions by the late 1960s, that Catholic clergy and laymen, proclaiming themselves "the voice of the voiceless," began diligently collecting information about its use.[10] The Papal Nuncio to Brazil presented a dossier on torture to Pope Paul in December 1969. Three months later, the Pope denounced torture specifically in his Easter Message, which many believe was directed at Brazil's military leaders. Although torture persisted in Brazil throughout the 1970s, the Pope's Easter Message heightened international awareness of the problem and proved to be a turning point for its domestic opponents. Brazilians began forming committees to press the authorities for an end to secret detentions and for full inquiries into the deaths of detainees. Political prisoners went on hunger strikes to protest torture. In 1977, President Geisel received a manifesto from 110 army and air force officres calling for an "end to censorship and inhuman repression" and for a return to full democracy. By 1980, the government had begun to respond to international and domestic pressure: Reports of torture, particularly in urban areas, became less frequent.

In Brazil, Chile, and Uruguay, as Stover and Nelson point out in Chapter 5, national medical societies have initiated disciplinary proceedings against members who have been co-opted in the service of torture. Health associations could support these efforts by calling on governments to cooperate with national societies that undertake disciplinary investigations. Many governments will disregard such requests, but at least they will be put on notice that the international health community takes seriously the obligations set out in the UN Principles of Medical Ethics and that it expects governments to do so as well. Warning governments in this way is not a fruitless gesture. An offending government's failure to cooperate could result in publicity over which the government would have no control. Political leaders may as a result view accountability as less costly than adverse international publicity.

Information on incidents of torture is often difficult to obtain. Of all the health-related institutions in the world, the International Committee of the Red Cross (ICRC) probably possesses the most detailed information on the use of torture today.[11] The ICRC is the only institution that, for more than a century, has made regular visits to prisoners and seen first-hand the physical and mental consequences of torture, an opportunity which it derives from its right to visit prisoners as specified in the Geneva Conventions. Each year the committee visits large numbers of political prisoners worldwide to ensure that their detention conditions conform to internationally accepted standards.

Opportunities available to the ICRC to document torture and prevent its practice are substantial but limited. "Sometimes," the ICRC acknowledges, "governments simply refuse to accept the [organization's] offer of its services, either in violation of the Geneva Conventions or—in internal situations—by invoking national sovereignty." Furthermore, even countries that allow the ICRC to visit prisoners of war or civilian detainees usually grant authorization to do so only *after* interrogation, the period in which torture is mostly likely to have taken place. Moreover, ICRC reports on prison visits are transmitted to governments or the "Detaining Power" in confidence and thus are not open to public scrutiny. If the government receiving an ICRC report publishes any part of it, however, the organization requests that it be published in full; otherwise, the ICRC reserves the right to publish the report in full itself.

Unfortunately, most of the ICRC's documentation on torture remains confidential. Thus, if other groups wish to obtain information on torture and make it public, they must create their own means of documentation. Health professionals are in a good position to obtain such information, either through medical-society disciplinary hearings against members who participate in torture or through medical examinations of persons who claim to have been tortured.

Governments often claim, however, that allegations of torture are unjustified; thus it is important to obtain good medical documentation in support of these protests. Some torture techniques leave no traces. Even visible traces do not always constitute proof because they are open to other interpretations, but they do reverse the burden of proof, particularly if it can be shown that the traces of torture found on several persons from the same country constitute a pattern. Medical examination of torture victims is also useful because it enables systematic collection of data on the occurrence and nature of various forms of torture, identifies the circumstances under which torture takes place, and establishes the immediate and long-term implications of deliberate physical and mental abuse.

Medical research teams in several countries already possess detailed information on the epidemiology of torture and its effects on victims. But for the most part this information remains underutilized. What needs to be done, in our opinion, is to establish a systematic, centralized means of collecting, storing, and disseminating this information more widely.

The International Medical Commission for Health and Human Rights, now being established in Geneva, could appropriately provide these services. Because the commission is nonpartisan and is located in a major international center, it will be in a good position to act as a clearinghouse for information on torture gathered by health professionals and other persons throughout the world. The commission could also study, possibly in conjunction with other health associations, the effectiveness of medical codes of ethics in preventing medical complicity in torture. A better understanding of why health personnel participate in torture could begin, for example, with a concerted effort to seek out and obtain testimonies from those who have participated in such acts. Better links could be established with prison health personnel, who often work in isolation from their national and international colleagues, and who are thus particularly susceptible to governmental pressure. The commission could also conduct research on neglected epidemiological implications of torture, perhaps drawing on the expertise and experience of the Centers for Disease Control in the United States. Approaching the problem of torture on a country-by-country basis, the commission could also evaluate the domestic means available to torture victims who wish to obtain legal redress.

Further research also needs to be carried out on the behavior of the perpetrators of torture. The purpose of research on this little understood and controversial topic is not to forgive or vindicate brutal behavior, but to understand better the conceptual underpinnings of institutionalized torture. Robert Jay Lifton has suggested that one of the key concepts underlying Nazi medical killings was belief in the legitimacy of destroying "life unworthy of life."[12] The Auschwitz doctors, he says, could act as healers at one moment and at the next select people for experimentation or killing because the doctors considered their prisoners to be subhuman. Lifton, who has interviewed 28 former Nazi doctors, suggests that the Auschwitz doctors sometimes experienced ethical conflicts but were able to resolve them through a process he describes as "doubling": namely, by creating an "Auschwitz self" as well as a humane husband-father self. The "Auschwitz self," he says, held a detached view of the killings as necessary "in order to heal," that is, to eliminate Jews and thereby control human evolution. But even as the doctors killed, Lifton maintains, they held on to the idea that they were healers, finding solace in professional discussion groups, in laboratory research projects, in providing small favors to detainees selected for experimentation, and in working with physicians who were inmates in the medical blocks where prisoners selected to live were treated. More recently, survivors of Argentina's secret detention centers operated by the military and police in the 1970s have noted that camp guards treated Jews more brutally than non-Jews because they considered the former subhuman.[13] A better understanding of the conceptual underpinnings of institutionalized torture might, as Robert J. Lifton says, enable us to "imagine the future holocausts that threaten us, and thereby take steps to avoid them." Better understanding might also help international organizations to place the agreed-upon right of freedom from torture in a context that would be more meaningful to violators and perhaps would deter them.

Another important aspect of torture that has received little attention is its use by armed opposition groups. Reports of ill-treatment and brutality, amounting to torture, carried out by terrorist groups are appearing more frequently.[14] This is a serious development because there is no possible redress for the victim. The International Medical Commission, in conjunction with the International Commission of Jurists, should examine this problem and suggest what can be done about it.

Most importantly, the International Medical Commission could file, or help others file, allegations of torture or violations of the human rights of health personnel with the appropriate international and regional organizations. Individual health professionals and national societies are often uneasy about submitting complaints because they fear reprisals or lack an adequate understanding of the complaint process to carry it to conclusion.

Legal Actions Against Torture

Torture is forbidden by international law and by domestic legislation or constitutional provisions in over 55 countries. The basic human right of freedom from torture is not only binding on the more than 55 states in which torture is forbidden by national statute and on states which have acceded to the 35 or more multilateral treaties on human rights; it is also generally binding on all nations as a rule of customary international law.

Several legal and human rights scholars argue that in certain situations the most effective means of protecting human rights is enforcement of these rights by national courts.[15] Nirmala Chandrahasan, for example, maintains that: "Domestic implementation translates international aspiration into reality by providing citizens with an available forum in which to obtain redress for violations. National courts, through interpretation and application, lend substance and dimension to the general, often vague concepts contained in international resolutions and conventions."[16]

But the obvious benefits of domestic enforcement are often vitiated by national courts that either are corrupt or lack independence from the executive arm. Furthermore, national courts often refuse to hear cases involving human rights violations. That these barriers are real is well illustrated by the Filártiga family's attempts to gain redress through the Paraguayan courts for the torture-murder of their 17-year-old son, Joelito (see Chapter 4). The family's lawyer was arrested, threatened with death, and then disbarred. Mrs. Filártiga and her daughter were briefly detained. Finally, the Paraguayan court dropped the case.

More promising, perhaps, are legal actions against torturers in foreign courts, again well illustrated in the Filártiga case. When a police official

Twelve-Point Program for the Prevention of Torture

1.   Official condemnation of torture
The highest authorities of every country should demonstrate their total
opposition to torture. They should make clear to all law-enforcement
personnel that torture will not be tolerated under any circumstances.

2.   Limits on incommunicado detention
Torture often takes place while the victims are held incommunicado—
unable to contact people outside who could help them or find out what is
happening to them. Governments should adopt safeguards to ensure that
incommunicado detection does not become an opportunity for torture. It is
vital that all prisoners be brought before a judicial authority promptly after
being taken into custody and that relatives, lawyers and doctors have
prompt and regular access to them.

3.   No secret detention
In some countries torture takes place in secret centres, often after the
victims are made to "disappear." Governments should ensure that
prisoners are held in publicly recognized places, and that accurate
information about their whereabouts is made available to relatives and
lawyers.

4.   Safeguards during interrogation and custody
Governments should keep procedures for detention and interrogation
under regular review. All prisoners should be promptly told of their
rights, including the right to lodge complaints about their treatment.
There should be regular independent visits of inspection to places of
detention. An important safeguard against torture would be the separation
of authorities responsible for detention from those in charge of
interrogation.

5.   Independent investigation of reports of torture
Governments should ensure that all complaints and reports of torture are
impartially and effectively investigated. The methods and findings of such
investigations should be made public. Complaints and witnesses should be
protected from intimidation.

6. No use of statements extracted under torture
Governments should ensure that confessions or other evidence obtained through torture may never be invoked in legal proceedings.

7. Prohibition of torture in law
Governments should ensure that acts of torture are punishable offences under the criminal law. In accordance with international law, the prohibition of torture must not be suspended under any circumstances, including states of war or other public emergency.

8. Prosecution of alleged torturers
Those responsible for torture should be brought to justice. This principle should apply wherever they happen to be, wherever the crime was committed and whatever the nationality of the perpetrators or victims. There should be no "safe haven" for torturers.

9. Training procedures
It should be made clear during the training of all officials involved in the custody, interrogation or treatment of prisoners that torture is a criminal act. They should be instructed that they are obliged to refuse to obey any order to torture.

10. Compensation and rehabilitation
Victims of torture and their dependents should be entitled to obtain financial compensation. Victims should be provided with appropriate medical care or rehabilitation.

11. International response
Governments should use all available channels to intercede with governments accused of torture. Inter-governmental mechanisms should be established and used to investigate reports of torture urgently and to take effective action against it. Governments should ensure that military, security or police transfers or training do not facilitate the practice of torture.

12. Ratification of international instruments
All governments should ratify international instruments containing safeguards and remedies against torture, including the International Covenant on Civil and Political Rights and its Optional Protocol which provides for individual complaints.

Amnesty International

A Doctor on Trial

In March 1985 Jacobo Timerman, editor of the Buenos Aires daily *La Razón*, brought charges against the former police doctor who, he claims, supervised his torture in a secret detention center seven years earlier. Based on the testimonies of Timerman and 21 other former detainees, a federal judge ordered the arrest of Dr. Jorge Antonio Berges for his role in the torture of prisoners in at least four clandestine detention centers operated by the military and police between 1976 and 1983.

Timerman presented written testimony to the court in which he described his first encounter with Berges in "Puesto Vasco," a secret detention center run by the Buenos Aires police. According to Timerman, Berges supervised the application of the *picana* (electric prod) and attended to detainees (see Introduction).

The federal judge ordered Berges's arrest at the request of a national human rights group, the Center for Legal and Social Studies (CELS). Marcello Parrilli, a CELS lawyer representing the former detainees, told the court that because Berges worked in several secret detention centers, he knows the names of those responsible for scores of "disappearances."

In the opening days of the court's investigation Berges's lawyer, a retired military judge, said that his client denied the charges of complicity in torture and of having knowledge of the whereabouts of the "disappeared" persons mentioned in the testimonies. Should Berges be convicted, he could receive a sentence of from eight to twenty-five years. In addition, the Medical Association of Quilmes (Colegio Médico de Quilmes) opened an investigation of Berges's medical activities, which could result in his explusion from the association.

Eric Stover

---

responsible for Joelito's death was located in the United States, the Filártigas brought suit against the official in a district court in New York City under the Alien Tort Claims Act. Eventually the US courts ruled in favor of the Filártiga family, proclaiming the torturer an "enemy of mankind." That action helped place the US judiciary on a course that many hope will improve the enforcement of international human rights standards and prompt other domestic courts to take similar actions.

Psychiatrists and other physicians can play an important role in cases of torture tried before national courts by providing expert testimony. During the court's deliberation on the amount of damages to be awarded the

Filártigas, for example, the presiding judge reviewed several medical reports describing the effects of torture on victims and their families. The US court's ruling held out the prospect that health professionals who participate in torture may also eventually become liable for such wrong-doing—inside or outside of their own country. An encouraging move in that direction has already taken place in Argentina. In response to the military's use of torture during its self-proclaimed "dirty war" against subversion in the 1970s, Argentine legislators, in 1984, laid down stiff penalties for those found guilty of torture and provided especially heavy sentences for doctors who assist, directly or indirectly, in its use.[17]

Domestic courts can also be used in defending health professionals who have been detained for reasons of conscience or for treating victims of torture. National health associations could follow the example set by the Chilean Medical Association which, in 1981, filed a writ of *habeas corpus* on behalf of three Chilean doctors held incommunicado for treating victims of torture. The association's quick response through the courts not only gained the government's immediate attention but also interested the press in publishing a number of articles on the issue of torture, both from a medical and legal point of view. Clearly the legal profession has made significant contributions to the protection of basic human rights, and the medical profession could learn a great deal from its experience.

Treatment and Rehabilitation of Torture Victims

The growing network of health professionals and institutions concerned about torture has made treatment accessible to many more victims than in the past. Nevertheless, there are still an untold number of torture victims, residing in their own countries or living in exile, who, for various reasons, have not sought medical care. "Most of the people who have been tortured don't want to talk about it," says Nelson Diaz, a 37-year-old Uruguayan who was imprisoned and tortured before emigrating to Canada. "They carry their sickness with them until they find someone to trust."[18]

Some torture victims, of course, may learn to cope with the trauma they experienced and are not compelled to seek assistance. For example, in his study of concentration camp survivors in Norway and Israel, Leo Eitinger concluded that it is an error to assume that all survivors lead significantly impaired lives as a result of their concentration camp experience.[19] Other writers suggest that labeling the aftereffects of torture as an individual illness is a form of medical reductionism that may lead to "iatrogenia"—an illness induced inadvertently by doctors or by medical treatments.[20] To classify the aftereffects of torture as primarily a medical illness and then to establish special institutions for medical treatment of its victims, they argue, may, in some cases, cause victims to view themselves as people set aside and stigmatized.

Although research on the aftereffects of torture and means of treating these effects is still in its infancy, medical studies such as those described in Chapter 3 indicate that the predominant symptomatology found in torture victims, sometimes years after their torture, includes feelings of helplessness, anxiety, insomnia, impaired memory, and inability to concentrate, and nightmares. "In my nightmares, I don't suffer torture," a Chilean doctor and former torture victim says, "but I see someone else, a good friend, being tortured and killed." The 45-year-old gynecologist, who is now receiving therapy in Toronto, links his nightmares to his experiences in a Chilean detention center, where he was held following the military coup of 1973: "They used to throw people who had been badly tortured, with broken bones and in very bad shape, into my cell. And they would say, 'Here's a doctor for you,' and laugh."[21]

A recent study of victims of violence, including 15 torture victims, carried out by physicians and psychiatrists in Chile found that in 12 of the 15 cases the use of testimony led to alleviation of anxiety and other acute symptoms. As a therapeutic instrument, the Chilean doctors concluded, the experience of torture narrated through testimonials had several beneficial effects:

> Paradoxically, the testimony is the very confession that had been sought by the torturers and that was withheld by the victims at the cost of extraordinary personal suffering. But through testimony, confession becomes denunciation instead of the betrayal it may have been perceived as earlier . . . it channeled the patients' anger into a socially constructive action—production of a document that could be used as an indictment against the offenders. . . . In this context testimony works as a means of prevention of future mental illness, because it does not simply express the emotional trauma, but facilitates its personal and social elaboration.[22]

For those torture victims who seek treatment, or perhaps an opportunity just to talk about their experience, several groups of health professionals and centers around the world provide appropriate services. Two centers— one in Denmark and the other in Canada—now administer to a growing number of refugees seeking assistance.

The Danish center, the International Rehabilitation Centre for Torture Victims, was established in 1982 and now maintains facilities at the University Hospital of Copenhagen. In addition to providing treatment and rehabilitation to victims and their families, the center trains health professionals from various countries in the latest methods of treatment. Physicians including psychiatrists at the clinic have treated several dozen torture victims—usually two or three at a time as space allows—from many different countries, including Afghanistan, Chile, Iraq, Iran, and several African states. Most victims treated at the center simply arrive in Denmark as refugees and learn of the program by word of mouth.[23]

The clinic's doctors follow three basic principles in treating torture victims. First, they employ psychotherapy and physiotherapy (such as massages or care for old wounds) in conjunction with one another. Second, the doctors provide counseling for family members when possible while they treat the victim. The objective is to keep families together and to approach the problem from a wholistic perspective. Finally, the staff attempts to provide a therapeutic environment that will not remind victims of their past torture. Patients spend several days or even weeks in the hospital, while they are interviewed and a treatment plan is developed. The clinic's doctors have found that much of what goes on in a hospital may resemble torture in the eyes of the victims. For example, patients often fear medical instruments that resemble the tools of torture and may dread dental treatment because they feel trapped in the dentist's chair, a situation very close to the torture situation.[24]

The Canadian Center for the Investigation and Prevention of Torture, established in Toronto in 1983, currently provides help to about 50 refugees who are torture victims, and has a waiting list of 35. Founded by Federico Allodi and Philip Berger, the center maintains a network of about three dozen doctors in the Toronto area to assist victims. In his treatment of torture victims, Allodi uses dynamic psychotherapy—a traditional therapy designed to help patients understand the emotional and psychological bases for their feelings and actions. Allodi believes that torture victims, because of their experiences, may have lost the ability to deal with people and may no longer trust anyone. Allodi tries to establish a therapeutic alliance between himself and his patients that will encourage patients to feel that their values and goals are important. After several sessions, he gradually urges patients to relive and recount the emotional trauma they suffered at the hands of their torturers. Sharing their experiences in the safety of the psychiatrist's office, Allodi says, helps patients regain their perception of the world as a fairly safe and secure place, where trust can again be placed in others. (See Chapter 3.)

In addition to treatment, the Canadian center assists immigration lawyers seeking documentary evidence of torture in order to secure political refugee status for the victims. Refugee status can be obtained in Canada, as well as other countries, if there is a well-founded fear that an individual will face persecution upon return to his or her home country. These centers provide

243

valuable services, but only to a fraction of those who need help. The existing centers can help other groups establish centers in places of refuge for victims of torture.

Dual Loyality and the Prevention of Psychiatric Abuse

There is also much that can be done to end psychiatric abuse and to aid its victims. Involuntary psychiatric confinement for nonviolent political reasons rather than for genuine medical reasons is both a violation of international human rights and a serious breach of medical ethics. Prevention of psychiatric abuse, like prevention of torture, requires the accumulation of accurate documentation on individual cases of abuse, followed by international exposure and pressure on the offending governments. Much of the responsibility for preventing the political misuse of psychiatry rests with the mental health profession itself. However, states, and all citizens within a state, also have the responsibility of ensuring that psychiatrists, like everyone else who hold positions of power in a society, are accountable for their actions.

All of the contributing authors in Part II agree that there are two ways of looking at Soviet suppression of dissent through psychiatric hospitalization. First, they maintain that unethical behavior on the part of Soviet psychiatrists is directly attributable to that country's political system, which uses psychiatry as a tool for quashing opposition to state polices. Second, they acknowledge that Soviet psychiatrists employ such broad diagnostic criteria for establishing mental illness that they come to view dissident behavior as abnormal. The authors disagree, however, on which of these views is primary.

Bloch and Reddaway (Chapter 6) believe that most Soviet psychiatrists knowingly misuse their profession for political ends. They argue that even if some dissidents are truly believed to be mentally ill, their psychiatrists fail to provide treatment appropriate for the conditions diagnosed. Chodoff, who shares Bloch and Reddaway's view, points to the manner in which political dissidents are treated after having been labelled "sluggish schizo-phrenics." "Even if such an illness exists," he writes, "it certainly is not severe enough to necessitate hospitalization of these well-functioning people whose family and friends do not see them as ill. There is no need to incarcerate them in special hospitals. . . . There is no need to give them drugs for punitive rather than therapeutic purposes, to threaten them with perpetual imprisonment unless they recant, to deprive them of the ordinary decencies of life . . ."[25]

Reich, on the other hand, contends that Soviet psychiatrists really see their patients as schizophrenic because of the dictates of the official diagnostic system. Soviet authorities and psychiatrists, he argues, base their understanding of mental illness on the diagnostic concept developed during the 1960s by Andrei V. Snezhnevsky, the founder of what has come to be called the Moscow School of Psychiatry.[26] The Snezhnevsky approach to mental illness imposes on the Soviet psychiatrist a monochromatic vision of psychopathology. There is no room for a second opinion, Reich says, for essentially there is no opinion other than that established by the Snezhnevsky school. Because Soviet dissidents behave and speak in ways that differ from their fellow citizens, psychiatrists, the KGB, members of the legal profession, and indeed much of the population actually believe that dissidents are mentally ill.

It might seem that the differing views of Soviet psychiatry expressed here are, for the most part, academic. But to dismiss them as such undermines the significance that these two views can play in shaping strategies aimed at preventing psychiatric abuse and in aiding its victims in the Soviet Union and elsewhere.

It can be argued in retrospect that the decision of several national society members to force the expulsion of the Soviet Union from the WPA was ill-conceived and that other measures should have been tried first, such as barring Soviet psychiatrists from official positions within the association or refusing to hold WPA-sponsored meetings in the Soviet Union. But that is all in the past. What should be done now, in our opinion, is to reestablish contact with Soviet psychiatry and invite the Soviets to the next WPA world congress, scheduled to be held in 1988, provided that they can demonstrate, to the satisfaction of Western colleagues, that they are making substantial progress in terminating political abuse of psychiatry. The reasons for the Soviet withdrawal, for example, are not altogether clear. There is considerable speculation that the decision to quit did not occur at the level of the psychiatrists but at a higher, more political level. If this was the case, WPA officials should make use of it, without compromising their stance, in meetings with Soviet psychiatrists. Snezhnevsky's imminent retirement as head of the powerful Moscow Institute of Psychiatry should be watched closely. New leadership in the Soviet psychiatric community could portend change, however slight, and such openings should be taken advantage of.

But most of all, the Soviet withdrawal should serve to reinforce the efforts of mental health professionals and others to speak out against the involuntary hospitalization of political and social nonconformists in the Soviet Union. More than ever, international attention needs to be focused on the plight of psychiatrists, like Anatoly Koryagin, who question the abuse of Soviet psychiatry and pay the consequences, for they are now in even greater isolation.

Walter Reich underscores why it is so important that we understand what has happened to Soviet psychiatry:

> [The Soviet experience] has much to teach about the ways in which an official diagnostic system can shape psychiatric vision and skew diagnostic practice, ensnaring people who elsewhere would be considered mentally well in the broad net that defines them irrevocably, as mentally ill. [It] is important because it exemplifies, in pure and extreme form, a trend that is only now developing in other countries; because its effects can be documented in multiple ways; and because it demonstrates, with grim clarity, how a system that appears to have only scientific origins and professional goals can, simply by virtue of its own nature as a systematic psychiatric technology, result in significant human harm.[27]

The abuse of the psychiatric discipline is not confined to the suppression of visible political activists in the Soviet Union, or Yugoslavia, or other countries. Controversy has raged in the United States, for example, over the status of homosexuality as a mental disorder. Not until 1968 did the American Psychiatric Association declare that "homosexuality . . . by itself does not constitute a psychiatric disorder." Before that time, the association had defined homosexuality as abnormal.[28] Other issues which pose tremendous legal, moral, and ethical delimmas for the psychiatric profession and the public at large include defining the criteria of dangerousness to self and others or the competency to stand trial, the insanity defense, the ethical aspects of psychotherapy, drug treatment, and surgical interventions in the brain to alter behaviors.[29]

South Africa's apartheid system raises several moral and ethical questions for the psychiatric profession as well. Given an entrenched government policy based on racial segregation, the possibility always exists that some white South African psychiatrists* could view dissidence on the part of blacks as somehow abnormal and subject such "troublemakers" to involuntary hospitalization. As discussed in the Introduction, no evidence of the misuse of psychiatry to suppress political dissent such as it exists in the Soviet Union has been found in South Africa, but the potential remains.[31]

What then should psychiatrists both inside and outside South Africa do? Should South African psychiatrists be treated as pariahs by their foreign colleagues? We believe little would be gained in ostracizing South African psychiatrists or their professional organization, the Society of Psychiatrists of South Africa (SPSA).[32] On the other hand, psychiatrists in South Africa and elsewhere should condemn apartheid because it proclaims that blacks are inferior beings, thereby undermining their self-esteem and, by doing so, their mental health. Further, if Lifton's hypothesis described earlier is

---

* At the time of writing, there are 150 psychiatrists in South Africa, of whom none are black, for a population of approximately 25 million.[30]

correct—that policies which promote racial superiority facilitate brutal acts—then apartheid creates an environment conducive for torture. It is not surprising, therefore, that political detainees in South Africa have been tortured, and, in some cases, so traumatized by it, that they have required urgent psychiatric care.[33] Until recently, the SPSA had not explicitly spoken about apartheid and torture. On 31 January 1985, at its annual meeting, the Society drew up a statement of policy on apartheid:

> (1) The Society of Psychiatrists recognises and deplores potentially harmful psychological effects on the people of South Africa as a result of any form of discrimination based on race, colour, gender, or creed. The Society does and will strive for the elimination of all forms of discrimination that adversely affect mental health.
>
> (2) The Society declares its opposition to any disparities in the quality of psychiatric services for all.
>
> (3) The Society declares its committment to insist that its members practise their profession as laid out in internationally accepted ethical codes in the declarations of Helsinki, Hawaii, and Tokyo and its determination to resist any form of abuse of psychiatric knowledge and skills for political ends or for any other purpose contrary to the best interests of the patients and their personal welfare.
>
> (4) The Society has by its representation and actions been responsible for many improvements in the services for all psychiatric patients in South Africa. The Society steadfastly declares its intention to continue these efforts.[34]

This statement is most appropriate and most welcome. We hope that the Society will continue its efforts and will work to inform the public of the pernicious effects of apartheid on victims and society at large. The SPSA deserves the support of colleagues worldwide in this work.

"Abuse," US Judge David L. Bazelon writes, "is imminent whenever psychiatrists abandon their role as the patient's ally and use their skills to serve institutional purposes."[35] The first step in combatting these dangers is to identify those practices which contain the seeds of abuse and develop safeguards appropriate to each situation. Judge Bazelon suggests that there are three areas in which the psychiatric profession could help remove "the impurities of institutional bias, pressures and interests" which may color psychiatric judgments in public institutions:

> First, psychiatrists must be able to understand and identify those situations in which they assume an alliance with a public or social institution rather than with the patient. Recognition of the inevitable conflict of interest must be legitimized rather than silenced by rote repetition of the Hippocratic Oath.

Second, the conflict of interest must be made explicit to the patient. It is nothing short of dishonest to encourage a patient to communicate freely by allowing him to assume that the psychiatrist is acting solely as his agent. The patient is entitled to at least one statement . . . of the risks involved in the relationship.

Third, the [psychiatric] profession should encourage forms of third-party review of its most critical decisions. This already exists in the case of judicial review of involuntary commitments, and review by the Veterans Administration of military psychiatric discharges and disability awards [in the United States].[36]

If psychiatrists and their associations worldwide succeed in reaching these goals, the profession and, most importantly, those in need of psychiatric care, would be well served, and the misuse of psychiatry for suppressing political dissent, as in the Soviet Union, would cease. Though it is difficult to influence Soviet psychiatry, scrupulous attention to the responsibilities of psychiatrists as citizens and to their accountability both to patients and to society would form a firmer base from which to improve the ethical practice of psychiatry everywhere.

Conclusion

Health professionals and other persons have a moral imperative to speak out against the misuse of medical knowledge and skills whenever and wherever it occurs. Yet health and biomedical professionals, particularly in the United States, have not been sufficiently involved, perhaps because neither they nor the general public have been made aware of the nature and magnitude of the problem, or perhaps because they view intervention as a political act or as futile. But there are frequent references in this book to situations where outside intervention has had beneficial results. Clearly, in countries with repressive governments, health professionals who protest abuses of human rights or seek to uphold the ethical standards of their profession place themselves in a precarious situation. Support from their colleagues abroad would provide assistance should they also become victims of repression.

Once awareness of the problem has risen sufficiently within the health professions, a more extensive network of professional societies and associations could be effective in research, in fact-finding, and in exerting pressure when abuses occur. American health professionals, particularly physicians, often view such matters as political and therefore fail to act. However, the misuse of medical knowledge for political reasons can be dealt with in a nonpolitical fashion. Codes of ethics in particular are not political, and their wide distribution will help to safeguard those health professionals who want to act ethically but who have little support for their actions. Silence condones: once awareness exists, it is both unethical and unthinkable to remain silent.

Both torture and psychiatric abuse violate internationally recognized human rights and involve the misuse of a health professional's special knowledge, skills, and social duties. In this book we have provided a sample of the kinds of misuse of medical knowledge and skills that occur in the world today, and of the progress that is being made to combat such abuse and to assist its victims. It is hoped that by making this information available in one place, health professionals and the public will become more aware of these problems. The health professions' action on behalf of human rights increases public awareness of these issues and, in turn, public awareness creates a supportive environment for the actions of professionals.

If systematic physical and mental brutality—vividly described by George Orwell in *1984* and portentously linked by him to medical irresponsibility— are to be avoided, it will not be for lack of technical ability. As Orwell's nightmare anticipated, we are now capable of breaking bodies and minds effectively on a large scale. To put Orwell's fears of 1984 behind us, we must put medical ethics and internationally defined human rights in front of us. And in this endeavor the health professions must take the lead.

Notes and References

1. Robert Jay Lifton, "The Concept of the Survivor," in Joel E. Dimsdale, ed., *Survivors, Victims, and Perpetrators: Essays on the Nazi Holocaust* (New York: Hemisphere Publishing Corporation, 1980), p. 125.

2. Amnesty International, *Torture in the Eighties* (London: Amnesty International, 1984).

3. The three commonly cited categories of prevention activities—primary, secondary, and tertiary—are defined as follows:

    Primary prevention includes activities that promote health or are undertaken prior to the development of disease or injuries, such as vaccinations, fluoridation of the water supply, automobile speed limits and emission controls, restriction on the purchase of handguns, or limitations on the sale of alcohol. Secondary prevention includes the detection of disease in early (asymptomatic) stages and intervention to arrest its progress—for example, screening for incipient hypertension, for phenylketonuria in newborns, or for precancerous changes in cells of the cervical epithelium. Tertiary prevention involves intervention after the development of a clinically manifest disease in order to reverse, arrest, or delay its progression—for example, administration of Vitamin B_{12} to prevent the recurrence of the manifestations of pernicious anemia, or administration of phenothiazines to prevent the recurrence of schizophrenic episodes. As will readily be recognized, tertiary prevention merges with conventional treatment.

Elena O. Nightingale, Mary Cureton, Vicki Kalmar, and Michelle B. Trudeau, *Perspectives on Health Promotion and Disease Prevention in the United States*, a staff paper (Washington, D.C.: Institute of Medicine of the National Academy of Sciences, 1978), pp. 21–22.

4. Amnesty International, *Amnesty International Report 1984* (London: Amnesty International, 1984) p. 3.

5. H. Tristram Engelhardt, "Rights and Responsibilities of Patients and Physicians," in Tom L. Beauchamp and Leroy Walters, eds., *Contemporary Issues in Bioethics* (Belmont, Calif.: Wadsworth, 1982), p. 134.

6. The issue of the medical consequences of nuclear war exemplifies this duty. See Eric Chivian, Susanna Chivian, Robert Jay Lifton, and John E. Mack, eds., *Last Aid: The Medical Dimensions of Nuclear War* (San Francisco: W. H. Freeman and Company, 1982).

7. See, for example, Farooq Hassan, "The Doctrine of Incorporation: New Vistas for the Enforcement of International Human Rights," *Human Rights Quarterly* 5, no. 1 (Winter 1983): 68–86; Richard A. Falk, "Responding to Severe Violations," in Jorge I. Dominguez, Nigel S. Rodley, Bryce Wood, and Richard A. Falk, *Enhancing Global Human Rights* (New York: McGraw Hill, 1979), pp. 207–247.

8. Statement made by Martin Ennals at the International Colloquium on How to Combat Torture, Geneva, 28–29 April 1983 (sponsored by Amnesty International and the Comité Suisse Contre la Torture).

9. See Inter-American Commission on Human Rights, *Report on Situation of Human Rights in Argentina* (Washington, D.C.: General Secretariat, Organization of American States, April 1980).

10. Amnesty International, *Torture in the Eighties*, pp. 62–76.

11. Article 126 of the Third Geneva Convention gives the ICRC the right to see prisoners of war from the beginning of their captivity. The Fourth Geneva Convention gives the ICRC the right to see civilian detainees, comparable to the right it has with regard to prisoners of war, with one important exception: The "Detaining Power" is permitted to suspend access to detainees suspected of activities hostile to the security of the State. However, signatories to the Conventions are required to grant the ICRC access to prisoners of war as well as civilian detainees during international conflicts. In civil wars, the signatories may deny ICRC teams rights of visitation at will. For more information about the conventions see, for example, these ICRC publications: *The ICRC and Torture* (Geneva: ICRC, 1976) and *The ICRC and Human Rights* (Geneva: ICRC, 1979), and *Bibliography of International Humanitarian Law Applicable in Armed Conflicts* (Geneva: ICRC, 1980).

12. Remarks made in a talk delivered by Robert J. Lifton at the Annual Meeting of the American Psychiatric Association on 20 May 1982 and at a Southern California Psychoanalytic Society conference on "The Violation of Human Rights: The Quest for Understanding," September 1984. The results of Lifton's interviews with 28 Nazi doctors is the subject of his forthcoming book entitled *From Healer to Killer: The Doctors of Auschwitz*.

13. Jacobo Timerman, *Prisoner without a Name, Cell without a Number* (New York: Knopf, 1981).

14. See Amnesty International, *Report on Torture* (New York: Farrar, Straus and Giroux, 1975), pp. 240–242.

15. See International Law Commission, *Draft Articles on State Responsibility*, [1980] 2 Summary Records of the 1635th Meeting 26, UN Doc. A/CN.4/L.318; Article 38(1) of the Statute of the International Court of Justice at the Hague provides, *inter alia*, that "international custom, [is] evidence of a general practice accepted as law." As such, international customary law can be inferred from multilateral declarations of common policy among states, domestic constitutions that overwhelmingly uphold a given norm, and the acceptance by domestic and international courts of internationally agreed standards.

16. Nirmala Chandrahasan, "Freedom from Torture and the Jurisdiction of Municipal Courts: Sri Lanka and United States Perspectives," *Human Rights Quarterly* 5, no. 1 (Winter 1983):58–67.

17. Article 144(4) of the revised Argentine Penal Code provides "Any public official who fails to prevent torture . . . when he was in a position to do so, will face a prison sentence of from 3 to 10 years. . . . If the official is a doctor the prison sentence will be doubled and he will be barred from exercising his profession."

18. Quoted in Sheila Whyte, "Medical Group Seeks Funds to Open Centre for Immigrant Torture Victims," *The Globe and Daily Mail*, 8 July 1983, p. 11.

19. Leo Eitinger, "The Concentration Camp Syndrome and Its Late Sequelae," in Joel E. Dimsdale, ed., *Survivors, Victims, and Perpetrators: Essays on the Nazi Holocaust* (New York: Hemisphere Publishing, 1980), pp. 127–161.

20. Unpublished paper by Silvia Amati on "Psychotherapy and the Torture Victim."

21. Quoted in Les Whittington, "Toronto Center Strained by Influx of Salvadoran Torture Victims," *Washington Post*, 12 June 1984, p. A13.

22. Ana Julia Cienfuegos and Cristina Monelli, "The Testimony of Political Repression as a Therapeutic Instrument," *American Journal of Orthopsychiatry* 53, no. 1 (January 1983):43–51.

23. Inge Kemp Genefke and Ole Aalund, "Rehabilitation of Torture Victims— Research Perspectives," *Manedsskrift for praktisk laegegerning*, January 1983.

24. *Ibid*.

25. Unpublished letter from Paul Chodoff to the Editor, *New York Times*, dated 1 February 1983.

26. See Walter Reich, "Psychiatric Diagnosis as an Ethical Problem," in Sidney Bloch and Paul Chodoff, eds., *Psychiatric Ethics* (Oxford: Oxford University Press, 1981), pp. 61–88.

27. Ibid., p. 64–65.

28. *Diagnostic and Statistical Manual of Mental Disorders*, 2d edition (Washington, D.C., American Psychiatric Association, 1968).

29. See, for example, Sidney Bloch and Paul Chodoff, eds., *Psychiatric Ethics*.

30. "Apartheid and Psychiatry," *The Lancet* (1 December 1984):1252–1253.

31. See American Psychiatric Association, "Report of the Committee to visit South Africa," *American Journal of Psychiatry* 136 (1979):1498 and Royal College of Psychiatrists, "Report of the Special (Political Abuse of Psychiatry) Committee on South Africa," *Bulletin of the Royal College of Psychiatrists* 6 (1982):178.

32. *Ibid.*

33. *Rand Daily Mail*, 27 February 1982.

34. The Society of Psychiatrists of South Africa, "Notes and News," *The Lancet* (2 March 1985).

35. David L. Bazelon, Report to the Board of Trustees of the American Psychiatric Association of the Ad Hoc Committee on the Use of Psychiatric Institutions for the Commitment of Political Dissenters from the Ad Hoc Committee's meeting of 21 April 1972. Judge David L. Bazelon's remarks, quoted here, were attached as a separate statement to the Ad Hoc Committee's report.

36. Ibid.

Appendix A

Codes of Ethics and Declarations on Abuse

Convention Against Torture and Other Cruel, Inhuman or Degrading Treatment or Punishment (United Nations)

Hippocratic Oath

Prayer of Moses Maimonides

Declaration of Geneva (World Medical Association)

Physician's Oath of the Soviet Union

Islamic Code of Medical Ethics

Principles of Medical Ethics (American Medical Association)

Regulations in Time of Armed Conflict (World Medical Association)

Declaration of Tokyo (World Medical Association)

Declaration of Hawaii (World Psychiatric Association)

Resolution of Singapore (International Council of Nurses)

Statement on the Nurse's Role in Safeguarding Human Rights (International Council of Nurses)

Codes for the ethical guidance of physicians, nurses, psychiatrists, and other health professionals have been promulgated over many centuries in many different countries and many different cultures. This appendix is a selection of codes and declarations for health professionals that are pertinent to the protection of people against torture and other forms of abuse.

One of the most important documents on torture is the Convention against Torture and Other Cruel, Inhuman, or Degrading Treatment or Punishment, adopted by consensus of the UN General Assembly on 10 December 1984. Among other things, it obliges states to make torture a punishable offense and provides for the extradition of torturers and the compensation of victims. The UN Principles of Medical Ethics Relevant to the Role of Health Personnel, Particularly Physicians, in the Protection of Prisoners and Detainees against Torture and Other Cruel, Inhuman, or Degrading Treatment or Punishment (1982) can be found in Chapter 5. (Editors)

Convention against Torture and Other Cruel, Inhuman or Degrading Treatment or Punishment

(United Nations, 1984)

PART I

Article 1

1. For the purposes of this Convention, torture means any act by which severe pain or suffering, whether physical or mental, is intentionally inflicted on a person for such purposes as obtaining from him or a third person information or a confession, punishing him for an act he or a third person has committed or is suspected of having committed, or intimidating or coercing him or a third person, or for any reason based on discrimination of any kind, when such pain or suffering is inflicted by or at the instigation of or with the consent or acquiescence of a public official or other person acting in an official capacity. It does not include pain or suffering arising only from, inherent in or incidental to lawful sanctions.
2. This article is without prejudice to any international instrument or national legislation which does or may contain provisions of wider application.

Article 2

1. Each State Party shall take effective legislative, administrative, judicial or other measures to prevent acts of torture in any territory under its jurisdiction.
2. No exceptional circumstances whatsoever, whether a state of war or a threat of war, internal political instability or any other public emergency, may be invoked as justification of torture.
3. An order from a superior officer or a public authority may not be invoked as a justification of torture.

Article 3

1. No State Party shall expel, return ("refouler") or extradite a person to another State where there are substantial grounds for believing that he would be in danger of being subjected to torture.
2. For the purposes of determining whether there are such grounds, the competent authorities shall take into account all relevant considerations including where applicable, the existence in the State concerned of a consistent pattern of gross, flagrant or mass violations of human rights.

Article 4

1. Each State Party shall ensure that all acts of torture are offences under its criminal law. The same shall apply to an attempt to commit torture and to an act by any person which constitutes complicity or participation in torture.
2. Each State Party shall make these offences punishable by appropriate penalties which take into account their grave nature.

Article 5

1. Each State Party shall take such measures as may be necessary to establish its jurisdiction over the offences referred to in article 4 in the following cases:

   (a) When the offences are committed in any territory under its jurisdiction or on board a ship or aircraft registered in that State;

   (b) When the alleged offender is a national of that State;

   (c) When the victim is a national of that State if that State considers it appropriate.
2. Each State Party shall likewise take such measures as may be necessary to establish its jurisdiction over such offences in cases where the alleged offender is present in any territory under its jurisdiction and it does not extradite him pursuant to article 8 to any of the States mentioned in paragraph 1 of this article.
3. This Convention does not exclude any criminal jurisdiction exercised in accordance with internal law.

Article 6

1. Upon being satisfied, after an examination of information available to it, that the circumstances so warrant, any State Party in whose territory a person alleged to have committed any offence referred to in article 4 is present, shall take him into custody or take other legal measures to ensure his presence. The custody and other legal measures shall be as provided in the law of that State but may be continued only for such time as is necessary to enable any criminal or extradition proceedings to be instituted.
2. Such State shall immediately make a preliminary inquiry into the facts.
3. Any person in custody pursuant to paragraph 1 of this article shall be assisted in communicating immediately with the nearest appropriate repre-

sentative of the State of which he is a national, or, if he is a stateless person, to the representative of the State where he usually resides.

4. When a State, pursuant to this article, has taken a person into custody, it shall immediately notify the States referred to in article 5, paragraph 1, of the fact that such person is in custody and of the circumstances which warrant his detention. The State which makes the preliminary inquiry contemplated in paragraph 2 of this article shall promptly report its findings to the said States and shall indicate whether it intends to exercise jurisdiction.

Article 7

1. The State Party in territory under whose jurisdiction a person alleged to have committed any offences referred to in article 4 is found, shall in the cases contemplated in article 5, if it does not extradite him, submit the case to its competent authorities for the purpose of prosecution.

2. These authorities shall take their decision in the same manner as in the case of any ordinary offence of a serious nature under the law of that State. In the cases referred to in article 5, paragraph 2, the standards of evidence required for prosecution and conviction shall in no way be less stringent than those which apply in the cases referred to in article 5, paragraph 1.

3. Any person regarding whom proceedings are brought in connection with any of the offences referred to in article 4 shall be guaranteed fair treatment at all stages of the proceedings.

Article 8

1. The offences referred to in article 4 shall be deemed to be included as extraditable offences in any extradition treaty existing between States Parties. States Parties undertake to include such offences as extraditable offences in every extradition treaty to be concluded between them.

2. If a State Party which makes extradition conditional on the existence of a treaty receives a request for extradition from another State Party with which it has no extradition treaty, it may consider this Convention as the legal basis for extradition in respect to such offences. Extradition shall be subject to the other conditions provided by the law of the requested State.

3. States Parties which do not make extradition conditional on the existence of a treaty shall recognize such offences as extraditable offences between themselves subject to the conditions provided by the law of the requested State.

4. Such offences shall be treated, for the purpose of extradition between State Parties, as if they had been committed not only in the place in which they occurred but also in the territories of the States required to establish their jurisdiction in accordance with article 5, paragraph 1.

Article 9

1. States Parties shall afford one another the greatest measure of assistance in connection with criminal proceedings brought in respect of any of the

offences referred to in article 4, including the supply of all evidence at their disposal necessary for the proceedings.

2. States Parties shall carry out their obligations under paragraph 1 of this article in conformity with any treaties on mutual judicial assistance that may exist between them.

Article 10

1. Each State Party shall ensure that education and information regarding the prohibition against torture are fully included in the training of law enforcement personnel, civil or military, medical personnel, public officials and other persons who may be involved in the custody, interrogation or treatment of any individual subjected to any form of arrest, detention or imprisonment.

2. States Parties shall include this prohibition in the rules of instructions issued in regard to the duties and functions of any such persons.

Article 11

Each State Party shall keep under systematic review interrogation rules, instructions, methods and practices as well as arrangements for the custody and treatment of persons subjected to any form of arrest, detention or imprisonment in any territory under its jurisdiction, with a view to preventing any cases of torture.

Article 12

Each State Party shall ensure that its competent authorities proceed to a prompt and impartial investigation, wherever there is reasonable ground to believe that an act of torture has been committed in any territory under its jurisdiction.

Article 13

Each State Party shall ensure that any individual who alleges he has been subjected to torture in any territory under its jurisdiction has the right to complain to and to have his case promptly and impartially examined by its competent authorities. Steps shall be taken to ensure that the complainant and witnesses are protected against all ill-treatment or intimidation as a consequence of his complaint or any evidence given.

Article 14

1. Each State Party shall ensure in its legal system that the victim of an act of torture obtains redress and has an enforceable right to fair and adequate compensation including the means for as full rehabilitation as possible. In the event of the death of the victim as a result of an act of torture, his dependants shall be entitled to compensation.

2. Nothing in this article shall affect any right of the victim or other persons to compensation which may exist under national law.

Article 15

Each State Party shall ensure that any statement which is established to have been made as result of torture shall not be invoked as evidence in any proceedings, except against a person accused of torture as evidence that the statement was made.

Article 16

1. Each State Party shall undertake to prevent in any territory under its jurisdiction other acts of cruel, inhuman or degrading treatment or punishment which do not amount to torture as defined in article 1, when such acts are committed by or at the instigation of or with the consent or acquiescence of a public official or other person acting in an official capacity. In particular, the obligations contained in articles 10, 11, 12 and 13 shall apply with the substitution for references to torture or references to other forms of cruel, inhuman or degrading treatment or punishment.

2. The provisions of this Convention are without prejudice to the provisions of any other international instrument or national law which prohibit cruel, inhuman or degrading treatment or punishment or which relate to extradition or expulsion.

PART II

Article 17

1. There shall be established a Committee against Torture (hereinafter referred to as the Committee) which shall carry out the functions hereinafter provided. The Committee shall consist of 10 experts of high moral standing and recognized competence in the field of human rights, who shall serve in their personal capacity. The experts shall be elected by the State Parties, consideration being given to equitable geographical distribution and to the usefulness of the participation of some persons having legal experience.

2. The members of the Committee shall be elected by secret ballot from a list of persons nominated by States Parties. Each State Party may nominate one person from among its own nationals. States Parties shall bear in mind the usefulness of nominating persons who are also members of the Human Rights Committee established under the International Covenant on Civil and Political Rights and are willing to serve on the Committee against Torture.

3. Elections of the members of the Committee shall be held at biennial meetings of States Parties convened by the Secretary-General of the United Nations. At those meetings, for which two thirds of the States Parties shall constitute a quorum, the persons elected to the Committee shall be those who obtain the largest number of votes and an absolute majority of the votes of the representatives of States Parties present and voting.

4. The initial election shall be held no later than six months after the date of the entry into force of this Convention. At least four months before the

date of each selection, the Secretary-General of the United Nations shall address a letter to the States Parties inviting them to submit their nominations within three months. The Secretary-General shall prepare a list in alphabetical order of all persons thus nominated, indicating the States Parties which have nominated them, and shall submit it to the States Parties.

5. The members of the Committee shall be elected for a term of four years. They shall be eligible for re-election if nominated. However, the term of five of the members elected at the first election shall expire at the end of two years; immediately after the first election the names of these five members shall be chosen by lot by the chairman of the meeting referred to in paragraph 3.

6. If a member of the Committee dies or resigns or for any other cause can no longer perform his Committee duties, the State Party which nominated him shall appoint another expert from among its nationals to serve for the remainder of his term, subject to the approval of the majority of the States Parties. The approval shall be considered given unless half or more of the States Parties respond negatively within six weeks after having been informed by the Secretary-General of the United Nations of the proposed appointment.

7. States Parties shall be responsible for the expenses of the members of the Committee while they are in performance of Committee duties.

Article 18

1. The Committee shall elect its officers for a term of two years. They may be re-elected.

2. The Committee shall establish its own rules of procedure, but these rules shall provide, *inter alia*, that:

   (a) Six members shall constitute a quorum
   (b) Decisions of the Committee shall be made by a majority vote of the members present.

3. The Secretary-General of the United Nations shall provide the necessary staff and facilities for the effective performance of the functions of the Committee under this Convention.

4. The Secretary-General of the United Nations shall convene the initial meeting of the Committee. After its initial meeting, the Committee shall meet at such times as shall be provided in its rules of procedure.

5. The State Parties shall be responsible for expenses incurred in connection with the holding of meetings of the States Parties and of the Committee, including reimbursement to the United Nations for any expenses, such as the cost of staff and facilities, incurred by the United Nations pursuant to paragraph 3 above.

Article 19

1. The States Parties shall submit to the Committee, through the Secretary General of the United Nations, reports on the measures they have taken to

give effect to their undertakings under this Convention, within one year after the entry into force of this Convention for the State Party. Thereafter the States Parties shall submit supplementary reports every four years on any new measures taken, and such other reports as the Committee may request.

2. The Secretary-General shall transmit the reports to all States Parties.

3. Each report shall be considered by the Committee which may make such comments or suggestions on the report as it may consider appropriate, and shall forward these to the State Party concerned. That State Party may respond with any observations it chooses to the Committee.

4. The Committee may, at its discretion, decide to include any comments or suggestions made by it in accordance with paragraph 3, together with the observations thereon received from the State Party concerned, in its annual report made in accordance with article 24. If so requested by the State Party concerned, the Committee may also include a copy of the report submitted under paragraph 1.

Article 20

1. If the Committee receives information which appears to it to contain reliable indications that torture is being systematically practised in the territory of a State Party, the Committee shall invite that State Party to submit observations with regard to the information concerned.

2. Taking into account any observations which may have been submitted by the State Party concerned as well as any other relevant information available to it, the Committee may, if it decides that this is warranted, designate one or more of its members to make a confidential inquiry and to report to the Committee urgently.

3. If an inquiry is made in accordance with paragraph 2, the Committee shall seek the co-operation of the State Party concerned. In agreement with that State Party, such an inquiry may include a visit to its territory.

4. After examining the findings of its member or members submitted in accordance with paragraph 2, the Committee shall transmit these findings to the state Party concerned together with any comments or suggestions which seem appropriate in view of the situation.

5. All the proceedings of the Committee referred to in paragraph 1–4 shall be confidential. After such proceedings have been completed with regard to an inquiry made in accordance with paragraph 2, the Committee may, at its discretion, decide to include a summary account of the results of the proceedings in its annual report made in accordance with article 24.

Article 21

1. A State Party to this Convention may at any time declare under this article that it recognizes the competence of the Committee to receive and consider communications to the effect that a State Party claims that another State

Party is not fulfilling its obligations under this Convention. Such communications may be received and considered according to the procedures laid down in this article only if submitted by a State Party which has made a declaration recognizing in regard to itself the competence of the Committee. No communication shall be dealt with by the Committee under this article if it concerns a State Party which has not made such a declaration. Communications received under this article shall be dealt with in accordance with the following procedure:

(a) If a State Party considers that another State Party is not giving effect to the provisions of this Convention, it may, by written communication, bring the matter to the attention of that State Party. Within three months after the receipt of the communication the receiving State shall afford the State which sent the communication an explanation or any other statement in writing clarifying the matter which should include, to the extent possible and pertinent, reference to domestic procedures and remedies taken, pending, or available in the matter.

(b) If the matter is not adjusted to the satisfaction of both States Parties concerned within six months after the receipt by the receiving State of the initial communication, either State shall have the right to refer the matter to the Committee, by notice given to the Committee and to the other State.

(c) The committee shall deal with a matter referred to it under this article only after it has ascertained that all domestic remedies have been invoked and exhausted in the matter, in conformity with the generally recognized principles of international law. This shall not be the rule where the application of the remedies is unreasonably prolonged or is unlikely to bring effective relief to the person who is the victim of the violation of this Convention.

(d) The Committee shall hold closed meetings when examining communications under this article.

(e) Subject to the provisions of subparagraph (c), the Committee shall make available its good offices to the States Parties concerned with a view to a friendly solution of the matter on the basis of respect for the obligations provided for in the present Convention. For this purpose, the Committee may, when appropriate, set up an *ad hoc* conciliation commission.

(f) In any matter referred to it under this article, the Committee may call upon the States Parties concerned, referred to in subparagraph (b), to supply any relevant information.

(g) The States Parties concerned, referred to in subparagraph (b), shall have the right to be represented when the matter is being considered by the Committee and to make submissions orally and/or in writing.

(h) The Committee shall, within 12 months after the date of receipt of notice under subparagraph (b), submit a report.

(i) If a solution within the terms of paragraph (e) is reached, the Committee shall confine its report to a brief statement of the facts; and of the solution reached.

(ii) If a solution within the terms of subparagraph (e) is not reached, the Committee shall confine its report to a brief statement of the facts; the written submissions and record of the oral submissions made by the States Parties concerned shall be attached to the report.

In every matter, the report shall be communicated to the States Parties concerned.

2. The provisions of this article shall come into force when five States Parties to this Convention have made declarations under paragraph 1 of this article. Such declarations shall be deposited by the States Parties with the Secretary-General of the United Nations, who shall transmit copies thereof to the other States Parties. A declaration may be withdrawn at any time by notification to the Secretary-General. Such a withdrawal shall not prejudice the consideration of any matter which is the subject of a communication already transmitted under this article; no further communication by any State Party shall be received under this article after the notification of withdrawal of the declaration has been received by the Secretary-General, unless the State Party concerned has made a new declaration.

Article 22

1. A State party to this Convention may at any time declare under this article that it recognizes the competence of the Committee to receive and consider communications from or on behalf of individuals subject to its jurisdiction who claim to be victims of a violation by a State Party of the provisions of the Convention. No communication shall be received by the Committee if it concerns a State Party to the Convention which has not made such a declaration.

2. The Committee shall consider inadmissible any communication under this article which is anonymous, or which it considers to be an abuse of the right of submission of such communications or to be incompatible with the provisions of this Convention.

3. Subject to the provisions of paragraph 2, the Committee shall bring any communications submitted to it under this article to the attention of the State Party to this Convention which has made a declaration under paragraph 1 and is alleged to be violating any provisions of the Convention. Within six months, the receiving State shall submit to the Committee written explanations or statements clarifying the matter and the remedy, if any, that may have been taken by that State.

4. The Committee shall consider communications received under this article in the light of all information made available to it by or on behalf of the individual and by the State Party concerned.

5. The Committee shall not consider any communications from an individual under this article unless it has ascertained that:

(a) The same matter has not been, and is not being, examined under another procedure of international investigation or settlement;

(b) The individual has exhausted all available domestic remedies; this shall not be the rule where the application of the remedies is unreasonably prolonged or is unlikely to bring effective relief to the person who is the victim of the violation of this Convention.

6. The Committee shall hold closed meetings when examining communications under this article.

7. The Committee shall forward its views to the State Party concerned and to the individual.

8. The provisions of this article shall come into force when five States Parties to this Convention have made declarations under paragraph 1 of this article. Such declarations shall be deposited by the States Parties with the Secretary-General of the United Nations, who shall transmit copies thereof to the other States Parties. A declaration may be withdrawn at any time by notification to the Secretary-General. Such a withdrawal shall not prejudice the consideration of any matter which is the subject of a communication already transmitted under this article; no further communication by or on behalf of an individual shall be received under this article after the notification of withdrawal of the declaration has been received by the Secretary-General, unless the State Party concerned has made a new declaration.

Article 23

The members of the Committee, and of the *ad hoc* conciliation commissions which may be appointed under article 21, paragraph 1 (e), shall be entitled to the facilities, privileges and immunities of experts on mission for the United Nations as laid down in the relevant sections of the Convention on the Privileges and Immunities of the United Nations.

Article 24

The Committee shall submit an annual report on its activities under this Convention to the States Parties and to the General Assembly of the United Nations.

PART III

Article 25

1. This Convention is open for signature by all States.

2. This Convention is subject to ratification. Instruments of ratification shall be deposited with the Secretary-General of the United Nations.

Article 26

This Convention is open to accession by all States. Accession shall be effected by the deposit of an instrument of accession with the Secretary-General of the United Nations.

Article 27

1. This Convention shall enter into force on the thirtieth day after the date of the deposit with the Secretary-General of the United Nations of the twentieth instrument of ratification or accession.
2. For each State ratifying this Convention or acceding to it after the deposit of the twentieth instrument of ratification or accession, the Convention shall enter into force on the thirtieth day after the date of the deposit of its own instrument of ratification or accession.

Article 28

1. Any State Party to this Convention may propose an amendment and file it with the Secretary-General of the United Nations. The Secretary-General shall thereupon communicate the proposed amendment to the States Parties to this Convention with a request that they notify him whether they favour a conference of States Parties for the purpose of considering and voting upon the proposal. In the event that within four months from the date of such communication at least one third of the State Parties favours such a conference, the Secretary-General shall convene the conference under the auspices of the United Nations. Any amendment adopted by a majority of the State Parties present and voting at the conference shall be submitted by the Secretary-General to all the States Parties for acceptance.
2. An amendment adopted in accordance with paragraph 1 shall enter into force when two thirds of the States Parties to this Convention have notified the Secretary-General of the United Nations that they have accepted it in accordance with their respective constitutional processes.
3. When amendments enter into force, they shall be binding on those States Parties which have accepted them, other States Parties still being bound by the provisions of this Convention and any earlier amendments which they have accepted.

Article 29

1. Any dispute between two or more States Parties concerning the interpretation or application of this Convention which cannot be settled through negotiation, shall, at the request of one of them, be submitted to arbitration. If within six months from the date of the request for arbitration the Parties are unable to agree on the organization of the arbitration, any one of those Parties may refer the dispute to the International Court of Justice by request in conformity with the Statute of the Court.
2. Each State may at the time of signature or ratification of this Convention or accession thereto, declare that it does not consider itself bound by the

preceding paragraph. The other States Parties shall not be bound by the preceding paragraph with respect to any State Party having made such a reservation.

3. Any State Party having made a reservation in accordance with the preceding paragraph may at any time withdraw this reservation by notification to the Secretary-General of the United Nations.

Article 30

1. A State Party may denounce this Convention by written notification to the Secretary-General of the United Nations. Denunciation becomes effective one year after the date of receipt of the notification by the Secretary-General.

2. Such a denunciation shall not have the effect of releasing the State Party from its obligations under this Convention in regard to any act or omission which occurs prior to the date at which the denunciation becomes effective. Nor shall denunciation prejudice in any way the continued consideration of any matter which is already under consideration by the Committee prior to the date at which the denunciation becomes effective.

3. Following the date at which the denunciation of a State Party becomes effective, the Committee shall not commence consideration of any new matter regarding that State.

Article 31

The Secretary-General of the United Nations shall inform all members of the United Nations and all States which have signed this Convention or acceded to it, of the following particulars:

(a) Signatures, ratifications and accessions under articles 25 and 26;

(b) The date of entry into force of this Convention under article 27, and the date of the entry into force of any amendments under article 28;

(c) Denunciations under article 30.

Article 32

1. This Convention, of which the Arabic, Chinese, English, French, Russian and Spanish texts are equally authentic, shall be deposited in the archives of the United Nations.

2. The Secretary-General of the United Nations shall transmit certified copies of this Convention to all states.

Hippocratic Oath

(Fifth century B.C.)

Hippocrates (c. 460–377 B.C.), born on the Aegean island of Cos, was the most celebrated physician of antiquity. It is not certain that he wrote the oath that bears his name, but it was probably written during his lifetime.

The earliest surviving references to the oath date from the first century A.D. These suggested that the oath was seen as an ideal rather than a norm, and it was not until the fourth century that a doctor was obliged to take the oath before practicing.

I swear by Apollo Physician and Asclepius and Hygieia and Panaceia and all the gods and goddesses, making them my witnesses, that I will fulfil according to my ability and judgment this oath and this covenant.

To hold him who has taught me this art as equal to my parents and to live my life in partnership with him, and if he is in need of money to give him a share of mine, and to regard his offspring as equal to my brother in male lineage and to teach them this art—if they desire to learn it—without fee and covenant; to give a share of precepts and oral instruction and all the other learning to my sons and to the sons of him who has instructed me and to pupils who have signed the covenant and have taken an oath according to the medical law, but to no one else.

I will apply dietetic measures for the benefit of the sick according to my ability and judgment; I will keep them from harm and injustice.

I will neither give a deadly drug to anybody if asked for it, nor will I make a suggestion to this effect. Similarly I will not give to a woman an abortive remedy. In purity and holiness I will guard my life and my art.

I will not use the knife, not even on sufferers from stone, but will withdraw in favor of such men as are engaged in this work.

Whatever houses I may visit, I will come for the benefit of the sick, remaining free of all intentional injustice, of all mischief and in particular of sexual relations with both female and male persons, be they free or slaves.

What I may see or hear in the course of the treatment or even outside the treatment in regard to the life of men, which on no account one must spread abroad, I will keep to myself holding such things shameful to be spoken about.

If I fulfil this oath and do not violate it, may it be granted to me to enjoy life and art, being honored with fame among all men for all time to come; if I transgress it and swear falsely, may the opposite of all this be my lot.

(*Ancient Medicine: Selected Papers of Ludwig Edelstein*, edited by Oswei Temkin and C. Temkin, Baltimore: Johns Hopkins University Press, 1967.)

Prayer of Moses Maimonides (excerpts)

(Twelfth century)

Moses Maimonides (1135–1204) was court physician to the sultan Saladin, the famous Muslim military leader. The prayer attributed to Maimonides is second only to the Hippocratic Oath in its influence on medical ethics.

Almighty God, Thou hast created the human body with infinite wisdom. . . . Thou hast blest Thine earth, Thy rivers and Thy mountains with healing substances; they enable Thy creatures to alleviate their sufferings and to heal their illnesses. Thou hast endowed man with the wisdom to relieve the sufferings of his brother, to recognize his disorders, to extract the healing substances, to discover their powers and to prepare and to apply them to suit every ill. In Thine Eternal Providence, Thou hast chosen me to watch over the life and health of Thy creatures. I am now about to apply myself to the duties of my profession. Support me, Almighty God, in these great labours that they may benefit mankind, for without Thy help not even the least thing will succeed.

Inspire me with love for my Art and for Thy creatures. Do not allow thirst for profit, ambition for renown and admiration, to interfere with my profession, for these are the enemies of truth and of love for mankind and they can lead astray in the great task of attending to the welfare of they creatures. Preserve the strength of my body and of my soul that they ever be ready cheerfully to help and support rich and poor, good and bad, enemy as well as friend. In the sufferer let me see only the human being. Illumine my mind that it may recognize what presents itself and that it may comprehend what is absent or hidden. . . .

Should those who are wiser than I wish to improve and instruct me, let my soul gratefully follow their guidance. . . .

Imbue my soul with gentleness and calmness. . . .

Let me be contented in everything except the great science of my profession. Never allow the thought to arise in me that I have attained to sufficient knowledge, but vouchsafe to me the strength, the leisure and the ambition ever to extend my knowledge. For Art is great, but the mind of man is ever expanding.

Almighty God! Thou has chosen me in Thy mercy to watch over the life and death of Thy creatures. I now apply myself to my profession. Support me in this great task so that it may benefit mankind, for without Thy help not even the least thing will succeed.

(Abraham Joshua Herschel, *Maimonides*, translated by Joachim Neugroschel, London: Faber, 1982.)

Declaration of Geneva
(World Medical Association, 1948, 1968, 1983)

Formed in 1947, the World Medical Association placed the formulation of a modern equivalent of the Hippocratic Oath high on its initial list of priorities. First adopted by the Second World Medical Assembly in 1948, the declaration was amended in 1968 and again in 1983.

At the time of being admitted as a member of the medical profession:

I solemnly pledge myself to consecrate my life to the service of humanity;

I will give to my teachers the respect and gratitude which is their due;

I will practise my profession with conscience and dignity;

The health of my patient will be my first consideration;

I will maintain by all the means in my power, the honor and the noble traditions of the medical profession;

My colleagues will be my brothers;

I will not permit considerations of religion, nationality, race, party politics or social standing to intervene between my duty and my patient;

I will maintain the utmost respect for human life from its beginnings, even under threat, and I will not use my medical knowledge contrary to the laws of humanity;

I make these promises solemnly, freely and upon my honor.

Physician's Oath
of the Soviet Union

Having attained the high calling of physicians and entering medical practice I solemnly swear:

to devote all my knowledge and strength to the preservation and improvement of the health of man, to the curing and prevention of diseases, to work conscientiously wherever the interests of society demand;

to be ever ready to render medical aid, to be attentive and thoughtful of the patient, to maintain medical confidence; constantly to perfect my medical knowledge and physician's skills, to further by my work the development of medical science and practice;

to turn, if the patient's interest demand it, for advice to my professional colleagues and that I myself will never refuse advice and help to them;

to preserve and further the noble traditions of our native medicine, and that I will in all of my actions be guided by the principles of communist morality, ever to bear in mind the high calling of the Soviet physician, and of my responsibility to the people and the Soviet state.

I swear that I will be faithful to this oath throughout the rest of my life.

(Originally published in *Meditsinskaya Gazeta*, 20 April 1971. English translation in *Survey*, Autumn 1971, p. 114.)

Islamic Code of Medical Ethics

(Selections from the Declaration of Kuwait, adopted by the International Conference on Islamic Medicine in January 1981)

The Physician's Oath

I swear by God, The Great;

To regard God in carrying out my profession;

To protect human life in all stages and under all circumstances, doing my utmost to rescue it from death, malady, pain and anxiety;

To keep people's dignity, cover their privacies and lock up their secrets;

To be, all the way, an instrument of God's mercy, extending my medical care to near and far, virtuous and sinner and friend and enemy;

To strive in the pursuit of knowledge and harnessing it for the benefit but not the harm of mankind;

To revere my teacher, teach my junior, and be brother to members of the medical profession joined in piety and charity;

To live my Faith in private and in public, avoiding whatever blemishes me in the eyes of God, His apostle and my fellow Faithful;

And may God be witness to this Oath.

Principles of Medical Ethics
(American Medical Association, 1980)

Preamble: the medical profession has long subscribed to a body of ethical statements developed primarily for the benefit of the patient. As a member of this profession, a physician must recognize responsibility not only to patients, but also to society, to other health professionals, and to self. The following Principles adopted by the American Medical Association are not laws, but standards of conduct which define the essentials of honorable behavior for the physician.

I. A physician shall be dedicated to providing competent medical service with compassion and respect for human dignity.

II. A physician shall deal honestly with patients and colleagues, and strive to expose those physicians deficient in character or competence, or who engage in fraud or deception.

III. A physician shall respect the law and also recognize a responsibility to seek changes in those requirements which are contrary to the best interests of the patient.

IV. A physician shall respect the rights of patients, of colleagues, and of other health professionals, and shall safeguard patient confidences within the constraints of the law.

V. A physician shall continue to study, apply and advance scientific knowledge, make relevant information available to patients, colleagues, and the public, obtain consultation, and use the talents of other health professionals when indicated.

VI. A physician shall, in the provision of appropriate patient care, except in emergencies, be free to choose whom to serve, with whom to associate, and the environment in which to provide medical services.

VII. A physician shall recognize a responsibility to participate in activities contributing to an improved community.

(Adopted by the American Medical Association, Chicago, 1980.)

Regulations in Time of Armed Conflict

(World Medical Association, 1956, 1957, 1983)

These regulations or guidelines set out the WMA's standards on the medical ethical position of the physician during a period of war or other armed conflict. The statement was approved by the 10th World Medical Assembly in Havana in 1956, was edited by the 11th Assembly meeting in Istanbul the following year, and was amended by the 35th World Medical Assembly in 1983.

The amended text reads as follows:

Regulations in Time of Armed Conflict
1. Medical Ethics in time of armed conflict is identical to medical ethics in time of peace, as established in the International Code of Medical Ethics of the World Medical Association. The primary obligation of the physician is his professional duty; in performing his professional duty, the physician's supreme guide is his conscience.
2. The primary task of the medical profession is to preserve health and save life. Hence it is deemed unethical for physicians to:
   A. Give advice or perform prophylactic, diagnostic or therapeutic procedures that are not justifiable in the patient's interest.
   B. Weaken the physical or mental strength of a human being without therapeutic justification.
   C. Employ scientific knowledge to imperil health or destroy life.
3. Human experimentation in time of armed conflict is governed by the same code as in time of peace; it is strictly forbidden on all persons deprived of their liberty, especially civilian and military prisoners and the population of occupied countries.
4. In emergencies, the physician must always give the required care impartially and without consideration of sex, race, nationality, religion, political

affiliation or any other similar criterion. Such medical assistance must be continued for as long as necessary and practicable.

5. Medical confidentiality must be preserved by the physician in the practice of his profession.

A PHYSICIAN SHALL use great caution in divulging discoveries or new techniques or treatment through non-professional channels.

A PHYSICIAN SHALL certify only that which he has personally verified.

Duties of Physicians to the Sick
A PHYSICIAN SHALL always bear in mind the obligation of preserving human life.

A PHYSICIAN SHALL owe his patients complete loyalty and all the resources of his science. Whenever an examination or treatment is beyond the physician's capacity he should summon another physician who has the necessary ability.

A PHYSICIAN SHALL preserve absolute confidentiality on all he knows about his patient even after the patient has died.

A PHYSICIAN SHALL give emergency care as a humanitarian duty unless he is assured that others are willing and able to give such care.

Duties of Physicians to Each Other
A PHYSICIAN SHALL behave towards his colleagues as he would have them behave towards him.

A PHYSICIAN SHALL NOT entice patients from his colleagues.

A PHYSICIAN SHALL observe the principles of the "Declaration of Geneva" approved by the World Medical Association.

Declaration of Tokyo

(World Medical Association, 1975)

Preamble
It is the privilege of the medical doctor to practise medicine in the service of humanity, to preserve and restore bodily and mental health without distinction as to persons, to comfort and to ease the suffering of his or her patients. The utmost respect for human life is to be maintained under threat, and no use made of any medical knowledge contrary to the laws of humanity.

For the purpose of this Declaration, torture is defined as the deliberate, systematic or wanton infliction of physical or mental suffering by one or more persons acting alone or on the orders of any authority, to force another person to yield information, to make a confession, or for any other reason.

Declaration

1. The doctor shall not countenance, condone or participate in the practice of torture or other forms of cruel, inhuman or degrading procedures, whatever the offence of which the victim of such procedures is suspected, accused or guilty, and whatever the victim's beliefs or motives, and in all situations, including armed conflict and civil strife.

2. The doctor shall not provide any premises, instruments, substances or knowledge to facilitate the practice of torture or other forms of cruel, inhuman or degrading treatment or to diminish the ability of the victim to resist such treatment.

3. The doctor shall not be present during any procedure during which torture or other forms of cruel, inhuman or degrading treatment is used or threatened.

4. A doctor must have complete clinical independence in deciding upon the care of a person for whom he or she is medically responsible. The doctor's fundamental role to alleviate the distress of his or her fellow men, and no motive whether personal, collective or political shall prevail against this higher purpose.

5. Where a prisoner refuses nourishment and is considered by the doctor as capable of forming an unimpaired and rational judgement concerning the consequences of such a voluntary refusal of nourishment, he or she shall not be fed artificially. The decision as to the capacity of the prisoner to form such a judgement should be confirmed by at least one other independent doctor. The consequences of the refusal of nourishment shall be explained by the doctor to the prisoner.

6. The World Medical Association will support, and should encourage the international community, the national medical associations and fellow doctors, to support the doctor and his or her family in the face of threats or reprisals resulting from a refusal to condone the use of torture or other forms of cruel, inhuman or degrading treatment.

Declaration of Hawaii

(World Psychiatric Association, 1977, revised 1983)

Ever since the dawn of culture, ethics has been an essential part of the healing art. It is the view of the World Psychiatric Association that due to conflicting loyalties and expectations of both physicians and patients in contemporary society and, the delicate nature of the therapist-patient relationship, high ethical standards are especially important for those involved in the science and practice of psychiatry as a medical speciality. These guidelines have been delineated in order to promote close adherence to those standards and to prevent misuse of psychiatric concepts, knowledge and technology.

Since the psychiatrist is a member of society as well as a practitioner of medicine, he or she must consider the ethical implications specific to psychiatry as well as the ethical demands on all physicians and the societal responsibility of every man and woman.

Even though ethical behavior is based on the individual psychiatrist's conscience and personal judgement, written guidelines are needed to clarify the profession's ethical implications.

Therefore, the General Assembly of the World Psychiatric Association has approved the following ethical guidelines for psychiatrists, having in mind the great differences in cultural backgrounds, and in legal, social and economic conditions which exist in the various countries of the world. It should be understood that the World Psychiatric Association views these guidelines to be minimal requirements for ethical standards of the psychiatric profession.

1. The aim of psychiatry is to treat mental illness and to promote mental health. To the best of his or her ability, consistent with accepted scientific and ethical principles, the psychiatrist shall serve the best interest of the patient and be also concerned for the common good and a just allocation of health resources. To fulfill these aims requires continuous research and continual education of health care personnel, patients and the public.

2. Every psychiatrist should offer to the patient the best therapy available to his knowledge and if accepted must treat him or her with the solicitude and respect due to all human beings. When the psychiatrist is responsible for treatment given by others he owes them competent supervision and education. Whenever there is a need, or whenever a reasonable request is forthcoming from the patient, the psychiatrist should seek the help of another colleague.

3. A psychiatrist aspires for a therapeutic relationship that is founded on mutual agreement. Such a relationship requires confidentiality, cooperation and mutual responsibility. Such a relationship may not be possible to establish with some patients. In that case, contact should be established with a relative or other person close to the patient. If and when a relationship is established for purposes other than therapeutic, such as in forensic psychiatry, its nature must be thoroughly explained to the person concerned.

4. The psychiatrist should inform the patient of the nature of the condition, therapeutic procedures, including possible alternatives, of the possible outcome. This information must be offered in a considerate way and the patient

be given the opportunity to choose between appropriate and available methods.

5. No procedure shall be performed or treatment given against or independent of a patient's own will, unless because of mental illness, the patient cannot form a judgement as to what is in his or her own best interest and without which treatment serious impairment is likely to occur to the patient or others.

6. As soon as the conditions for compulsory treatment no longer apply, the psychiatrist should release the patient from the compulsory nature of the treatment and if further therapy is necessary should obtain voluntary consent. The psychiatrist should inform the patient and/or relatives or meaningful others, of the existence of mechanisms of appeal of the detention and for any other complaints related to his or her well being.

7. The psychiatrist must never use his professional possibilities to violate the dignity or human rights of any individual or group and should never let inappropriate personal desires, feelings, prejudices or beliefs interfere with the treatment. The psychiatrist must on no account utilize the tools of his profession, once the absence of psychiatric illness has been established. If a patient or some third party demands actions contrary to scientific knowledge or ethical principles the psychiatrist must refuse to cooperate.

8. Whatever the psychiatrist has been told by the patient, or has noted during examination or treatment, must be kept confidential unless the patient relieves the psychiatrist from this obligation, or to prevent serious harm to self or others makes disclosure necessary. In these cases however, the patient should be informed of the breach of confidentiality.

9. To increase and propagate psychiatric knowledge and skill requires participation of the patients. Informed consent must, however, be obtained before presenting a patient to a class, and if possible, also when a case history is released for scientific publication, whereby all reasonable measures must be taken to preserve the dignity and anonymity of the patient and to safeguard the personal reputation of the subject. The patient's participation must be voluntary, after full information has been given of the aim, procedures, risks and inconveniences of a research project and there must always be a reasonable relationship between calculated risks or inconveniences and the benefit of the study. In clinical research every subject must retain and exert all his rights as a patient. For children and other patients who cannot themselves give informed consent, this should be obtained from the legal next-of-kin. Every patient or research subject is free to withdraw for any reason at any time from any voluntary treatment and from any teaching or research program in which he or she participates. This withdrawal, as well as any refusal to enter a program, must never influence the psychiatrist's efforts to help the patient or subject.

10. The psychiatrist should stop all therapeutic, teaching or research programs that may evolve contrary to the principles of this Declaration.

Resolution of Singapore:
Role of the Nurse in the Care of Detainees and Prisoners

(International Council of Nurses, 1975)

Whereas the ICN Code for Nurses specifically states that:

1. The fundamental responsibility of the nurse is fourfold: to promote health, to prevent illness, to restore health and to alleviate suffering.
2. The nurse's primary responsibility is to those people who require nursing care.
3. The nurse when acting in a professional capacity should at all times maintain standards of personal conduct which reflect credit upon the profession.
4. The nurse takes appropriate action to safeguard the individual when his care is endangered by a co-worker or any other person, and

Whereas in 1973 ICN reaffirmed support for the Red Cross Rights and Duties of Nurses under the Geneva Convention of 1949, which specifically state that, in case of armed conflict of international as well as national character (i.e., internal disorders, civil wars, armed rebellions):

1. Members of the armed forces, prisoners and persons taking no active part in the hostilities:
   a) shall be entitled to protection and care if wounded or sick,
   b) shall be treated humanely, that is:
   —they may not be subject to physical mutilation or to medical or scientific experiments of any kind which are not justified by the medical, dental or hospital treatment of the prisoner concerned and carried out in his interest,
   —they shall not be willfully left without medical assistance and care, nor shall conditions exposing them to contagion or infection be created,
   —they shall be treated humanely and cared for by the Party in conflict in whose power they may be, without adverse distinction founded on sex, race, nationality, religion, political opinion, or any other similar criteria.
2. The following acts are and shall remain prohibited at any time and in any place whatsoever with respect to the above mentioned persons:
   a) violence to life and person, in particular murder of all kinds, mutilation, cruel treatment and torture;
   b) outrages upon personal dignity, in particular humiliating and degrading treatment.

Whereas in 1971 ICN endorsed the United Nations Universal Declaration of Human Rights and, hence, accepted that:
1. "Everyone is entitled to all the rights and freedoms set forth in this

Declaration without distinction of any kind, such as race, colour, sex, language, religion, political or other opinion, national or social origin, property, birth or other status (Article 2)".

2. "No one shall be subject to torture or to cruel, inhuman or degrading treatment or punishment (Article 5)," and

Whereas in relation to detainees and prisoners of conscience, interrogation procedures are increasingly being employed which result in ill effects, often permanent, on the person's mental and physical health;

Therefore be it resolved that ICN condemns the use of all such procedures harmful to the mental and physical health of prisoners and detainees; and

Further be it resolved that nurses having knowledge of physical or mental ill-treatment of detainees and prisoners take appropriate action including reporting the matter to appropriate national and/or international bodies; and

Further be it resolved that nurses participate in clinical research carried out on prisoners, only if the freely given consent of the patient has been secured after a complete explanation and understanding by the patient of the nature and risk of the research; and

Finally be it resolved that the nurse's first responsibility is towards her patients, notwithstanding considerations of national security and interest.

Statement on the Nurse's Role in Safeguarding Human Rights
(International Council of Nurses, 1983)

Responding to requests from national member associations for guidance on the protection of human rights of both nurses and those for whom they care, the Council of National Representatives of the International Council of Nurses adopted the statement given below at its meeting in Brasilia in June 1983.

Statement on the Nurse's Role in Safeguarding Human Rights
This document has been developed in response to the requests of national nurses associations for guidance in assisting nurses to safeguard their own human rights and those for whom they have professional responsibility. It is meant to be used in conjunction with the ICN Code for Nurses and

resolutions relevant to human rights. Nurses should also be familiar with the Geneva Conventions and the additional protocols as they relate to the responsibilities of nurses.

The current world situation is such that there are innumerable circumstances in which a nurse may become involved that require action on her/his part to safeguard human rights. Nurses are accountable for their own professional actions and must therefore be clear as to what is expected of them in such situations.

Also conflict situations have increased in number and often include internal political upheaval, and strife, or international war. The nature of war is changing. Increasingly nurses find themselves having to act or respond in complex situations to which there seems to be no clear cut solution.

Changes in the field of communications also have increased the awareness and sensitivity of all groups to those conflict situations.

The need for nursing actions to safeguard human rights is not restricted to times of political upheaval and war. It can also arise in prisons or in the normal work situation of any nurse where abuse of patients, nurses, or others is witnessed or suspected. Nurses have a responsibility in each of these situations to take action to safeguard the rights of those involved. Physical abuse and mental abuse are equally of concern to the nurse. Over or under treatment is another area to be watched. There may be pressures applied to use one's knowledge and skills in ways that are not beneficial to patients or others.

Scientific discoveries have brought about more sophisticated forms of torture and methods of resuscitation so that those being tortured can be kept alive for repeated sessions. It is in such circumstances that nurses must be clear about what actions they must take as in no way can they participate in such torture, or torture techniques.

Nurses have individual responsibility but often they can be more effective if they approach human rights issues as a group. The national nurses' associations need to ensure that their structure provides a realistic mechanism through which nurses can seek confidential advice, counsel, support and assistance in dealing with these difficult situations. Verification of the facts reported will be an important first step in any particular situation.

At times it will be appropriate for the NNA to become a spokesman for the nurses involved. They may also be required to negotiate for them. It is *essential* that confidentiality be maintained. In rare cases the personal judgment of the nurse may be such that other actions seem more appropriate than approaching the association.

The nurse initiating the actions requires knowledge of her own and others' human rights, moral courage, a well thought through plan of action and a commitment and determination to see that the necessary follow-up does occur. Personal risk is a factor that has to be considered and each person must use her/his best judgment in the situation.

Rights of those in need of care
—Health care is a right of all individuals. Everyone should have access to health care regardless of financial, political, geographic, racial or religious considerations. The nurse should seek to ensure such impartial treatment.
—Nurses must ensure that adequate treatment is provided—within available resources—and in accord with nursing ethics (ICN Code) to all those in need of care.
—A patient/prisoner has the right to refuse to eat or to refuse treatments. The nurse may need to verify that the patient/prisoner understands the implications of such action but she should not participate in the administration of food or medications to such patients.

Rights and duties of nurses
—When considering the rights and duties of nursing personnel it needs to be remembered that both action and lack of action can have a detrimental effect and the nursing personnel must be considered accountable on both counts.
—Nurses have a right to practise within the code of ethics and nursing legislation of the country in which they practise. Personal safety—freedom from abuse, threats or intimidation—are the rights of every nurse.
—National nurses' associations have a responsibility to participate in the development of health and social legislation relative to patients' rights and all related topics.
—It *is a duty* to have informed consent of patients relative to having research done on them and in receiving treatments such as blood transfusions, anesthesia, grafts, etc. Such informed consent is a patient's right and must be ensured.

Appendix B

Selected Organizations Concerned with Torture and/or Psychiatric Abuse

Hazel Sirett, Human Rights Internet

Many organizations throughout the world work actively to abolish torture, end psychiatric abuse, and promote medical ethics. The nature of these organizations varies greatly—from those with substantial budgets that can organize high-level investigative missions to offending countries to those with limited resources that are staffed by volunteers and can only publish an occasional newsletter or organize a local demonstration. However, all are driven by the belief that the use of torture and psychiatric repressions are inhuman and unlawful instruments of rule.

Some of the more important of these groups follows, along with information on their activities and how they may be contacted. For a more complete list and further information, see two directories from which much of the following material has been drawn: *The North American Human Rights Directory* (1984), which describes over 700 organizations in the United States and Canada that are actively promoting human rights; and the *Human Rights Directory: Western Europe* (1982), which describes over 800 organizations based in Western Europe that are concerned with issues of human rights and social justice.

American Association for the Advancement of Science (AAAS)
Clearinghouse on Science and Human Rights of the AAAS Committee on
Scientific Freedom and Responsibility
1515 Massachusetts Avenue, N.W., Washington, D.C. 20005
(202) 467-5239

The Clearinghouse on Science and Human Rights, established in 1977, disseminates information on members of the scientific community in foreign countries whose human rights or scientific freedoms have been violated.

The clearinghouse works to help such scientists through its contacts with scientific societies, US and international government agencies, and private human rights groups. Upon receiving an inquiry or expression of concern about a particular scientist who is believed to be the victim of a violation of human rights, the clearinghouse refers the case to an AAAS-affiliated professional society whose discipline relates to that of the persecuted scientist. The clearinghouse also organizes missions of inquiry to countries where scientists have been imprisoned.

The clearinghouse also investigates cases in which members of the medical profession are suspected of participating in torture or psychiatric abuse. Such information is then brought to the attention of national and international health professionals, who are then informed of the role that codes of medical ethics can play in preventing the use of torture and psychiatric abuse.

Publications: Clearinghouse Report on Science and Human Rights (occasional newsletter); *Human Rights and the Medical Profession in Uruguay since 1972* (1981); *Human Rights and Scientific Cooperation: Problems and Opportunities in the Americas* (1981); *Scientists and Human Rights in Argentina since 1976* (1981); *Report of a Medical Fact-Finding Mission to El Salvador* (1983); *Report of a Fact-Finding Mission to the Phillipines* (1984).

American College of Physicians (ACP)
655 15th Street, N.W., Washington, D.C. 20005
(202) 393-1650

The American College of Physicians was founded in 1915 to uphold high standards in medical education, medical practice, and medical research. Today it represents over 60,000 doctors of internal medicine, physicians in related nonsurgical specialities, and physicians-in-training. The College's membership includes private practitioners providing primary care, medical specialists (in such fields as gastroenterology, endocrinology, oncology, and cardiology), medical educators, and researchers. It is the largest organization of general internists and allied subspecialists in the world.

In 1983, the College approved the formation of the Subcommittee on

Human Rights and Medical Practice with the charge of responding, in the name of the College, to documented abuses of human rights of physicians (because of their professional work) and to other circumstances involving the medical profession in apparent violations of human rights. In 1983, the College joined the American Association for the Advancement of Science and other professional associations in support of a fact-finding mission to the Philippines to investigate health and human rights conditions.

American Psychiatric Association (APA)
1400 K Street, N.W., Washington, D.C. 20005
(202) 682-6000

The American Psychiatric Assocation was founded in 1884 to improve and advance the rehabilitation of the mentally ill and to promote the standards of all psychiatric endeavors. The association opposes abuses of psychiatry and medical ethics.

The APA maintains two committees that monitor the abuse and misuse of psychiatry in the United States and abroad: the Committee on International Abuse of Psychiatry and Psychiatrists and the Committee on Abuse or Misuse of Psychiatry in the United States. In addition, the association has established a Task Force on Human Rights to respond to cases of violations of human rights of foreign psychiatrists.

The APA dispatches missions to investigate allegations of psychiatric abuse, sponsors letter-writing compaigns addressed to Congress and to governments that violate human rights, and initiates human rights resolutions at APA meetings.

American Public Health Association (APHA)
1015 15th Street, N.W., Washington, D.C. 20005
(202) 789-5600

The American Public Health Association, established in 1875, is an organization of public health workers. In recent years the APHA has established a number of task forces to investigate allegations of abuses in the field of public health. For example, in 1981 the association joined the American Association for the Advancement of Science and other professional associations in investigating the detention of three physicians held by the secret police in Chile. The association has also participated in missions to Guatemala and El Salvador to investigate violations of human rights and medical neutrality.

Amnesty International (AI)
1 Easton Street, London WCIX 8DJ, United Kingdom
US Branch: 322 Seventh Avenue, New York, New York 10001
(212) 807-8400

Amnesty International, recipient of the 1977 Nobel Peace Prize, grew out of a public appeal by British lawyer Peter Benenson for the "forgotten prisoners." The appeal was made in *The Observer* (London) and *Le Monde* (Paris) on 28 May 1961. Articles in other European newspapers publicized the appeal, and Mr. Benenson's idea immediately achieved worldwide support.

Amnesty International is currently the strongest international pressure group for the advancement of human rights, comprising over 500,000 individual members, subscribers, and supporters in some 160 countries or territories. It is a worldwide movement independent of any government, political grouping, ideology, economic interest, or religious creed. Amnesty International's activities focus strictly on those prisoners whose cases fall within its mandate: (1) It seeks the release of "prisoners of conscience"— persons who have neither used nor advocated violence and who have been detained anywhere on account of their beliefs, color, sex, ethnic origin, language, or religion; (2) it advocates fair and prompt trials for all political prisoners and works on behalf of such persons detained without charge or trial; and (3) it opposes torture and the death penalty and any other cruel, inhuman, or degrading treatment or punishment of all prisoners, without reservation.

AI acts on the basis of the UN Universal Declaration of Human Rights and other international human rights agreements. Through practical work for prisoners within its mandate, AI participates in the wider promotion and protection of human rights in the civil, political, economic, social, and cultural spheres.

Publications: Newsletter (international monthly account of AI's work for human rights in countries throughout the world, which includes a bulletin on the work of the Campaign for the Abolition of Torture); *Torture in the Eighties* (1984); *Amnesty International Handbook* (annual report). A wide variety of material is published throughout the year (see Appendix C for a selected bibliography).

Anti-Torture Research (ATR)
Trondhjemsgade 11, DK-2100 Copenhagen, Denmark

Founded in 1978, Anti-Torture Research is an international scientific society with the following objectives: (1) to compile and disseminate information among investigators that promotes research on the biomedical consequences of torture; (2) to sponsor, initiate, and coordinate biomedical research in all medical and scientific fields related to the effects of torture; (3) to arrange biomedical meetings, to publish biomedical results, and to assist generally in the broad distribution of information within ATR; (4) to assist in funding relevant biomedical research activities; and (5) to cooperate with other biomedical societies and other organizations to promote the objectives of ATR. Any qualified person who is studying problems coming under the society's objectives may apply to the ATR council for membership.

Publications: Rehabilitation of Torture Victims (by Ole Aalund in conjunction with the International Rehabilitation and Research Center for Torture Victims, 1983).

British Medical Association (BMA)
Tavistock Square, London WC1H 9JP, United Kingdom

The British Medical Association has from the start concerned itself with ethical questions as an integral part of the doctor's individual responsibility to his or her patients and profession. Since 1947 its Central Ethical Committee has considered ethical questions arising within the profession.

During the early 1970s, the British Medical Association was urged by certain doctors, particularly medical officers in the armed services, to provide guidelines on how they should act in circumstances surrounding the interrogation of persons detained under the Prevention of Terrorism Act. The BMA responded by stating categorically that "No doctor should take part, directly or indirectly, in interrogation procedures " (chairman's statement, BMA Central Ethical Committee, 24 August 1972).

A further issue that preoccupied the Central Ethical Committee was the forcible feeding of hunger-strikers in British prisons. The dilemma for attendant medical personnel was acute: They could help to prevent suffering but could be viewed as complying with unethical or undesirable actions. The resolution of this dilemma has always been based on the primacy of the doctor-patient relationship, which is no different in prison than it is outside: In respecting the patient's wishes, the doctor must exercise his or her own judgment regardless of external pressures and may accordingly withhold treatment when the patient so wishes.

British Psychological Society
St. Andrews House, 48 Princess Road East, Leicester LE1 7DR, United Kingdom

In 1976 the British Psychological Society, the chartered body representing professional psychologists in the United Kingdom, set up a working party to study abuses of psychology for political purposes, with special reference to the Soviet Union and Northern Ireland. In February 1978 this group recommended that the society endorse and implement the Resolution concerning Professional Ethics of Psychology, which was unanimously approved by the International Union of Psychological Science in 1976. This declared the IUPS's active opposition to the misuse of psychology to infringe "the inviolable rights of human beings."

Canadian Centre for Investigation and Prevention of Torture (CIPT)
10 Trinity Square, Toronto M5G 1B1, Canada
(416) 369-5974

CIPT is a nonprofit institution incorporated in March 1983 in the province of Ontario, Canada. The center's mandate extends only to victims of torture and their families. Within the limits of its resources, the center arranges for the care of torture victims who apply for help, particularly those who have settled in Canada or have come either as refugees or as people seeking refugee status.

The major activities of CIPT are treatment, research, and education in the area of torture and the prevention of torture. CIPT physicians and other health and social workers interview victims of torture and arrange assessments of their physical and psychological condition; one or more of its physician associates then administer appropriate treatment. Few of the more than 700 refugees who were victims of torture and were seen between 1978 and 1983 by Toronto physicians have needed hospitalization. Accordingly, the center combines physical and psychological treatment, integrating social, legal, and medical services with the support of exile organizations and trained volunteers.

The education of professionals and the public is a major concern of CIPT. Between 1978 and 1983, CIPT organizers made several presentations to regional, provincial, national, and international meetings of health professionals and to classes of medical and nursing students. During 1984 and 1985, CIPT organized a series of multidisciplinary seminars lasting from one to three days for physicians and other professionals working with survivors of torture.

Chilean Medical Association/Colegio Médico de Chile
Esmeralda 678, Casilla 639, Santiago, Chile

The Chilean Medical Association, established in 1948, has a membership of more than 9,000 physicians. When the military assumed power in 1973, all professional associations lost their right to elect their leaders; leaders were subsequently designated by the military authorities. However, in late 1981 the military government reinstated the right of professional associations to hold democratic elections. Since then, the association has worked actively to prevent medical complicity in torture and to defend physicians who have been imprisoned for their professional work or peacefully held political beliefs.

In August 1983, the association approved a code of ethics designed to guide the behavior of medical personnel who may be called on to torture prisoners or to examine torture victims while in detention. That same month, the association's ethics committee began an investigation into the role of five physicians who had allegedly participated in or covered up torture. In 1985, the association ruled that one of the physicians under investigation be suspended from the association for having certified that a woman, who had been interrogated by the military in 1982, was in good physical condition when in fact she had been tortured. The association has received information that from at least 30 to 40 doctors helped the military government abuse political prisoners. The association's president and the chairman of the ethics committee testified before the US Congress in 1984 about their efforts to stop professional complicity in torture.

In addition to its work against torture, the association has spoken out on behalf of imprisoned colleagues and has petitioned the government to investigate the whereabouts of 20 physicians who have been "disappeared" since 1973. The association has also established a committee to aid physicians, who have returned from exile, to find employment.

Publication: Vida Médica

Christian Action for the Abolition of Torture/Action des Chretiens Pour L'Abolition de la Torture (ACAT)
252, rue St. Jacques, 75005 Paris, France
US Branch: American Christians for the Abolition of Torture
300 W. Apsley Street, Philadelphia, Pennsylvania 19144

Christian Action for the Abolition of Torture was founded in 1974 to mobilize the Christian community in the struggle to end torture, the mistreatment of individuals, and the incarceration of political prisoners and dissidents in psychiatric hospitals. It also campaigns for the respect of human rights covenants and other international instruments concerning human rights. ACAT distributes, within the Christian and pastoral communities, information on torture and violations of human rights to heighten awareness of these situations and to encourage action. ACAT sponsors many activities on the pastoral level, including public prayer, reflection sessions, and fasts.

ACAT sends weekly urgent appeals (in response to information on political prisoners, specifically from Anmesty International) to government leaders; supports others organizations engaged in campaigns for the defense of human rights; communicates with embassies about human rights issues; and participates in Human Rights Day and in colloquiums (e.g., "Human Rights and the Gospel" on the 30th anniversary of the Universal Declaration of Human Rights).

Publication: Le Courier (quarterly).

Christian Churches' Social Assistance Foundation/Fundación de Ayuda
Social de las Iglesias Cristianas (FASIC)
Manuel Montt 2501, Santiago, Chile

FASIC is an ecumenical center, active in community assistance and health services. It has special programs concerned with the effects of repression, the reintegration of exiles, and problems of children whose parents or relatives have been "disappeared," detained, and/or tortured. FASIC is particularly concerned with the mental health problems in Chile, which have resulted from torture and other forms of repression. Since 1977, it has provided psychiatric care to hundreds of torture victims and their families. FASIC works closely with the unofficial National Commission Against Torture, the Vicariate of Solidarity of the Archdiocese of Santiago, and the Chilean Psychologists Association.

Publications: La Tortura en el Chile de Hoy—Experiencias Médicas (1981); *Informe acerca de la Participación de los Médicos en la Tortura* (1983); *La Tortura, Un Problema Médico* (1984); *Atención Médico-psicológica de Personas Afectadas por la Represión Política en Chile* (1984); *Psicoterapia y Represión Política* (1984).

Committee for the Defense of Health, Professional Ethics, and the Human
Rights of the Argentine People/Comité para la Defensa de la Salud,
de la Etica Profesional y los Derechos Humanos del Pueblo Argentino
(CODESEDH)
México 479, Casa de la Paz 1097, Buenos Aires, Argentina

CODESEDH is an independent committee of health professionals and lawyers established in 1983 to promote the right to health and to create codes of ethics to increase the awareness of health professionals of their professional duties when faced with human rights abuses. The committee is independent of any political grouping, ideology, economic interest, or religious creed. The committee has worked with the Grandmothers of the Plaza de Mayo in their search for "disappeared" children and in the application of genetic analysis to determine grandpaternity.

Publication: La Salud, el Médico y los Derechos Humanos (1984).

Council for International Organizations of the Medical Sciences (CIOMS)
c/o World Health Organization, 1211 Geneva 27, Switzerland

The Council for International Organizations of the Medical Sciences was formed under the initiative of UNESCO in 1949. It is a nongovernmental organization that is officially recognized by UNESCO and the World Health Organization (WHO). The council continues in its original purpose, which is to organize international medical congresses. It publishes an annual calendar of medical congresses held around the world.

In 1976 CIOMS responded to an appeal by WHO to prepare "an outline of the principles of medical ethics which may be relevant to the protection of persons subject to any form of detention or imprisonment against torture and other cruel, inhuman or degrading treatment or punishment." The CIOMS sent a questionnaire to 205 organizations in its 29 member countries regarding the role of medical personnel in protecting persons from torture. The results of their research were used to draft a new code of medical principles, which was eventually submitted to WHO and later to the General Assembly of the United Nations. In 1982 the General Assembly adopted without a vote a modified version of the code.

Defense for Children International (DCI)
P.O. Box 92, CH-1226 Geneva-Thonex, Switzerland
US Branch: Defense for Children USA
534 Eighth Street, Brooklyn, New York 11215
(718) 965-0245

Established in 1979 during the International Year of the Child, the Defense for Children International was created to respond to gross violations of human rights affecting children throughout the world. DCI holds consultative states with the United Nations and has national chapters in various countries. DCI's membership has responded to 600 individual cases in which children have suffered human rights abuses, including torture and "disappearance."

Human Rights Internet (HRI)
1338 G Street, S.E., Washington, D.C. 20003
(202) 543-9200

Human Rights Internet (HRI) is an international communications network and clearinghouse on human rights with universal coverage. Founded in

1976, HRI has over 2,000 individuals and organizations contributing to its network.

Publications: HRI Reporter (bimonthly); *Teaching Human Rights* (1981); *Human Rights Directory: Latin America, Asia, and Africa* (1981); *Human Rights Directory: Western Europe* (1982); and *The North American Human Rights Directory* (1984).

Institute of Medicine (IOM) of the National Academy of Sciences
2101 Constitution Avenue, N.W., Washington, D.C. 20418
(202) 334-2000

The Institute of Medicine was established in 1970 to address the problems of providing adequate health services to all sectors of society. The IOM identifies, for study and analysis, important issues and problems that relate to health and medicine. In 1982 the governing council of the IOM voted: (1) to assist in referring victims of torture for needed treatment; (2) to inform the membership of the IOM about transgressions against human rights on a regular basis; and (3) to take other appropriate actions on behalf of health personnel whose human rights have been violated.

In 1983 the Institute of Medicine joined the National Academy of Sciences, the American Association for the Advancement of Science, the New York Academy of Sciences, and the International League for Human Rights in sponsoring a medical fact-finding mission to El Salvador to investigate abuses directed against health professionals.

International Association against Torture/Association Internationale Contre la Torture (AICT)
Case Postale 207, 1211 Geneva 16, Switzerland

The International Association against Torture was formed in Milan, Italy, in 1977 to combat torture and state terrorism in Latin America. The organization carries out its objectives through conferences, debates, meetings, slide shows, films, circulation of petitions, sending telegrams, and letters of protest.

Publication: Un Continent Torturé: Torture et Disparitions Forcés en Amerique Latine—Un Système de Gouvernment [A tortured continent: torture and forced disappearances in Latin America—a system of government] (1984).

International Association on Political Use of Psychiatry/Association Internationale Contre L'Utilisation de la Psychiatrie a des Fins Politiques (IAPUP)
Dr. G. Bles, IAPUP, Domus Medica, 60 boulevard de Latour-Maubourg, 75007 Paris, France

The International Association on Political Use of Psychiatry was founded in December 1980 "to try to prevent the corruption of medicine by politics and to try to help those individuals who suffer from such corruption or from seeking to oppose it." At present, the IAPUP unites "small, voluntary, humanitarian, non-political groups in six countries and some individuals."

Publication: Information Bulletin (occasional, in English and French).

Participating Committees:

1. Working Group on the Internment of Dissenters in Mental Hospitals, c/o Christine Shaw, 17 Norland Square, London W11, United Kingdom.

The Working Group was set up in 1971 in response to a dossier of detailed evidence of psychiatric abuse in the Soviet Union, which was sent to the West by Vladimir Bukovsky and for which he was subsequently arrested. The material he collected was translated by the group and disseminated to professional colleagues and humanitarian organizations in Britain and overseas, and this work has continued on the basis of information that filters through to the West. One immediate result of the initial material was a letter to the *Times* (London), signed by 44 psychiatrists. The letter affirmed that the psychiatrists could find no medical basis for the forcible interment of the subjects listed in Bukovsky's dossier, and it concluded that this practice represented a grave violation of professional ethics by Soviet psychiatry.

The group has continued to focus its work on the translation and evaluation of documents, sending articles and letters to editors of the medical and lay press, organizing lectures and meetings, lobbying psychiatric and humanitarian groups, and placing phone calls to Moscow and the heads of Soviet prison hospitals. The working group aims to alert the psychiatric profession to the issues at stake in the misuse of psychiatric institutions for political ends, particularly but not exclusively in the Soviet Union. It also monitors abuses in other countries, and its first *News Bulletin on Psychiatric Abuse* (June 1977) cited abuses in Romania, East Germany, Argentina, Chile, and South Africa. The group's active membership remains small, and comprises a mixture of psychiatrists, psychologists, humanitarians, and Soviet specialists, with a wide range of contacts with analogous groups throughout North America and Western Europe. The working group also maintains close contact with human rights activists in the Soviet Union.

Publications: The Political Abuse of Psychiatry in the Soviet Union (1977); *The Imprisoned Conscience of Soviet Psychiatry* (Dr. Semyon Gluzman, 1977); *News Bulletin on Psychiatric Abuse in the Soviet Union* (1977, 1979, 1980); *Soviet Opponents of Police Psychiatry: Their Aims, KGB Suppression of Them, and How to Help Them* (1980); *Soviet Political Psychiatry: The Story of the Opposition* (1983).

2. Le Comité des Psychiatres Français Contre L'Utilisation de la Psychiatrie a des Fins Politiques (Committee of French Psychiatrists against the Use of Psychiatry for Political Purposes), 82, rue d'Alesia, 75014 Paris, France.

3. Deutsche Vereinigung Gegen Politischen Missbrauch Der Psychiatrie (German Association against the Political Abuse of Psychiatry), Konradstrasse 9, 8045 Ismaning, West Germany.

4. *International Podrabinek Fund,* c/o Stichting V. Boekovski, Postbus 51049, 1007 EA Amsterdam, Netherlands.

5. *L'Association Suisse Contre les Abus de la Psychiatrie a des Fins Politiques* (Swiss Association against Psychiatric Abuse for Political Purposes), Avenue Krieg 28, 1206 Geneva, Switzerland.

6. *Psychiatrists against Psychiatric Abuse,* Dr. J. Jeffries, 250 College Street, Room G.99, Toronto M5T 1R8, Ontario, Canada.

International Commission of Jurists (ICJ)/Commission Internationale de Jurists (CIJ)
The Center for the Independence of Judges and Laywers (CIJL)/Center pour l'Independance des Magistrats et des Avocats (CIMA)/Centro para la Independicia de Jueces y Abogados (CIJA)
P. O. Box 120, 109 route de Chêne, 1224 Chêne-Bougeries, Geneva, Switzerland

The International Commission of Jurists was founded in 1952 to promote the understanding and observance of the rule of law throughout the world. The ICJ's work "is devoted to the legal promotion and protection of human rights and fundamental freedoms in all parts of the world. The Rule of Law is seen as a dynamic concept to be used to advance not only the classical civil and political rights of the individual, but also his economic, social, and cultural rights, and to promote social and development policies under which members of the community in which he lives may realize their full poten-tiality."

Major work of the ICJ includes: international conferences and seminars; press statements concerning flagrant violations of the rule of law wherever they occur; and sending legal-observer missions to major trials to monitor the correctness and fairness of trial procedures and the extent to which the rights of the defense are respected.

The Centre for the Independence of Judges and Lawyers, formed by the ICJ in February 1978, has as its dual tasks: (1) to inform lawyers and lawyers' organizations throughout the world of their colleagues in many countries who are persecuted or harassed for their professional work in upholding the principles of the Rule of Law; and (2) to mobilize such lawyers and lawyers' organizations to support their colleagues. The ICJ's activities have included investigations of the use of confessions obtained under torture in court cases.

Publications: ICJ Review (twice yearly, in English; also available in Spanish edition, *Revista*)—the *Review* includes sections on human rights in the world, commentaries, articles, and judicial applications of the Rule of Law. *ICJ Newsletter* (quarterly, in English)—this contains a report on the activities of the ICJ and on recent events relating to the work of the secretariat. *Bulletin of the Centre for the Independence of Judges and Lawyers* (twice yearly, in English)—special studies and reports on conferences and seminars on the findings of inquiries and investigations; reports regarding torture and international law. *How to Make the Convention against Torture Effective (1979); States of Emergency: Their Impact on Human Rights* (1983).

International Committee of the Red Cross (ICRC)/Comité International de la Croix-Rouge
17, avenue de la Paix, CH-1211 Geneva, Switzerland

The International Committee of the Red Cross was founded in Geneva in 1863 as the International Committee for Relief of Wounded Soldiers. Its current name was adopted in 1880. It promoted the Geneva Conventions of 1864, 1906, 1929, and 1940 and works for their continual improvement and promulgation. It founded the Central Prisoner of War Agency (which operated from 1870 to 1871, 1911 to 1918, and 1939 to 1945), now known as the Central Tracing Agency (1960). It is also a founder of the International Red Cross movement. It is registered in accordance with Swiss law and recognized by the Geneva Conventions of 1929 and 1949.

The ICRC is an independent institution, governed by its own statutes (these were amended on 25 September 1952 to conform to the statutes of the International Red Cross). It upholds the fundamental principles of the Red Cross, namely: impartiality; action independent of any racial, political, religious, or economic considerations; the universality of the Red Cross; and the equality of the national Red Cross societies. It maintains close contact with governmental authorities and any national or international institutions whose assistance it considers useful.

Each year the ICRC visits large numbers of political prisoners worldwide to ensure that their detention conditions conform to internationally accepted standards. In 1981 the ICRC visited 489 places of detention, and between 1971 and 1981 its delegates carried out approximately 15,000 visits in some 80 countries.

Publications: The International Review of the Red Cross (bimonthly); *ICRC Bulletin* (monthly). Numerous publications, details of which may be found in the ICRC's *Catalogue of Publications, 1964–1980.* Human rights publications include the following: *Respect of Human Rights in Time of Armed Conflict* (1971); *The ICRC and Torture* (1976); *The ICRC and Human Rights* (Dietrich Schindler, 1979); *Guerilla et Droit Humanitaire* (Michel Veuthy, 1983).

International Council of Nurses (ICN)
37, rue de Vermont, 1211 Geneva 20, Switzerland

The International Council of Nurses was founded in 1899 to provide a means of communication among nurses of all nations and to afford facilities for the interchange of international hospitality. It provides opportunities for nurses from all over the world to confer on questions relating to the welfare of their patients.

In 1971 the ICN's Council of National Representatives adopted a policy statement on human rights in which it endorsed the Universal Declaration of Human Rights. Other policy statements have been adopted since concerning equal pay for equal work, the rights of children, quality of life, and the role of the nurse in the care of detainees and prisoners. The ICN has a "Code of Nurses" enumerating principles that are basic to the equality of rights for women and men.

International Medical Commission for Health and Human Rights (IMC)
Case Postale 157, 1211 Geneva 4, Switzerland

At a 1980 meeting in Geneva of physicians, allied health professionals, and others committed to and experienced in the defense of human rights, it was resolved to create an International Medical Commission for Health and Human Rights. A committee was set up to pave the way for the commission, which, it is hoped, will be formally established in 1985.

The aims of the IMC will be to secure the active support of physicians and other health workers throughout the world in promoting and protecting human rights and to encourage their personal involvement and commitment in a spirit of solidarity that crosses national, political, and other boundaries. This aim will be pursued in various ways, including (1) securing the widest possible commitment of physicians and other health workers, both individually and collectively, to respect human rights and medical ethics and to keep watch over failures to observe these principles; (2) investigating general situations and individual cases in which activities in the health field do not appear to conform with established principles of human rights, and taking action to secure observance of these principles; and (3) promoting an exchange of information among physicians and other health workers on the ethical principles of health work and human rights. The guidelines for IMC's work will be: the Universal Declaration of Human Rights; the International Covenant on Economic, Social, and Cultural Rights; the International Covenant on Civil and Political Rights; and other international instruments recognized by the international community.

The IMC's actions will be directed towards three objectives: (1) to secure observance of human rights principles in all interactions between health systems and other systems; (2) to promote observance of accepted codes of medical ethics in a changing world; and (3) to promote the right to health for all.

The commission will be independent of any national, political, or religious affiliation: Its members will be selected as individuals, and they will not represent any organization or government. The commission's work will cover all parts of the world. The commission shall be composed of no more than 50 members, who possess a variety of professional expertise.

International Rehabilitation and Research Center for Torture Victims (RCT)
University Hospital, Rigshospitalet, Unit 7013, Juliane Mariesvej 26, DK-2100 Copenhagen OE, Denmark

The International Rehabilitation and Research Center for Torture Victims is the world's first center devoted to the treatment and rehabilitation of torture victims and their families. With a staff of 20—including nurses, physicians, psychologists, physiotherapists, dentists, interpreters, and administrative personnel—the center hopes to admit dozens of torture victims a year for mental, physical, social, and legal rehabilitation. When necessary, this work will be extended to the wives, husbands, and children of victims. The center also offers international training courses and seeks to familiarize medical students with the injuries caused by torture by insuring that the subject is included in textbooks.

The annual cost of running the center is estimated at $1 million, and potential donors include both governments and private individuals, as well as the UN Voluntary Fund for Torture Victims.

Publication: Rehabilitation of Torture Victims—Research Perspectives (by Inge Kemp Genefke in conjunction with Ole Aalund, Anti-Torture Research, 1983).

Latin American Social Work Collective/Colectivo Latinoamericano de Trabajo Psicosocial (COLAT)
Rue du Gouvernement Provisoire 32, 1000 Bruxelles, Belgium

COLAT was formed in 1976 to develop a community-based mental health program for Latin American exiles in Europe. It is composed mainly of Latin American psychiatrists, psychologists, doctors, sociologists, and social workers—all under the academic supervision of the Catholic University of Louvain.

COLAT has become well-known in the Latin American community in Europe for the publication of the review *Franja*, as well as for organizing social and cultural activities for young people and providing counseling and therapeutic services for the exile community.

Publications: Franja; Así Buscamos Rehacernos.

Medical Action Group (MAG)
Room 504, PDC Building, 1440 Taft Avenue, Ermita, Metro Manila, Philippines

The Medical Action Group is composed of Filipino physicians and nurses who strive to implement the humanitarian ideals of the medical profession by providing community-based health care in economically depressed areas and by bringing public attention to the plight of health workers.

Through a network of provincial chapters, MAG provides legal assistance to health workers who have been detained or otherwise restricted in carrying out their professional duties. According to MAG, rural health workers in the Philippines are often singled out by local security forces because their work brings them into contact with peasant trade unions and church groups critical of the government.

Publications: MAG Bulletin (occasional).

Medical Committee for Exiles/Comité Medical pour les Exiles (COMEDE)
78, rue du General Leclerc, 94270 Kremlin-Bicetre, France

COMEDE was formed in April 1979 by members of a number of organizations concerned with providing aid to exiles in France—Amnesty International, Comité Inter-mouvements Auprès des Exiles, and Group Accueil et Solidarité.

Since its establishment, COMEDE has provided care for some 5,000 refugees. Approximately one-fourth of COMEDE's patients have been victims of torture or ill-treatment, the majority of whom have been Turks and Iranians. COMEDE's premises at the Kremlin-Bicetre Hospital are provided by the Minister of Health. COMEDE undertakes almost 1,000 consultations a month, not all of which involve victims of torture. Two general surgeries are held daily, as well as a biweekly gynecological surgery and a weekly dermatology surgery. A physiotherapist and social worker work at the center from time to time, but COMEDE hopes to supply the services of these professionals more regularly in the future. Reports of medical findings and the effects of torture and ill-treatment on victims are documented for the French Office for Refugees and the Stateless (OFPRA).

National Academy of Sciences (NAS)
2101 Constitution Avenue, N.W., Washington, D.C. 20418
(202) 334-2000

In 1976 the National Academy of Sciences created the Committee on Human Rights. The committee was established in response to the increased concern of academy members about the repression of scientists and scientific research in many areas of the world. With the information obtained by the committee, the academy added the voice of its membership to that of its officers and established a group of volunteer correspondents that now exceeds 570 academy members. The committee takes action only in cases of extreme oppression, when a fellow scientist is being tortured, is detained without formal charges or trial, or is imprisoned for a statement or an action that to the committee is no crime; the committee acts to safeguard what the Universal Declaration of Human Rights declares to be the birthright of every person. The committee is funded by the academy's endowment income.

Royal College of Psychiatrists
17 Belgrave Square, London SW1X 8PG, United Kingdom

An autonomous, professional body, the Royal College of Psychiatrists has passed a number of strongly worded resolutions on the abuse of psychiatry in many countries, especially in the Soviet Union. In January 1973, as the debate on psychiatric abuse began to get under way in Britain, the Royal College of Psychiatrists declared itself "firmly opposed" to the use of psychiatric facilities for detaining persons solely because of their political dissent, no matter where such action occurs. In November of the same year, following a visit by psychiatrists to the Soviet Union, it issued a less-guarded resolution which "deplores the current use of psychiatry in the Soviet Union for the purpose of political repression and condemns the activities of doctors who lend themselves to this work."

In November 1975, the Royal College took the then-unprecedented step of expressing its readiness to dispatch a commission of inquiry jointly with the Bar Council to report on alleged abuses of psychiatry in the Soviet Union. This offer was rejected by the Soviet authorities. An additional resolution of 1976 reiterated the Royal College's refusal to tolerate the abuse of the skills of their profession for achieving political ends.

In addition to much detailed work and investigation, the committee submitted a motion to the June 1979 Council and Annual General Meeting for approval. The motion requested that the World Psychiatric Association be asked to apply the resolution passed at the General Assembly to people being persecuted for bringing the abuse of psychiatry to the attention of the world, as well as those guilty of its abuse. The Special Committee has also considered allegations of psychiatric abuse in other countries, including Argentina, Chile, and South Africa.

Swiss Committee against Torture/Comité Suisse Contre la Torture
Case Postale 2402 CH-1002 Lausanne, Switzerland

The Swiss Committee against Torture was set up in 1977 to help prevent torture by organizing visits to detention centers. In recent years the committee has been active in promoting the adoption by the UN General Assembly of an International Protocol to the International Convention on Torture.

Publication: Bulletin d'Information (occasional).

University of Cape Town, Institute of Criminology
Private Bag, Rondebosch 7700 Cape, South Africa

The University of Cape Town's Institute of Criminology recently instituted a project entitled "The Psychological Processes of Detention and Torture in South Africa," which aims to document the physical and psychological aftereffects of torture on former detainees held by the South African security police. Social workers and psychologists have interviewed some 300 former detainees who claim to have been tortured while in official custody. The results of their research will be published in 1985.

United Nations Voluntary Fund for Victims of Torture
Division of Human Rights, United Nations, Palais des Nations, CH-1211 Geneva 10, Switzerland

The UN General Assembly established the UN Voluntary Fund for Victims of Torture in December 1981. Its objective is to receive voluntary contributions from UN member states and to distribute the funds to provide medical, psychological, legal, financial, and social aid to individuals who are victims of torture and their families. By October 1984 the fund had received $1.1 million from 16 governments and nongovernmental organizations and individuals.

In March 1983 the fund drew up a program of activities for 1984 through 1986. The program emphasized providing financial assistance to projects for the direct medical and psychological rehabilitation to individual victims and their families. The board also emphasized training courses for medical personnel to provide the experience and knowledge required to deal effectively with torture victims. In August 1984 the fund recommended disbursing $500,000 for treatment and rehabilitation centers for torture victims in Denmark and Canada and 13 projects in eight different countries. Both the projects and the countries in which they are carried out are kept confidential because of their sensitive nature.

World Medical Association (WMA)
28, avenue des Alpes, F-01210 Ferney-Voltaire, France

The World Medical Association, formed in 1947, is an international organization whose membership consists of one recognized medical association per member country. There are currently 48 national medical associations affiliated with the WMA.

Over the years, the WMA has issued important declarations and ethical codes for the profession. These include the 1948 Declaration of Geneva, considered its basic code of ethics, and the 1975 Declaration of Tokyo, with specific guidelines for physicians regarding torture and other cruel and degrading treatment.

Since the adoption of the Tokyo declaration, the WMA has continually sought to keep the stringent language of the declaration from being superseded by what it considers to be the less restraining language contained in draft codes of medical ethics and torture presented to the United Nations by the Council for International Organizations of Medical Sciences and the World Health Organization. The principles of medical ethics pertaining to the role of physicians who are faced with torture that were adopted by the General Assembly of the United Nations in December 1982 reflect the WMA's strict position that under no circumstances should a physician participate in torture.

World Psychiatric Association (WPA)
Lazarettgasse 14, A-1090 Vienna, Austria

Founded in 1961, the World Psychiatric Association has member bodies in more than 63 counries and is concerned with upholding the professional ethics of psychiatry throughout the world.

Following the Sixth World Congress of Psychiatry in Hawaii in 1977, the WPA established a Committee to Review Abuses of Psychiatry. The committee investigates alleged human rights abuses against psychiatrists, and, if appropriate, requests that the member association in the country concerned bring the matter to the attention of its government. The WPA also maintains a Committee on Ethics, which monitors violations by psychiatrists and psychiatric institutions of those ethical guidelines adopted at the World Congress of 1977. The guidelines emphasize that as a practitioner of medicine and a member of society, the psychiatrist must consider "the ethical implications specific to psychiatry, as well as the ethical demands on all physicians and the societal duties of every man and woman."

The use of psychiatry to suppress political dissent became a major issue at the general assembly of the Seventh World Congress of Psychiatry, which met in Vienna in July 1983. The delegates voted to give permanent constitutional status to the Committee to Review the Abuse of Psychiatry. The delegates also acknowledged the resignation of the Soviet All-Union of Society of Psychiatrists and Neuropathologists, and said that the Soviets would not be welcomed back without "sincere cooperation and evidence before hand of amelioration of the political use of psychiatry." The assembly also voted to give honorary membership to Dr. Anatoly Koryagin, a Soviet psychiatrist who protested the abuse of his profession and who was subsequently imprisoned for his efforts.

Appendix C

Selected Bibliography

Some publications not listed below are listed in Appendix B under the name of the organization that publishes them.

Torture

General Reading

Ackroyd, C., et al. *The Technology of Political Control*. Middlesex, United Kingdom: Penguin, 1977.

"Aggression and Torture." *World Medical Journal* 23, no. 5 (September–October 1976): 65–69.

Amnesty International. *Report on Torture*. New York: Farrar, Straus and Giroux, 1975.

Amnesty International. *Torture in Greece: The First Torturers' Trial 1975*. London: Amnesty International, 1977.

Amnesty International. *"Disappearances": A Workbook*. New York: Amnesty International, 1981.

Amnesty International. *Iraq: Evidence of Torture*. London: Amnesty International, 1981.

Amnesty International. *Detention without Trial and Torture in South Africa*. London: Amnesty International, 25 October 1982.

Amnesty International. *Chile: Evidence of Torture*. London: Amnesty International, 1983.

Amnesty International. *Torture in the Eighties*. London: Amnesty International, 1984.

Commission on CIA Activities within the U.S.: Report to the President. Washington, D.C.: US Government Printing Office, 1975.

Gellhorn, A. "Violations of Human Rights: Torture and the Medical Profession." *New England Journal of Medicine* 229 (1978):358–359.

Goldstein, R., M.D., and A. Gellhorn, M.D. *Human Rights and the Medical Profession in Uruguay since 1972.* Washington, D.C.: American Association for the Advancement of Science, 1982.

Jin, B. "Torture as State Policy: The Medical Community Fights Back." *University of Toronto Medical Journal* (1980):71–75.

Korovessis, P. *The Method.* London: Allison and Busby, 1970.

Lea, H. C. *Torture: With Documents on Theory and Practice of Judicial Torture.* Philadelphia: University of Pennsylvania Press, 1973.

Lippman, M. "The Protection of Universal Human Rights: The Problem of Torture." *Universal Human Rights* (now *Human Rights Quarterly*) 1, no. 4 (October–December 1979):25–55.

Naquet, P. V. *Torture: Cancer of Democracy.* Middlesex, United Kingdom: Penguin, 1963.

Osnos, P. "Danish Clinic Fights Torture's Aftershocks." *The Washington Post,* 16 May 1983.

Pilisuk, M., and L. Ober. "Torture and Genocide as Public Health Problems." *American Journal of Orthopsychiatry* 46, no. 3 (July 1976):388–392.

Rivas, F. "La Tortura." *Vida Médica,* September 1983, 53–57.

Simonies. "On Behalf of Victims of Pseudo-Medical Experiments: Red Cross Action" Extract. *International Review of the Red Cross,* January 1973.

Timerman, J. *Prisoner without a Name, Cell without a Number.* New York: Knopf, 1981.

"Torture as State Policy." *Time,* 16 August 1976.

Wynen, "The Physician and Torture." *World Medical Journal* 28, no. 2 (March–April 1982):18–19.

Medical Involvement

Aziz, P. *Doctors of Death.* Geneva: Ferni Publications, 1976.

Colligan, J. "New Science of Torture." *Science Digest,* July 1976, 44.

"Doctors Who Make Pain." *Newsweek,* 1 August 1983:25–26.

Jadresic, A. "Doctors and Torture: An Experience as a Prisoner." *Journal of Medical Ethics,* 6, no. 3 (September 1980):124–128.

Kandela, P. "Cause for Concern: Doctors Who Take Part in Torture." *World Medicine,* 4 April 1981.

Keogh, J. P., and D. Spodick. "Physicians and Torture." *New England Journal of Medicine* 297, no. 12 (22 September 1977):675.

Kosteljanetz, M., and O. Aalund. "Torture: A Challenge to Medical Science." *Interdisciplinary Science Reviews* 8 (1983).

Lowry, D. "Ill-treatment, Brutality and Torture: Some Thoughts upon the 'Treatment' of Irish Political Prisoners." *De Paul Law Review* 22 (Spring 1973):553–581.

Mitsherlich, A., and F. Mielke. *Doctors of Infamy.* New York: H. Schuman, 1949.

Mitsherlich, A., and F. Mielke. *The Death Doctors.* London: Elek, 1962.

Shapiro, S. "Medical Work against Torture: The Case of Steve Biko." *New England Journal of Medicine* 303, no. 13 (September 1980):761.

Szasz, T. S., et al. "Political Torture and Physicians." *New England Journal of Medicine* 295; no. 18 (28 October 1976):1018–1020.

Medical Studies: Epidemiology, Diagnosis, and Treatment

Aalund, O. "Sequelae to Exposure of Porcine Skin to Heat and Electricity." *Acta Medical legalis et Socialis* 30(1980):33–44.

Allodi, F., M.D. "The Psychiatric Effects of Political Persecution and Torture in Children and Families of Victims." *Canada's Mental Health* 28(September 1980):8–10.

Allodi, F., M.D., and G. Cowgill. "Ethical and Psychiatric Aspects of Torture: A Canadian Study." *Canadian Journal of Psychiatry* 27(1982):98–102.

American Journal of Forensic Medicine and Pathology 5, no. 4 (December 1984).

Amnesty International. *Evidence of Torture: Studies by the Amnesty International Danish Medical Group.* London: Amnesty International, 1977.

Amnesty International. "Sequelae and Rehabilitation of Concentration Camp Victims, Sailors from the Second World War, Hostages and Torture Victims." Seminar. *Danish Medical Bulletin* 27(1980):213–250.

Amnesty International. Danish Medical Group. *Results of Examinations of 14 Argentine Victims of Torture.* London: Amnesty International, 1980.

Berger, P. "International Seminar Reviews Progress in Scientific Study of Torture Effects." *Canadian Medical Association Journal,* 22 April 1978.

Bexton, W. H., W. Heron, and T. H. Scott. "Effects of Decreased Variation in the Sensory Environment." *Canadian Journal of Psychology* 8 (1954):70–76.

Biderman, A. D. "Communist Attempts to Elicit False Confessions from Air Force Prisoners of War." *Bulletin of the New York Academy of Medicine* 33 (1957):616–625.

Biderman, A. D. "Social-Psychological Needs and 'Involuntary' Behavior as Illustrated by Compliance in Interrogation." *Sociometry* 23, no. 2 (June 1960).

Cathcart, L. M., P. Berger, and B. Knazan. "Medical Examination of Torture Victims Applying for Refugee Status." *Canadian Medical Association Journal* 28(1979):179–184.

Cienfuegos, A. J., and C. Monelli. "Testimony of Political Experiences as a Therapeutic Instrument." *American Journal of Orthopsychiatry* 53, no. 1 (January 1983):43–51.

Daly, R. "Psychiatric After-Effects of Irish Prisoners Subjected to Ill-treatment and Torture." *New Scientist*, 5 August 1976, 272–273.

Danielson, L., et al. "Electrical and Thermal Injuries in Pig Skin—Evaluated and Compared by Light Microscopy." *Forensic Science International* 12 (1978):211–225.

Federn, E. "The Endurance of Torture." *Complex* 4 (1951):34–41.

Gordon, E., and A. K. Mant. "Clinical Evidence of Torture—Examination of a Teacher from El Salvador." *Lancet* 1, no. 8370 (28 January 1984):213–214.

Haward, L. R. "Investigations of Torture Allegations by the Forensic Psychologist." *Journal of Forensic Sciences* 14, no. 4 (October 1974):299–309.

Jensen, T. S., M.D., et al. "Cerebral Atrophy in Young Torture Victims." *New England Journal of Medicine* 307, no. 21 (18 November 1982):1341.

Karlsmark, T., et al. "Tracing the Use of Torture: Electrically Induced Calcification of Collagen in Pig Skin." *Nature* 301 (6 January 1983):75–78.

Kral, V. A., L. H. Pazder, and B. T. Wigdor. "Long-Term Effects of a Prolonged Stress Experience." *Canadian Psychiatric Association Journal* 12 (1967):175–181.

Milwertz, J. "Victims of Torture." *World Health*, August 1983, 2–4.

Nielsen, K. G., O. Nielsen, and H. K. Thomsen. "Device and Methods for the Measurement of Energy Transfer in Experiments Involving thermal and Electrical Injuries of Skin." *Forensic Science International* 17(1981):203.

Nightingale, E. O., et al. "Special Report: Support Urged for Syrian Doctors." *New England Journal of Medicine* 310 (1984):803–804.

Rasmussen, O. V., and I. Lunde. "Evaluation of Investigation of 200 Torture Victims." *Danish Medical Bulletin* 27(1980):241–243.

Shallice, T. "The Ulster Depth Interrogation Techniques and Their Relation to Sensory Deprivation Research." *Cognition*, 1973.

Shurley, J. T. "Stress and Adaptation as Related to Sensory/Perceptual Isolation Research." *Military Medical* 131(1966):254–258.

Thomsen, H. K., et al. "Early Epidermal Changes in Heat and Electrically Injured Pig Skin." *Forensic Science International* 17(1981):133–143. Reprint. Copenhagen: Anti-Torture Research Index, ATR Publication nos. 3 and 4.

Wexler, D., et al. "Sensory Deprivation." *Archives of Neurology and Psychiatry* (Chicago) 79(1958):225–233.

World Health Organization. "Psychosocial Aspects of Violence." Symposium at The Hague, 8–11 April 1981. Geneva: World Health Organization, 1981. Mimeo.

Zubek, J. P., ed. *Sensory Deprivation: Fifteen Years of Research*. New York: 1969.

Zuckerman, M. "Perceptual Isolation as a Stress Situation: A Review." *Archives of General Psychiatry* 11(1964):255–276.

Zuckerman, M., et al. "Experimental and Subject Factors Determining Responses to Sensory Deprivation, Social Isolation, and Confinement." *Journal of Abnormal Psychology* 73(1966):183–194.

Ethics: Medical and Legal Perspectives

Anonymous. *The Gangrene.* New York: Lyle Stuart, 1960.

Bassiouni, M. C., and D. Derby. "An Appraisal of Torture in International Law and Practice: The Need for an International Convention for the Prevention and Suppression of Torture." *Revue Internationale de Droit Penal* 48, no. 17 (1977).

Beecher, H. *Research and the Individual.* Boston: Little, and Brown, 1970.

Belknap, R. "Commentary: Torture and Ethics of Medicine." *Man and Medicine* 4, no. 1 (1979):53–57.

Berger, P. B. "Medicine and Torture: The Struggle for Human Rights." *Canadian Medical Association Journal* 124(1 April 1981):839–840.

Bernard, C. *An Introduction to the Study of Experimental Medicine* (1865). Translated by H. D. Greene. New York: H. Schuman, 1949.

"Biomedical Ethics and the Shadow of Nazism: A Conference on the Proper Use of the Nazi Analogy in Ethical Debate." *Hastings Center Report*, 6, no. 4 (August 1976):1–19.

British Medical Association. *The Handbook of Medical Ethics.* London: British Medical Association, 1981.

Burges, S. H. "Doctors and Torture: The Police Surgeon." *Journal of Medical Ethics*, 6 September 1980.

Cooperman, E. M. "Doctors, Torture and Abuse of the Doctor-Patient Relationship." *Canadian Medical Association Journal* 116(1977):707–710.

Crozier, B. *A Theory of Conflict.* New York: Scribner, 1975.

Curran, W. J. "Official Torture and Human Rights: The American Courts and International Law." *New England Journal of Medicine* 304, no. 22 (28 May 1981):1342–1343.

Dooley-Clarke, D. "The Hunger Strike in Northern Ireland: Medical Ethics and Political Protest." *The Hastings Center Report*, December 1981, 5–8.

D'Zurilla, W. "Individual Responsibility for Torture under International Law." *Tulane Law Review* 56, no. 1 (December 1981).

Ewing, A. C. *The Morality of Punishment.* London: Kegan, Paul, 1929.

Favre, J. "Ethical Problems for the Physician Exposed by Torture; A propos of a Personal Experience." *Acta Medicinae Legalis et Socialis* (Liege) 30, no. 1 (1980):71–74.

Gellhorn, A. "Medicine, Torture and the United Nations." *Lancet*, 23 February 1980, 428–429.

Genefke, I. K. "Medical Work against Torture." *New England Journal of Medicine* 303(1980):229.

Heijder, A. "Professional Codes of Ethics against Torture." In *Professional Codes of Ethics*, edited by Amnesty International. London: Amnesty International, 1976.

International Commission of Jurists. "Law and the Prevention of Torture." *ICJ Review* (December 1973):23–27.

International Commission of Jurists. *Torture: How to Make an International Convention Effective.* Geneva: International Commission of Jurists, 1979.

Jones, G. E. "On the Permissibility of Torture." *Journal of Medical Ethics* 6, no. 1 (1980):11–15.

Levin, M. "The Case for Torture." *Newsweek,* 7 June 1982, p. 13.

Leys, S. "The Case for Torture: A Rebuttal." *Newsweek,* 5 July 1982, p. 8.

Mufson, M. "Political Torture and Overpopulation." *New England Journal of Medicine* 297, no. 1 (7 July 1977):63–64.

Murton, T. "Prison Doctors." In *Humanistic Perspectives in Medicine,* edited by M. Visscher. Buffalo, N.Y.: Prometheus Books, 1972.

O'Boyle, M. "Torture and Emergency Powers under the European Convention on Human Rights: Ireland v. United Kingdom." *American Journal of International Law* 71 (1971):687.

Paskins, B. "What's Wrong with Torture?" *British Journal of International Studies* 2 (July 1976):138–148.

Shokeir, M. H. K. "Doctors and Torture." *Lancet* 2 (1973):1439–1440.

Shue, H. "Torture." *Philosophy and Public Affairs* 7, no. 2 (Winter 1978):124–143.

Sieghart, P. "Medicine and Torture–Legal Aspects." In *I Diritti dell'Uomo nell'Ambito della Medicina Legale,* Universitá degli Studi di Messina, 24–29 March 1980, 260–272.

"Torture and Philosophy." *Journal of Medical Ethics* 6, no. 1 (1980).

"Torture as a Tort in Violation of International Law." *Stanford Law Review* 33 (January 1981):353–369.

World Health Organization. "Health Aspects of Avoidable Maltreatment of Prisoners and Detainees." Paper presented at Fifth United Nations Congress on the Prevention of Crime and the Treatment of Offenders, Toronto, Canada, 1–12 September 1975.

World Medical Association. "Torture." *World Medical Journal* 28, no. 2 (March–April 1981).

Psychiatric Abuse
General Reading

Alexaeyeff, S. "Abuse of Psychiatry as a Tool for Political Repression in the Soviet Union." *Medical Journal of Australia* 1, no. 5 (31 January 1976):122–123.

Amnesty International. *The Political Abuse of Psychiatry in Romania.* London: Amnesty International, 1980.

Amnesty International. "Confinement of Prisoners of Conscience in Psychiatric

Institutions." In *Yugoslavia: Prisoners of Conscience*. London: Amnesty International, 1982.

Amnesty International. *Mental Health Aspects of Political Imprisonment in Uruguay*. New York: Amnesty International, 1983.

Amnesty International. *Political Abuse of Psychiatry in the USSR*. New York: Amnesty International, 1983.

Bauer, R. A. "Brainwashing: Psychology or Demonology." *Journal of Social Issues* 13 (1957):41–47.

Biderman, A. D. "Communist Attempts to Elicit False Confessions from Air Force Prisoners of War." *Bulletin of the New York Academy of Medicine* 9 (September 1957):33.

Biderman, A. D. "Socio-Psychological Needs and 'Involuntary' Behavior as Illustrated by Compliance in Interrogation." *Sociometry* 23 (June 1960):2.

Bloch, S., and P. Reddaway. *Psychiatric Terror*. New York: Basic Books, 1977.

Bloch, S., and P. Reddaway. *Soviet Psychiatric Abuse: The Shadow over World Psychiatry*. London: Victor Gollancz, 1984.

Bukovsky, V., and S. Gluzman. "A Manual of Psychiatry for Dissidents." In *Psychiatric Terror*, written by S. Bloch and P. Reddaway, app. 6. New York: Basic Books, 1977.

Deeley, P. *Beyond the Breaking Point: A Study of the Techniques of Interrogation*. London: Arthur Barker, 1971.

de Meeus, A. *White Book on the Internment of Dissenters in Soviet Mental Hospitals*. Brussels: International Committee for the Defence of Human Rights in the USSR, 1974.

Drucker, H. "Psychotropic Drugs and Imprisonment in a Psychiatric Hospital for Political Reasons." *Acta Med Leg Soc* (Liege) 30, no. 1 (1980):189–210.

Farber, I. E., et al. "Brainwashing, Conditioning and DDD." *Sociometry* 40, no. 4 (December 1957).

Field, M. G. *Doctor and Patient in Soviet Russia*. Cambridge: Harvard University Press, 1957.

Fireside, H. *Soviet Psychoprisons*. New York: Norton, 1979.

Hinkle, L. E., Jr., and H. G. Wolff. "Communist Interrogation and Indoctrination of the Enemies of the State." *Archives of Neurological Psychiatry* (Chicago) 76 (1956):115–174.

Jones, K. "Society Looks at the Psychiatrist." *British Journal of Psychiatry* 132 (1978):321–332.

Lader, M. *Psychiatry on Trial*. Harmondsworth, United Kingdom: Penguin, 1977.

Letters (from an anonymous psychiatrist testifying to a policy of systematic internment during the Stalin period). *American Journal of Psychiatry* 126 (1970): 1327–1328; 127 (1970): 842–843; 127 (1971): 1575–1576; 131 (1974): 474.

Letters (from Soviet physicians in defense of Soviet psychiatric practices). *The Guardian*, 29 September 1973; *British Medical Journal*, 10 August 1974.

Muller-Hegemann, D. "Psychotherapy in the German Democratic Republic." In *Psychiatry in the Communist World*, edited by A. Kev. New York: Science House, 1968.

National Institute of Mental Health. *The Report of the First US Mission on Mental Health to the USSR*. Public Health Service Publication no. 1893. Chevy Chase, Md.: National Institute of Mental Health, 1969.

Nekipelov, V. *Institute of Fools: Notes from the Serbsky*. London: Gollancz, 1980.

Ochberg, F. J., M.D., and J. Gunn. "The Psychiatrist and the Policeman." *Psychiatric Annals* 10, no. 5 (May 1980):30–44.

Pisarev, S. P. "Soviet Mental Prisons." *Survey* 77, no. 3 (1977):175–180.

Podrabinek, A. *Punitive Medicine*. Ann Arbor, Mich.: Karoma, 1980.

Reddaway, P. *Uncensored Russia*. London: Cape, 1972.

Rich, V. "Internees in Poland: Psychiatric Abuse Claim." *Nature* 299 (30 September 1982):386.

Santucci, P. S., and G. Winoker. "Brainwashing as a Factor in Psychiatric Illness." *Archives of Neurology and Psychiatry* 74 (1955):11–16.

Sedman, G. "Brainwashing and Sensory Deprivation as Factors in the Production of Psychiatric States: The Relationship between Such States and Schizophrenia." *Confinia Psychiatrica* 4 (1961):28–44.

Solzhenitsyn, A. *The Gulag Archipelago*. New York: Harper & Row, 1973.

Stone, A. "In the Service of the State: The Psychiatrist as Double Agent." Special supplement to *Hastings Center Report*, April 1978.

Stone, I. F. "Betrayal by Psychiatry." *New York Review of Books*, 10 February 1972.

Tonge, W. L. "Psychiatry and Political Dissent." *The Lancet*, 20 July 1974.

United Nations. Economic and Social Council. Commission on Human Rights. Subcommission on Prevention of Discrimination and Protection of Minorities. 35th Session. Item 11. *Report of the Sessional Working Group on the Question of Persons Detained on the Grounds of Mental Ill-Health*. E/Cn.4/Sub.2/1982/17. Geneva, 5 September 1982.

United Nations. General Assembly. *Human Rights and Scientific and Technological Developments*. Report by the Secretary General. E/Cn.4/Sub.2/446. 15 July 1980.

US Congress. Senate. Committee on the Judiciary. Subcommittee to Investigate the Administration of the Internal Security Act and Other Internal Security Laws. *Hearings on Abuse of Psychiatry for Political Purposes*, 26 September 1972. Reprint. New York: Arno Press, 1973.

Wade, N. "Technology in Ulster: Rubber Bullets Hit Home, Brainwashing Backfires." *Science* 176 (1972):1102–1105.

Wing, J. K. "Psychiatry in the Soviet Union." *British Medical Journal* 1 (1974):433.

Case Studies of Medical Involvement

Amnesty International. *The Political Abuse of Psychiatry in Romania*. London: Amnesty International, 1980.

Bukovsky, V. *My Life as a Dissenter*. London: Deutsch, 1978.

Chorley, Lord. "The Case of Dr. A. J. Kraus." *Association of University Teachers Bulletin*, April 1970.

Gorbanevskya, N. *Red Square at Noon*. London: Deutsch, 1972.

Grigorenko, P. *Memoirs*. Translated by Thomas P. Whitney. New York: Norton, 1982.

Khodorovich, T., ed. *The Case of Leonid Plyushch*. London: C. Hurst, 1976.

Koryagin, A. "An Appeal from a Soviet Labor Camp." In *Matchbox*, edited by Amnesty International USA, May 1982, p. 5.

Labedz, L. *Solzhenitsyn: A Documentary Record*. Harmondsworth, United Kingdom: Penguin, 1972.

Medvedev, Z. *The Rise and Fall of T. D. Lysenko*. New York: Columbia University Press, 1969.

Medvedev, Z. *The Medvedev Papers*. London: Macmillan, 1971.

Medvedev, Z., and R. Medvedev. *A Question of Madness*. London: Macmillan, 1971.

Mee, C. *The Internment of Soviet Dissenters in Mental Hospitals*. London: Working Group on the Internment of Dissenters in Mental Hospitals, 1971.

Plyushch, L. *History's Carnival*. London: Collins/Harvill, 1979.

Steinberg, I. Z. *Spiridonova: Revolutionary Terrorist*. London: Methuen, 1935.

Tarsis, V. Y. *Ward 7*. London: Collins/Harvill, 1965.

Weissbrot, D., ed. *Selected Poems by Natalya Gorbanevskaya with a Transcript of Her Trial and Papers Relating to Her Detention in a Prison Psychiatric Hospital*. Oxford: Carcanet Press, 1972.

Psychiatric Concepts and Possibilities for Abuse

Bazelon, D. L. Introduction to *Forensic Psychiatry*. (Translation of the most authoritative and comprehensive work in the field of mental illness and the law.) White Plains, N.Y.: International Arts and Sciences Press, 1970.

Hite, C. "Bridging the US-Soviet Psychiatric Gap." *Psychiatric News* 9 (1974):6–17; 19 (1974):30–31, 40.

Holland, J., and I. V. Shakhmatova-Pavlova. "Concept and Classification of Schizophrenia in the Soviet Union." Unpublished manuscript, 1974.

Holland, J. "Schizophrenia in the Soviet Union." In *Annual Review of Research in Schizophrenia*, vol. 6, edited by R. Cancro. New York: 1977.

Kazanetz, E. "Differentiating Exogenous Psychiatric Illness from Schizophrenia." *Archives of General Psychiatry* 36 (1979):740–745.

Morozov, G. V., and I. M. Dalashnik, eds. *Forensic Psychiatry*. New York: International Arts and Science Press, 1970.

Reich, W. "The Spectrum Concept of Schizophrenia: Problems for Diagnostic Practice." *Archives of General Psychiatry* 32 (1975):489–498.

Reich, W. "Diagnosing Soviet Dissidents." *Harper's Magazine*, August 1978, 31–37.

"Report of the Ad Hoc Committee on the Use of Psychiatric Institutions for the Commitment of Political Dissenters." Unpublished manuscript. 1972. Summary in *Psychiatric News*, 5 July 1972,

Rosenhan, D. L. "On Being Sane in Insane Places." *Science* 179 (19 January 1973):250–258.

Snezhnevsky, A. V. "Symptom, Syndrome, Disease: A Clinical Method in Psychiatry." In *The World Biennial of Psychiatry and Psychotherapy*, vol. 1, edited by S. Arieti. 1971.

Snezhnevsky, A. V. "The Symptomatology, Clinical Forms and Nosology of Schizophrenia." In *Modern Perspectives in World Psychiatry*, edited by J. G. Howells. New York: Brunner/Mazel, 1971.

Snezhnevsky, A. V., and M. Vartanyan. "The Forms of Schizophrenia and Their Biological Correlates." In *Biochemistry, Schizophrenia, and Affective Illness*, edited by H. E. Himwich. Baltimore: Williams & Wilkins, 1970.

Szasz, T. *Ideology and Insanity: Essays on the Psychiatric Dehumanization of Man*. New York: Doubleday, 1969.

Szasz, T. *Psychiatric Slavery—When Confinement and Coercion Masquerade as Cure*. London: Macmillan, 1977.

United Nations. Economic and Social Council. Commission on Human Rights. Subcommission on Prevention of Discrimination and Protection of Minorities. 35th Session. *Human Rights and Scientific and Technological Developments: Guidelines, Principles and Guarantees for the Protection of Persons Detained on Grounds of Mental Ill-health or Suffering from Mental Disorder*. E/Cn.4/Sub.2/1982/16. Geneva, 31 August 1982.

United Nations. Economic and Social Council. Commission on Human Rights. Subcommission on Prevention of Discrimination and Protection of Minorities. 35th Session. Item 11. *Report of the Sessional Working Group on the Question of Persons Detained on the Grounds of Mental Ill-Health. E/Cn.4/Sub.2/1982/17. Geneva, 5 September 1982.*

World Health Organization. Report of the International Pilot Study of Schizophrenia. Geneva: World Health Organization, 1973.

World Health Organization. "Apartheid and Mental Health Care." *Objective: Justice* (UN Office of Public Information) 9, no. 1 (Spring 1977):39.

Ethics: Medical and Legal Perspectives

American Psychiatric Association. Committee on Medical Ethics. "The Principles of Medical Ethics, with Annotations Especially Applicable to Psychiatry." *American Journal of Psychiatry* 130 (1973):1057–1064.

Balint, M. *The Doctor, His Patient, and the Illness.* New York: International Universities Press, 1957.

Bloch, S. "The Political Misuse of Soviet Psychiatry: Honolulu and Beyond." *Australian and New Zealand Journal of Psychiatry* 14 (1980):109–114.

Bloch, S., and P. Chodoff, eds. *Psychiatric Ethics.* Oxford: Oxford University Press, 1981.

"Can Psychiatry Police Itself Effectively?" *American Journal of Psychiatry* 133 (June 1976):653–655.

Chalidze, V. *To Defend These Rights: Human Rights and the Soviet Union.* London: Collins/Harvill, 1975.

Curran, W. J., and T. W. Harding. *The Law and Mental Health: Harmonizing Objectives.* Geneva: World Health Organization, 1978.

Institute of Society, Ethics and the Life Sciences. *A Conference on Conflicting Loyalties.* Special supplement. Hastings-on-Hudson, N.Y.: Institute of Society, Ethics, and the Life Sciences, April 1978.

Moore, R. A. "Ethics in the Practice of Psychiatry: Origins, Functions, Models and Enforcement." *American Journal of Psychiatry* 135, no. 2 (February 1978):157–163.

Roth, L. "Mental Health Commitment: The State of the Debate, 1980." *Hospital and Community Psychiatry* 31 (1980):385–396.

Stone, A. A. *Mental Health and Law: A System in Transition.* National Institute of Mental Health, Center for Studies on Crime and Delinquency, Department of Health, Education and Welfare Publication no. (ADM) 74-176. Washington, D.C.: US Government Printing Office, 1975.

Szasz, T. *The Myth of Mental Illness.* New York: Harper & Row, 1961.

Szasz, T. *Law, Liberty and Psychiatry.* New York: Macmillan, 1963.

Thornberry, T. P., and J. E. Jacoby, *The Criminally Insane.* Chicago: University of Chicago Press, 1979.

Index

Fainberg, Viktor, 159–160
Filártiga, Dolly, 87–100
Filártiga, Joel, 28–29, 79–100, 120,
   237–241
Filártiga, Joelito, 28–29, 79–100, 120,
   237–241
Filártiga, Nidia, 83–100, 237–241
Filártiga v. Pēna-Irala, 90–100, 237–241
Filatova, A. P., 178
Forensic implications of schizophrenia,
   145–146
Forensic Medical Officers Association,
   119
Forensic sciences, 19–21, 110–113, 119
France, 9, 32, 27, 102
   Amnesty International, 105
   Comité Medical pour les Exiles
      (COMEDE), 295
   Fundación de Ayuda Social de las Iglesias
      Cristianas (FASIC), 287

Genetic analysis and grandpaternity,
   113
Geneva Conventions, 9, 230, 234
Germany, 10, 12, 30–31
Geschwind, Norman, 186, 196, 203
Gluzman, Semyon, 157–159
Gonzalez, Juan L., 115
Gorbanevskaya, Natalya, 140, 146
Grandmothers of the Plaza de Mayo,
   60, 113
Greece, 11, 13, 32, 33
Grigorenko, Andrei, 188
Grigorenko, Oleg, 184
Grigorenko, Pyotr G., 131, 140–141,
   155–160, 176, 183–205, 217–218,
   221
Grigorenko, Zinaida, 184, 188
Guatemala, 9, 10
   American Association for the
      Advancement of Science, 122
Guilt and victims of torture, 74–75
Gulag Archipelago, 8
Gunn, John, 16

Habeas corpus, 10, 82, 103, 122, 241
Hallucinations, 195
Hawk, David, 39

Heijder, Alfred, 103
Helfeld, David, 82
Helsinki Rules of Conduct, 105
Herzog, Vladimir, 114
Hippocratic Oath, 30–31, 42, 104, 230,
   247, 265–266
Holland, 73
Human Rights Internet (HRI), 280, 288
Hungary, 17
Huxley, Aldous, 130

Iatrogenia, 241–242
Indonesia, 9–10
Institute of Medicine (IOM) of the
   National Academy of Sciences, 289
Inter-American Commission on Human
   Rights, 51, 233
International Association Against
   Torture, 289
International Association on the
   Political Use of Psychiatry (IAPUP),
   16–17, 289–290
International Commission of Jurists
   (ICJ), 237, 291
International Committee of the Red
   Cross (ICRC), 17, 292
International Conference on Islamic
   Medicine, 269–270
International Convention Against
   Torture, 95
International Council of Nurses (ICN),
   276–279, 292–293
International Covenant on Civil and
   Political Rights, 90
International Human Rights Law
   Group, 90
International League for Human
   Rights, 82, 90
International Medical Commission for
   Health and Human Rights (IMC),
   235–237, 293–294
International Pilot Study of
   Schizophrenia, 143
International Police Academy (IPA), 12
International Rehabilitation and
   Research Center for Torture
   Victims (RCT), 242–243, 294
International Rescue Committee, 55

Iran, 10, 13–14, 243
Iraq, 243
Irish Republic Army, 102
Irwin, Robert, 119–120
Isern, D. R., 7
Islamic Code of Medical Ethics, 269–270
Islamic *Shari'a* law, 13
Israel, 14, 75, 241
Italy, 228
Ivanov, Yury, 115, 159
Izurieta, Zulma, 50

Japan, 8, 12
  International League for Human Rights, 18
  Japan Civil Liberties Union, 18
Japan Civil Liberties Union (JCLU), 18
Jones, Barbara P., 186, 203

Kant, Immanuel, 36–37
Kashchenko Psychiatric Hospital, 137–138
Kekilova, Annasoltan, 160
KGB, 152, 155–159, 167, 175, 179–180, 190, 209, 217, 219, 220, 245
Khartoum Hospital, 13
Khmer Rouge, 15, 39
Khrushchev, Nikita, 136, 137, 189
Klebanov, Vladimir, 168
Kofas, Dimitrios, 33
Kokorev, V. V., 160
Kolb, Lawrence C., 187
Koryagin, Anatoly, 129–130, 159, 164–174, 227, 245
Kosterin, A. E., 190
Kraepelin, Emil, 142, 193–194
Krajger, Sergej, 225
Kushkun, V., 177
Kuznetsov, A. I., 136

Lambrakis, Grigoris, 32
Landau, Yakov, 152–153
Lanuscou, Matilde, 111–113
Latin American Social Work Collective (COLAT), 294
Lawyers Committee for International Human Rights, 90

Leaf of Spring, A, 139
Lifton, Robert J., 75, 229, 236, 246–247
Lorca, Federico García, 11
Lunts, Daniil, 146, 148, 152–154, 158
Lyubarskaya, Lydia, 160

Maltsev, Yury, 140
Manual on Psychiatry for Dissenters, 158
Mauritania, 13
Mbareté, 82
Medical Action Group (MAG), 232, 295
Medical Association of Quilmes, 240
Medical Association of South Africa (MASA), 109, 120
Medvedev, Roy, 150
Medvedev, Zhores, 141, 150–151, 156, 210
Metz, Ruth Eugenio, 50–51
Mollnow, Carl, 17–18
Morimura, Seiichi, 12
Morozov, Georgy V., 141, 145, 148, 151–154, 158, 194, 217
Morozov, V. M., 160
Moscow Institute of Psychiatry, 245
Murton, Tom, 33–34

Nacht und Nebel, 10
Nadzharov, Ruben, 148, 151, 211
Katasone, Yasuhiro H., 18
National Academy of Sciences (NAS), 123, 289, 295–296
Nazi concentration camps, 8, 10, 14–15, 30–31, 75, 231, 241
Nepal, 12
Neuroses, 195, 208
Nikitin, Alexei V., 130, 180–181, 164–174
1984, 130, 249
Northern Ireland, 119
  Amnesty International, 70
  Forensic Medical Association and, 119
Norway, 14, 75, 241
Nuremberg trials, 30–32
Nurse(s)
  International Council of, 276–279
  Role of, in the Care of Detainees and Prisoners, 276–277
  Role of, in Safeguarding Human Rights, Statement on, 277–279

315

316

Role of the Nurse in the Care of
  Detainees and Prisoners, 276–277
Romania, 16–17
Romero, Maria Elena, 50
Romero de Metz, Graciela, 50–51
Roslan, A., 177, 179–180
Roslik, Vladimir, 116
Royal Australian and New Zealand
  College of Psychiatrists, 224
Royal College of Psychiatrists, 224, 293–
  294
Royal Ulster Constabulary (RUC), 119

Sakharov, Andrei, 150
Samizdat, 134, 157, 158
Samsonov, Nikolai, 136–137, 160
Sanabria, Carlos, 45–57
Sanatorio la Esperanza, El, 82–100
São Paulo Forensic Medical Institute,
  109
São Paulo State Medical Council, 109
Satter, David, 172
Savitch, Viktor, P., 165
Schizophrenia, 208–209, 213
  borderline, 211–213
  continuous, 144, 213
  definition of, 142–143
  dissenter and, 146–148
  forensic implications of, 145–146
  genetic factors and, 145
  latent, 143
  malignant, 144–145, 213
  mild, 144–145, 213
  moderate, 144–145
  paranoid, 194–195
  periodic, 144–145, 213
  pseudoneurotic, 142–143
  rapid, 144–145
  recurrent, 213
  shiftlike, 144, 213
  sluggish, 144–145, 213–214, 218–219
  Soviet method of diagnosis of, 142–
    148
Schneider, Kurt, 142
Serbsky Institute for Forensic
  Psychiatry, 135–137, 141, 143–144,
  146, 148–149, 151–152, 154–155,
  157–158, 189–195, 217

Serebrov, Feliks, 169, 171
Serebryakova, Zoya, 151–152
Shari'a law, 13
Shibata, Harry, 109, 114
Shimozato, Masaki, 12
"60 Minutes," 17–18
Snezhnevsky, Andrei V., 143–144, 148–
  151, 153–154, 160, 185, 206–222,
  245
Snow, Clyde, 110–113
Society of Psychiatrists of South Africa
  (SPSA), 246
Solzhenitsyn, Aleksander, 34, 158
South Africa, 108–109, 246–247
  American Psychiatric Association, 17,
    226–227
  apartheid, 17, 246–267
  Black Consciousness Movement, 108
  Medical Association of South Africa,
    109, 120
  psychiatric care, 17, 246–247
  Royal College of Psychiatrists, 17
  Society of Psychiatrists of South
    Africa, 246
  UN Centre Against Apartheid, 17
  University of Cape Town, Institute of
    Criminology, 294
  World Health Organization, 17
South African Medical and Dental
  Council, 109
South American Refugee Program
  (SARP), 55
*Soviet Psychiatric Abuse: The Shadow over
  World Psychiatry*, 141
Soviet Union. *See also* Dnepropetrovsk
  Special Psychiatric Hospital;
  Kashchenko Psychiatric Hospital;
  KGB; Moscow Institute of
  Psychiatry; Serbsky Institute for
  Forensic Psychiatry
  Academy of Medical Sciences, 148,
    149, 206, 211
  Action Group for the Defense of
    Human Rights, 140
  All-Union Society of Psychiatrists and
    Neuropathologists, 209, 211, 224
  American Psychiatric Association,
    131, 226